Telling Stories
Taking Risks

Journalism Writing at the Century's Edge

Alice M. Klement

University of Oklahoma

Carolyn B. Matalene

University of South Carolina

Wadsworth Publishing Company

I(T)P® An International Thomson Publishing Company

Belmont, CA • Albany, NY • Bonn • Boston • Cincinnati • Detroit • Johannesburg
London • Madrid • Melbourne • Mexico City • New York • Paris • Singapore
Tokyo • Toronto • Washington

COMMUNICATIONS EDITOR: Randall Adams
EDITORIAL ASSISTANT: Megan Gilbert
MARKETING MANAGER: Mike Dew
PROJECT EDITOR: Vicki Friedberg
PRODUCTION: Melanie Field, Strawberry Field Publishing
PRINT BUYER: Barbara Britton
PERMISSIONS EDITOR: Robert M. Kauser
COVER AND INTERIOR DESIGN: Dare Porter/Real Time Design
COPY EDITOR: Carol Dondrea
COMPOSITOR: TBH Typecast, Inc.
PRINTER: Maple-Vail Book Manufacturing

For more information, contact Wadsworth Publishing Company, 10 Davis Drive, Belmont, CA 94002, or electronically at http://www.thomson.com/wadsworth.html

International Thomson Publishing Europe
Berkshire House 168-173
High Holborn
London, WC1V 7AA, England

International Thomson Editores
Campos Eliseos 385, Piso 7
Col. Polanco
11560 México D.F. México

Thomas Nelson Australia
102 Dodds Street
South Melbourne 3205
Victoria, Australia

International Thomson Publishing Asia
221 Henderson Road
#05-10 Henderson Building
Singapore 0315

Nelson Canada
1120 Birchmount Road
Scarborough, Ontario
Canada M1K 5G4

International Thomson Publishing Japan
Hirakawacho Kyowa Building, 3F
2-2-1 Hirakawacho
Chiyoda-ku, Tokyo 102, Japan

International Thomson Publishing GmbH
Königswinterer Strasse 418
53227 Bonn, Germany

International Thomson Publishing Southern Africa
Building 18, Constantia Park
240 Old Pretoria Road
Halfway House, 1685 South Africa

Library of Congress Cataloging-in-Publication Data
Telling stories/taking risks : journalism writing at the century's
    edge / [compiled by] Alice M. Klement, Carolyn B. Matalene.
        p.   cm.
    ISBN 0-534-52272-6
    1. Journalism.   I. Klement, Alice M.   II. Matalene, Carolyn B.
PN4726.T45   1997
071'.3–dc21   97-21540

*This book is printed on
acid-free recycled paper.*

We dedicate this book to our mothers,
Waltressa Lunt Burrows and Elinor F. Klement—
our first and best storytellers,
teachers, and coaches.

About the Editors

ALICE M. KLEMENT

A wrangler of words and images, Alice Klement moves from coast to coast, country to country. En route, she leads a hyphenated life: writer-editor, lawyer-journalist, coach-researcher, a dealer in fact, a fan of fiction.

For more than a decade, she reported stories—in Chicago gang haunts and White House corridors, from night court to Supreme Court, Alaskan boondocks to Miami vicelands—for community newspapers, The National Law Journal, *a ma-and-pa weekly, and* The Miami Herald. *She also traveled to all 50 states and more than 100 countries, freelancing from several continents. After writing two guide-books, she still welcomes wanderlust.*

She earned degrees in journalism (Northwestern, 1972) and law (DePaul, 1978) before teaching in South Florida and, from an endowed chair, at the University of Oklahoma. She's consulted at a fake Tribune *for a CBC/CBS-TV series and coached in dozens of newsrooms. In 1997, she served as a Fulbright Fellow in Indonesia and a Research Fellow with The Poynter Institute for Media Studies.*

In classrooms or newsrooms, with groups or one-on-one, her approach is consistent. She attends *to writers and editors, figuring how to untangle thoughts, tantalize readers, and accentuate the authentic. To her, such efforts are not incidental diversions, but the very* stuff *of life: ideas in heads, fears and hopes in hearts.*

CAROLYN B. MATALENE

Carolyn Matalene teaches composition and rhetoric at the University of South Carolina—when she's not teaching somewhere else. She has been an exchange professor in China, a teacher of teachers in Liberia, a Fulbright Scholar and visiting professor during three visits to Finland, as well as a writing coach in businesses, state agencies, and newsrooms. Originally an English major of the novel-reading sort, she earned a B.A. from Northwestern and an M.A. and Ph.D. from the University of Pennsylvania. Then she revised herself into a writing specialist to direct USC's freshman English program. Her research on writing can be found in Worlds of Writing, Professional Writing in Context, *and numerous journal articles.*

Winner of many teaching awards, she was recently recognized by graduate students for her "outstanding classroom presence." Students in her popular advanced writing course can't believe how much writing she requires. She keeps them focused with favorite maxims: Know your audience, Form is power, Revision goes on even unto death, Keep your belt and your sentences short. And she insists students master rhetorical theories—from Aristotle to Kenneth Burke. But reading great writing beats studying principles, so she edited this book to showcase some writers too good to go unnoticed. As Ezra Pound said, "Literature is news that stays news."

Contents

CHAPTER 1: TELLING THEIR STORIES

CHAPTER 2: TELLING STORIES FROM INSIDE

CHAPTER 3: TELLING STORIES THAT PERSUADE

CHAPTER 4: TELLING OUR STORIES

(P)Review

At the Century's Edge

As many good stories do, *Telling Stories/Taking Risks* has a beginning, middle, and end. And, as many good storytellers know, the beginning and the end can often be switched–to dramatic effect. So if you're a journalist or student of the media, you might feel comfortable starting from the first chapter, learning to tell others' stories before you tell your own. But if you're a devotee of literature or student of composition, you might feel more comfortable starting from the fourth chapter, telling first your stories and then the world's.

However, this book is not about comfort. It is about risk. In fact, we'd like you to be a tad uncomfortable, much like the writers and editors who shaped these stories. They're trying to break rules, sometimes in form, sometimes in content. And, along the way, they take risks.

We offer more than 50 stories, from newspapers, magazines, and newspaper magazines, from Ken Fuson's one sentence to Gary Smith's many. To find these, we invaded annual National Writers' Workshops sponsored by major newspapers and The Poynter Institute for Media Studies. Then we called newsroom coaches, culled contests, and Nexised names. We did not ignore mainstream media, but we did pursue alternatives, scanning 'zines, tracking Web homepages, and perusing Net chatrooms. We also followed whim, though not as far as one reporter who explored *The Joy of Risk* by bungee jumping.

We hope that the journalists here are distinctive in what they say and how they say it. Hear their voices: a veteran from The Associated Press, an editor for *Esquire,* a college professor who freelances, and at least one reporter unsure of whether she's dealing in fact or fiction. Their strategy is clear: Get involved, get others involved. Their advice is also clear: Be willing to try something different, whether it's a new style or a new source.

Though these journalists take risks, they also take care, as writers concerned about process, committed to craft. So follow them to the millennial edge. Sometimes, as they do, move in close, with an "I." Sometimes, as they do, stand back, adjusting delivery. If you write long, get gutsy and go short. If you're content to introspect, go down the block, or around the world, to inspect. And, whether you join these reporters as a wannabe or as a reader, delve in. After all, that's the highest compliment you can pay storytellers: to read their stories.

ALICE M. KLEMENT, McMAHON CENTENNIAL PROFESSOR, 1994–96
University of Oklahoma School of Journalism and Mass Communication

Acknowledgments

Alice Klement thanks colleagues Carole Rich, Mark E. Jones, and Nelly Polhaupessy; organizers of The National Writers' Workshops at the *Orange County Register, The Des Moines Register, The Albuquerque Tribune,* and The Poynter Institute for Media Studies; director David Dary and staff at the University of Oklahoma's School of Journalism and Mass Communication, and journalists at *The Detroit News* and *The Oklahoma Daily,* especially senior Nicole Koch and adviser Jack Willis. Deep gratitude goes to friends who eased her way along the road.

Carolyn Matalene would like to thank research assistants Keith Perry, Paige Haggard, and Nell Anderson for reading, searching, and errand running; the English department of the University of South Carolina for support both financial and clerical; Patricia Wheeler of the Writing Center for her sharp eyes and good taste; and her husband and daughter for diversions on land and sea and devotion day after day.

We'd also like to thank the following reviewers for their thoughtful comments and suggestions:

Sharon S. Brock, *The Ohio State University;* Jon Franklin, *University of Oregon;* Robert C. Kochersberger, *North Carolina State University;* Beverly G. Merrick, *New Mexico State University;* Avis Meyer, *Saint Louis University;* Bernadette Pruitt, *Southwest Missouri State University;* Carl Sessions Stepp, *University of Maryland;* and K. Tim Wulfemeyer, *San Diego State University.*

Foreword

Donald M. Murray

Telling Stories/Taking Risks does just that for both English and journalism. Nonfiction makes up a large proportion of what is published and read today—though the contemporary vitality of the literature of experience is routinely overlooked by English departments. Here students and teachers will discover how to speak of their concerns in the voices of their times.

In its presentation of powerful personal voices finding their way into print, this collection is just as radical for journalists, despite the traditional prejudice against such writing in most newsrooms. Such writing, I believe, can help save print journalism by articulating readers' immediate and private concerns.

So I read *Telling Stories/Taking Risks* with admiration—and with sadness and anger that such a book was not available to me when I was a student, beginning my lifelong apprenticeship to the writer's craft.

I came to college as a bookaholic. I read new books and old books, good books and bad books, books for story and books for information with a glorious promiscuity. I intended to spend my life reading and, if I were lucky, writing—and I would make books and swallow more books, whole libraries of books following wherever my hungers took me.

Then my English professors introduced me to the canon, the aesthetic and intellectual aristocracy of literature. I had come to college from the other side of the tracks, and now, having climbed to the academy on the hill, I was sent back across the tracks.

I couldn't just read. I had to read the way they read—with aesthetic propriety. British literature was good; American literature was doubtful. When I was an undergraduate English major, no course in American literature counted for credit. Then I discovered there was something called genre and it had a precise hierarchy:

1. Poetry—formal poetry in traditional form, no free verse. I took a whole semester of Browning, considered the equal of Shakespeare and Chaucer. Stephen Vincent Benét was then the greatest American poet because of his book-length, epic poems.
2. Drama—if poetic and written before Shakespeare's death. After that, it went to the drama department and no longer counted as literature.
3. Novels—especially 19th-century ones and especially ones by Dickens and Trollope.
4. Some short stories—if they were literary.
5. A few essays—but only if not personal.
6. No books of nonfiction.

Although I could study poetry and fiction, I was not to write it. I was to write formal pieces of literary criticism in an acquired, impersonal, academic voice. And as I read, I was urged to travel backward. Old was good; new–after 1850 or so–was suspect. When I explored getting a doctorate in British literature of the 1880s and 1890s, Harvard told me that was far too modern.

And so I graduated to a life of writing. I wrote what I had not studied, the nonfiction genres that I thought I was qualified to write because they were pedestrian, not literary, and therefore appropriate to my talents. When my talents flowered–I did not realize they would not flower from disuse–then I would write poetry and fiction, great poetry and great fiction.

My daily professional challenge was nonfiction in which, at first, I reported the experiences of others and then, eventually, my own thoughts and feelings. The more personal I became, the more I was published and read. But even 10 years after I had won a Pulitzer for editorial writing, even after the number of articles and books I had published became ridiculously long, I did not call myself a writer. What I wrote did not fit the English department canon–or the hard news canon of the newsroom.

Even now, almost 50 years after I was granted a B.A. in English literature and went to work at a newspaper, I feel that the 400-plus essays I have published as newspaper columns or magazine articles or books do not quite count.

That makes me angry, and it also moves me to celebrate *Telling Stories/Taking Risks*. The canon is being rewritten. Nonfiction can stand as tall and proud as fiction and poetry.

–DONALD M. MURRAY

Donald M. Murray publishes poetry, fiction, textbooks on writing, and a weekly column in The Boston Globe. *He is an award-winning journalist and teacher.*

Foreword

Don Fry

I majored in English because I wanted to study the human mind. At Duke in the fifties, the psychology department confined itself to rats and pigeons, and let its students extrapolate to people. But if you want to understand human beings, novels and poems and plays get you there more quickly than mazes. And the best journalists can get you there even faster.

After a brief flirtation with a career as a Navy pilot, I chose writing, following the example of my high school colleague, novelist Reynolds Price. But somehow, the writers I studied had more to say than I did, and I ended up teaching and writing *about* the writers rather than imitating them.

Late in life I discovered journalism, a profession that serves the information junkie I've always been, and also satisfies my raging curiosity about human beings and their funny ways of living in this strange world. As a journalism teacher, I simply recycled what every literature major knows about storytelling.

Journalists have several advantages over creative writers:

- They can get access to anyone, and ask people anything they want to know.
- They work in sociable teams rather than alone in an attic.
- They have editors who help them make sense.
- They have colleagues who can make pictures to help explain things.
- They have lots of readers every day.

Having practiced and taught journalism for a while, I just started writing my first novel. This new venture has shown me that journalists also have some disadvantages:

- They can't make up the characters or what the characters say.
- They can't put their enemies in their stories as villains.
- They can't have all the space they want.

Journalists cover the world of facts and real people because facts and real people are just as interesting as the Trojan War, British aristocratic families, or Bohemias with seacoasts. One of the great pleasures of journalistic life is telling each other stories we've just uncovered, and quoting people saying things we could never imagine. We listen, and shake our heads, and say, "You can't make stuff like that up."

To paraphrase the late James Reston, journalists write letters to friends they don't know, about interesting things their friends didn't have time to find out about. And the best ones use storytelling as their vehicle.

Newspaper "stories" don't necessarily tell stories. Sometimes they package facts in space. And that's the problem that this anthology, *Telling Stories/ Taking Risks*, takes risks to avoid. It includes real stories by authors who don't believe they have to sound like everybody else in the newsroom. Real stories by authors who believe that storytelling best explains things that people need to know to manage their complex lives. Real stories by authors who believe that readers like to read.

These authors use all the tools of the creative writer creatively: dialogue, characterization, appropriate story structures, imagery and telling detail, irony and juxtaposition–you name it. They often write about themselves–not wallowing in their emotions like Romantic poets, but using their lives and feelings as springboards for reporting.

Here's the main difference between literature and journalism. Poets look inward and pound words into shape to describe what they find inside. Journalists look outward into the world and bring that world kicking and screaming onto their pages. Everybody in journalism knows that all good journalism writing depends on good reporting. And now that I've played in both worlds, I believe that all great writing, factual or fictional, comes from great reporting.

–DON FRY, WRITING COACH

Don Fry has always regarded himself as a failure because he hasn't written The Great North Carolina Novel. He has managed to publish 18 other books, though, on Beowulf, Norse sagas, coaching writers, and excellent newspaper writing. But he has almost finished a World War II bomber novel, so there's still hope.

Introduction

Writing is very easy, really.
All you have to do is keep a bright continuous stream
before your reader's eyes.
–John Gardner

John Gardner actually said this once in a talk, but maybe he didn't believe it. Certainly, the writers I teach and coach don't find writing "very easy, really." But then writers of nonfiction can't invent their material. They have to go with the facts, sometimes spending weeks discovering what the facts are, and they have to go with the words their sources speak, sometimes coaxing them to talk at all. Then they have to be sure that the "bright continuous stream" is fair and ethical and provable and readable–and not just readable but surprising. Somehow they succeed. Publishers and editors, booksellers and book buyers, readers and writers, all know that this is the first great age of nonfiction.

Recent linguistic work called "relevance theory" offers an explanation of what readers want from what they read. Readers want the greatest contextual effect for the smallest processing effort. They want the most surprising or mind-bending or hunch-confirming information packaged so that it can be read easily–the biggest bang for the smallest buck. If both the story and the telling are familiar, they won't bother to read it. But if both are radically strange, they won't be able to.

As we learn what readers want–and of course they are us–we have to abandon the old pairs we have used for talking about writing, like form and content or reporting and writing. Gathering a bunch of facts and stuffing them into tired forms gets yawns. Questioning the usual sources and dumping notes into files wins no prizes. The writers here don't work that way. Instead, they write *and* report from the beginning as they labor to give us a mind-bending read. Instead of thinking of the traditional categories–profiles, features, news stories, obits, sports, and the like–as forms to fill, they treat them as genres, responses to recurring social needs. Take the obituary, for example; a time-honored function of journalism is recognizing death. In this book you will find obits you will hardly recognize. The best writers stretch the limits of the genres they are writing in, using new strategies for unexpected subjects and purposes.

They also question the oldest assumption of journalism: that language is a transparent medium. Old time reporters–those guys in the movies who smoke cigarettes, wear fedoras, and call in their stories on crank telephones– maintained a cheerful but antique positivism about the relationship of language to the world. As David Brinkley once explained in a TV interview: "Journalism is very simple really. Reporters tell people what happened today and if they understand, they tell people what it means. That's all there is to it."

These writers don't find the process nearly so simple or straightforward. They believe that the world we inhabit is in part—some argue in large part—constructed by the language we use to talk about it. So the act of writing is always—no matter how "factual" the story—an act of selecting and creating, naming and foregrounding, leaving out and marginalizing. Today's most exciting journalists call attention to their own acts of writing, asking self-conscious questions: How should this story be told? What if the sources do the telling? What is my role? How has covering this story changed who I am? What about my own story?

Telling Stories/Taking Risks is organized according to the degree of the reporter's own involvement or presence in the story. It begins with writers who remain invisible and it ends with writers who have decided they must be seen. Thus, the stories in Chapter 1, "Telling Their Stories," are written in the third person. But each of these writers has taken a risk, either by seeing more, knowing more, using an unexpected structure, or by telling stories of those seldom spotlighted. Several of these writers let those who were part of the story do all the telling, remaining absent even as fact-gatherers. One writer makes the accumulation of minute detail carry the point, whereas another changes the angle of the news through relentless reporting—not stopping with an account of a shooting, but adding up the exact costs of one gunshot wound. Just as the writing of history has expanded from stories of presidents and generals and kings to accounts of how ordinary people work and live and die, so too are journalists now writing about those who don't make news except as they face life-threatening diseases, struggle with poverty, or simply live their lives in odd and funny ways.

In Chapter 2, "Telling Stories from Inside," our writers get on the bus and take us along for the ride, admitting to the role of perceiver and sometimes to more. They teach us on the way, sometimes explaining the inside story of a whole industry, sometimes describing the way an unusual mind works. They go behind events to look for causes: What does snake-handling have to do with religious faith, or how do crab pickers feel about their work? They are betrayed by a source or beaten at Scrabble or fascinated by city folk. Here we sense the presence of an observer, calling attention to the complicated and problematic act of storytelling.

Another tradition broken by the writers here is the long-standing journalistic practice of not taking a stand—except on the op-ed page. Reporters are supposed to maintain balance and fairness, tell us both sides of the story, then stop. In Chapter 3, "Telling Stories That Persuade," the reporters find the facts, but these become an argument. Most journalists pretend that reporting is not persuasion, but these writers select and arrange their evidence to direct us to specific conclusions about our world. Some enter their own stories, staring down a defendant or questioning the nature of their own involvement.

But the most radical risk taken here is the admission of the personal. In Chapter 4, "Telling Our Stories," the writers refuse their roles as transmitters of information or invisible onlookers with notepads. Instead, they reveal themselves as persons with memories and experiences and histories, persons who when pricked, bleed, sometimes forever. Their admissions make us realize that print journalism is produced by people, not by processes.

All of the stories here, we believe, offer some kind of bang for the reader's buck as they stretch the limits of journalism. But one tradition that is not broken is the writer's commitment to the reader. Readers structure stories according to abstract plans–cause-effect or problem-solution, for example–but they are moved by images, pictures, and sensory details. The writing that helps us understand our world offers us radically changing levels of abstraction, moving up to offer us more complex levels of explanation, but also swooping lower to provide us with more of the grittiness of the actual world. Explaining *and* exemplifying. Reporting *and* writing. Telling stories, taking risks.

Is print journalism over? Not yet. Not for me. Newspapers and magazines and books are still amazingly efficient–packable, permanent, and wireless. But even if paper goes, writing won't–because we're hard-wired for language, programmed to tell our stories, forever trying to tell them in new ways.

Carolyn B. Matalene
Professor of English
University of South Carolina

Chapter

Telling
Their Stories

Greg Raver-Lampman

Charlotte's Millions

"How can we get today's readers to buy tomorrow's paper?" editors ask. One solution is to keep your readers hanging–with a serial. When Greg Raver-Lampman, of The Virginian-Pilot, *looked into the form, he studied some famous practitioners like Charles Dickens and Wilkie Collins. But they wrote fiction. Raver-Lampman wanted to write about real people and events. That's risky.*

First, you need to understand the form. "A serial has a plot that builds to a climax and usually gets told from the viewpoint of a central character," Raver-Lampman says. That's different from a series, a group of stories on the same topic. Second, you can't write a serial the way you would a traditional news or even a feature story because you mustn't pull readers out of the time sequence. "You must be scrupulous to keep the reader in the moment, observing what happens through the eyes of a protagonist." So when he teaches the form, Raver-Lampman tells students to "kill the reporter so the characters can speak." "Charlotte's Millions" has no quotes spoken to the writer but much reported dialogue, and that meant extensive reporting. "When Charlotte and Chip were driving around at 3 A.M. talking about cars, I knew what they were saying because I was there," says Raver-Lampman.

There's also the problem of pacing. Raver-Lampman figured that out by reading medieval romances and quest stories. "You need to discover the natural climax and the peaks leading to it," he says. That means not telling the ending until the end, contrary to the newsroom tradition of placing the most dramatic element in the lead. In Charlotte's story, the dramatic tension is psychological. "Charlotte is a penny-pinching night nurse and coupon clipper who must reconcile herself to being a millionaire. Her inability to spend any of this money culminates with a splurge inconceivable only days before."

Raver-Lampman has learned from Jon Franklin and his book Writing for Story *–"a must for anyone attempting to write drama-driven stories." Maybe he learned something too from specializing in Greek literature at Berkeley, earning a B.A. in 1979. After all,* The Odyssey *is our first cliff-hanger. Since earning a Pulitzer nomination for his serials, he has taught journalism at Norfolk State University. Currently, he's on leave from the newsroom to write novels.* Magic and Loss *and* The Secret of the Mango Tree *have been published;* White Tribes *is on the way. It's probably a page-turner.*

–CM

Greg Raver-Lampman, Charlotte's Millions, *The Virginian-Pilot/The Ledger-Star,* July 14–19, 1991. Reprinted courtesy of *The* (Norfolk, VA) *Virginian-Pilot.*

Coupon-clipper hits Lotto fortune

SHAD POINT, Md.–If there was a way to turn a dime into a dollar, Charlotte Jones was for it. Whether she was cutting coupons or yanking the handle of a quarter slot, she never passed up a chance to double her money.

Charlotte had taken coupon cutting to a near science. When she went to Super Giant, she lugged her coupons in an accordion file, craftily cross-indexed. Those dime-off discounts were free money, pennies from heaven. Checkout clerks moaned when they saw her coming.

One time Charlotte clipped 31 half-off coupons for Scott paper towels. Then she spotted a double-coupon sale at the Super Giant. The way Charlotte figured things, double value for a half-off coupon meant free paper towels. She gathered up her coupons and toted home 31 free rolls of paper towels–although they'd made her pay the sales tax. Unsatisfied, Charlotte figured another angle: She could drive to Delaware, where there is no sales tax, and walk away with the paper towels absolutely free.

A love of gambling ran just as deep. Before Charlotte had even learned long division, her Aunt Lenora would take her to Pennyland, an Ocean City arcade. There was a slot machine stashed behind a curtain there, out of view of most customers. Aunt Lenora would take young Charlotte behind the curtain, shove in quarters and let her pull the handle, over and over. The machine would jangle and colorful fruit symbols would dance before her eyes. Sometimes, quarters cascaded out.

The next hook was bingo. In grade school, Grandma Lillie took Charlotte to the local hall. Charlotte won. She called out "bingo!" and picked a prize, a metal wastebasket with a pedal that opened the lid. She has haunted bingo halls ever since, sometimes four times a week, laying out as much as $30 dollars a night.

Today, jackpots come in cash, not trash cans.

About five years ago, Charlotte got hooked on lotteries. She read tales of big-time winners and snatched up several tickets every week. She'd buy Maryland tickets at the Brown Derby in Fruitland. When Virginia launched a lottery, friends Charlotte knew only as Mr. and Mrs. Teapot would buy her five tickets a week in Chincoteague.

Charlotte also liked to drive up to a truck stop in Delaware where she could play instant games like "Whole Lotta Scratchin' Goin' On."

Charlotte loved to win, even if only a few bucks. One time she hit for $1,500 at bingo. About six years ago, she scored $860 in the Maryland lottery.

Like all players, she fantasized about hitting the big one. It would be enough to let her take vacations. Nothing fancy, nothing wasteful. Charlotte never imagined for a moment that she could win enough to quit her job.

When Virginia's lottery jackpot climbed to $21.4 million in June, Charlotte went all out. The Teapots bought her 10 tickets in Chincoteague and a friend, Chip Fields, bought her another 10 at T's Corner, a souvenir and fireworks shop near the Virginia-Maryland border.

On a hot, humid Sunday, June 16, the day after the numbers were drawn, Charlotte checked the 10 tickets the Teapots had bought for her. Nothing. Then she remembered the other 10 in the glove compartment of her 1984 Volkswagen Rabbit.

One of the tickets startled her. She had five numbers. That could be worth a couple thousand bucks. A big win.

She phoned the lottery office to check. While her sister, Margaret, worked on tomato plants in the garden, Charlotte stood in the screened-in porch, covered with sweat, holding the telephone, listening to the recording, jotting numbers on the back of an old lottery ticket: 8-22-23-41-42-44.

The shock hit when she hung up. She seemed to have all *six* numbers. She figured she'd written one number wrong. She called back. She checked again.

"Sister," Charlotte called out, "I think I've got all six numbers on the Virginia Lottery." Charlotte's eyes teared up. Her sister ran in.

"We can go to Alaska," Charlotte thought.

"Have you got the numbers written down right?" Margaret asked. "Are you sure?" Charlotte continued making calls, and all verified that she had the winning ticket. Somebody from the lottery had even gone to T's Corner to verify that the ticket was sold there.

Suddenly her eyes seemed to dry out. Even her sweat seemed to dry up. She felt numb.

This wasn't another $1,500 win. This was beyond the scope of her imagination. She was talking *millions.* Charlotte, who had spent so much of her life calculating the exact savings on a roll of paper towels, struggled too comprehend the concept of seemingly unlimited riches.

She had seen pictures of people winning–cooks and sailors and assembly line workers–but those people were just faces on TV.

But now . . . she was every gambler's dream, the biggest single lottery winner in Virginia history.

Still, it wouldn't seem real. Not until the lottery people verified her ticket and cut her a check.

Charlotte stuck her lucky ticket between the pages of a Harlequin romance, "Fantasy Lover" by Kami Lane. She wrapped a rubber band around it.

She and her sister talked. Tomorrow they'd set out on a long trip: Down the shore, across the bay, through Norfolk, then all the way up to Richmond.

But if everything was true, by the end of the trip she'd be a multimillionaire.

Free money has a price, winner told

Before giving big check, state has gentle warning

When Charlotte Jones arrived in Richmond on June 17, lottery officials led her into a conference room and sat her down in front of a TV set. They had a little film they wanted her to watch.

Charlotte felt a bit dumbfounded. She had already decided to quit her job. She had tossed and turned all night, thinking about what life would be like as a millionaire. In all, she had slept an hour.

As the lottery people rolled the video tape, Charlotte didn't know what to expect.

It opened with pictures of celebrating lottery winners holding up big mock checks with lots of zeroes. The soundtrack played Glenn Miller's lazy Dixieland version of the 1940s classic, "I Haven't Time To Be a Millionaire."

As the clarinets and saxophones died out, the video cut to a balding man in a black suit. Letters on the screen identified him as Ken Thorson, Virginia's lottery director.

"Congratulations," Thorson said in a calm voice, staring out of the TV screen at Charlotte. "Today you are going to join a growing list of Virginia lottery players who've won a very significant prize."

He seemed very serious.

"Being a winner means many things," he intoned. After telling Charlotte she was going to carry home a large check, Thorson seemed to grow even more somber, his voice soothing, like an undertaker's.

"With all this happiness and good feeling," Thorson said, "there are going to be some new responsibilities and some changes in your life. Things are going to be different—financially, socially and, yes, even *psychologically.*"

Charlotte hadn't thought of "social" and "psychological" change when she fantasized about the lottery. She had fantasized about *winning.*

"Like most people," Thorson continued, "you've probably had almost no experience dealing with the news media, or with people asking you for donations, or making decisions about investing large sums of money. Well, that's all going to change."

The video dispensed technical information about the rate of payouts, about the need to name beneficiaries, about dealing with reporters, and about taxes.

At one point, the video cut to David Snyder, a Lynchburg man who had won $10.9 million.

Snyder told how his minister dropped by to warn him about people trying to mooch money. As Snyder explained it, the minister gave him this advice:

"You've just got to say to yourself, 'Hey, I don't have a guilty conscience about rejecting people and saying no.'

"You cannot cure the world's poor. So don't even attempt it."

The stuff about not curing the world's ills made good sense to Charlotte. She'd remember that.

At the end of the tape, Virginia's first lottery winner, C. Anthony Palermo of Virginia Beach, talked about the changes that come with winning.

"It takes a lot of getting used to," Palermo said. "Maybe next year I'll start getting used to it. Maybe I'll never get used to it. I don't know."

The video ended. Charlotte had to sign papers, verify that she had made out a will. Lottery people encouraged her to step into the next room and give the media a look at the big winner.

They led her into a room where a long, brown formica table stood in front of a Virginia Lottery banner. TV cameras, lights, reporters and photographers were jammed in there. Charlotte walked in alongside Thorson.

Thorson read a news release the Lottery Department had prepared in the back room while Charlotte stood holding the backs of two plastic chairs, her eyes locked on him. She kept her purse slung on her shoulder.

Occasionally, Charlotte glanced out at all the reporters. She had seen these news conferences before, but it looked so different from this side of the table.

"Now, I'd like to present her this check, our ceremonial check," Thorson said, holding up a 6-foot-long green cardboard check, made out for $21.4 million. Charlotte held one side, Thorson the other. Lights flashed. Charlotte laughed.

"Our congratulations to you," Thorson said, reaching across to shake her hand for the perfect canned photo opportunity. There was another rush of clicks and flashes.

"Thank you very much," Charlotte said, and the press gallery burst into applause.

Thorson explained to the media, to all these reporters, that Charlotte was "available for questions." She heard a voice ask in a slow drawl: "When did you find out that you won?"

Charlotte looked at the reporter. The guy was dressed impeccably. He had styled hair and a dark, even tan. She figured he must be from one of the TV stations.

"Yesterday afternoon," Charlotte said. She went into some detail.

"Are you scared and nervous right now?" the same newsman asked.

"Yes," Charlotte said, breaking into laughter.

"What do you plan on doing with it?" the guy asked.

"Have a lot of fun," Charlotte said.

"What does that mean?"

"Well," Charlotte said . . . and she realized she didn't know the answer. "I've got family. And, uh, we like to travel. That's the main thing, right now."

"You plan on traveling to Europe or something?" the guy drawled.

"No, not Europe," Charlotte said. She had never been even slightly interested in seeing Europe.

"Where do you plan on traveling?"

"Umm, maybe Alaska," Charlotte said. Then she paused and added, "Canada." She paused again. "Hawaii," she said. Then she figured, what the heck. "Australia . . . New Zealand."

The room burst into laughter. Charlotte let out a big belly laugh.

"What are your plans?" asked a woman sitting next to the TV guy. "I understand you're going to quit your job. What else? Give us a rundown of what you're going to do."

"I have no idea," Charlotte said. "I haven't been able to think of anything." People laughed again.

"I really haven't," she said. "Your mind just goes and goes and goes and goes. You feel like you're beginning to go a little bit . . ."–Charlotte made the look of a crazy person.

In a few minutes it was over.

Back in the conference room, the lottery people gave her the real check for $812,562.96, her first annual payout. The lottery director took out a fountain pen, signed his name, then blew on the check to dry the ink.

They also gave her a Virginia Lottery goodie bag with a T-shirt, a cap, a potato-chip-bag clip, a lottery pin, a key ring and a hot-and-cold travel cup, all inscribed with the Virginia Lottery logo. Charlotte got a kick out of that. She always liked freebies.

Charlotte walked down the stairs, lugging her goodie bag. People applauded and shook her hand. Guards led her out the back of the building to her sister Margaret's van.

After all the ceremony, after all the paperwork and the video and the news conference and the private discussions, the reality still hadn't sunk in.

As she and Margaret set out for the long ride from Richmond to their home in Shad Point, Md., Charlotte thought about all that the lottery officials had told her. They stopped at the snack shop on the Chesapeake Bay Bridge-Tunnel and got a dinner of candy bars, soft pretzels and lemonade.

Charlotte had decided that she wanted to donate two fetal heart scopes, which cost about $600 each, to the hospital where she worked. Other than that, she had no plans.

She was sailing uncharted waters here. What really happens when, suddenly, you're unbelievably rich?

Charlotte had no idea.

She was about to find out.

It's time to celebrate new riches

But reality of wealth remains unfathomable

Charlotte Jones, newly declared millionaire, rolled up the driveway of her home in Shad Point, Md., to find the house full of nieces and nephews and cousins.

Her sister Margaret's sons, Buck and Al, were there with wives and children. A "congratulations" banner fluttered outside the screened porch, near the hummingbird feeder. On the porch was a mylar balloon reading "$21.4 million!"

When she walked into the house, Charlotte found thousands of phony dollar bills thrown around the house by her 9-year-old grandniece, Katie. On the mirror in Charlotte's room was a sign showing a hand clutching a bag of loot, inscribed with the words: "Today is the first day of the rest of your life."

Katie asked if Charlotte would take her to Disney World. Charlotte said she'd think about it. She also suggested that Charlotte buy a Porsche.

"I'm *not* getting a Porsche," Charlotte said.

The Jones clan had always been close. Charlotte, who has never married, lives with her sister Margaret, who is 12 years older. Margaret's sons and daughter always included Charlotte in parties, holidays and vacations.

Charlotte and Margaret had different interests. Charlotte had dragged Margaret to bingo games, but bingo bored Margaret. She didn't care much for slot machines or pinball, either. Margaret tended to stay home, weaving baskets or painting still-lifes.

Buck and Al and the grandchildren were often at the house, where they'd munch pizza, hot dogs or one of Margaret's specialties, bread with cheese and bacon bits cooked in the toaster oven. Margaret sometimes bought packs of cold cuts. As she made the sandwiches, Margaret would ask whether people wanted "round or square" meat.

Margaret did a good deal of the cooking and cleaning around the house. Her husband, who passed away 10 years back, once told Charlotte: "You're a wonderful nurse. The best nurse Peninsula General has ever had. Other than that, you're not worth a damn."

Charlotte still laughed about that.

The night when Charlotte returned with her winnings, she drank a beer, her first since May. She wasn't much of a drinker. She conked right out and drifted off to sleep.

The next day, Charlotte went to breakfast at Denny's with some night-shift nurses. Then she set about doing chores unique to millionaires.

Charlotte already had a stockbroker and an accountant and saw no reason to change them. She understood that she needed "financial planning," but had just one investment in mind: AT&T stock. Somehow, it seemed so blue-chip. That was the stock rich people owned.

That morning, Charlotte went to the bank to deposit her lottery winnings.

When she walked in, bank employees broke into applause. As she filled out her deposit slip, Charlotte examined the lottery check. It came with a stub, like a paycheck. The gross amount was $1,069,161.78. The "one" with all those figures behind it represented a *million dollars.*

There was a deduction of more than $213,000—almost a quarter of a million dollars—for federal taxes. The state tax deduction of $42,766.47 was more than Charlotte earned in a year as a nurse. The net amount of the check was $812,562.96.

She followed her usual paycheck-deposit routine of filling out a deposit slip for a round figure—$800,000 in this case. The extra money was pocket change. Then it hit her. The "pocket change" would amount to more than 12 *thousand* dollars in *cash.*

She tore up the deposit slip and wrote a new one.

After she deposited the check, someone asked her whether she had a regular or premium account.

"What's the difference?" Charlotte asked.

"Sixth-tenths of 1 percent," came the answer.

"So what?" she said. Someone suggested it could mean $15,000 in interest.

It was stunning. Charlotte tried to do the calculations herself, but the figures were so big. One years' interest on $812,000 would amount to more than a year's pay.

It was overwhelming. The local newspaper had calculated that Charlotte's $812,000, broken down to a 40-hour workweek, came to $390 an hour. Charlotte, the woman who had worried years about maximizing her money, who played bingo every week dreaming of a jackpot of maybe $1,000, suddenly had this money in the bank, growing, proliferating, breeding, expanding.

The longer she left the money alone, the more there would be to spend.

When she got home, it was a madhouse. The telephone rang non-stop. Friends and neighbors trooped to the house to congratulate her.

A news crew came out to interview her. Someone told Charlotte that the TV weatherman said on the air that he'd be happy to be her pet dog.

Even Margaret got calls. Margaret heard from a banker in Baltimore whose bank had handled a small trust account for her. The banker wanted to drop by for a visit.

The banker from Baltimore—from the big city where everyone looks down on the Eastern Shore yokels—would barely have taken Margaret's call a week ago. Now he wanted to drop by for a social call. Charlotte laughed.

Margaret said thanks, but no thanks.

With all the turmoil, Charlotte tried to maintain her routine. The next morning, a Wednesday, she showed up at her monthly breakfast club at the Pittsville Diner. When she got back home, there were more visits, more phone calls.

At one point, Margaret came over with the phone.

"Charlotte," she said, "It's Hazel Massey."

When Charlotte was 12 years old, she had been hospitalized with rheumatic fever. Hazel Massey was in the next bed. They had exchanged Christmas cards for years.

"Oh my god!" Charlotte laughed into the phone. "How you doing?"

For Charlotte, those first days were wonderful, hearing from friends she hadn't even thought of for years, people from grade school. It was like being on "This is Your Life" 24 hours a day.

Friends kept trooping by to congratulate her. Her grandniece, Katie, continued to hint about Disney World and the Porsche.

One old friend sat on the screen porch and said, matter-of-factly, "You're going to have a lot of people after you."

"I don't doubt that," Charlotte said. "And they're going to go right past me, too."

That was one of many warnings. Among the congratulations, people offered advice.

Be careful, Charlotte, some would say.

Watch yourself.

Don't do anything foolish.

Don't forget your friends.

Some people called the money a "mixed blessing."

With everything going on, Charlotte wanted to make it clear she wasn't about to come unhinged, or snooty, or arrogant. She made every effort to do what she had done before becoming filthy rich. Those first days, however, she spent almost all her time fielding phone calls, talking to relatives.

On Wednesday, June 19, Charlotte decided it was time to venture out into the world again to show she hadn't changed.

It was time to play some bingo.

Bingo! It's time for some fun

New riches don't weaken love of all the old hangouts

Charlotte rolled her 1984 Volkswagen Rabbit into St. Francis De Sales, next to a car with a bumper sticker that read, "Happiness is yelling bingo."

For Charlotte, bingo was an important ritual.

After all this fuss over the millions, the hubbub, the pressure of decisions, Charlotte was returning to a world that made her comfortable, to good friends, to the rhythms of the smoke-filled bingo parlor.

Bingo players, like Charlotte, take pride in the contributions the games have made to St. Francis, a Catholic school. Charlotte could point to the new wing that bingo built.

Of course, a good cause isn't everything. Bingo players enjoy the fact that this collection plate can sometimes run in reverse, dumping money back into their laps.

St. Francis was just one nocturnal haunt. Charlotte also played bingo at the local synagogue and at the Improved Order of Redmen, Tony Tank Tribe No. 149, the lodge of a local men's club.

She also enjoyed playing pinball at a truck stop up the road and cruising the streets of Salisbury after midnight with her old pal, Chip Fields.

This was Charlotte's world, populated by friends she'd had for decades. If being a millionaire meant leaving this behind, Charlotte wanted no part of it.

Someone spotted her as she got out of the VW.

"Lord have mercy," Charlotte's old buddy shouted, "Do I get to touch a multimillionaire?"

When Charlotte walked into the bingo parlor, people flocked to her, asked to hug her, to touch her hand.

"I'm glad you came," one woman said.

"I never thought about not coming," Charlotte said. "I love bingo."

As the turmoil died, Charlotte bought her usual allotment: 34 hard bingo cards, six specials, eight bonanzas, eight kenos and two quickies.

She unpacked her blue plastic bingo bag, like a doctor opening his kit and laying out his scalpels. Inside were tools and talismans: magnetic bingo wands, bingo daubers, and her good-luck charms—a stuffed Garfield cat, a small blue plastic elephant and a Babar's World Tour Growth Chart Storybook.

Charlotte spread her cards out on the table and lit a cigarette.

A popper sent up numbered Ping-Pong balls, and the game was on. A caller shouted out the number: "N-47."

Beginning players marked single cards. Charlotte tracked 34 at a time while juggling her magnetic bingo wand, her cigarettes and a fistful of intricate side games.

Marty Huebschman, a stooped, 84-year-old man from Salisbury, shuffled over as he spotted Charlotte.

"How can you do it?" asked Marty, a bingo helper and aluminum can collector. "How can you play bingo?"

"Because I love bingo," Charlotte said.

"You must," said Marty.

He leaned over and hugged her.

"Charlotte," he whispered, "do what you say you want to do. Travel the world."

"Hey, Marty," somebody shouted from the back of the room, "are you proposing to Charlotte?" Marty walked away as everyone laughed.

Another number popped out. Charlotte scanned her cards and realized she had a winner.

"Bingo!" she called.

There was a collective groan, then everyone burst into laughter.

Charlotte played for about four hours. She won twice, raking in $50, more than she'd paid for all those cards. She let everyone know: Fifty bucks or $21.4 million, winning was just as sweet.

For Charlotte, there was more to a night on the town than a game of bingo. Whenever she won, she sprang for pinball. She telephoned her friend Chip, and the two headed out for the Oasis, a truck stop across the line in Delaware.

Charlotte and Chip had a lot in common. They both liked to check out fancy cars and diesel rigs, or listen to police scanners and follow ambulances and firetrucks into the night.

When they walked into the Oasis, the waitress came out from behind the orange formica counter. "I didn't figure I'd see you in here," she said to Charlotte. "I figured you bought your own pinball machine."

A trucker in a T-shirt and baseball cap recognized Charlotte. "You want to go into the trucking business, lady?" he said.

At the cash register there were two different Delaware instant lottery games. "I want five of each," Charlotte said, pointing to the lottery cards, "and a roll of quarters."

Charlotte's favorite pinball machines were Whirlwind and Secret Service. She and Chip pumped quarters in and played until about 2 A.M. Sometimes the game would make a loud click, a sound she loved because it meant she'd won a free game.

When they walked out of the Oasis, the night was still warm and humid. A handful of cars cruised by. In the parking lot, dozens of massive rigs rumbled, spitting out a gritty exhaust. Truckers were asleep inside. Charlotte and Chip scanned the parking lot, looking for money. They'd done that ever since Charlotte found a dollar bill lying flat in a puddle long ago.

They climbed into Chip's pickup.

"You want to go through here and look at the trucks?" Chip asked.

It was part of their ritual. She didn't see any reason to change the routine because she was rich.

"Just a quickie," Charlotte said. Chip maneuvered his pickup between lines of 18-wheelers, admiring the chrome and the lights on the massive rigs.

"There's a good one," Chip said. "A double-decker."

"National Food Express," Charlotte said, reading off the side of the truck. "I've *heard* of them."

"There's another double-decker," Chip said. "That's a Ford."

"But it doesn't have a huge cab on it," Charlotte said. They looked over the trucks for about 10 minutes, then headed for home. The world seemed asleep.

There was one more stop to make. As they drove into Salisbury, Chip and Charlotte turned into a Cadillac dealership. They'd been doing this for more than a year, long before she'd won the lottery. The night watchman, Joe Barnett, knew them.

They cruised through the lot, spellbound by Fleetwoods and El Dorados and Coup De Villes. "Oh, cars, cars, cars, cars," Chip said, his headlights splashing against the line of Cadillacs.

He pulled up to a tan-and-brown truck. "That two-tone," Chip said. "That's pretty."

"That *is* pretty," Charlotte said.

Chip grew quiet for a moment.

"Ah, if I ever win the lottery . . . " he said, his voice trailing off.

There was a moment of silence.

Charlotte gazed around at all these cars with leather seats and every luxury, cars she'd dreamed about owning. People kept asking when she was going to buy a Cadillac, a Rolls, a Porsche. But Charlotte figured you don't just jump in and buy a car. No matter how many millions you have, no matter how fast your money multiplies, you don't waste. You shop around, you look for deals.

Maybe Charlotte would be comfortable walking into a showroom to buy a Cadillac sometime soon.

But she wasn't ready yet.

Everyone asks for piece of Lotto prize

With money in the bank, time for Disney World

They were coming out of the woodwork.

About the time Charlotte was getting back to her routine, the mail started to change. She figured she didn't have to worry about junk mail because her address wasn't listed in the phone book. But three days after she went to Richmond to pick up her winnings, among cards and letters from old friends she found an envelope addressed to "Charlotte Jones, Shad Point, Md.," with no street address.

She was amazed that the letter had gotten through.

"Congratulations on your big win," the letter said. "I wish you all the happiness that your new found fortune can possibly bring you.

"Enclosed you will find a brochure of my lovely home on the Chickahominy River."

This guy wanted Charlotte to buy a house, a mansion.

"From the article in the paper," the letter continued, "you seem to be a family oriented person. Our home is a wonderful family house. The neighborhood is very quiet, but lends itself to entertainment if you so desire."

Enclosed was a picture of a massive estate on the banks of the Chickahominy. It reminded Charlotte of the spreads she'd see in the back of *Town & Country* magazine. When she'd look at those homes, she'd think: What kind of person could live there? Charlotte liked living in Shad Point in her sister's two-bedroom home, with its knickknacks and puzzles, with the mugs and visors and baskets and souvenirs. Charlotte didn't see any reason to move. Ever.

But now, someone figured she needed a mansion.

"Prestige on the water," the brochure said. The house, according to the prose, had its own pier, on deep water. It also had a 7-foot-long bathtub with eight water jets.

The list price: $545,000.

For Charlotte, the letter was a bizarre joke. But it hammered home how much money she had. She could buy this house, outright, and have money to spare from just her first check. It boggled the mind.

Over the next few days, more letters came, addressed to "Charlotte Jones, Shad Point, Md." Some were hilarious. One man wrote to say he had bought five lottery tickets the week Charlotte won. He wanted Charlotte to refund his five bucks.

A company mailed a card with a picture of Charlotte in the middle of a mock newspaper story, under the headline, "Prominent citizen makes today's news." Inside, the company was offering to sell her an alarm system.

One inventor from northern Virginia wanted Charlotte to help develop a new computer keyboard. The corporation would even put her on the company's board of advisers—if she invested.

A man phoned Peninsula General Hospital from Virginia and said he had seen Charlotte's picture in the newspaper. He wanted her to appear in his next movie. He left his name and telephone number.

An insurance agent sent a letter offering to plan her estate. But he made a crucial mistake: The letter arrived with 14 cents postage due.

Other people wrote offering to "manage" her money. Now that she had money, everyone wanted to help her.

These letters didn't bother Charlotte. She gathered her mail each morning and tried to separate the friendly cards from the "trash."

"It's going to be fun," Charlotte told her sister. "The trash we're going to laugh at and the rest we're going to enjoy."

Then the really desperate letters started to trickle in.

One man wrote saying that he had declared bankruptcy and needed $3,000 to pay off the IRS and "get them off my back."

"I definitely don't want you to give me anything," the letter said. "Only for a loan which I *will* repay."

One woman, who claimed to be a schoolteacher, wrote a letter in pencil. It was full of misspellings. The woman said her fallopian tubes had been tied, but, due to some mistake, she ended up with four children instead of three. She wanted cash.

Another woman had heart trouble. She needed a new home with a ventilation system. She not only described her disease, but sent a few EKG strips as well.

One letter came in from Dale City, Va.

"Dear Mrs. Jones," it began. "I am sure you have had several letters by now from people in my situation and I don't really know why I am writing but, who knows. First, let me congratulate you on your winnings. That's a lot of money and I hope it will bring your happiness. This is *my* story." The letter then launched into a plea for cash.

One week after Charlotte won the lottery, she went to clear out her locker at work at Peninsula General Hospital. There were a lot of hugs and jokes. Taped to her locker were more letters. These were addressed to Charlotte Jones, lottery winner, care of Peninsula General.

One of them caught Charlotte's attention. It was typed, two pages long, single-spaced, from a Filipino woman in Richmond who cleaned houses and worked as a convenience store clerk. She included a picture of herself, sitting on a couch.

The letter rambled on about the Lord and destiny and life. The lady mentioned that her parents lived near Mount Pinatubo, the volcano erupting in the Philippines. Finally she wrote:

"I know how to cook, do the laundry, clean your mansion, and do whatever you wants me to do and still receive better pay than housekeeping and 7-Eleven."

Some people seemed desperate. Charlotte heard one story that especially upset her. A gray-haired woman in a nurse's uniform had shown up at a store near Charlotte's home. The woman told the store clerk that she worked with Charlotte and wanted to congratulate her. She wanted to know where Charlotte lived.

That gave Charlotte the creeps. Anybody who worked with her knew where she lived. Did this woman disguise herself to try to find Charlotte? And what did she want?

For the first time, Charlotte started to feel a bit unsettled. She skipped going to the Oasis, the truck stop, on Saturday night. She figured there might be a lot of people there, people drinking. There might be some trouble.

She didn't want to take any chances. The first weekend after she'd won all that money, she spent Saturday clipping coupons.

On Tuesday, June 25, a cousin from Colorado arrived for a previously scheduled visit. The whole clan gathered on the porch to eat chicken wings, salmon salad, veggies and ice cream. It was a family party like dozens they'd had before.

Everyone talked about the lottery. Charlotte's grandniece, Katie, helped stitch up a "book of wants" made up of old bingo paper, held together by sewing thread. In the book, Katie wrote that she wanted a horse named "Time," plus a bridle and a saddle. Katie kept asking when Charlotte was going to buy a new car, like a Porsche. At one point, Katie said she wanted to go to Jamaica to get her hair done up in corn rows.

"You can get your hair done here, cheap," Charlotte said. "You don't have to go to Jamaica to get your hair done."

The cousin, Shirley Cowart, joked about Charlotte buying a Rolls-Royce.

Charlotte's niece, Noralynn, said she still had a hard time comprehending what had happened. "I still don't understand $21 million," Noralynn said to Charlotte. "What is $21 million?"

The fact that Charlotte was a millionaire didn't seem to register at all. If the family had gathered in a mansion, been driven home in a Rolls with Charlotte decked in jewels, waited on by a maid, the reality of the lottery might seem more tangible.

But what is money if it's not spent? What does it mean to have $800,000 in the bank, growing, expanding, and buying nothing?

Charlotte had read about misers who died and left behind dilapidated cars and run-down houses. People later found millions stashed in the bank, or stuffed in mattresses or hidden in old books or newspapers. In some ways, those miser millionaires were lucky. They were anonymous. Nobody knew about their wealth. They didn't have to contend with begging letters, the entreaties from car dealers and stockbrokers and sick, broken, miserable people.

Charlotte didn't want to go down in history as a millionaire miser. But she wanted to preserve her values, wanted to be cautious, wanted to keep her friends, the way of life she loved.

"When did it really hit you?" Shirley asked at one point that night.

Charlotte paused.

"It hasn't," she said.

As the relatives gathered, everyone started talking about Disney World. The talk of Cadillacs and trips to Alaska and New Zealand were all nebulous fantasies. But the talk of a family vacation to Disney World had started to take shape. Relatives had checked their calendars, looking for time off. They would have to go before school started in September.

"We've shortly got to make arrangements for that trip," said Charlotte's sister, Margaret.

There was no putting this one off.

The time had come to spend some money.

Learning the limits of wealth

Money talks, but some don't listen

Ten days after she hit Virginia's Lotto jackpot, Charlotte Jones trundled into the American Automobile Association office in Salisbury, Md., hurrying because she hoped to drive to Philadelphia that afternoon to visit a sick aunt.

The travel agent recognized her.

"That's right," said the agent. "You won all the money."

Charlotte had been to triple A many times. That was when a vacation meant a long drive in a hot car. Usually when Charlotte came to triple A, she had a ceiling on how much she could spend, a *certain amount* she couldn't exceed, no matter what. A little extra money on a hotel room meant a little less to spend on meals.

Charlotte was planning her first big splurge, a family vacation to Disney World. It was the first time she'd ever gone shopping without that *certain amount* factored in. Still, Charlotte remained convinced: You don't waste money, no matter how much you have.

Charlotte plopped down into a chair. The travel agent's nameplate read "Abby Turner."

"This is kind of short notice," Charlotte said. "There will be 13 of us. We're going to Disney World."

Charlotte explained that she wanted the cheapest air fair and a hotel *in* Disney World, so her nieces and nephews wouldn't have to drive to the Magic Kingdom every day.

There was one major requirement: The entire clan had to stay together.

Abby jotted everything down.

The air fare was a piece of cake. All 13 could fly coach, round-trip, for $3,444, less than $300 per adult. "That's not bad," said Charlotte. On short notice, she'd expected to get soaked.

"Just go ahead and do it."

Then Abby dove into the hotel negotiations. That's where everything started to crumble.

Abby yanked out a fistful of Disney World brochures and pointed out one of the most expensive hotels, the Grand Floridian.

"This one is *very* posh," Abby said. "People drive up in Rolls-Royces."

"I *don't* want that," Charlotte snapped. "We're not Rolls-Royce people."

Abby asked about camping.

No way.

Charlotte said she just wanted something that would allow the family to stay together. Abby showed Charlotte two- and three-bedroom Disney World villas, each of which could hold five or six people.

"There's no such thing as one villa that would hold us all?" Charlotte asked.

"No," Abby said.

Charlotte was disappointed. She'd always figured that if you had money, you could get whatever you wanted.

"Can you see if you can get something side by side?" Charlotte asked. "I don't want to be spread out from here to yonder."

Abby dialed Disney World, talked to someone at the reservation center, then turned to Charlotte: "She's saying they can't guarantee that you'll be together."

"Lord," Charlotte thought, "I've got all this money and I can't do what I *want?*"

The triple A office manager, Judy Skrip, pulled rank and offered to make some calls.

Charlotte watched as Judy punched the buttons of her telephone.

"Do you mind," Judy asked Charlotte, "if I tell them your situation?"

"No," Charlotte answered. Of course, Charlotte's "situation" was that she was rich beyond belief.

"I have a *V.I.P.* here," Judy said, when she finally reached someone on the phone. "This lady has just won—and I'm not kidding you . . ."

Judy put her hand over the mouthpiece and turned to Charlotte: "How much?" she asked.

"Twenty-one point four million," Charlotte answered matter-of-factly.

Judy talked into the telephone again. "Twenty-one point four million dollars." Charlotte listened, convinced that Judy would come away with a promise that the family would be together.

Abby got Charlotte some coffee.

Judy tried to persuade a number of people at the reservation center that Charlotte's villas needed to be together. But Judy spent most of her time on hold. Almost an hour had passed.

After one especially long pause, someone came back on the line.

"Even under *special* circumstances?" Judy asked. It was clear they were telling Judy that the family couldn't get rooms together.

"So," Judy said into the telephone in an angry tone, "instead of doing *that,* you'd rather have us take all *this* somewhere *else?*"

Charlotte recognized a threat. Still, it was an empty threat. She didn't *want* to go anywhere else. She wanted to go to Disney World. That's where her grand-niece Katie wanted to go. Disney World was *it.* That's where Mickey Mouse was. Katie wanted to see Mickey Mouse.

Judy made more calls, and spent more time on hold, while Charlotte sat, waiting, drinking her coffee, flipping through brochures, fidgeting, increasingly frustrated.

For the past week, Charlotte had been treated like a big shot in Salisbury. Now she was being treated like just another schmo in the land of Mickey and Donald. Fantasies may come true in Disney World, fairies may wish upon stars, but just try booking rooms together.

Charlotte watched over the next 10 minutes as Judy pulled every string she could think of. Those posters of Greece and Jamaica were getting old.

Judy talked on the phone some more, then turned to Charlotte. "They're telling me 99 percent of the time they're together."

For Charlotte, getting rooms together seemed a simple request. If being a millionaire didn't count for much, maybe *acting* like one would.

"I don't *want* 99 percent," Charlotte snapped. "I'll *buy* a home in Disney World for a week. I can afford it."

Abby, who was listening in, chuckled. "You rich people are so picky," she joked.

Judy hung up the telephone and suggested that Charlotte come back the next day. "Let us play with it," Judy said. Judy implied that some heavy string-pulling would take place.

Before Charlotte walked out, Judy spoke up again.

"Do you want to fly first class?" she asked.

Charlotte had never even considered first class. She'd made her position on first class known before: It was a waste of money. Charlotte asked Judy to look into the price, partly out of curiosity, but she didn't commit to anything.

"My sister will kill me if I waste too much money," Charlotte said.

Charlotte walked out, still burned that she couldn't get what she wanted. She spent that evening with an ailing aunt in Philadelphia, then drove back to Shad Point about midnight. Charlotte spent a bit of time thinking about the vacation.

What did it mean to be a millionaire if you couldn't get something as simple as a family vacation at Disney World?

She returned to the triple A office the next morning, intent on keeping her family together.

When Charlotte sat down, Judy explained that she had found accommodations, a hotel room for the whole family.

Charlotte was relieved.

Judy explained. Disney World's Contemporary Hotel, the concrete pyramid with the monorail going through it, had added on a presidential suite. It was a luxurious, three-bedroom spread with a parlor and five bathrooms.

"They say it's brand-new," Judy said. "It's a *huge* accommodation."

Charlotte said to book it.

Judy added up the bill for the suite for a week.

It came to $11,000.

Then Judy started talking about flying first class again.

The price was more outrageous than Charlotte's worst nightmare. It came to $20,481 for the group of 13 people. That was $17,000 *more* than coach fare.

Unlike the presidential suite, flying first class was *not* necessary. Judy could book the coach seats for $3,444. The Joneses would get to Disney World just as fast. First-class travel just meant wider seats and some pampering–for the price of a new pickup truck.

While Charlotte stared at the paper with the $20,481 scrawled on it, Judy said she could probably whittle the price down. Judy telephoned the airline. She signed Charlotte and her relatives up for frequent flier discounts. Judy also got a senior citizen discount for Charlotte's sister, Margaret, and another 10 percent discount for Charlotte, since she would be accompanying a senior.

It was just like cutting coupons, only on a grander scale. In a few minutes on the phone, Judy had managed to shave the first-class fare down to $9,734.

For Charlotte, it was mind boggling. Judy had managed to *save* $10,000.

Still, the first-class fare was $6,000 more than coach.

The vacation bill was adding up fast. Sure, Charlotte didn't have any *certain amount* budgeted. Even so, she had no desire to throw money away.

She'd already committed *$11,000* for a hotel room–and now Judy was talking about springing for $6,000 *extra* just to sit in the front of the plane. Six thousand dollars was more than Charlotte could save clipping coupons for God knows how long–*years*.

As Charlotte sat there, Judy was ticking off benefits of flying first class.

"You could almost get the whole first-class compartment and party the whole way down," Judy said at one point. They could get better meals, plus free champagne and orange juice.

Charlotte could picture it. Buck and Al at the windows. Charlotte and her sister sitting together. Charlotte's nieces enjoying first-class service and fancy meals. Katie soaking it up. Charlotte could even picture some schoolteacher or businessman getting the only other seat in the first-class cabin, surrounded by the Jones clan.

It was a wonderful image. So different somehow from the image of sitting in coach, a few seats back, behind the first-class curtain. But was that first-class fantasy really worth an *extra* $6,000?

"Well . . ." Charlotte said after a moment's hesitation.

Why not?

Julie Sullivan

Desperate Days at the Merlin

Julie Sullivan, a feature writer at The Spokesman-Review *in Spokane, Washington, lauds writing short as storytelling at its purest: the fewer the words, the sharper the focus. But the short form, she concedes, is fraught with risk for reporter and reader. "It can be paralyzing," she says, to deal with a whole story, in 10 or fewer column-inches.*

Her strategy, she explains, works best for breaking news and profiles of "ordinary people doing ordinary things," though it requires extraordinary courage. "Write with authority," she advises colleagues. "Your perspective matters. Trust yourself. Trust your material. You need confidence to select, rather than compress."

Sullivan's own confidence is hard won. Raised in a poor mining town in Montana, she learned to care about words from parents who taught English and woke her by reciting poems. In 1985, with a bachelor's degree in journalism from the University of Montana, she headed to a weekly newspaper in Alaska. To land the job at The Review *three years later, she pledged to work harder than anyone else. And she did, finding "no story too small, too demeaning."*

Sullivan is passionate about small–that is, short. At writing workshops, she seeks converts. Be practical, she advises. After all, twice as many short stories fit space hogged by a long one. Wrap short stories around those nearby, as Krystal Wilhelm's profile complemented "Desperate Days." Be persistent, she urges. Short-form writers must fight newsroom disdain, where short often equals lightweight. Or be funny. Negotiate a contract to get paid by the word.

Above all, as Sullivan knows, be professional. Respect deadlines. She had only three days and limited space to deliver "Desperate Days." Then, as Sullivan did at 34, you might win recognition. She has two national awards that acknowledge short: in 1991 from the American Society of Newspaper Editors and in 1996 from the American Association of Sunday and Feature Editors.

Sullivan also keeps that promise to work hard. Here's how: Go to the scene, ask lots of questions, find the character, look for the icon. Write from memory, but check notebooks for crucial details. Then, risk. Forget some rules: Don't set up quotes. Limit sources. Don't do deep background. Only suggest complex issues, but don't elaborate. Start strong. Use simple words and simple transitions. End strong.

–AK

Julie Sullivan, Desperate Days at the Merlin, *The Spokesman-Review*, February 25, 1990. Reprinted courtesy of *The* (Spokane, WA) *Spokesman-Review*.

Krystal Wilhelm crouches on the seventh stair of the Merlin Apartments, thin knees pulled against her 16-year-old stomach, insides cramping.

She's dope sick. Not from withdrawal, but from injecting cocaine she suspects was cut with lidocaine, a local anesthetic.

Living in the Merlin, one cracked cement step from the street, the Coeur d'Alene girl knows impure drugs are an occupational hazard.

She rocks with cramps. But she needs $2 for a pack of cigarettes and that means going upstairs, finding her shoes and heading out into the cold for a "date."

She'll make $100 a day getting into cars with strangers, but she can spend twice that much on cocaine. Her last meal was a box of macaroni and cheese, made with water, no butter, no milk.

"I like the high," she says softly. "It keeps me from being depressed all the time."

At 5-foot-1 and 100 pounds, Wilhelm says she's been running away since she walked to Rathdrum at age 9. She married at 14, had a baby at 15, and watched the state of Washington take the child after a boyfriend snuffed out a cigarette on her son's tiny 2-month-old fist.

None of it shows. Wilhelm's face is an expanse of unlined innocence. She says she loves her parents, but couldn't care less what they think. She'd die if her son ever used drugs, but her arms are so scarred by needles it looks like razors have been used to slice her skin.

Traveling with a hairbrush and a short, tight black skirt, Wilhelm puts on her third borrowed coat of the week. Renting rooms by the night, she shares bed, board and clothes, but not needles. Fear of AIDS also keeps a condom in her pocket.

She wants to quit drugs, she says over and over.

Maybe on March 4, after spending her last $100 on two "8-balls" of cocaine. One last blowout, the day she will turn 17.

Warren Harding, Unexpectedly

Roddy Ray's "Real Life" appeared in the Detroit Free Press *from 1993 to 1995, when he left the paper because of the newspaper strike, one that lasted nearly two years. Readers continue to miss his version of the human interest column. Brief and beautifully wrought, Ray's slices of life served up the human comedy in portions sometimes zany, sometimes heartbreaking.*

"Give me a person and I'll give you a story," he says. "Give me my Uncle Chad, I'll give you a thousand." Ray keeps his stories short to keep his readers rapt. "Writing is a pain and I'd rather get it over with," he adds. Like O. Henry, Ray was born in Greensboro, North Carolina, and the coincidence has not escaped him.

Ray is a stuntman. The almost surreal Warren Harding piece displays his deft timing, suspending the resolution for maximum whee. The tale of honest living reveals Ray at his best—writing short, holding the story together with offbeat names for money, then pulling readers in with a witty ending. The story of Doug came as a fresh breeze to a writer fatigued by countless tales of good deeds and warmth, and though fate choreographed that story's finale, the headline was pure Roddy Ray.

"When everything's done it might look easy," he says, "but doing it again and again and again took everything I had." He resists explaining his genius for connecting with readers. "If I could explain that dance," he quotes a friend, "I wouldn't have to dance it."

He tries to comb his stories till they're smooth as silk and believes emerging writers would do well to specialize. "Find what's you and hone it," he says. "Writing's a wide-open field and there's room for all sorts." Books that are too long he reads few, but he loves Barbara Pym. "Her stories are thrilling to me because she conveys so well the delicate emotions and heartaches of life."

Ray fell into journalism at the University of Michigan—"no tests and the papers were short"—and graduated in 1984. After an internship with the Free Press, *he became a staff reporter, then Europe correspondent before beginning "Real Life."*

Since leaving, Ray has been turned down by a dozen top papers in the United States and London. When interviewed for this book, he was in debt and living in a weekly room with money he earned writing utility bill inserts. Such, he says, is real life.

−CM

Roddy Ray, Real Life: Warren Harding, Unexpectedly, *Detroit Free Press,* November 2, 1994. Reprinted courtesy of *Detroit Free Press.*

I n 1923, President Warren Harding went to Alaska and called it the world's pictureland. He got sick soon after—food poisoning, presumably—and died in San Francisco.

Things went better for Jessie Scott. Then 13, the St. Louis girl was in the early years of what would be a respectably long life.

She took up painting, studying under various teachers; the avocation lasted for decades. Her style ranged from realism to abstraction. She was not a wealthy woman—she retired as an IRS clerk at 65—so she bought many of her frames secondhand, in thrift shops and the like.

Framing was expensive, so often she would paint to the size of a frame she'd bought, or at least paint to a standard frame size. Sometimes a pretty frame would inspire her to paint a picture. And sometimes she'd find inspiration in the pictures she removed from the old frames.

All of this left Jessie Smith with a basement cluttered with picture frames she'll never get around to using. Though she retired only last year from teaching painting to seniors for Detroit's Parks and Recreation Department, she does not paint nearly as much as she used to.

She was sorting through these frames one recent day at her home on Detroit's east side, planning to give them to former students, when, upon taking apart a certain frame, she suddenly was taken back 71 years, to Harding's trip to Alaska. She seemed to remember his penchant for cursing. And didn't he say, "The buck stops here?" No, she concluded, that was Truman.

But what about this Boston preacher, the Rev. George Lyman Paine, whose career was threatened by accusations he kissed a pretty female church member against her will? Were things so different then from now?

Jessie quit what she was doing and took a chair to remember 1923, when Lionel Barrymore—such a lover!—married Irene Fenwick in Rome.

Then the iceboxes—you could get one for $25. Most were top loaders, but here was a side loader. Imagine replenishing ice in your icebox every so often, Jessie thought, wondering, how did I survive that?

And so, that recent day, Jessie, who is 84, got sidetracked by her discovery in an old picture frame of a yellowed *Free Press* from July 15, 1923. She thought it a wonderful surprise. Though enriched by her brief trip back in time, she laments her frame project is still far from complete.

Where Honest Living Will Get You

J eanette Andrew had her mind on other things Saturday evening when the cashier at the Taylor Meijer store counted out the change from her paycheck.

Roddy Ray, Real Life: Where Honest Living Will Get You, *Detroit Free Press*, November 16, 1994. Reprinted courtesy of *Detroit Free Press*.

As she headed to the parking lot with her bagels, orange juice, and so forth, the wad of money in her purse, something knocked at her brain: a little fact, saying please let me in.

When she got to the van, where her sister, Mary Alexander, waited with their four kids, she gave Mary the wad and said, "I think she gave me too much money."

"It's $322," Mary said upon counting it.

Wow, they thought: an extra Ben Franklin! (Well, two Ulysses Grants.)

There was that moment, that millisecond, yes, during which Jeanette contemplated keeping the excess $100. But the cashier hugged and kissed her when she returned the money. Jeanette felt good.

The sisters took the kids to eat Mexican, then went home and did some crafts. Mary made a Styrofoam turkey. The kids went to bed and the sisters stayed up talking.

By 3 A.M., Jeanette groggily was getting ready to leave for work; she's an independent merchandiser of McCormick spices, and her work takes her to stores in various towns—this time it was Monroe.

Soon she was rolling down Telegraph in her white '94 Aerostar, coffee in hand, Patty Loveless loud on the speakers. She was tired—Jeanette, that is; she'd only slept a couple of hours.

Going through Flat Rock, she was jolted to notice that the speed limit in that stretch of Telegraph drops from 55 to 35. About the same moment, she saw the red and blue lights in her rear-view mirror; she pulled over, angry at herself.

The cop told her she was going 20 over the limit, took her license and went to his car. When he returned to her window, he told her that 20 over the limit draws a hefty fine.

A hundred Washingtons, to be exact. Funny how a cool $100 should come up twice in a matter of hours.

She didn't make the connection then, but when she finally did, it reaffirmed her belief that what goes around, comes around.

Had she not given the $100 back to the cashier, she believes the cop, before warning her to put on her seat belt and take it easy through his city, wouldn't have done what he did, and let her go.

If you can prove otherwise, Real Life will give you a shiny new Lincoln.

You Might Run into Doug One Day

A t 5 years old, Doug Kelly tried to pet a German shepherd and it bit him on the head; he got stitches.

At 10, he was riding his bike on a Woodward sidewalk when a driver

Roddy Ray, Real Life: You Might Run into Doug One Day, *Detroit Free Press*, August 22, 1994. Reprinted courtesy of *Detroit Free Press*.

exited the entrance of a parking lot, hitting him, rolling him onto the hood of her car. She was horrified. "I'm OK," he insisted.

The same year, he was on 13 Mile crossing Woodward on a moped when he says a driver going north ran a red light; he hit the car. The ambulance took him to nearby William Beaumont Hospital; he was treated and released.

At 17, the summer before his senior year at Royal Oak Kimball, he was on his way to work at a restaurant, riding his moped through an alley near Normandy and Woodward, when a driver backed into him from the Midas parking lot, knocking him to the ground. The driver sped off. Doug got stitches in his elbow.

At 18, he was visiting a friend at Western Michigan University in Kalamazoo when he jogged into a moving car—another red-light runner, he says—and banged his knee. Nothing too serious, but police wrote a report.

By now Doug had a reputation. Friends called him a "car magnet," and kidded him that they didn't want to cross the street with him.

At 21, when he was at Lansing Community College, he was walking on a side-walk when a driver pulled out of a McDonald's parking lot and nailed him, man-gling his knee. He landed on his face in the eastbound lanes of Grand River Avenue, breaking his nose. At Lansing's Sparrow Hospital that night he won-dered, "What can I do? I can't stay inside all the time."

The Monday before last, the Auburn Hills man, 25, was driving through downtown Pontiac, on his way to have lunch with his brother, when a car ran a red light and smacked into him. The driver was ticketed.

Doug's left elbow—the same one that had stitches 8 years ago—was broken and cut; he got stitches in it, and in his left temple.

The doctor who put those stitches in removed some stitches from his ankle; he'd cut it on a broken bottle about a week earlier when he was taking out the garbage at a pizza place where he works.

Doug says he is not more careless than most of us, just unlucky. He wonders how to break the spell.

He did not show up as agreed to be photographed Friday; one had to wonder what kept him.

Life, by Nelson J. McCumby

Unable to find work in Mackinaw City, Clarence persuaded Nelson to hop a night train to Midland, about 175 miles away. They got on about 10 P.M. It was cold—there was nothing but the winter sky above—but now and then, when the firemen below opened a trap door for coal, warmth arose.

Roddy Ray, Real Life: Life, by Nelson J. McCumby, *Detroit Free Press,* January 26, 1994. Reprinted courtesy of *Detroit Free Press.*

During a stop about halfway there, before they knew what was happening, they were drenched with water from an elevated tank. So cold. They huddled together.

In Midland, nearly frozen, they found a small heated building full of sand used to help trains get a grip on the icy rails. Clarence and Nelson fell asleep in paradise, about 65 years ago, only to awake at dawn itching, ridden with fleas.

About 10 years ago, after Clarence Erwin had died, Nelson, retired and living with his wife, Leona, in Florida, bought a yellow legal pad.

A piece at a time, in a silent room, Nelson J. McCumby wrote the story of his life, beginning back in Bliss Township, Mich., when he was 5 and soldiers brought diphtheria back from World War I. The cemetery across the street from his home was like a circus every day.

He wrote of the 1928 train trip from Mackinaw City to Midland, of how he and Clarence found no jobs and soon returned home. He wrote of his retirement from construction after 47 years in East Lansing. He wrote of his five children and how they'd done all right, and his many grandchildren.

Eventually Nelson McCumby, who left school after fourth grade, completed the story of his life. It was a good life.

He tried to get his story published, but it came back in the mail after some weeks with a polite note. He says an editor explained that, "being that no murder took place in it or any such thing like that, some drastic thing, they didn't think the public would really buy it at the present time."

But the editor held out hope, saying, "There may come a day when all that will change, and we may be checking back with you."

Ten years later, Nelson, 81, living in Traverse City, says they never got back to him. He's still got the 11-page manuscript and doesn't plan to try again. The literary world will have to be satisfied with this brief summary.

Nancy Shulins

Timeless Love

"Think globally, act locally," reads Nancy Shulins's favorite bumper sticker. It's her writing mantra. She loves the local part, the treasure hunt of unravelling the mystery of a person. "There's no such thing as too much reporting," she says. "I'd like to analyze the DNA and dental records of the people I profile." She loves the global part too, finding a theme with universal appeal to make the story cohere.

"Timeless Love," provided both title and theme for a story so amazing that a reporter could hardly miss–except for the difficulty of understanding a person from a culture as alien as the paleolithic. Shulins' solution then–she was 37–is also her tip for writers now: "People reveal themselves over time, not in an hour or so, and you have to be there." So there she was, watching the Good family's home-made videos, taking trips, eating burgers, and shopping at the mall. Finally, she had enough local knowledge to juxtapose the mind sets of husband and wife as well as the right metaphors to convey the fairy tale quality of this, the ultimate mixed marriage. (And to win AP's story of the year award for feature writing.)

Shulins attended Northeastern University as a work-study student, but liked the work more than the study. So she dropped out, went back home, and started writing stories–35 cents an inch–for the Valley News *in West Lebanon, New Hampshire. In 1976, she went to work for The Associated Press in Montpelier, Vermont, became a correspondent in 1978, and went to Indiana the next year as a one-woman bureau. Joining the National Writing Team in New York in 1981, she soon entered "The Poets' Corner," the veteran feature writers, aka AP Newsfeatures. Here she worked with editor Jack Cappon–"the best thing that can happen to you," Shulins says. "He could look at a mess and tell you how to make it sing." In 1990, AP named her "Special Correspondent"–the first time this honorary title went to a woman.*

Cappon got her started as a writing coach. "Dare to be different," she tells writers around the country, "but don't take a risk to say 'look at me.'" Simple and direct is best–the way her favorite writer Jane Smiley achieves her effects. "I went through a period of complexity," Shulins says. "And I came out on the other side. We're not here to obfuscate but to be clear and precise."

–CM

RUTHERFORD, N.J. (AP)–Yarima Good is leaving the shopping malls, traffic jams and fast-food franchises of the suburbs this winter for a journey 10,000 years into the past. She'll be among Earth's most primitive people, with no written language and no concept of numbers or time; naked Indians who feast on termites and tarantulas and have yet to invent the wheel.

In effect, she will be in the Stone Age.

In fact, Yarima will be home.

Five years have passed since the love of a man brought Yarima out of the Amazon jungle, through the looking glass and into the 20th century. Five years since she first wore clothes or walked in shoes; since she learned to make light by moving a little stick on the wall; since she crouched under a bush to hide from the terrible beast with glowing eyes that turned out to be her first car.

Now the mother of three in a suburban jungle, she can laugh at her early fears: that her reflection would spring from mirrors and attack her, that toilets would bite her if she sat on them.

In 1975, when anthropologist Kenneth Good went to Venezuela to study Yarima's people, the Yanomama, she was a child, and he was the first "nabuh," or outsider, she'd ever seen.

He ended up staying 12 years. The child who'd shared her plantains and fishing spots with him grew up. So did their fondness for one another. Against all odds, it bloomed into love.

Now Ken is her husband and it's Yarima who's a stranger in a strange land, the land of the nabuh, where everything's different–everything except love.

That alone is the same: strong enough to bridge the 10,000 years between her world and his. There is much in this baffling wonderland that delights her: Macy's sportswear and McDonald's french fries. Michael Jackson and NFL football.

Automatic dishwashers and disposable diapers.

Still, it's a staggering transition from life in a jungle tribe, surrounded by every friend and relative she'd ever known, to life in a two-bedroom apartment in a New York City suburb. If it weren't for her children, Ken says, Yarima would sooner go home.

Sometimes her dreams carry her back to the jungle, and she imagines herself lying in her hammock surrounded by friends. She dreams she's walking through shallow streams with her sister and brother. The water feels cool on her bare feet and crabs nibble her fingers as she scoops them up in her hands.

Then she wakes up.

Those dreams and the videotapes Ken made in the jungle are Yarima's only links to her past. Short of an arduous and expensive journey back through the looking glass, she has no way of communicating with family, no way of knowing they're alive.

In the jungle, says Ken, every day is the same. "In the morning, the women go out to the forest. They make a fire, sit and talk, laugh, watch each other's babies and take turns going off to gather food, which will be shared. Then they go to the stream, wash their babies, themselves and the food, and come home with flowers in their ears.

"If you're a woman, you're a gatherer. If you're a man, you're a hunter. This is what life is reduced to in the jungle."

By contrast, this is what life is like in the land of the nabuh: English lessons, which Yarima likes; housework, which she hates; TV, which she watches religiously.

She has David, 5, and Vanessa, 3, the only Yanomama children on Earth who can name all four Teenage Mutant Ninja Turtles. She has 7-month-old Daniel, a tiny echo of her with his straight black hair, almond eyes and high cheekbones.

And she has Ken, the only adult this side of the looking glass who understands her language and her loneliness.

He's everything to her: lover, provider, teacher, interpreter and friend.

Just as she once led him along jungle paths, he now guides her through her strange new world, with its perplexing cast of characters: Jesus Christ, Betty Crocker, Pee-wee Herman, Uncle Sam.

Ken's twice her size, with a long, husky body unlike that of any man she'd ever seen. As a child, she called him "Long Feet" and "Big Forehead," and touched his black, wiry beard in awe. Yanomama men are small, smooth-cheeked, and unlike Ken, who at 49 is thinning, never go bald.

"She's seen those ads for Hair Club for Men," he says, "and she's bugging the hell out of me." He's not an easygoing man, nor is he good at hiding annoyance when confronted by a traffic jam or a ketchup stain. "A type Triple A," he says.

But when Yarima's in the room, he speaks more gently and smiles more easily, mustering all the patience he withholds from the rest of the world.

"I never really get mad at her. I realize what she's going through is enough."

There's an easy warmth between them as they sit together on the sofa, murmuring in their secret, shared language, smiling at the baby's antics and at each other.

They do not kiss, an odd custom to the somewhat reserved Yanomama. There are other ways of showing affection. Once, when Ken had been away from the jungle, Yarima amazed him by throwing her arms around him in front of everyone. They also caused a sensation by becoming the first couple to sleep together in the same hammock.

The fierce resistance to change that's enabled the Yanomama to remain a Stone Age people into the 20th century makes Yarima that much more of an anomaly. She moves through her new world with equanimity and grace, smiling and humming as she mixes baby formula or watches MTV.

What is she thinking? What is she feeling? "I'd give anything to know what's going on in her head," Ken says.

The three days a week that he teaches anthropology at Jersey City State College, he can guess what she's feeling: Boredom. Tuesdays through Fridays, she has 90-minute sessions with tutor Rachel Schwartz. Then she and the kids walk downtown. Otherwise, there's little to do but watch TV and wait for Ken.

To break up the monotony, he takes them to Burger King, Kentucky Fried Chicken, rural Pennsylvania, New York's Central Park. There are also visits to Willowbrook Mall where, pushing a stroller flanked by wheedling kids, Yarima vanishes into a bobbing sea of mothers. In some ways, she fits right in, proudly displaying David's construction-paper frog on her refrigerator and stocking cupboards with bagels, Wheaties and other nutritious snacks. She dresses the children in colorful, cuddly outfits befitting the savvy shopper she's become. And included in her small but growing vocabulary are phrases any mother would recognize: "No more Coke," she admonishes. "Milk. Your teeth fall out."

She can't read road signs, yet she's the one who points the way to the mall and remembers where they parked. She also operates the VCR.

Rachel is teaching her to count, an alien notion for a Yanomama, whose entire numerical system consists of "one," "two," and "many." The written word is another new concept. So is the idea of marking time. Ken figures Yarima's around 26, but there's no way of knowing for sure.

Having so much to learn is difficult, but "though I've seen her discouraged, she never gives up," Rachel says. Yarima dreams of learning to drive and buying a red sports car. She also wants to move back to Pennsylvania, her first home outside the jungle.

It was there, at Bryn Mawr Hospital, that she delivered her first baby.

Barely arrived in America, she was still breaking in her first shoes, size 2 Buster Browns. Sixteen months later during a visit home, she delivered her second child, on a banana leaf. David and Vanessa love to tell new acquaintances the stories of their births, savoring the shock value.

How will they regard their heritage as they get older? Will they feel proud or self-conscious? Special or different? "My endeavor in life is to make both equally proud of how and where they were born," Ken says.

At the moment, though, he has more pressing concerns. He's about to trek into the Amazon with three suburban preschoolers, one of whom, Vanessa, gets hysterical at the sight of an ant. The kids are excited about going to the jungle in much the way they get excited about going to Burger King. To prepare them, Yarima plays videotapes, pointing out relatives and coaching them in Yanomama, a language they understand but don't speak. "I'm hungry," says David. "Not 'hungry.' 'Ohi.'" This is fun, for a while. Eventually, David's scowl signals the end of the game. "Stop talking jungle," he says. The visit to Yarima's village, Hasupuweteri, near the headwaters of the Oronoco River, will be Yarima's first since Vanessa was born. The petite, self-assured woman in black leggings bears little resemblance to the naked Indian who walked out of the jungle five years ago. The tiny holes through which she inserted her facial sticks have closed. Nowadays, she wears eyeliner.

This trip, she hopes to entice others with necklaces of plastic beads to gather her firewood for her. For the record, she'd sooner make the last leg of the journey by helicopter than on foot. How will her family regard her, with her American children and Western ways? "I think we'll be seen as the rich people," says Ken.

As her husband, he's proud of how well Yarima's adjusted. As a scientist, he's acutely aware of having upset the balance, disturbed the symmetry, of both their worlds. To never truly belong in either—that is the terrible price the time traveler pays.

Ken knows his children couldn't survive in the jungle, though Yarima has yet to accept that. "The answer," he says, "is to go back and forth, nine months here, three months there." The problem is how to pay for it. Each trip costs roughly $30,000.

Several potentially lucrative projects are in the works. *Into the Heart*, Ken's account of his Amazon adventure, was published this year by Simon & Schuster. The paperback is due out any day.

Reviews have been favorable. One British journalist, though, berated Ken for introducing Yarima to pop culture and fast food instead of classical music and haute cuisine. "It's a Jingle Out There," read the headline.

The article struck a nerve in Ken, who hates fast food and prefers Beethoven, but says Yarima's preferences are just that—hers, not his.

She has many: traffic jams, gold chains, action films, county fairs. He does his best to indulge them all, though he did cancel pay-per-view TV after receiving a $189 cable bill. Yarima had watched "Rocky V" seven times.

"I feel I'm doing the best I can, and that reduces the guilt somewhat," says Ken. Still, "I come home from work and I look at her and I realize she's been sitting on the couch all day.

"In the jungle, she never knew loneliness. Here she has no one to talk to, day after day, week after week."

Nonetheless, he says, they are happy.

"It's a very simple relationship. We just live. We're not overburdened with trying to figure it out. We're just happy to be together." He can't say why, nor can he pinpoint the moment when tenderness turned to love. It was boundless and intoxicating but when he thought about all they'd have to give up to stay together, he kissed her forehead, gazed at her tear-streaked face and left. He can't describe his sadness. Nor can he explain what drove him back to her again and again, despite eight bouts of malaria, despite every obstacle disparate cultures could pose.

Finally, they knew. They belonged together. As Yarima instructed Ken to tell the judge who officiated at their wedding: "Tell the pata that I am your wife. Tell him that even if you become sick, I will still be your wife. If you cannot leave your hammock, I will go down to the river and get you water. I will harvest plantains and roast them for you on the fire. Tell the pata that I will gather fruit and honey for you. I will care for you and do all these things even when you are very old. Even then I will be your wife."

Still, it is hard—hard to watch her listen to tapes of loved ones with tears running down her cheeks; hard to hear her struggle to count to 10; hard to watch her walk into Dunkin' Donuts with the note he has written for her that says "two frosted crullers," words she still can't pronounce. "All this stuff makes her seem like a child, so helpless," says Ken.

"But in the jungle, she kept me alive. She can get food from the inside of a log. In the jungle, she's a complete adult."

And so, they are going back to her world, if only for a few weeks. Yarima is eager to show off her children and see her family, to kick off her shoes and eat roasted snake, to go to the forest and come back with flowers in her ears.

The trip will, of course, be a logistical nightmare; it's tough enough taking three kids to Disney World, let alone to the Amazon jungle. They'll travel by car, plane and boat. When they reach the headwaters of the Oronoco, they'll walk.

Finding the seminomadic tribe could take some doing. But when they do, they'll be warmly greeted. The children will be admired. Yarima and Ken will be chided for having stayed away so long.

The past and the present will touch, linked by a love strong enough to encompass them both, a love supple enough to stretch from the Stone Age to the suburbs, and back.

John Dorschner

A Fighting Chance

When John Dorschner replayed the first interview taped for "A Fighting Chance," he decided to embrace as direct a writing style as a reporter can. He crafted a story about breast cancer using only direct quotes. Faced with language so honest, he concedes, "anything I could do to tell the story in my own words would be excessive, overly emotional." But let sources control a story? Even in a story where truth is undisputed, with no snake oil to sell, that's risky.

So Dorschner's editor at Tropic magazine was understandably hesitant: "Is this the way to do this?" Alternatives seemed too tame, however, and Dorschner said so. He didn't want the story to come across as "soft and weepy." After all, he had a patient who spoke no bullshit. (After five years free of cancer, Lisa Boccard still speaks straightforwardly.) To Dorschner, 50 when he told this story, the all-quotes tactic seemed mature. "I try to let the material tell itself. The essence of journalism is material."

In another risky step, Dorschner helped the material speak. Together, writer and editor eliminated many of the ellipses that traditionally mark gaps in quotations. In "A Fighting Chance," Lisa's quotes are direct—but not continuous. So the draft . . . when Lisa wandered . . . or followed a tangent . . . looked awkward . . . typographically . . . and confused readers. Tightening quotes let the narrative flow, yet it may be deemed controversial.

At 15, Dorschner volunteered as a sports writer for his hometown weekly in Illinois. Later, at the University of Colorado at Boulder, he abandoned journalism classes after one course. Instead, the history major headed into the college newsroom, where he eventually became editor. After graduating in 1967, he edited features for a magazine published by a telephone company. In 1970, an ad led him to The Miami Herald. After one stint of editing, Dorschner found that he prefers writing for one of the few newspaper magazines still stuffed inside Sunday editions. He produces about two dozen stories a year. Some take two days; others, six weeks.

Like counterparts nationwide, Tropic magazine faces shrinking resources and readership. But Dorschner is philosophical: "Time is more precious. Space is more precious." To cope, he follows the same advice he offers newcomers. "The main thing is to work—to write," he says. "Go out and get the experience. Talk with people and see things."

—AK

John Dorschner, A Fighting Chance, Tropic, July 3, 1994. Reprinted courtesy of Tropic, The Miami Herald.

At first, some of her photos seem like pure glamour, almost cheesecake, but you look closer and you see something unusual, even haunting, about the depiction of this young woman. And that is the point.

When the photos were first taken, Lisa Boccard's breast was racked with cancer. She wanted the photos to jolt people's perceptions about the power of disease.

"I lost my hair but not my inner beauty," she says. "So I asked a photographer to photograph me bald. It helped me cope."

These days, she displays her photos in an exhibit she calls The Cure Package—spreading a message that she hopes will reach men as well as women. "I want brothers to understand it. I want boyfriends not to walk away from girlfriends because they lose their breasts."

She has become evangelical. Wherever she can, she displays the intimate photographs shown on these pages. Her personal message has inevitably blended with the political. Last fall, she was one of 100 women who went to the East Room of the White House—to present a petition with 2.8 million signatures demanding more money for breast cancer research, a disease that afflicts 180,000 a year—a number that keeps increasing at an alarming rate.

When she appeared on a local television talk show, the typed underline on the screen summed her up like this: "Cancer Survivor and Advocate for Life." Advocate for life? It sounds like a vague New Age buzz phrase, but Lisa believes that positive thinking and a hunger for life can make a dramatic impact on how long, and how well, cancer patients live.

She knows that is not as simple as it sounds. She has struggled through highs and lows, endured physical and psychological pain so brutal she admits that at least once she wanted to give up the fight. She didn't.

Three years ago, the cancer in her body was so widespread and virulent that doctors said her chances of living were "abysmal." Now she is in remission. For two years doctors have been unable to find cancer in her body. Why? Doctors credit a powerful new kind of chemotherapy so toxic it nearly killed her. But they also say Lisa's ability to survive the treatment, and respond to it, may have a lot to do with her will to live, a force medical science is beginning to take very seriously.

What follows is Lisa's story, in her own words, and those of friends and doctors, who all share the belief that what she has to say needs to be heard.

Lisa: "In 1991, I was basically doing what a 29-year-old girl does. I was office manager at the Towers of Quayside, a North Miami condominium complex. I had a boyfriend in Key West, and I was going down there a lot. I was planning to move there after the first of the year.

"In March, I was exercising at the Quayside spa, and the next day, I had pain up and down my left arm. I couldn't even grab the phone, the pain was so intense. A friend of mine is a doctor. We kind of work out together. He gave me some Naprosyn, and anti-inflammatory medicine, figuring it was a muscle pull. After five days, it wasn't getting better. He doubled the prescription. It didn't help. Then he did an examination of my breast and said, 'Lisa, go see your doctor. Something doesn't feel right.'

"I saw my gynecologist, and he said I was too young to have breast cancer. He said, 'Lisa, what you're feeling is the fact you're turning 30 and you haven't had

children. Your body is going through changes.' Then he put his pinkie in my face
–I'll never forget this–and he said, 'If you had cancer, it'd be about the size of a
pea, and I don't feel anything that feels like a pea.'"

**Steven Silvers, a gynecologist who was a leader in studying breast cancer
while chief resident at Jackson Memorial:** "Most gynecologists don't know
enough about breasts. A lot of things get blown off with the younger patients
because the percentages are so low that it might be breast cancer. Pain is a hard
one in a young woman. It's really difficult to know what it means. But you don't
just blow it off. You have to listen to the patient."

Lisa: "Months went by. The pain was getting worse. My friend the doctor did an
examination of my breast, and he said, 'Go get a mammogram.' I got a mammogram. The test was so painful, tears were streaming down my face. I went back
to my gynecologist. He sent me to another doctor. He aspirated my breast–that's
put a needle in my breast. He decided I had fibrocystic disease, which is very
common in women. The pain kept getting worse. Finally, I saw Dr. Daniel Weingrad at North Shore Hospital. This was like September–six months after the first
pain. He felt my breast, and he said, 'Lisa, we need to do a biopsy.' I said, 'No
problem.'

"I had the biopsy, and the next day in his office, he told me I had cancer. I
wasn't surprised, I guess. It was just so obvious that something wasn't right.
Mentally, subconsciously I had prepared for the worst."

Her father, Matthew Boccard: "Her mother and I were with her. She was sitting between the two of us, and this was a proud moment. She got up, put her
hands on her hips and leaned over so she was just a few inches from his face,
and she said, 'OK, I've got cancer. What are we going to do about it?'

"A lot of people can't handle news like that. They just go to pieces. Lisa has a
very simple message for them–if you want to live, fight it."

Dr. Daniel Weingrad, cancer surgeon: "She had lobular carcinoma, which
accounts for about 9 percent of all breast cancers. Her tumor was everywhere,
and it's understandable it wasn't detected by a mammogram. Especially in
younger women, with the denseness of their breasts, it's harder for a mammogram to detect tumors.

"Cancer is the most intense assault on your emotions that you're ever going to
experience, and she was exceptionally strong in dealing with it."

Lisa: "I didn't cry in front of the doctor. But when I walked out to the car and
opened the door, I lost it. I don't think that I ever cried as hard as I did that afternoon. And when I saw my mom crying, I felt responsible for the pain she was
experiencing.

"I had so much support. We had–no lie–over 120 phone calls that night.
Twenty people came to the house. My father had been involved in politics and
had been the mayor of El Portal. My brother had been the El Portal police com-
missioner. So our family knew a lot of people. And then people from Quayside
called. And old friends. And that really helped.

"My boyfriend called me the same night I had the biopsy, and I told him. He
said, 'OK, we're going to work on this together. I'll be there for you.' And my family was very supportive.

"I think part of my strength is that I had such a great support team that I didn't want to disappoint them. I think that's why I was so determined and focused on going forward."

Her Father: "We didn't want to bury her with sympathy, like she was dying. We just treated her normally."

Dr. Sanford Cohen, a psychiatrist who's head of the University of Miami's division of biobehavioral medicine and has spent much of his life researching brain–body relationships: "All the studies show that the single most important factor is social and family support. When the support system is positive and strong, patients do better psychologically, and they do better physically. There are reports that women with breast cancer who are feisty, who have more of a fighting spirit, who plan their life actively, who feel in control of things –they do better than the more passive.

"There are studies of voodoo. Look at a person who's convinced he's hexed or cursed. Is it possible he might die? My answer is yes, and there's some evidence to support that. You've created a sense of despair, of hopelessness, of depression. Death could occur by ventriculating arrhythmia or cardiovascular arrest. There are many cases in the literature that report this. The victim has to believe the hex works. And he's more likely to believe if his friends and relatives treat him like the hex will work.

"The similarities between this hexed person and the modern cancer patient are striking. Sometimes the patient dies too quickly for the malignancy to have had time to kill. Sometimes relatives treat the patient as if he's already dead. They go through preparatory rituals, drawing the shades, lowering voices. These are gestures of complete capitulation and abandonment."

Lisa: "I went to an oncologist, Dr. Michael Troner. He said we'll have to take it step by step. I had four treatments of chemotherapy to shrink the tumor."

Dr. Michael Troner: "I don't know why the rates of breast cancer keep going up. It's a disease of Western civilization. It's not a disease of people who have low-fat, non-Western diets. Everybody suspects it has something to do with our diet or our environment. There's this classic study of women in Japan, where breast cancer strikes 1 in 20 or 1 in 30. But when Japanese women move to Hawaii, within two generations, their breast cancer frequency is like American women–1 in 8 or so. So clearly it's not genetic."

Lisa: "Thirteen days after the first treatment, I lost my hair. I was in Key West, with my boyfriend. I woke up in the morning and took a shower. As I was washing myself, I saw my hand was full of hair. I started shaking. It was very intense. I knew it was going to happen, but still, there's no way you can prepare for it. It made me realize I was seriously ill. I probably spent 40 minutes in that shower, crying.

"There was nothing he could do for me that day. *Nothing.* I came out of the shower crying, and he says, 'What's wrong?' And I say, 'Look.' And I go like this, pulling out a handful of hair. All that day, as we went around, crazy person that I am, I'd go pulling out handfuls of hair.

"Every weekend after that, he was more distant. He just avoided me. I started staying in a bed and breakfast. Losing the hair ended the relationship. Mutual friends told me he couldn't handle it, and he started seeing another girl. He didn't even have the courtesy to tell me.

"I was so hurt and angry. Not only am I dying, but the person I cared for very much dumps me. I asked myself, 'What do I deal with first? Well, I have to live, and I can deal with him later, or not at all.'

"I still kept going to Key West though, almost every weekend. After four months, everybody knew I had cancer, and I just couldn't get away from it in Miami. Sometimes I just needed a break. I didn't want to be Lisa Boccard, cancer patient, *all* the time.

"Key West is a small-town atmosphere. The people are fantastic. I couldn't pay for a drink, in any bar, anywhere. That made me feel special. Riding my bike at 3 in the morning with the moon out–it was so perfect. One time, I went hang gliding."

Dr. Cohen: "If they stop living, they die quicker. But if you go on with your living, first of all you're going to feel better. Second, you're going to cope better. The cancer patients who do the best have a sense of being in control. They are master of the life that remains. That's the key."

Lisa: "And I was developing a new relationship–with a male nurse. I'd first met Keith in the holding room, when I was being prepared for the biopsy. He was holding my hand, and I thought, 'Wow, this is really neat. This hospital makes you so relaxed and so welcome.' He asked why are you here, and I said, because I might have breast cancer, and his whole face went to a completely different attitude–more caring, more goodness. And he said, 'I promise after the surgery, when you wake up in the recovery room, I'll be there.'

"And he was. When I started chemotherapy, he came over to my mom and dad's house and brought things for the mouth sores. Then he'd come over to my apartment and see how I was doing. We'd sit by the pool and talk. There came a point where it hit me that he was really special. And we began a relationship. Here I was a bald person, I couldn't have been very attractive, but he cared for me, and that helped a lot.

"About this time, I decided to do the photos. I just really, *really* thought it would be neat to show myself bald. Every time you see a beautiful picture of a woman, she's got long hair and big boobs, and I'm none of that now. I'm just bald. I wanted to show in pictures that having cancer didn't mean you couldn't be beautiful. And I wanted to show what it was like having cancer.

"I had been a photographer for my high school yearbook, so I knew some things, and I had a couple of ideas. I found Lynn Parks, a commercial photographer. I brought all the props I wanted to the studio–the Key West T-shirt, the mannequins. We had a makeup artist come in. She worked on my face. It took over an hour and a half to do my makeup. I had no eyebrows, no eyelashes. . . .

"In December, the doctor told me the chemotherapy had shrunk the tumor, but it was still too big. He said I had to remove my breast. And I said OK. No hesitation. When you're fighting for your life, I guess you do anything that you have to do to live. I mean, at the time, I was thinking of it like it was a driving trip to Disney World. How do you drive there? Well, you drive up the turnpike, and then you get off at this exit, and you go this way, and then you go that way. That's how I was thinking. What do I have to do to survive?

"But it wasn't easy, I admit. On the eve of my surgery, my boyfriend and I were together. That was a big emotional moment. All my life, the only thing I had going for me was my chest. You know, meeting men, I was always complimented. 'Lisa, you have nice hooters.' Stuff like that . . . Not that I was consumed with my chest as *me*. But . . . well, yeah, it was devastating. This was part of *me* that they were cutting out."

Her dad: "We were waiting in the hallway. It seemed like it was three hours later when the surgeon came out. He came down the hallway very, *very* slowly, with his head down. I went up to him, 'Hey doctor, how'd we make out?' For a moment, he didn't give me an answer. Then he said it was pretty bad. I asked what are her chances? He said about 20 percent."

Dr. Weingrad: "Something like 14 or 16 lymph nodes were involved. That meant the cancer had spread. More than 10 is considered an outstandingly poor prognosis. Her prognosis was just abysmal."

Lisa: "I was hoping when I woke up, it would be the end of it. But it wasn't. He told me in my hospital room. I was really angry. I felt I had been through enough. I was thinking, 'Come on, God. You made me go through the treatment. You took away part of my body.' Oh was I angry. But survival was at stake. And I immediately became determined to do whatever I had to do.

"The first couple of days I couldn't move. My girlfriend Charlotte would come over when Mom went to work, and she would take me to the shower, and bathe me, and my oldest brother came down from Jacksonville, and he stayed with me."

Her dad: "Five days after surgery, she was at her desk."

Lisa: "I had a sling and pillows to prop up my one arm. I was in such pain. My chest felt like they had driven stakes through me. The whole left side of my body hurt. In fact, up till a couple months ago I still used the pillow, and my arm cramps up sometimes, and I can't move it for a couple of minutes, because I have nerve damage in my arm. That's one of the side effects that I have to deal with.

"But every step of the way I worked. Work kept me going. It made me feel I still had a place to go. Here I had lost my breast, my hair, my possible future, but I still had a place to go. . . .

"I have my beliefs in God, but I don't go to church every Sunday like I should. Only because I don't like to be told when to kneel, when to stand up. I like going to church when no one's there, just kind of do my thing with God. That helped me a lot. It was so strange, every time I went to church I found myself crying. I feel like I'm really going to Him now. It was like one on one. I felt His presence there. It was like a cleansing for me.

"At this time, a lot of people were praying for me, all over the United States. My uncle's a bishop in Louisiana, and people in his office were sending me stuff, and even friends of mine who are Jewish prayed."

Dr. Cohen: "There have been studies, still open to some question, where prayers seem to have a positive effect. If persons are aware of the prayers and believe in them, that could be the voodoo or faith healing effect. There's one study in California where people were praying for patients who supposedly didn't know about the prayer, and it showed positive results, but there was some suggestion that the patients *did* know about the prayers. But the main point is that those who believe in things will often feel better psychologically and do better physically."

Her brother, Vince: "I always tried to make a joke out of it. I used to call her Mrs. Clean. I did a cartoon of her with just one breast. I used to draw cartoons of her bald head, in some kind of embarrassing situation."

Lisa: "Like riding my bike down Duval Street in Key West and I'm bald."

Vince: "After her surgery, we went looking for a prosthesis. That was fun. It was a tiny store in North Miami Beach. We went in and I asked, 'Do you have any 38 double-D's?'"

Lisa: "This was just a couple days after my surgery, because I didn't want to be walking around lopsided. It's depressing when you walk in there. She had old lady clothes, old lady things. She went and fitted me. And Vinnie asked if they had a nipple. I didn't even think of that."

Vince: "They *had* a nipple. A little suction cup thing. I stuck it on my forehead."

Dr. Cohen: "Norman Cousins wrote a book about getting over a serious illness by watching Marx Brothers movies. Purely on a psychological basis, humor allows one to put things in a less threatening perspective. Anything that makes you feel a little more in control of things is better. We don't have a lot of evidence, but there's a possibility that, just as depression may cause chemical changes that produce negative body effects, it's not inconceivable that developing more positive aspects could bring psychological changes that might help ameliorate the symptoms of cancer."

Lisa: "After the mastectomy, I thought it was important I didn't allow the disease to stop me. I continued to date my nurse. I worked. I went to Key West–this was crazy–like two weeks after the mastectomy. I had pills and two tubes coming out of me for draining fluid. The fluid went into a cup, and every so often I had to empty it. It was filled with puss and blood. But I went. I wasn't going to let it stop me from doing what I enjoyed. I danced. After a few beers, I felt nothing. It was my way of being–of expressing life, of *rejoicing* in life. . . .

"But a lot of issues weren't easy to deal with. For a woman, it's not easy to go to a doctor. You're sitting there bare-breasted for an hour. They're touching the breasts, and then they're on the phone, and you're just sitting there, and what do you do? It's embarrassing, and that's how Dr. Weingrad was at first. Then he got to know me as a person. After the mastectomy, I remember this one day when he got ready to examine me, he made sure one side was covered, when he examined the other side. Then he switched, covering the other side. Even though there was nothing there on this one side, he covered it up. I though wow–that was very interesting. I had become a person. It's not like he was treating a sack of meat. . . .

"I had some tough choices to make. Dr. Troner said, 'If I give you normal chemotherapy, I can see only one year more for you.' And I said, 'OK, what are the alternatives?' And he said stem-cell rescue.

"He warned that there would be numerous side effects. 'And one of them is going to upset you. You won't be able to conceive children.'

"Later, I wrote how I felt: *This was something I had always wanted to do . . . to experience the growth of life inside of me. . . . I had already lost the old Lisa, lost my hair . . . lost my breast . . . and now not being able to do the one thing in life a woman lives for–creating a life. Well, I couldn't get out of Dr. Troner's fast enough. . . . The first thing I did was call Keith. Then I sat in my car and felt completely alone, and cried. It was like losing two lives–mine and the one I may have had one day.*

"This treatment involved really powerful chemo. I had to sign a contract with the treatment center. The paper warned the treatment was a life-threatening situation, and you could die from it–the *treatment.*"

Dr. Troner: "We found over the years that breast cancer responds to chemotherapy. But if we give them very high doses of chemotherapy, you can also wipe out the bone marrow, which constructs the white cells and platelets that keep you alive. In stem-cell rescue, you collect the white blood cells in advance and then after the treatment, you give them back the white cells and platelets. They have to have a good heart and good kidneys. To say the least, it's tough."

Lisa: "One interesting thing about the illness: For the first time, it was *my* life. It was the first time I made all the decisions. Like going down to Key West after the surgery. My parents said, 'Honey, you need to rest.' But I went because I wanted to go. My mom and dad didn't make the decision about the stem-cell protocol. I did. Because it was *my* body.

"But before I began the stem-cell program I was with Keith in my apartment. I'll never forget that. Later, I wrote about this moment: *As we always did, we were wrestling around like two people in love, and for some reason I just started to cry. I remembered telling him that I didn't want to die. I just kept saying it over and over. The tears rolled down my face, and I began to shake, and I couldn't stop crying. Then he began to cry. He said, 'I don't want you to die, either.'* . . .

"*Here I was, bald, sick, and in love with the most caring and warm loving man, who didn't care how I looked or what I had. Here we were, two people live in love, having fun with one another, like puppies playing in the yard, and then, boom, it could all end in a matter of a few months. It just seemed so sad to me, at that moment. All I ever wanted to do was to grow old with him, and not be a memory of his past.*

"Just before I started the treatment, I lit a candle for myself. I never did that before. A lot of people lit candles for me. I stopped by my church and lit a candle and said, 'OK, I'm ready. Let's go.'

"They started the treatment in February 1992. This was three straight days hooked up to Adriamycin, one of the heaviest chemos there is. I went every morning at 9 and I stayed every day until after *Oprah*, which was over at 5. It's very wearing on your body. There was vomiting and diarrhea. Over the weekend, I was sent home with a bag, they were giving me fluids, because I could dehydrate, through the Porta-Cath. This was a device they hooked up to me–a tube connecting to a vein that went straight to the heart, so they could get stuff in quickly, with maximum effect.

"I had a briefcase full of drugs, fed through the Porta-Cath, and I had a nurse who'd come in every three or four hours. If I wanted to go to the bathroom, I had to drag this briefcase with me. Then I had to be rushed to the hospital, because I had contracted a fever. My white count was low, you know, the cells you need to fight off infection. So I was in the hospital for five days. My hair fell out again.

"The first time I lost my hair, everyone said, 'Oh yeah, we'll shave our heads for you.' The idea was so you'll feel more comfortable. But nobody did it, and I didn't expect anyone to. But then the second time, I went over to see Charlotte Briggs, my girlfriend, one night, and I walked in the door, and she's bald. She has shaved her head! And she hugged me. I laughed and said, 'What? Are you crazy?' She said, 'I promised you I'd do it.'"

Charlotte Briggs: "One day, when her hair was falling out, she started crying on the phone. She was down, very down. That same night, I had my son do it. He was 16 or 17 at the time. He said, 'Are you crazy?' I said, 'Well, I'm a little bit crazy, and I hope you can understand. Lisa is down, and not doing too well.' When she came through the door, she couldn't believe that I did it. It was fun. We got wigs together. She made it fun."

Lisa: "For the second step of the stem-cell replacement, they hooked me up to this machine. They were literally taking the blood out of my body—I could see it through the tubes. They were separating the white blood cells from the red blood cells. They were collecting the white cells so that after my second heavy dose, they'd put them back in me.

"Six to eight weeks later, again I had three straight days of heavy chemo, from 8 in the morning to after *Oprah*. On the last day, they took my frozen white cells and put them back in me. Then I was put in a hospital isolation ward. See, my white blood cell count was so low I was considered an AIDS patient. If I got a cold, I would die, because I had no immune system. If someone came into the room, they had to wear gloves and mask. Flowers weren't allowed. No candy, because the most minute germ could take my life. Friends and relatives could come in, but they had to wear masks, and they couldn't touch me.

"That was an incredible experience. I couldn't eat. I couldn't get anything down my throat. I couldn't walk. I couldn't talk. By day eight, I was totally out of it. I couldn't breathe, because the blisters were so bad in my throat. That was a side effect from the chemo. I vomited on myself. I had no control of my body. One time my blisters were so bad I was choking."

Her mom: "She jumped out of bed, hooked to this thing, through the Porta-Cath that went directly to the heart. She wanted to throw up, and she ran to the bathroom, and she fell by the toilet bowl, and the IV came out of her Porta-Cath. The nurse came in, and I was holding the tube to the machine, to keep it from dripping, and the nurse got all excited. He said, 'Forget the machine. You should have your finger on the port in her chest.' Air could have gotten in, and an embolism would have gone straight to her heart. That could mean cardiac arrest."

Lisa: "They rushed me to the emergency room. That was the worst moment. . . .

"I came out of isolation on April 2, 1992. I had been in for 12 days. I lost 20 pounds. I call that my second birthday. Then I had 25 treatments of radiation. That's part of the protocol. My last treatment was in August of '92. That was like graduation to life, and ever since then, they have detected no cancer. They check me every three months."

Dr. Troner: "If you look at the statistics for a case like hers, they're really dismal. Most of these patients are dead within five years. But recent data with stem-cell protocol is that 60 to 65 are disease free at three or four years. We'll see. Are we really curing them, or are we giving them a few more years?"

Dr. Cohen: "We don't know whether feeling better and feeling in control would actually cause a remission of cancer. There are reports by many traditional oncologists and surgeons of what they call 'spontaneous remissions.' There have been over 3,000 medical reports over the past 15 years of *remarkable*–I won't say miraculous–remissions. Now, can we attribute that to psychological changes? They seem to be connected, but we can't say for certain. There is some very serious research going on about these cases now.

"Dave Spiegal in California has made observations of women with metastatic breast cancer. He compared women who had group therapy versus a control group. It turned out that the women who went through therapy lived 36 months versus their controls, who lived 18 months. That study is considered one of the best that's been done.

"Another study was done by Fawzy I. Fawzy. He provided group psychotherapy sessions to one group, but not another. Those who had group therapy felt better, coped better, lived longer and there were some changes in their bodies. It looked like there was an immuno-enhancing effect."

Teri Amar, psychotherapist: "Most physicians feel we are separated at the neck, that the mind and the body are not connected. But we all have cancer cells running around in our body all the time. Those of us who have intact immune systems, we have lymphocytes that come along and kill the cancer cells and eat them up, but if our immune system is suppressed, then the cancer cell grows and multiplies. . . .

"People need reasons to live. So in my groups we talk about finding a dream, to lead a really rich life. Our goal is to 'Live Juicy.' It means rolling down a grassy hill, doing those things that bring out your best, most magic self. And when people do that, their immune system seems to perk up and say, 'Hey! This person might be a passionate person worth saving.'

"I never make outlandish claims. I don't think that we as human beings are powerful enough to give ourselves an illness, and I don't know that we're powerful enough with our mind to cure it. If we could give ourselves illnesses, how do you explain babies who are born with cancer? I *don't* see this work as an alternative therapy. I believe in modern medicine. I believe this work is complimentary."

Lisa: "I meet with her meditation group twice a month. One meeting we had, it was like 12 or 13 people, nine were women with breast cancer. You sit in the circle. We talk about anything. If there's a person in the group that's having a tough time, then the evening is focused on them.

"I've learned about meditation. There's also visualization, which Teri promotes in the group. You concentrate on focusing on something that kills cancer cells. One guy in the group, he visualizes popcorn being the cancer cells, and he's gone as far as tape recording popping sounds, and when he hears it, he thinks of cancer cells blowing up. For me, at the beginning, I had a gun in my hand, like at a carnival. I'm shooting like a target. Or it could be like a bomb blowing up a cancer cell. Whatever it takes for you. It's positive thinking. I don't know how it works, but I believe it works.

"In August of last year, I had a bone scan done, and a spot came up on my ribs. I'll be honest with you, I wasn't ready to go through the treatment again. I felt, 'All right, let's just get it over with.' I was depressed. Things were happening personally. I wasn't happy at work, and I didn't want to fight. When I said, I didn't want to take treatment, my brother got mad at me, and we got in a fight. I was thinking why should I go through it? Is this going to happen every year? But Teri totally changed my mind."

Teri Amar: "She was very depressed. But we got to talking. She said, 'I have these pictures. Can I show them to you?' She didn't have any of the captions on them yet. And this idea evolved: Maybe these pictures could help other people. That gave her something to live for, some reason to go through the torture that she might have to face again. No matter what they did to Lisa, there was a very wise piece of her that knew she was not her breast, that somewhere inside of her was the woman, separate from the woman with breasts, the women with hair. And that her glamour was not about her breasts or about her hair."

Lisa: "There was a shadow, but they keep testing it, and they don't see anything more. The cancer markers came back negative. So I haven't needed treatment. . . .

"In the last year, I've become an advocate concerning breast cancer. I'd wanted to do something all along, but everyone said, worry about your treatment first. The way I was brought up, in a family that was always involved in government, there was always the idea of giving something back to society. I felt I had a responsibility to give back what I had learned.

"Anyway, I got involved with the National Breast Cancer Coalition because of a column by Dave Lawrence in The Miami Herald. He interviewed Alex Stolfi, a nurse who was asking for help for the coalition. I called, and I said, 'I'll staple papers. I'll lick envelopes. I'll do anything.'"

Alex Stolfi: "My phone didn't stop ringing. I got a message from someone who was helping me: 'Alex, you must call this woman right now. She's called several times. Please don't wait.' I called her. We clicked instantly. Working on the campaign, we were really together day and night.

"We're trying to raise awareness about breast cancer in younger women. In 1993, 11,000 women under the age of 40 had breast cancer, and 29,000 women in their 40s had breast cancer.

"We needed to show that this is not just a woman's issue. There's the husband, children. If you have 183,000 women with breast cancer in 1993, that means you have 180,000 families dealing with breast cancer. And 46,000 died. One in nine women now get breast cancer. Thirty years ago it was one in 14. Why? It's controversial to call this an epidemic, but that's what some people are calling it.

"Breast cancer has been an ignored subject, and we wanted to present the White House with a huge petition, from people all over the country, demanding more money for breast cancer research."

Lisa: "I met Alex, and we went to this steering committee meeting. All these people were there—doctors and nurses and socialites and just little old me, cancer survivor.

"Mainly, I worked hard on getting signatures. My brother Vinnie gave me a lot of help. We went all over the place. I admire the AIDS activists. You see people wearing red ribbons on the Academy Awards, and I hope sometime they'll be wearing pink ribbons to symbolize breast cancer. A lot of women don't like to talk about it or think about it. And the longer they sweep under the carpet, the more of us are going to die.

"I talk to a lot of breast cancer patients, breast cancer survivors, and they're all down. They don't think they're going to get their life back together. I tell them, yes, it's an awful thing, Yes, we lost our breasts. Yes, we may still die. Yes, we have to live with this disease. Tomorrow, Dr. Troner could tell me, 'Lisa, it's back. A bone scan shows it.' But we can still be *alive* now.

"That means what I do today—from the time I wake up to the time I go to bed at night is everything I want to do. I've learned I don't like to be around negative people. Because negative people sit around and complain. I can't relate to it. It's such *trivial* stuff. I want to shout, 'Why don't you wake up?'

"Of course, it's still not easy sometimes. I've been going through reconstruction. They put an expander in my chest. The doctor fills it with fluid on a gradual basis. It inflates like a balloon, slowly, stretching the skin like a pregnancy. The new skin stretches around it. It hurt.

"And my personal life—well, that's a rough subject. When I was seeing the male nurse, he was separated. The wife moved out. It was OK to date like that. But then his wife moved home. We're still friends, but not as close as before. That's all right, because I'm getting Lisa back together again with my exhibit and my breast cancer advocacy. Everything's OK."

Keith: "It was a time in both of our lives that we needed each other, and right now we're friends. I'm really supportive of the message she's carrying. Like the picture with myself shows what's important is what's inside a person. There was no way I was going to look at Lisa and say, 'Gosh—one breast.' She was *Lisa*."

Dr. Weingrad: "She still has a high risk. Basically, she has the moment. That's all she can count on, and she makes the most of it."

Lisa: "I talked to Teri the other day, and I told her if the cancer comes back, it's OK. I'm ready to die, because I understand it all, and I don't know if I can explain it to everybody, but I understand it. I'll continue to fight—for myself, for my mom and dad, for my friends, my boyfriend. But if it doesn't work, it's OK.

"It's not the amount of time you have. It's the quality of time that you have. Last July, I went to the Amazon. I was sitting on the top of the boat. It was 3 o'clock in the morning, and it was absolutely incredible. No one was around. You could hear the birds and the bats—jungle sounds. All of a sudden, I looked up at the moon, and it just hit me. I don't know how to describe it. This is why I survived. It was like God tapped me on the back and said you did it, you survived the test."

E. Jean Carroll

Young Doctor Thompson

E. Jean Carroll was a beauty queen and cheerleader back home in Indiana, so she needs an audience. "There was nothing to do but turn to writing," she says. After majoring in communication–"an F in the only journalism course I took"–she flooded magazines and for five years received mimeographed rejections. "I have stacks of them. Rejection means nothing. Keep going," she advises. The sixth year the slips were handwritten, but the seventh, Esquire bought a story, and she was on her way.

Now her bio reads: "E. Jean Carroll is a modest woman who was nominated for an Ace award for her television show, **Ask E. Jean,** an Emmy for writing for **Saturday Night Live** and let's just interrupt this so-called 'bio' right here and frankly admit that it's not going to have the really interesting facts. . . . "

Like how she got the story, "Young Doctor Thompson," arriving unannounced at Hunter's place, Owl Farm, at midnight. He let her in and the fun began. "The second night I'm sitting on the side of his great hot tub, he's in the tub with Dove bars, margaritas, and assorted substances when he pulls me in and whacks off every last stitch of my clothing with a foot long knife–most fun I ever had in my life," she says. And she was 45 at the time.

But back to her bio: ". . . a contributing editor to **Esquire,** she has also written for the usual fish-wraps, **GQ, Rolling Stone, Playboy;** she's a correspondent to **Outside,** and writes the famed **ASK E. JEAN** column for **Elle** (the most popular column for young women in America) which has spawned the **ASK E. JEAN** TV show, the **ASK E. JEAN** books, the **ASK E. JEAN** audio tapes, not to mention the beautiful **ASK E. JEAN** bikini waxing kits."

How she loves that column–and, no, she doesn't make up the questions–it lets her use journalism as a weapon. "That's what it's for, to get people to think like you do," she says. If you ask E. Jean about writing, she tells you that you have to write six hours a day. "Nothing gets done unless you put in the hours." If you ask her about her reading, she says, "Chekhov is my god," and that she wishes she had written Pride and Prejudice, Gulliver's Travels, and Why I Won the Nobel Prize for Literature.

–CM

E. Jean Carroll, Young Doctor Thompson, *Esquire*, February 1993. Reprinted courtesy of the author from *Esquire*.

COMMONWEALTH OF KENTUCKY; BUREAU OF VITAL STATISTICS;
CERTIFICATE OF BIRTH
FULL NAME OF CHILD: Hunter Stockton Thompson.
PLACE OF BIRTH: Norton Infirmary, Louisville, Kentucky.
SEX: Male. LEGITIMATE? Yes. FULL-TERM? Yes.
DATE OF BIRTH: July 18, 1937. WEIGHT (N.O.R.): 11 pounds.
FATHER: Jack Robert Thompson, white, 42, Horse Cave, Ky.
MOTHER: Virginia Davidson Ray, white, 29, Louisville, Ky.
FATHER'S TRADE: Insurance engineering, First Kentucky Fire Insurance Co.,
10 years.
MOTHER'S TRADE: Housewife, 1½ years.

HUNTER WAS THE POLE around which trouble would occur. He was a good-looking boy who could outthink you and outperform you. But I believe he had great sadness. He was a serious, important child–chairman of the board of the gang. He knew how to bestow attention. His approval was extremely important because he had so many skills. And so you spent your whole time bouncing up and down, waiting for Hunter to approve.

–JOHN BRUTON, now a businessman in South America

BEARGRASS CREEK WAS A CONCRETE culvert going through Louisville. And black dudes would be walking down there, and we would ambush them. We'd have BB guns with us. When they'd come down the creek, we'd shoot at them. And that became part of the Hunter mythology.

–GERALD TYRRELL, known as "Ching," retired bank executive;
now a partner in a Louisville literary agency

OH, HE WAS A FOX! I mean, well, you daydreamed about Hunter. At twelve I'd go home to my bedroom and think, *God, I'd like to kiss Hunter. I'd like to pull his pants down and see what his penis looks like.*

He was just sexy. Sexy, but beyond that. There was a quality in Hunter that I think has always stayed with me, that I always look for in a man. Arrogance. He had a walk that was cool. I wonder if he still walks that way. And he was a leader. Hunter was the leader of the gang that we had–I still have this fantasy! I daydream of being in bed with Hunter. If Hunter and I ever got together, good God!

–"GINNY DANIALS" (does not wish her true name revealed)

THERE WAS A LOT OF STRESS involved in being around Hunter. You didn't want to cross him. He would become physically aggressive and physically violent. With his fists. And kicking. He was well coordinated and also effective. He would win. He would rile somebody up and then he would go at them like a windmill. He had a bad temper as a child. Also, he had this way of standing outside the problem, so he could never get caught. Lying was the thing he did best. He did it with total cool and total confidence.

–JOHN BRUTON

A lot of girls felt like I did. But a lot of girls were afraid of Hunter. Because he was dangerous. They said that he was wild. But he thrilled me. When we had slumber parties, it was like, "OOOO*ooooooo*, Hunter!"

Hunter would be the one that we would try to call and ask, "What do you look like naked?" But some girls said, "Oh, my mother thinks he's just too wild." But I never said that, because I secretly always wanted to be . . . Hunter's girl.

−Ginny Danials

I was always unnerved by his presence. Always minding my p's and q's and watching my step. Why? To my knowledge, all he ever did was twitch my ears at the dining-room table. He did it until I was ready to kill him. I pleaded with everyone at the table. "Can anyone do anything about this guy?" And it used to take until I was actually ready to burst into tears. And my mother would say, "Hunter, for God's sake!" or "Damn it!" When she was really mad she'd say, "Damn it." And everybody would freeze. But that's the only physical contact we ever had.

−Jim Thompson, HST's youngest brother, former disc jockey

We got off the bus and my dog always used to come and meet me. My little dog named Dubby. She was just this little black dog. Whenever my sister and I would fight, the dog would get all excited and bite my sister. And so I was telling Hunter this story, and "So," I said, "you better never hurt me while my dog is around because she'll bite you." And Hunter said, "Oh, yeah?" And I said, "Yeah." So he hauls off and kicks my dog across the street.

−Judy Wellons Whitehead, now a businesswoman in Mexico

When his father was alive he used to sit on the front porch with his little radio and watch us play in the front yard.

He was a lot older. He was a retired, white-haired, stone-faced guy who didn't say much. He was a big sports fan. He would listen to the Louisville Colonels baseball team while sitting on the porch. I think Hunter respected him. His mother had no power over him but had great influence. His father could discipline him up until the end.

−Gerald Tyrrell

−Tell me about your father.
−*(Silence)*
−You never talk about him.
−Well, read what I've written!
−I've read everything that you've ever written. You've never mentioned him.
−*(Silence)*
−Tell me about him.
−He had a great outlook on life.

−Hunter Thompson, interview

In fights, Hunter's technique was always to provoke action and then do something startling, to throw the other person off balance psychologically as well as physically. He created situations of confusion and perhaps even fright or disorientation.

When we played war, there would be five or six boys to a side. We were usually bare-chested and wore helmet liners–army surplus from World War II–and carried Daisy air rifles, BB guns, and, of course, rocks. A lot of Louisville had vegetation. Lots of squirrels, rabbits, minks. So there were places for ambushes. There was a woods near us. There were plenty of rocks. My mother was terrified. Because, of course, we could have been blinded by the BB guns and the rocks. But this was Kentucky. And Hunter is very Kentucky. Kentucky is a very violent place.

–Walter Kaegi, now a professor of history at the University of Chicago

I was down from Shelbyville seeing Hunter. We were either walking or riding our bikes. But anyway, we were over on Lexington Road, where there was this little grocery store. And Hunter walked into that grocery store and just picked up what he wanted–candy bars, potato chips, and I think he even took a soft drink–and put it in his pocket and just walked out! Scared me to death! I said, "My Lord, I'd be in jail for that!" Walked right on out. I never have forgotten it! It scared the hell out of me, to tell you the truth.

–Lewis Mathis, lawyer from Shelbyville, Kentucky

Probably it's not important, but I realized I told a tale wrong and want to correct it. The story about my dog who would always protect me. I think I said that Hunter kicked the dog–*wrong!* He slapped the hell out of *me*. He wanted to see if my dog would attack anyone who hurt me, as I claimed. Of course, the dog did nothing while I reeled in whirling stars. I don't know how I got that so wrong. As I remember, Hunter always liked dogs.

–Judy Wellons Whitehead, in a midnight fax

We boys just constantly read about war. Mainly the Civil War. We knew quite a bit about the southern generals and read in detail about the battles. Next to us on Bates Court there was a woods, and that's where we played North-South. That's the critical thing, North-South. We passed letters back and forth over enemy lines. Hunter was General Thompson of the Virginia Second Cavalry. His base was Fort Lee. Mine was the Army of Central Georgia. We made special control stamps and special cancellations.

–Walter Kaegi

I've always felt like a southerner. And I always felt like I was born in defeat. And I may have written everything I've written just to win back a victory. My life may be pure revenge.

–Hunter Thompson, interview

Hunter was a southerner, but Rhett Butler and Hunter had nothing in common.

–Judy Wellons Whitehead

It was the end of a social era. When you got to be sixteen in Louisville, and you were in this certain echelon of male acceptability, every single night in the summer–from the day that school ended until the day that school started–every day of the Christmas vacation, there was a major, major party. Sometimes two and sometimes three, given by the debutantes.

And what this meant was extravagant, free alcohol for underage drinkers. I mean, total free bars. Not bottles, cases. Anything you wanted. And it all had the blessing of the establishment of Louisville. The mayor, the mayor's daughter, or the banker's daughter or Sally Bingham, whose father owned the newspaper, or whatever. You were untouchable. Hunter was in Athenaeum, the most prestigious literary association in Louisville, and so he was an untouchable. We all started drinking at about fourteen.

−PORTER BIBB, former publisher of Rolling Stone,
now corporate finance director of a major investment firm

WE LOVED GOING UP TO the Shelby County Fair. That's where we saw our first stripper. She was in a tent and not particularly attractive. She was old, or she seemed old to us little boys at the time . . . and she popped a Ping-Pong ball out of her vagina, which we all thought was pretty amazing! And she was pretending to smoke a cigarette with her nether lips. She just stuck it in there, and Hunter, Lewis [Mathis], and I clapped.

−GERALD TYRRELL

THE STRIPPERS WERE just in an old tent. And people started throwing money at them. We didn't have any money. So Hunter tried to steal some from the girls off the stage.

−LEWIS MATHIS

HUNTER HAD AN EXOTIC APPEAL for the very richest girls in Louisville. I mean, Arabella Berry [name changed]. Her father was one of the two or three richest people in five states. He shot at Hunter one night when he brought Arabella home late.

−PORTER BIBB

WE WERE IN THE HABIT of stealing five or six cases of beer on weekends to drink. That night was the Friday night after my expulsion. We did our normal run and stole about five or six cases. We took one of them and put it on the school superintendent's lawn at one o'clock in the morning and very carefully put twenty whole bottles right through every pane in the front of his house.

−HUNTER THOMPSON, in an interview with Ron Rosenbaum in High Times

WHITE BUCKS, KHAKIS, white button-down Brooks Brothers shirt, leather belt, and a Shetland sweater. That was the uniform. Crew cut. We all wore crew cuts. Castlewood Athletic Club was a feeder to Athenaeum. It was like a farm system. And Hunter was a big star of Castlewood. But only a very small proportion of Castlewood guys got into Athenaeum. Very small proportion. And that gave Hunter a lot of currency. So he was kind of multilevel.

He hobnobbed with several cliques. The very top athletes who were untouchable in high school, they all knew Hunter. He was a gentleman athlete. He was not a competitive athlete. He never went out for anything. I don't know why. I always wondered. I thought he could have played football. He was probably not quick enough for basketball. And Hunter was also friends with the real shady element. The greaser element.

−PORTER BIBB

THERE WAS SOMEBODY who broke into churches, broke into schools—petty vandalism. Notes were left: "The Wrecker." A lieutenant on the police force shadowed Hunter for a year. But he couldn't pin it on him. To this day nobody knows if Hunter was the Wrecker.

−GERALD TYRRELL

−Are you the Wrecker?
−Call the AAA or Robin Leach.

−HUNTER THOMPSON, interview

HUNTER WAS DIFFICULT from the moment of his birth.

−VIRGINIA RAY THOMPSON, his mother

THE ONLY MAN IN MY LIFE until the time I was fourteen years old to tell me that he loved me was Hunter . . . He was dashing. I remember when he literally carried my books and rode the bus home with me. And I remember his arm touching mine, and I remember the hairs on my arm stood up straight. I don't know how we parted. I don't know when we broke up. Yes. I remember. My mother laid down the law. She said if I ever saw Hunter again, I would never see him again. I would be sent away.

I don't think Hunter ever knew how much I loved him. I want to tell him now. I want him to know it. Every time I was getting ready to tell him a long time ago, he would do something destructive and I couldn't tell him.

−LOU ANN MURPHY ILER, high school sweetheart; artist.
Thompson still has her picture up in his kitchen

HE HAD A LOT of confidence. It came from an intuitive understanding that he was smarter, stronger, and quicker than the kids we were running with in society.

−PORTER BIBB

MY MOTHER GAVE HIM carte blanche. Take the car, take the keys, come back anytime you want. . . . He often stayed out all night long. And my mother would sit up. She would sit there at the window. I hated to see Mummy sitting up smoking by the window.

−JIM THOMPSON

HUNTER WENT TO JAIL several times. Never for any lengthy period. After he and several others trashed the filling station on Bardstown Road, I know he ended up in jail. They caused some serious damage. And I think that might have been the time the police came and got him from Male High. They came and took Hunter away in handcuffs. I was at Male then. I did not see him being taken away, but others did.

−GERALD TYRRELL

Tearful Youth is Jailed Amid Barrage of Pleas

Should I Give Him Medal? Judge Asks Mother

Juvenile court judge Louis H. Jull yesterday ordered a tearful high school senior to County Jail for sixty days.

When the sixty days are up, Jull said he will make a final disposition of the case of Hunter S. Thompson, seventeen, of 2437 Ransdell. Thompson was one of three youths involved in a scrape in Cherokee Park early on the morning of May 11.

They were accused by police of robbing Joseph E. Monin, twenty, of 1824 Bonnycastle. . . . At the time Monin and another youth were parked near Hogan's Fountain with two girls. . . .

Jull explained that Thompson had been before the court many times as a result of three previous arrests and had always promised to mend his ways, but never had. Thompson's previous offenses, chief probation officer Charles Dibowski said, involved drinking and destruction of property. . . .

The girls told a reporter that they had not known Thompson at the time of the offense but were now on first-name terms with him. . . .

—Louisville Courier Journal, *June 16, 1955*

I used to go visit him in jail. That's where Hunter started writing. That's where he took a correspondence course before he left for the Air Force. He was about to graduate from high school, but he couldn't graduate because he was in jail. He was seventeen years old! Terrible. But Sam Stallings and Ralston Steenrod [the two boys who were arrested with Thompson] didn't go to jail.

Everybody else had money. And got out and went to college. Steenrod went on to Princeton. And Hunter was the only one, 'cause he couldn't afford—nobody could afford—to pay his way. So he went to jail.

The jail was horrible. It was just dirty, the Jefferson County Jail. Oh, it was just nasty. When I went to visit him, it was through one of those glass [partitions] with smudged-up lip prints. I mean, he was such a child to be going through this. And those horrible people that were in there with him!

He didn't cry. But he was sad. He wasn't Hunter at all. He looked terrible, you know, like everybody looks in jail; he wasn't eating anything. And he was so ashamed. He was just really embarrassed. I mean, his life had just been taken away from him! And Hunter was not a person you would ever confine—I'm sure you can see that now—so you couldn't picture him confined. And it was just—he was seething.

But that's really where he started writing. It was the beginning of his life all over again.

—*Judy Wellons Whitehead*

Headquarters; Eglin Air Force Base, Florida

23 Aug 1957

Attn: Base Staff Personnel Officer

Personnel Report: A/2C Hunter S. Thompson

A/2C Hunter S. Thompson, AF 15546879 has done some outstanding sportswriting but . . . this airman has little consideration for military bearing or dress and seems to dislike the service and want out as soon as possible. . . .

—*W. S. Evans, USAF colonel; chief, Office of Information Services*

I PLAYED BASKETBALL at Eglin when Hunter was the sportswriter for the base paper. And he made up the craziest stories! A little something would happen in the gym and he'd make a great big story! When I left Eglin, he wrote that I was going up to the Boston Celtics! He had one story where I hit nine forty-foot jumpers, and then he took a picture of me reenacting a ninety-foot jumper that I threw the length of the floor.

The last trip I made with him, we went to New Orleans. I had a new car. A brand-new Chevy Bel Air. I won the money for it at the blackjack table in Thule, Greenland. I don't remember much about the trip to New Orleans. Hunter burnt a hole in the seat. We had a lot of beers. Hunter had a great sense of humor. We spent an awful lot of time together. The only time he got strange was when he started writing.

We never talked literature. I'm from Montana. He probably thought I wasn't intelligent enough. Now, tell me. What's Hunter famous for? Oh! Is he? I didn't know that. I'll be durned! I'll be durned! Uncle Duke? I'll be durned!

—GENE ESPELAND, Montana basketball coach

I WAS AT STEPHENS COLLEGE. I hadn't spoken to Hunter in about a year and a half. I don't know how he knew where I was. He had been flooding the U.S. Government with as much correspondence as he could, trying to get out of the Air Force. Anyway, it was late at night. The middle of the night. I don't know where he got the number. My room was right across the hall from the pay phone on our floor. And it was ringing and ringing and no one answered it. So I got up and answered it. And it was Hunter.

He as at Eglin and he said all hell was breaking loose. He told me, and I remember his exact words, he said, "I may not surface for a while. If you read about anything in the paper and you don't hear from me, get me a lawyer."

He was hell-bent on getting out of the service. And he was going to get out anyway he could.

—LOU ANN MURPHY ILER

NEWS RELEASE
EGLIN AFB, FLORIDA [NOVEMBER 8]
    . . . A reportedly "fanatical" airman had received his separation papers and was rumored to have set out in the direction of the gatehouse at high speed in a mufflerless car with no brakes. An immediate search was begun for Hunter S. Thompson. . . .

—OFFICE OF INFORMATION SERVICES

HUNTER SAID, "You remember Gregory Corso, the fucking guy who wrote 'Boom'?" I said, "Yeah." "Well," said Hunter, "he's reading tonight at the Living Theater. Let's go." I said, "Fuckin' A!" So we put a case of beer in two big bags and got a cab to the Living Theater. Fourteenth Street.

We sit about in the middle of the theater and put the bags of beer between our legs. We pop a couple, and we watch. . . . We're both working at *Time* magazine as copyboys. The only thing *Time* requires of copyboys is they have no aspirations to journalism. . . . Now, the evening's entertainment is Frank O'Hara reading his poetry and then Gregory Corso. But Kerouac is sitting in the front row. And we're there with a case of beer between us, and we're ready to hear some fucking poetry. All we know about Corso is he wrote 'Boom.' "Boom boom you clouds, boom boom you wind. . . ." We're looking for a guy with hobnailed boots about six six, two hundred and forty-five, solid build, to stalk down there on the stage with his lumberjack pants and his lumberjack shirt, stick his ax into the canvas, and read his fucking screed. That's what we're looking for.

So up comes this mincing, miserable little fag. Well, by this time Hunter and I are pretty well fucking oiled. And one of the distractions of the evening is that when we finish a can of beer, we put it down beneath our feet and kick it, because it's a canted floor. And once the beer can gets sideways and rolling it goes *brrrrrrr* ding, *brrrrrrr* ding, *brrrrrrr* ding, *brrrrrrr*. So every time we have a beer, it goes *brrrrrrr* ding, *brrrrrrr* ding. Well, we ended up in a shouting dialogue with Corso. Hunter was convinced the rest of the audience was going to lynch us.

Corso would not go on reading. He was insulted. He said to the audience in general, these are his words, precisely: "You're all a bunch of *baaaystuds.*" *Baaaystuds.* That's what he said. And he pointed at Hunter, and he said, "And you are a *cweep!*" A *cweep.* And he stormed off the stage.

To save the evening, Kerouac came up and read *Doctor Sax.* He was totally unintelligible. Well, *Doctor Sax* is totally unintelligible. But it was Jack Kerouac. And we all enjoyed him.

–Gene McGarr, director and producer of commercials

I went down one spring vacation and visited Hunter in New York after he'd been up to see me at Yale. He was in a very bleak apartment in Manhattan, with absolutely no food except a jar of peanut butter. He smoked a pipe. Wore a long overcoat buttoned up to his neck. And he was thin. I think he was enjoying New York, from an impoverished point of view. He drove this old car and parked it with impunity wherever he wished.

He had absolutely no money. We walked around and rode in his car. It was okay. It was interesting. But to be perfectly honest, I never went back to see him again. Maybe it's the snobbishness in me, but just as a practical manner, in that really stark and unattractive flat, without a guest room, sleeping on the couch and waking up to peanut butter and, you know . . .

–Gerald Tyrrell

One hot night, Hunter, my soon-to-be wife, Eleanor, and another young lady and I went swimming at the LeRoy Street Pool. It's a city pool. Big fence around it. So we hoisted the ladies over, it was absolutely empty, it was 1:00 in the morning, so we hoisted over, stripped down to bathing suits or underwear, and dove in the water and had a good time. Until five or six guys came over the fence.

It was an Italian neighborhood. And they started kicking our clothes in the water. Hunter and I grabbed a couple of them and beat the shit out of them. They went over the fence and escaped, and we started picking up our clothing. Then ten guys came over the fence. And immediately we're into it again. Well, shit, after a few punches we beat the hell out of them too! They went back over the fence. We finished picking up our clothing, turned, and the fence was now black with people. There must have been fifty guys.

So we hoisted the girls over the fence and told them to run like hell. As soon as Hunter and I got down they came at us. There were so damn many of them they were interfering with one another. They used bottles, sticks. It was less than a minute of heavy action. They disappeared when the cops arrived. Hunter was lying in a fetal position. They kicked the shit out of him—*once they got him down*. But I think it's enough to say that Hunter is as brave as any man I've ever met.

The cops sent us to the hospital, where they had to use hoses. They put us in a tiled room, stripped us, and hosed us down to get the glass off. They wanted to keep Hunter. His eyes didn't look good. He had a concussion. But he refused to stay, and I was ambulatory, so we left.

—Gene McGarr

McGarr gave Hunter a run for his money. Gene McGarr was a very influential personality himself. And he and Hunter together were the wild boys. I arrived right after they got beaten to a pulp at the swimming pool. They were standing there bloody and really in bad shape. McGarr had a kind of aggressive personality. I think Hunter has a penchant for finding partners who will rise to the occasion and then create this kind of gladiator combat.

—"Peter Flanders," close friend in the '50s, '60s, and '70s; currently a historian, does not wish his true name used

The first time I really saw him was in a basement apartment in the Village. Standing in the doorway. The doorway was kind of short and Hunter loomed in under it in his madras shorts and white alligator shirt. And he had a big, thick manuscript under his arm. And he stood there in the doorway. He hadn't said a word. And I remember I was in this little alcove bed thing. Lying on the bed. The McGarrs and Peter Flanders were there, and we were all being very serious. Serious beatniks. Life was very serious. And I looked at Hunter in the doorway and I was absolutely gone. My heart just leapt out of my body.

—Sandra Dawn Thompson Tarlo

Hunter came over one night. I was out working. I never bothered locking my door, because anybody who wanted to climb five flights of stairs and rob from me, they were welcome to. This was a hot summer night. All the windows on the block were open. Hunter, apparently feeling a little frisky and being bored waiting around for me and not knowing when I was coming home, went into the front room, the windows opening out on the street, took off his belt, and started whipping the wall. You know, this loud thwack! Every time he'd thwack the wall, he'd yell, "*Ahgggh! Ahghhh! Aghhhh!*"

Then he'd stop the thwacking and in another voice would say, "Do it again. Do it again. Keep doing it." And then this *thwaaaack!* So apparently there were people hanging out of windows, yelling, "You son of a bitch! You can't get away with that! . . ." Then Hunter put his belt back on and sat down.

Well, about five minutes later there were the thundering hoofbeats of two New York City policemen, who, by the time they had climbed five flights of stairs, were truly apoplectic. They banged on the fucking door.

Now, Hunter sat with, you know, his cigarette in one hand, beer in the other, and said, "Who's there?" Two cops came in. They wanted to know what the fuck was going on. They had heard the complaints. They wanted to know where the bodies were. They made Hunter take his shirt off. To show that he had no whip marks on him.

—Gene McGarr

Hunter called me from Viking. He was taking [his first novel] *Prince Jellyfish* around to publishers, and he asked to meet me for a drink. My heart raced! It was Christmas Eve.

We met at a bar on Christopher Street. We were both absolutely smitten. Just drinking away, getting drunker and more and more attracted. He wanted me to come up to the cabin with him that night. But I said I had to be with my father at his new house on Long Island and help decorate the tree. I took the last train, which was at 11:00. The whole way out there I was just flying on the train. I stood between the cars, outside, and I don't believe I have ever been higher in my life.

—Sandra Dawn Thompson Tarlo

Sandy was an exact Sixties-generation Xerox of Rosanna Arquette.

—Porter Bibb

Then he called me a couple of days before New Year's Eve. Three o'clock in the morning. I should have known right then! He said, "I'm coming to the city. Would you like to get together?" He came to my apartment. We just fell into each other's arms. We spent four or five days in my single bed in my teeny bedroom—we had a bottle of something, Christian Brothers or something awful, or rum or something—wrapped around each other. I was so happy. And he was so happy.

—Sandra Dawn Thompson Tarlo

Situations Wanted: Correspondents
Politics, travel, features. No hack work. Young, good experience, contacts. Advise needs, rates, Box 969.
—Hunter S. Thompson, ad in Editor & Publisher, *January 27, 1962*

Hunter was working on getting to South America with the *National Observer.* His grandmother, Memo, died, and he received $1,500. He bought a camera and then he bought a ticket to South America. The *Observer* promised to pay him per article.

Meanwhile, I was working in Queens for a company with these bright young scientists who were making speed as a little sideline. Anyway, the idea was that Hunter would send me a story, and I would type ten copies and send them to travel sections of newspapers. He wanted the articles individually typed. But it was okay, because now I was taking lots of speed!

—Sandra Dawn Thompson Tarlo

Hunter arrived in Brazil, and I was driving on Copacabana Beach in an open MG with a guy named Archie Dick, who was one of our gang down there, and I saw Hunter sort of loping along. And we picked him up and he'd been drinking a little bit and he was really damn glad to see us. He looked like death warmed over. Just really ragged. But the thing that really struck us was the fact that he had a monkey in his pocket. And the monkey was drunk. And had thrown up in his pocket. The monkey subsequently committed suicide. The maid was upset and yelling because the monkey jumped off the balcony. . . .

I remember there was no talk of Sandy coming down. And all of a sudden she was there.

—Robert Bone, *reporter with HST on the* Middletown Daily Record; *currently travel correspondent and author*

During Carnival. I love music and I love to dance. And there were groups of drummers in front of our apartment building. And I was kind of in this huddle, moving and dancing to the samba music, and this man came up in front of me or in back of me and started kind of rubbing himself up against me, and I was so happy and I was having such a good time, I just moved away. No big deal. And the next thing I knew, Hunter, who'd been out in the city drinking with his journalist buddies, was there and he had this guy literally by the neck. Off the ground!

And said to him, "*Tiene problemas?*"

And it was a big scene. And then, of course, Hunter took me upstairs, and you know what he did after that? He locked me in for the carnival.

He went out. But he locked me in. I was not to go out on the street. He literally locked me in.

—Sandra Dawn Thompson Tarlo

You have to remember that even after Brazil, even after he was with Sandy, I saw him with plenty of other girls. Including prostitutes. That was the very accepted thing down there. Prostitution was so much a part of the scene that you never thought much about it. First of all, it was safe, and second of all, it was an accepted part of social life.

Mainly we'd go to the Kit Kat club, a block and a half from Copacabana Beach. We'd stay till 5:00 or 6:00 in the morning, and we'd drink until that time or maybe sometimes pick up the women. But normally we'd just sit there and drink. Somehow or other the liquor seemed to flow a little bit more in Brazil. You didn't think twice about it. Being drunk was a kind of natural state.

—Robert Bone

This was the first time he'd ever really been with heavy reporters like the *New York Times* people and the major network reporters. And it was his first time drinking with the heavies, and I would guess he loved it.

He also swam every day. Swimming for Hunter was relaxing. He liked the backstroke. The backstroke was like meditation. It just totally calmed him.

—Sandra Dawn Thompson Tarlo

HUNTER AND SOME GUY decided they were going to go out and shoot rats in the dump in Rio. Hunter had a .357 magnum. So they were out shooting rats and somebody called the cops, and eventually Hunter was arrested and taken to jail. But Hunter, of course, with his considerable charm, began to make friends with the police. Naturally he had gotten rid of the gun. The other guy had taken it away. So there was some doubt whether it was really Hunter shooting, and he said it wasn't him. "I wasn't shooting the rats. It must have been those other guys." And eventually he and the cops were having coffee together and so forth, and then Hunter put his feet up on the desk and leaned back on the chair and the .357 magnum bullets rolled out of his pocket.

They threw him back in jail and the embassy was called.

−ROBERT BONE

HE NEEDED SOMEONE who was devoted, and I was devoted. It was decided that I should go back to the States while Hunter traveled to other countries for the *Observer,* and I went to Louisville to visit Hunter's mother and his brother Jim.

While I was there, Hunter came home. I don't know how long we intended to stay there, but one day Hunter called upstairs to me. He said, "Sandy! Put on a skirt!" I came down in a little green plaid skirt and a great big charcoal-gray sweater because I had my arm in a sling from a riding accident. And it was underneath the sweater.

And we all got in this little old white car. His brothers, Davison and Jim, were in the front seat. And Hunter and I were in the back, and Hunter was holding my hand. And I said, "Where are we going?" And Hunter told me, "Jeffersonville, Indiana." And I said, "*Indiana!*" I thought it was at least five hundred miles away. "Why are we going to Indiana?" I said.

And Hunter said it just like this: "Oh, to get married."

−SANDRA DAWN THOMPSON TARLO

SANDY APPEALED TO ALL OF US because she seemed to be so direct, so down-to-earth, and honest. Very beautiful too. I thought, *She's a great person for Hunter. She'll probably calm him down.*

−JIM THOMPSON

WE CONSUMMATED THE MARRIAGE in the backseat of that car.

−SANDRA DAWN THOMPSON TARLO

Life of the Party

Robin Chotzinoff writes about obsessed eccentrics who she thinks "ought to be famous." That's been her *obsession since 1983, when she began writing for Denver's alternative weekly,* Westword. *This newspaper is one of very few, she insists, that publish stories like "Life of The Party," about events "not very important that turn out to be."*

So Chotzinoff pursues the off-beat: the city's hippest bathroom attendant, Japanese poultry experts who identify the sex of turkeys, a taxi dispatcher who recites poetry over the airwaves "because it's not just for the elite." She also considers herself an expert in the more mundane topics of food, fashion, gardening and, of course, dead bodies "if they're not murdered."

Although Chotzinoff respects editors who "take the 'I' right out," her personal travails often reach print: press junkets filled with freebie doughnuts, a fast-talking Kirby salesman who sells her a $600 vacuum cleaner she doesn't need, excruciating waits at the post office to mail fiction manuscripts. (Waiting in nonfiction lines proved worthwhile. She has profiled gardeners in People with Dirty Hands *and oddball athletes in* People Who Sweat.)

She turned fanatical about books when, at 6, she decided to be a writer. As a reader, Chotzinoff moved from a laundry closet with a bare bulb, to a hammock on Long Island, to a pine stump in the Colorado woods. Her rituals continue. Now, at 37, she reads humorist S. J. Perelman quarterly and essayist E. B. White annually. Her formal education is limited to two years at Andover High School and one at Bryn Mawr College. She does not, as she explains, have a degree in anything.

Chotzinoff refuses to kowtow to bosses or literary fads, insisting that "people whom you work for don't own you." That attitude—*"I have to write it the right way"—wins awards. She attributes success to competitiveness ("I've got to get to* The New York Times") *and guilt that she cultivates ("It tells me when I'm in trouble").*

To avoid burnout, Chotzinoff heads far off the job by playing blues piano and singing (not very well) and tackling endurance races that mix running and biking, skiing and snowshoeing. Inevitably, her writing is as provocative as her approach to life. "About half the people I write about are mad at me," she says. "But only once did someone want to shoot me. It didn't work out."

—AK

Robin Chotzinoff, Life of the Party, *Westword*, February 14–20, 1996. Reprinted courtesy of *Westword*.

I
f I had it to do over again, I would use dry ice," Shaun Gothwaite says. "Louie began to turn a little purple without it."

Other than that, it was the perfect wake. No one who knew Louie Aran could imagine him filled with embalming fluid or laid out among waxy flowers in a funeral home. So they had an enormous party the day after he died of a heart attack, at home, at age fifty. Louie's wife, Shaun, stayed home to direct the revel, which stretched on into the week. Louie himself was in attendance, dead, on the sofa. Inside the house at 37th Avenue and Perry Street, at least a hundred people joined hands and walked through the rooms to the strains of live bagpipe music. The temperature outside stuck at zero, and the neighborhood block captain shoveled snow from the sidewalk with such intense concentration that he kept forgetting to blow his runny nose. Out of respect for the dead, and to avoid a traffic jam, no one parked at the karate academy up the street. The party ended and another began.

"There was one for the people who came to see the body and another for the people who got there too late, and the food and the booze and the flowers, ooooh, there were so many," Gothwaite says, brimming with details and tears. She paces around her living room, smoking. She has lost ten pounds since Louie died last week. He hasn't been dead long enough for the tense change to take effect—she says "he loves" when she means "he loved." But being a "weeping widow," as she likes to call herself, she can get away with it. Often, when she thinks she's talking, she's shouting.

The phone rings every five minutes. People from the Common Grounds coffeehouse, where Shaun hangs out; the Zip 37 gallery, where she shows her photographs; her massage-therapy clients; Louie's chemistry students from Metro State; his hippie friends from Texas; his comrades in arms from the Aurora Gun Club. Shaun lets it ring and works on her lists instead. One reads:

> Get new fire extinguisher
> Get chimney swept
> Check refrigerator

"The water pipe broke behind the washing machine," she recites. "The light switch in the bathroom doesn't work. The toilet wouldn't stop running."

The windows are wide open. The view is of large wood stumps, ready to be cut for the house's wood stove. "Oh, God," Shaun says, "I should learn to cut wood." A gust of wind blows off the coffee table a shred of paper on which Shaun has written "Louie, 50, chemist/cowboy."

"And what am I going to do about the obituary? I don't want it to be like the ones in the papers. 'So-and-so was a housewife. She was a member of the Eastern Star and a homemaker. She is survived by four grandchildren and eight great-grandchildren.' Please. What am I going to write? Where it all starts . . . You know where it all starts? When we met."

Shaun met Louie in 1987 when she agreed to deliver a book to him at the Metro State chemistry lab. He was, she remembers, "an older guy, a little guy. He didn't say much." But suddenly Shaun liked everything about the chemistry department—even its smell. She learned that Louie had been born in Spanish Harlem in 1945 but had always been enamored of cowboys and Indians and had moved to Texas in his late teens. Following a brief stint with a group of San Antonio radicals know as the "hippanos," Louie came to Denver to work for the U.S. Geological Survey, got his master's degree in chemistry and went to work for Metro State College as the chemistry-lab coordinator. He believed not just in astrology but in black-powder rifles. Shaun liked the contradictions. She liked to be around Louie, she says, because he was "content—he had the most amazing ability to do nothing. He called it Louie-ism. 'Do nothing,' he would say. 'There is nothing to do.'"

Married in 1989, Shaun and Louie settled in the northwest Denver house Louie had bought for cash in the early Seventies and remodeled until it looked like a cross between a New Mexico shaman's cottage and Grizzly Adams's place. To this ambience Shaun added shrines made of dead flowers and found objects. (Her most recent, in honor of Louie, contains two packages of Marlboro Lights, a vial of his ashes and his Aurora Gun Club membership card, among other things.) Their circle of friends, in the neighborhood and elsewhere, was huge. The marriage survived several hospitalizations—Louie had developed a bacterial heart infection—infidelity, and the usual lesser skirmishes.

"We were exact opposites," Shaun recalls. "We were two rocks in the tumbler, and the lock represented the marriage and the freedom to tumble and smash and maybe polish against each other. I stayed with him because I was so sure it wasn't finished between us. There was something between us like an umbilical cord."

On the night of January 26, in fact, Shaun and Louie discussed their marriage while walking their dogs. The talk ended peacefully. Shaun went to bed, but Louie stayed up—he planned to sharpen knives and then make bullets for the next day's shooting. He had his fatal heart attack within the hour.

"Ooooh, and his father died of a heart attack in that same room, in 1978—whaddaya think of that?" Shaun asks, scrabbling through her lists in search of cigarettes. "I seem to be smoking a lot. That's okay. Anyway, I came downstairs Saturday morning and saw him lying there, smiling, with one eye open, and the dogs were lying next to him. Ooooh. And my mouth went dry. I was scared. I knew he was dead, but I called 911 and screamed into the phone, and they said, 'Ma'am, ma'am, stay on the line,' but I screamed, '*Fuck you!*' and I hung up and called a friend."

By then, she could hear sirens. In minutes, paramedics were trying to revive Louie while Shaun stepped around them, trying to keep busy by making coffee for District One's Officer Marc Chavez, who told her it was good and strong and came back two hours later with candles from the local botanica.

"I filled out the piece of paper they gave me, and they told me Louie was dead, and I told them to leave the body with me, and they left," Shaun continues. At that point, she remembered what Louie wanted done with his remains: "He didn't want to be filled with fluids. He wanted to do the death thing right. He said, have a big party. Do what you have to do."

So Shaun moved Louie onto the living-room sofa, covered him with a blanket, and put Chap Stick on his lips, which were starting to look dry. Then she got out the phone and the Wild Turkey, and the mourners began to arrive.

"I started drinking, and I'm glad," she says, "because it helps. I was sad, glad, dancing, playing music, sobbing. The flowers started to come, and I love flowers. Between three and four hundred people came in and out of here."

Louie ended up hanging out with his friends for nearly 36 hours, despite the coroner's semiofficial position that "you don't want a dead body lying around, and 24 hours would be pushing it." Late Sunday afternoon, Louie was removed to the Horan & McConaty mortuary a few blocks away.

"I picked up what they call his 'cremains' that Saturday—just in time," she recalls, "because I had to shoot some of him out of his gun on Sunday. The Aurora Gun Club turned out in force to help Shaun load some of Louie into his favorite rifle. "The club," she says, "dedicated the whole shoot to Louie."

Then she went home and made more lists. "On Monday I was alone for the first time," she recalls. On Tuesday she filled several vials with Louie's ashes to give to his friends. On Wednesday she began making arrangements to scatter another handful of Louie over the mountains north of Black Hawk. "And I think I will sprinkle him in my garden this spring," she decides, "and a lot of our friends want him in their gardens, too. It's illegal, I hear, but whoever says so can kiss my ass."

The rest of Louie will stay in a small pine box in the living room, five feet from the new fire extinguisher and one wall away from the rapidly depleting woodpile.

"I have to maintain the place," Shaun says. "I have to learn how Louie did it. And then there's this obituary. I mean, what about it? Could *this* just be it?"

Yes.

Ken Fuson

Ah, What a Day!

Ken Fuson compares newspapers to boxes of Cracker Jack, giving readers a sur-prise, a prize, each day. He supplied a few of his own at The Des Moines Register, *where, at 38, he wrote "Ah, What a Day!"—a one-sentence, one-paragraph story. "This makes newspapers less ordinary and mundane," he insists. "We don't have to be so predictable."*

After reporting two hours by car and on foot, Fuson crafted 289 words into a story that fit entirely into the paper's daily budget of stories. He wisely warned edi-tors: "It's going to be weird" and "I know it's ridiculously long." Yet they left intact the riskiest sentence he's ever written. He willingly takes heat for such unorthodox efforts. "Some journalism profs will say it's not news; they'll say it's gimmicky. But," he insists, "that doesn't bother me."

Fuson so wants to reel in readers that he'll rely on italics, exuberant punctua-tion, even—horrors!—quote leads. When he writes a longer story, Fuson urges edi-tors, only half sarcastically, to tuck a toll-free number into the copy and offer free coffee to callers who read that far. He likes readers. He readily declares his loyalty, insisting that "I'll never consider myself anything but a reader." And he always tries mightily to follow his own advice: "Don't write a story that you won't read."

Fuson traces his start to John Steinbeck's The Grapes of Wrath, *the biggest novel that the librarian at his high school could find. ("The power of the words just overwhelmed me," he writes, stuffing yet another aside in the parentheses he prefers.) After that, he decided to major in journalism, heading to the University of Missouri and jobs at community newspapers in Missouri and Iowa.*

Though confident about story leads and ends, Fuson fusses over middles—what facts to include, what to exclude. "Structure is the one area of storytelling that we all struggle with most but talk about least," he confides. All this anxiety nets prizes, including an unprecedented three "Outstandings" in annual contests among almost 100 newspapers owned by Gannett Co., Inc. After winning a 1996 National Headliner Award, Fuson insisted, "It's not a matter of inspiration. It's a matter of craft." Then he headed to Baltimore to prove that for The Sun.

—AK

Ken Fuson, Ah! What a Day! *The Des Moines Register,* March 26, 1995. Reprinted courtesy of *The Des Moines Register.*

Here's how Iowa celebrates a 70-degree day in the middle of March: By washing the car and scooping the loop and taking a walk; by daydreaming in school and playing hooky at work and shutting off the furnace at home; by skateboarding and flying kites and digging through closets for baseball gloves; by riding that new bike you got for Christmas and drawing hopscotch boxes in chalk on the sidewalk and not caring if the kids lost their mittens again; by looking for robins and noticing swimsuits on department store mannequins and shooting hoops in the park; by sticking the ice scraper in the trunk and the antifreeze in the garage and leaving the car parked outside overnight; by cleaning the barbecue and stuffing the parka in storage and just standing outside and letting the friendly sun kiss your face; by wondering where you're going to go on summer vacation and getting reacquainted with neighbors on the front porch and telling the boys that—yes!yes!—they can run outside and play without a jacket; by holding hands with a lover and jogging in shorts and picking up the extra branches in the yard; by eating an ice cream cone outside and (if you're a farmer or gardener) feeling that first twinge that says it's time to plant and (if you're a high school senior) feeling that first twinge that says it's time to leave; by wondering if in all of history there has ever been a day so glorious and concluding that there hasn't and being afraid to even stop and take a breath (or begin a new paragraph) for fear that winter would return, leaving Wednesday in our memory as nothing more than a sweet and too-short dream.

Doug Bates, Tom Hallman, & Mark O'Keefe

Return of the River

When a record flood surged through the Pacific Northwest early in 1996, Jack Hart at The Oregonian *proved his claim that "regular collaboration is the key to risk-taking." As the Willamette River crested midday Thursday, the senior editor began guiding "Return of the River" by jotting a story theme and deploying three reporters. While they collected the necessary scenes in the necessary sequence, Hart stayed in the newsroom, massaging dictation from cell phones and feeds from computer modems.*

The narrative came in late Friday, on deadline for Sunday's edition. Once waters receded, chatter began among journalists and academics on the Net's Writer-L. (The moderator is Jon Franklin, who teaches creative nonfiction courses at the University of Oregon. To join, e-mail writer@pioneer.net)

But come out of cyberspace. Doug Bates tracked the headwaters for "Genesis" and followed the flow for "Illusions of Control," and "High-Tech in the Wet." (Luckily, he'd already read John McPhee's The Control of Nature.*) The coast is familiar territory for Bates. His 1968 bachelor's degree in journalism came from the University of Oregon. At 49, after reporting and editing for five newspapers from Seattle to San Diego, Bates is still near a river, as editorial page editor for* The Bend Bulletin.

Mark O'Keefe, writer of "Taking the Long View" and "Meeting the River," normally covers religious and social issues, not rushing water. But, at 35, after deadline duty for UPI wires in Milwaukee and seven years at The Virginian-Pilot, *he can handle anything. He prepped with two journalism degrees, a bachelor's from Marquette University (1983) and a master's from Regent University (1987).*

Tom Hallman, Jr., stayed closest to base for "Riding It Out in Portland" and "The End of the Line." At 40, the veteran crime reporter now focuses on features, earning honors as a finalist for the 1995 Pulitzer Prize in feature writing. In 1977, he received a bachelor's in journalism from Drake University. He then reported for magazines in New York City and weeklies in the Northwest.

At 49, Hart has the credentials to coordinate chaos: reporter, editor, Sunday magazine editor, educator at five universities. He earned journalism degrees from the University of Washington (B.A., 1968) and the University of Wisconsin (Ph.D., 1975). Like most editors, Hart reads everything, from billboards to blockbusters. On dry days he also reads skywriting.

–AK

Doug Bates, Tom Hallman, Mark O'Keefe, Return of the River, *The Oregonian*, February 11, 1996. Reprinted courtesy of *The* (Portland) *Oregonian*.

GENESIS

Headwaters of the Willamette
Thursday Morning, Feb. 8, 1996

At its birth, the flood looks benign and beautiful. Crystalline droplets, billions of them, trickle into the indigo waters of Waldo Lake, high on the headwaters of the great Willamette. The melt-off fashions fantastic shapes in the vanishing snowpack—miniature caves and arches and odd pinnacles of ice, all etched in the whitest of whites.

Out of this purity gushes the Willamette's wild North Fork, the only undammed arm of the river. No one gazing at such a breathtakingly pristine sight would easily imagine the roiling brown ugliness that will end up licking at the top of Portland's harbor wall.

Dan Ramsey, though, has a pretty good idea what's in store for the Willamette Valley.

"I've lived up here 11 winters," he says, "and I've never seen one like this. First, we got 203 inches of snow in just 14 days. Then, just as quickly, it warmed up. Now we're down to only 50 inches on the ground, and it's going fast."

Ramsey should be out driving a snowplow, but the roads are bare. He's part of the state highway crew stationed high on the western slopes of Oregon's Cascades and lives in a state-owned cabin in Willamette Pass. Portland, where his children live, is about 180 miles north.

"Say," he says, frowning, "have you heard anything from Portland today?"

If the man looks a little worried, it might be because all around him he sees signs that the worst flood in 32 years is bearing down on the part of the state his loved ones call home. "Quite a year, all right," says Ramsey, distractedly, as he repairs tire chains for his crew's idled equipment.

"Quite a year. . . ."

Something truly eerie is going on at the source of the Willamette. Here it is still deep winter, but it looks and feels like a day in May. Ramsey works amid melting snowdrifts, wearing no coat or gloves, just his orange jumpsuit, flapping open down the chest.

Then it begins to rain—hard—and that's strange, too. Where are the snowflakes? They should be burying the Willamette Highway this time of year.

Instead of snowy silence, the upper Willamette reverberates everywhere with the troubling sounds of hydrology: the dripping, trickling, gurgling and gushing of an extraordinary meteorological event that cannot bode well for those downhill. And from here, downhill includes the entire 11,000 square miles of the Willamette River Basin and most of Oregon's population.

In Portland, normal winter flows might reach to 8 feet on the gauge that measures water depth where the Willamette flows through the very center of the city. But the water already has begun a precipitous climb and has just passed 20 feet.

And more water is on the way. As the North Fork drops 1,500 feet from Waldo to Skookum Creek, a score of unnamed torrents taint the clear river by dumping their swollen contents and turning it to café au lait. Then comes a winding, 2,000-foot plunge to civilization and the accompanying muddy merges of dozens of other imaginatively named tributaries such as First Creek, Second Creek, Third Creek and so forth, all the way up to Ninth Creek.

By the time the North Fork roars under the covered bridge at tiny Westfir, all those creeks have turned it to dark coffee. The sight—and the sound—is unnerving.

"You've got to feel sorry for people downstream," says Dan Ramsey, back at the pass, gazing out at the rain dissolving the snowpack. He reflects a moment, then asks again, a hint of concern in his voice, "Heard any news from Portland?"

ILLUSIONS OF CONTROL
LOOKOUT POINT DAM
THURSDAY AFTERNOON, FEB. 8, 1996

Technically, the wild river that flows out of Waldo Lake is "The North Fork of the Middle Fork of the Willamette." The Middle Fork, which is the true main stem of North America's biggest north-flowing river, begins 25 miles south of Waldo in a tiny lake called Timpanogas.

"Everyone here agrees that Timpanogas is where the Willamette begins," says David Murdough, a U.S. Forest Service soil scientist working in the neighborhood of the river's headwaters. "It's all the creeks, though, that turn it into a river —Tumblebug Creek, Cold Creek, Swift Creek—there's a score of them that feed into the Middle Fork as it drops through Paddys Valley at the edge of the Willamette Forest."

Normally mere brooks, those creeks are torrents Thursday afternoon, turning the Middle Fork into the same swollen, deafening, chocolate mess that the North Fork has become.

With one enormous difference.

Just before the Middle Fork reaches Oakridge, the roaring river flattens out in a sprawling, unsightly basin lined with tree stumps and stratified mud.

It's the reservoir behind Hills Creek Dam, the first of a string of big flood control projects built to tame the mighty Willamette.

Floodgates at Hills Creek allow only a small stream to escape—just enough to protect fish habitat—so it's a gentle river that meets up with rampaging Salt and Salmon creeks in Oakridge. The creeks help turn the Middle Fork back into a fairly mean-looking flood threat by the time it passes through town and converges with the North Fork. At that point the river looks truly frightening. It races toward Eugene and the Willamette Valley, 40 miles away.

But the vast ugly tub called Lookout Point Reservoir absorbs the fury of the Middle Fork and spreads it over thousands of acres of stumps and mud flats. A naive observer might assume humanity has gained dominion over this wild river.

But below Lookout Point Dam, in offices next to the powerhouse, Dick Lamster knows better. This river, despite 14 flood-control dams throughout the Willamette Basin, has not entirely abandoned its ancient ways. It is always eager to return, to become what it once was, as if it wanted to remind us that no real taming has taken place—only partial confinement and the illusion of docility.

"We're just passing minimum flows right now," says Lamster, resource manager at Lookout Point for the U.S. Army Corps of Engineers. "It's local runoff from side streams that is causing the flooding. I'm afraid we can't control that, but we're doing everything we can to help out."

Lamster notes that the flood-control dams on Willamette tributaries control only 27 percent of the river basin. And Thursday night, as rain splashes against the windows of Lamster's office below the Lookout Point Dam, he grimly acknowledges that nature is firmly in control of the other 73 percent.

The numbers bear him out. In the past two days, the volume of water flowing past Eugene has tripled.

One of Lamster's co-workers leaves early Thursday. Though she works at the biggest dam on the main stem of the Willamette, there is little that she or her employer can do to spare her home in the farmlands north of Eugene.

By Thursday night, it will be under water.

HIGH-TECH IN THE WET

THE SONY PLANT IN EUGENE
THURSDAY NIGHT, FEB. 8, 1996

Once the Willamette passes Lookout Point and absorbs its Coast Fork and then the icy McKenzie, nothing blocks the bloated river between Eugene and Portland. No more dams, no more reservoirs—just 100 miles of flat, open flood plains and many more rivers with venerable Indian names such as Santiam, Molalla and Clackamas.

The Indians knew what was coming and moved to higher ground in Willamette winters. Descendants of the European settlers, however, turned the valley into year-round homesteads and farms. Today, it has been transformed into the high-technology corridor that some choose to call, in the hubris of our age, the "Silicon Forest."

By Thursday, a good portion of this so-called forest is surrounded by murky water. And the water is still rising. Down in Portland, it has rushed up past the 26-foot mark and shows no signs of slowing.

In Springfield, on the north side of town, some of the water headed downstream has detoured into one of the biggest and brightest examples of Oregon's techno-revolution. Muddy brown liquid is creeping into Sony's newly opened compact-disk manufacturing plant.

"We knew we'd built on a 100-year flood plain," says Monica Shovlin, Sony's local marketing-services manager. "What we didn't know was that we'd be this lucky."

"Lucky" is putting 100 employees to work in an extra shift, placing thousands of sandbags around the big brick building as floodwaters lap at the door.

Water gets knee-deep in the Sony cafeteria before the flooding Mohawk and McKenzie rivers crest, sending all that water north toward Portland. By Thursday night, the cafeteria is drained, except for whatever moisture and muck is left in the big room's expanse of carpet, being sucked dry by workers with whirring industrial vacuums.

Sony's hassle and inconvenience is exceeded only by the embarrassment of having the flood coincide with the arrival of company engineers from around the world for a conference at the gleaming new factory. The meeting must be moved to drier quarters at the Valley River Inn, across the freeway, in Eugene.

And long after the floodwaters recede from the great temporary wall around Sony's building, the rows and rows of soggy sandbags remain in place—a fitting metaphor, perhaps, for society's greatest conceit of all, the belief that it can really control nature.

The river, meanwhile, keeps rising and rushing toward Portland. At noon Friday, it climbs past the 28-foot mark in Portland Harbor.

TAKING THE LONG VIEW
OREGON STATE UNIVERSITY, CORVALLIS
FRIDAY MORNING, FEB. 9, 1996

For his entire career, he has studied the ways of the water, but until today, professor Stan Gregory never had experienced a major flood. When he heard it might be coming, he was like a kid from Florida waiting to see his first snowfall.

"It's an adrenaline rush," says Gregory, a member of the "stream team," a group of professors in the Department of Fisheries and Wildlife. The team members map and dissect floods as if they were performing an autopsy. For the rest of his career, Gregory will be analyzing this one, the Great Flood of 1996.

Still, as Gregory well knows, floods are not that big of a deal in the historical scheme of the Willamette valley. During the Ice Age, water filled the entire valley, forming the huge Lake Allison. Dozens of big floods have roared down the valley since record keeping started in the mid-1800s. This is by no means the biggest.

Gregory says Oregonians are starting to forget what wet really means.

"We've been in a drought since 1964," he says, his shoulder-length hair touching the collar of his faded jeans jacket.

But in nearby Portland, the scene looks anything but dry.

Bike paths that twisted through the park are several feet underwater. Trees that provided shade on sunny days stand like aliens in the brown liquid that rushes through the intersection of the Willamette and Marys rivers.

The gawkers—and they're out in force, taking pictures, pointing out flooded landmarks to their children—see destruction. Gregory sees creative renewal.

"The process of change is occurring right now," he says. "The river is exchanging nutrients with the surrounding land, and new habitats are being formed. The existing habitats are being made more complex and rich." Professor Peter Bayley, a fellow stream-teamer, nods. Neither wants to minimize the destruction of this flood, but this is nature's way, they say, whether it's on the banks of the Mississippi, the Amazon or the Willamette.

Bayley has studied flooding on all three. We can try to tame rivers with dams and dikes, he says, but they will rise again, as they are meant to do.

As he speaks, the Willamette downstream in Portland is climbing. If it nears 29 feet it will spill over the harbor wall and into the core of downtown.

City workers and hastily assembled volunteers are frantically working to build the wall higher.

"We need a little more humility in dealing with our environment," Bayley says. If Willamette Valley housing developments continue to sprout in areas Native Americans and early settlers repeatedly saw underwater, the two professors say, future damage will be even greater, especially if this 32-year spell of drier-than-normal weather comes to an end.

"The good thing about this is it provides the Willamette Valley a teachable moment," Gregory says. "Most of the time, someone else is doing the teaching. This time, Mother Nature is doing the teaching."

MEETING THE RIVER
Salem
Friday Morning, Feb. 9, 1996

In the pre-dawn darkness on the Mill Creek Bridge, Jason White hears the rushing water before he sees the house he rents. He lights a cigarette while his wife, Claudia, clutches their feverish 1-year-old son, Christian.

When they fled Los Angeles two years earlier to pick a new home, they never bargained for this. Before choosing Salem, they drove through much of the United States, to San Francisco, Seattle, Idaho, Chicago, New York and West Virginia. Oregon was the place they would put on their perfect postcard.

But this dark scene isn't one to write to Mom about. The yard that is normally on the bank of the creek is now part of the creek. Water surrounds the house.

But there is an encouraging sign. On Wednesday, the water was two feet above the door. This morning, it has receded to the walk leading up to the porch.

Claudia, wearing canvas high-top sneakers, stands on the sidewalk, which is dry.

"I'm not getting my shoes wet," she says. "I'm going to hang out here."

Jason makes two splashes in the water, then with a third stride hits the porch and grabs a note on the front door. It's from their landlord.

"Not as bad as I thought," the note says. Jason turns the key and walks in. Their couch is on milk crates. "Is the carpet dry?" Claudia asks.

"What's that, babe?"

"Is the carpet dry?"

"It's a little bit wet."

Jason flicks his cigarette lighter to help him see. He breathes easier as he heads to the baby's room, then their bedroom. No significant damage.

"I'm happy," says Jason, a janitor who had no renter's insurance. "Very happy. I thought I was going to lose everything, and we would have no place to live."

After evacuating on Wednesday, the couple headed to a public shelter, then to a Motel 6. The Court Street Christian Church, their Salem congregation, insisted on it, offering to pick up the tab.

It was late that night that Jason took his son to the Salem Hospital emergency room. The thermometer said 105 degrees.

But this morning, the fever has broken and the sun is starting to come up, making its first appearance in days. The couple heads to McDonald's for breakfast.

The parents push a plastic forkful of scrambled eggs toward the face of their son, who hasn't eaten since the fever hit.

The baby frowns, then turns his head away in disgust. Suddenly, though, he reconsiders. He takes a bite. Then he swallows it. The young parents smile, tension draining from their faces.

RIDING IT OUT IN PORTLAND
ABOARD THE TUG LASSEN
FRIDAY AFTERNOON, FEB. 9, 1996

Capt. Chris Satalich flips switches, and twin engines on the Lassen, a 70-foot-long Shaver Transportation Co. tugboat, roar to life. As Satalich checks his gauges, the wheelhouse vibrates.

Satisfied, he nudges the throttles, and the tug moves out of the harbor with the grace of a dancer.

The Willamette has crested at 28.5 feet in downtown Portland. But it refuses to drop, and water laps over the top of the harbor wall.

Satalich, 34, and his 24-year-old deckhand, Bob Dillon, are heading out to explore the final stretches of river—from the edge of the industrial park in Northwest Portland to the confluence with the Columbia River, where the Willamette dies.

The river always has been a part of the Sataliches' life. He grew up in a North Portland home that overlooked the river, and his father was a captain for Shaver in the 1950s and '60s. Satalich began riding tugs for fun when he was a boy. He's been working on them since he was 16—first as a deckhand and now as captain. His job is pushing grain barges and assisting ships.

It's a job.

That's all.

When it comes to this river, Chris Satalich is no romantic.

And yet he senses that this Friday is special.

"I've never seen the river like this," he says. He peers out the wheelhouse window, 35 feet above the water.

"Never," he says. He pulls back the throttles and moves the tug into the heart of the river he thought he knew so well.

Although the Lassen is one of the most powerful vessels in Shaver's fleet, Satalich must hold her back. "We have to go slow," he says. "Dead slow.

"Look at that dock."

He points toward Cathedral Park.

"That dock there is so fragile," he says, "that any little wake will tear it apart."

And so he idles downstream, keeping pace with a flotilla of debris that stretches as far as he can see. Satalich slows and watches it pass beneath him.

Trees.

A dock.

A green garbage can.

A blue fuel tank.

A folding oak chair.

"Hey, Bob," he calls. "You want a chair?"

He maneuvers the tug so that the chair is directly in front of them.

"Naw," says Dillon, "it's too messed up."

They head downstream.

Nothing on the river is normal. Piers that should exist are deep under water. Docks have disappeared. Landmarks that used to be below the tug now are at eye level. Even the water itself is new.

"I've seen brown water, but this is strange," Satalich says. "See how it looks almost like there's powder in the water, like there's a chemical reaction taking place."

The Willamette has a personality, he says. The Columbia River is the big brother, the Willamette always the younger sibling.

"Today," says Satalich, "little brother is angry."

THE END OF THE LINE

MOUTH OF THE WILLAMETTE

LATE FRIDAY AFTERNOON, FEB. 9, 1996

This stretch of the river just above Sauvie Island is usually calm, almost like a lake. Not today. Satalich estimates the current to be about 3 knots—nearly 5 mph.

It is as if the river has a job to complete. Today, it must finish reclaiming itself. The debris that flows toward the Columbia is simply a by-product of the river asserting its power.

A few miles away, cities are in a tizzy because the Willamette has disrupted human routine. Parking lots overflow. Basements fill with water. Volunteers scramble to fortify a harbor wall. The river has reached its absolute peak.

But here . . .

Here the river flows as it has always flowed.

The tug moves through the gap between Sauvie Island and Kelley Point Park.

In the distance, green hills roll to the horizon. Closer in, the wide Columbia welcomes and envelops its little brother.

Waiting out in the Columbia are 10 ships. They float at anchor, waiting for the Willamette to recede so that they can head upriver and dock. But they must wait. Sooner or later, human technology gives way to more powerful forces.

And nature, which for days on end has cloaked the Willamette Valley in dark clouds, blustery winds and drenching rains, finally seems to be relenting.

A bright sun has broken through.

The sky is clear, brilliant blue.

Birds swoop down along the river, and—for the first time in weeks—it is warm.

The city has disappeared behind the tug, hidden around an upstream bend.

Without landmarks—walls, buildings, bridges—the Willamette seems to run in a perfectly natural state. There is no evidence of a 100-year flood. There is only the rushing river.

It is impossible to see that anything ever even happened.

Patrick May

Society Pays Awful Price for Violence

When news gets wild, reporter Patrick May often gets a 911 from editors at The Miami Herald. *Murder, mayhem, weather amok–editors find him because he's quick, he gets folks to trust him, and he's willing to roam. "I'm a restless traveler at heart," May concedes.*

He first packed his bags more than two decades ago when, as an undergraduate bored with classes, he split to work construction in Seattle, drive a cab in San Francisco, grow roses in Boston, and play country-western in Alaska. Heading abroad, he circled the globe, north to south, east to west. The idea of getting paid to travel sparked his return to school, to San Francisco State University, where he graduated with a journalism degree in 1981.

May's close-up on crime began at The Florida Times-Union, *covering cops on a night beat. In 1983, he moved to a bureau at* The Miami Herald, *then downtown to the main newsroom. At 42, he plunged into South Florida's gun culture with a dozen stories. He found revealing faces: apartment neighbors alarmed over a kidnapping, petty practitioners of petty crimes. He also found revealing numbers: 90 bureaucratic pages to demolish a crack house and, in "Society Pays Awful Price for Violence," the cost of a single shooting.*

For "Society," May searched weeks for the right example and then worked for one month culling legal and medical records. He needed both sides of the ledger, and he went headlong after data. "I don't have an aversion to numbers," he says, tackling the risk that numbers often pose for readers. Ready to write, he split an IBM screen nine ways, moving from interview notes, to outline, to main story, always pulling from electronic databases.

After a complex story runs, May expects a malaise that can last for days or weeks. He fights doubts, asking nagging questions like "Why am I in this business?" Then, doubts overcome, he's "proud always to be a writer." Regardless of mood, May also fights routine. "Every time you're following a formula, break out of it," he says. "If you have half a brain, you can learn the inverted pyramid. That's the deadline form, but there are also plenty of other ways to tell a good story. Take the risk."

–AK

Derrick Hanna, 16, would-be car thief, pointed a .357 magnum at a kid in a driver's seat one night. "Get out!" he screamed at Lazaro Gutierrez, 17. Lazaro flinched. Derrick squeezed the trigger–five-eighths of an inch.

Patrick May, Society Pays Awful Price for Violence, *The Miami Herald,* July 25, 1993.
Reprinted with permission of *The Miami Herald.*

The upshot:

For Derrick, 50 years in prison.

For Lazaro, life in a wheelchair.

For the rest of us, $661,534.83.

Forget, for the moment, the wasted lives. Forget the arguments about gun control.

Think about the money.

The bullet that fragmented inside Lazaro's neck the night of Oct. 21, 1988, set off an awesome run of expenses, mostly underwritten by taxpayers with little idea of the medical-legal costs of America's gun culture.

There are costs of rescue: $638 for the seven-minute helicopter flight to Jackson Memorial Hospital.

Costs of respiration: $56,966 for pumping oxygen into the victim for 10 weeks.

Costs of rehabilitation: $82,580.74 for four months of therapy.

There are also the costs of justice.

Near a schoolyard on Southwest 192nd Street, two crime-scene detectives took photographs and lifted fingerprints for four hours: $120.

In a state attorney's office, court stenographers recorded depositions from 46 witnesses: $3,644. 45.

In a 10th-floor juvenile cell at the Dade County Jail, the shooter waited 18 months for trial: $29,090.21.

Then there is the unresolved lawsuit. Lawyers for the victim claim the Dade school board failed to provide adequate security near Southridge High the night Lazaro was shot. The two sides' legal costs thus far: $214,988.

That's by no means all the expenses. Although total current costs already stand over a half-million dollars, there's a lot more where those came from. The shooter isn't going anywhere. His projected release date is April 7, 2027. The projected prison cost: $839,452.

The victim isn't going anywhere, either. Care for a quadriplegic can run up to $100,000 a year. The bullet inside Lazaro Gutierrez is just a small piece of what some public-health experts are calling a national emergency. What happened to Lazaro happens again and again, day after day, year after year.

Each year in America, gunfire kills 35,000 people. In Dade and elsewhere, bullets now claim more lives than motor-vehicle accidents.

Counting the dead is easy. Counting the cost is not.

Only a handful of studies exist on the financial burden of gunshot injuries. The most ambitious, a federally funded survey by University of California San Francisco researchers, offers incomplete audit at best: $20.4 billion in 1990 for all firearm deaths and injuries.

But the figure is shaky. First, no one truly knows how many people survive. One estimate puts the wounded at 245,000 a year. Secondly, the report considers only victims, not law enforcement costs.

"The victim is often only half the equation," says Jim Mercy, chief of the epidemiology branch of the National Center for Injury Prevention and Control in Atlanta. "We are also paying for the apprehension and incarceration" of the shooter.

The key word there is "we."

"The public," says Mercy, "pays in excess of 80 percent of the costs of death and injury by firearm."

Amy Dunathan, an aide to Sen. John Chafee, R-R.I., says that "except for motor-vehicle crashes, no source of injury consumes more public funds" than firearms.

"Hospitals are closing," she says, "because trauma centers can't handle all the indigent getting shot up."

Harry Teter, Jr., executive director of the American Trauma Society, says 91 trauma centers have closed since 1983, often overwhelmed by the cost of urban violence.

How high are the costs? Researchers at the University of California at Davis Medical Center found gunshot victims ran up an average hospital bill of $13,200. And a General Accounting Office study found the lifetime bill, including lost wages, to be $373,520.

Victims often run up a $20,000 bill in their first hour in the emergency room, says Jeanne Eckes of Jackson's Ryder Trauma Center. "Just the cost of blood alone"–$140 per pint, or unit–"is incredibly high. The real bleeders can take 40 units."

At the Washington, D.C., Hospital Center, acute care sometimes hits $300,000 for a single weekend.

That's no surprise, says Dr. Mark Brown, chairman of orthopedics and rehabilitation at Jackson. Consider what bullets do:

"They usually shatter the bone," he says. "Particularly devastating is when the bullet penetrates the bowel, then hits a bone in the spine or hip, causing infection."

Says Eckes, "We also see more multiple shootings, probably because of the semi-automatic weapons. They tend to make a few more holes. The most expensive shooting is probably the multiple chest-and-belly combo."

At Cook County Hospital in Chicago, only 5 percent of persons admitted for gunshot wounds in 1984 had been shot more than once. By 1988, it was 20 percent.

But it is the bullets that hit the spine that carry the biggest price tag, says Barth Green, director of neurosurgery at Jackson and president of the Miami Project to Cure Paralysis.

"We average about four quadriplegics and paraplegics a month from gunshot wounds, and the average economic impact to society is over $1 million a case," says Green. "These patients require intensive care, about 10 times as much as routine hospital treatment. One bed sore, for example, can cost $75,000 to cure."

Lazaro Gutierrez, the kid behind the wheel of an '81 Chevy, needed intensive care for 39 days.

In the moments before a bullet wrecked his life, he picked up his cheerleader girlfriend after a football game. As he pulled out of the parking lot, someone yelled, "Yo!" Thinking the boy wanted a ride, Lazaro stopped. That's when Derrick Hanna appeared at the window, pointing a gun and demanding he get out.

"Gutierrez attempted to drive away," says the police report, "and the subject fired one shot, striking him in the neck."

Within 40 minutes, the victim began to run up a 182-page hospital bill, which now fills four accordion files and stands two feet high. Total: $307,452.30.

It took Metro-Dade detective Paul Law one month to catch up with the shooter, known on the street as both "Dog" and "Crazy." That was enough time for him to hold up a pizza delivery man who refused to give up his car. Derrick shot him in the face, too.

In the end, Derrick saved the state of Florida a few bucks. He pleaded no contest, avoiding the costs of a trial, and went off to prison. There he sits, another kid with a million-dollar trigger finger.

Lazaro Gutierrez sits, too—in a $3,400 electric wheelchair.

"That chair," he says, "costs more than the car I was shot for."

VICTIM'S COSTS

From the moment someone picked up a phone and dialed 911—11:16 P.M., Oct. 21, 1988 to be exact—the costs of keeping shooting victim Lazaro Gutierrez alive have continued to rise. Here are just some of the expenses that went into the total below:

A life is saved . . .

The call for help brings Engine 34 ($111 for 54 minutes) and Rescue 5 ($73). Seven rescuers use bandages, IV fluids, and other equipment ($1,000) to stabilize Lazaro. Air Rescue 3 flies him to Jackson in 7 minutes ($638). Total: $1,822.

. . . and the bill begins

Lazaro's 9-month stay at Jackson starts at midnight with a trauma center visit ($300). His 182-page bill opens with a 2-inch IV adaptor ($2), and includes oxygen and ventilator ($56,966), dressings and supplies like a rotating bed ($38,454) and lots of medicine ($12,463.54).

As state-of-the-art machines measure his every physiological move, Lazaro spends 39 days in a $900-a-day bed ($35,100) in ICU, watched over by his own nurse. As a "total quad," everything must now be done for him.

Total ER, ICU, and recovery: $224,871.56.

The expenses never cease . . .

There are months of IV solution ($7,150), CAT scans ($705) and X-ray diagnoses ($5,225). Anesthesia is used in the operating room ($2,578). Along the way, Lazaro ingests Maalox ($3.50 for a 6-oz. bottle), has his urine output monitored in measuring cups ($9 for 3 cups) and his wounds dabbed with sponges ($3 a box).

Lazaro and his family get counseling, too. On Oct. 24, for instance, a counselor spends 45 minutes ($69) with Lazaro and writes: "Pt is beginning to express anger regarding shooting. Pt's mother is experiencing an intense grief reaction. Will follow family on daily basis until crisis subsides."

. . . even on Christmas

Dec. 25, 1988—a typical day of treatment. It includes things like room and board ($415), blood tests ($54) and "chest physio-therapy" to help Lazaro's breathing ($270 for 6 sessions), where a therapist taps on his back for 15 minutes. There's the daily charge for his roto-bed ($145), along with an anti-coagulant medicine ($3.50) and a Tylenol ($3.50). Total Christmas costs: $1,192.08.

Rehab comes in tiny steps . . .

February 1989, the treatment focus shifts. For four months he receives occupational therapy ($11,997), including field trips to Bayside to practice wheelchair skills. And physical therapy ($13,353), such as exercises for strengthening the neck. Eventually, Lazaro is able to bring his hand to his mouth. On June 2, after 107 days in a $400-a-day room ($42,800), Lazaro leaves Jackson. Total rehab: $82,580.74.

. . . help comes from many directions

Lisa Hardeman, a victim's advocate for the state attorney's office, spends 16 hours helping Lazaro get $10,000 from the state's crime victim's compensation fund. "I did a lot of research for Lazaro, talking to people in wheelchairs, how to get a good one, what to pay. I also spent time talking with him and his parents." Total: $192.16.

Lazaro finally comes home . . .

He moves about in a Quickie 3Rx wheelchair ($3,400). His waterbed cost $400 and his shower wheelchair goes for $900 new. Another electric wheelchair costs $4,000.

With the help of his dad's labor, the family home is transformed with wheelchair ramps and a shower and sink he can use sitting down ($10,000). His van ($3,700) is outfitted, too, to accommodate the wheelchair ($1,750). His carport is paved in concrete to give him more space to more around ($1,000). Total: $25,150.

. . . and waits and waits

The costs of the shooting don't stop with the criminal case. In July 1989, attorneys for Lazaro file suit against the Dade school board, claiming security at Southridge the night of the incident was lacking.

Jackson places a lien on any settlement for unpaid bills charged to Lazaro, whose insurance company goes bankrupt shortly after the shooting.

Lazaro studies for his GED, while the lawsuit winds slowly toward trial, probably sometime in 1994. Both sides have already run up sizable bills for legal fees and costs, including investigators, filing fees, phone calls, and expert witnesses. Total: $214,988.

TOTAL TO DATE: $549,604.46.

And there's no end in sight.

"Odds are, there's no way he's going to go back to work," says UM economist William Landsea. "It just doesn't happen." Since his parents won't live forever, Lazaro must eventually hire either in-home help ($100,000 a year for two assistants) or move into an institution ($40,000 a year).

On lost wages: "If he worked steady year-round—and that's a big if—he could be a $30,000-a-year worker," says Landsea. "You're talking about 40 years of work." Total, without inflation: $1.2 million.

SHOOTER'S COSTS

The search for Lazaro's shooter was underway before the victim had even reached the hospital. Taxpayers picked up the bills, as well as the costs of the ensuing search for justice.

At the scene of the crime . . .

Two scene technicians spend four hours each gathering fingerprints and taking photos ($120) and another 4 hours processing what they find ($60).

Officer writes the report ($72), while a sergeant ($80), four officers ($288), and a corporal ($76) help with crowd control and a neighborhood canvas. Total: $696.

. . . the hunt is launched

Det. Paul Law is called from home and puts in 8 hours of OT ($228) talking to witnesses. He tries to call Lazaro at Jackson, but the victim is in surgery. For the next four days, Law works the case full-time, often on OT ($228) as he canvases the area and talks to the press ($152), and works with other detectives to compile a suspect list ($152).

There are plenty of leads . . .

Law interviews a guy who says he can find the shooter ($114), but then gets sidetracked by another kid who says "he knows who shot the Cuban boy," only to give a bad name ($114). In the following weeks, he visits Lazaro ($57), learns the shooter's nickname ($152) and re-interviews witnesses ($456).

. . . that finally pay off

Late November, Law catches up with Derrick, who blames the shooting on another kid ($380). He interviews Derrick's accomplice ($152), has Lazaro ID his shooter's photo ($152), then meets with prosecutors to prepare an arrest affidavit ($228). Total detective work: $4,104.

Other costs add up . . .

The bill comes in from the doctor who repaired the ankle Derrick broke while jumping a fence fleeing the crime scene ($327.50) and Derrick's court-appointed lawyer starts ringing up $40-an-hour charges, including setting up depos ($40), reading cop reports ($120) and waiting for depo subjects who never show ($220). Total: $8,224.

. . . while the case heads for trial

Prosecutors fly in Lazaro's girlfriend from New Port Richey for a depo ($438), one of their 13 depos ($713). "They're the meat of the case," says prosecutor Flora Seff. "This is our chance to speak to everyone expected to testify and to see the trial laid out months before it actually begins." Seff also spends six hours listening to police tapes ($186) and visits Lazaro at home three times ($186).

She consults with a Jackson doctor ($15.50) and a school official ($23.25), cajoles young witnesses to testify ($62).

As plea negotiations heat up . . .

Seff meets again and again with Derrick's lawyer as his client tries to decide what to do ($124), even as she prepares for trial with Det. Law ($124), rereads all depos ($93), confers with her supervisor about a plea bargain ($31), and roughs out opening statement and closing arguments ($93). Total prosecution cost: $3,408.

. . . other costs stack up

There are 24 court hearings with prosecutor ($31/hr), judge ($43.46/hr), bailiff ($10.19/hr), court clerk ($11.40/hr), calendar clerk ($9.24/hr) and corrections officer ($10.97/hr).

Stenographers do subpoenas ($216), court sessions ($113.75), and depos ($3,644.45)–even when witnesses don't show ($211.60). Subpoenas are served all over town ($560).

Derrick sits 563 days in jail ($29,090.21), 33 days at the South Florida Reception Center ($1,980) and, as of last week, 1,099 days at Charlotte Correctional Institution ($43,960).

Mary Lou Hanna drives to see her son once a month ($1,560), mails him $20 a month for snacks ($780), gives him $400 a year for shoes and toothbrushes ($1,300), accepts his collect calls ($7,800) and pays his subscription to *Ebony Man* ($64). Total: $95,498.37.

TOTAL TO DATE: $111,930.37.

And the bill keeps climbing . . .

With gain time, Derrick is scheduled to get out of prison April 7, 2027. He will have spent 12,315 more days behind bars. Prison officials say it now costs them $39.69 a day to house and feed an inmate, and they predict a 3 percent annual increase in those costs due to inflation.

Projected total from now until Derrick gets out: $839,452.

---

* SOURCES: Metro-Dade police, civil process bureau and fire-rescue; Dade County Jail; South Florida Reception Center; Florida Department of Corrections; Jackson Memorial Hospital and Ryder Trauma Center; University of Miami; victim's family members and attorneys; Dade's court administrator, clerk of the court, state attorney's office; Deering Hospital; Dade school board.

Madeleine Blais

The Arithmetic of Need

Madeleine Blais–award-winning journalist with a 1980 Pulitzer Prize for feature writing–would like others to think of her as Author, uppercase A. But she carries her hyphenate nervously, hustling as freelance, lowercase f.

In "The Arithmetic of Need," Blais profiles an ingenious New Englander whom she describes as "walking the edge, curiously undefeated." As a shortcut to intimacy, she opens in the first-person–"a way," Blais explains, "to code the reader that I, the writer, know this person." When editors at the Washington Post Magazine *opted for anonymity, fearful that readers would reject a subject outside its circulation, the writer had to be convincing.*

Detail by detail, Blais takes an approach that she calls "quiet and incremental," moving from particular to general, from individual to universal, teetering on that "fine line between enthralling readers or boring them." A favorite quote from poet William Carlos Williams–"No ideas but in things"–offers some reassurance. But she still frets: "Who's interested in this person besides me?"

Blais's obsession with details surfaced at 8, when she remembered newspaper headlines and at 17, when she decided to be a poet. But after majoring in English at the College of New Rochelle, the 1969 graduate turned practical. She headed to Columbia University for a master's in journalism. Then, when The New York Times *did not call, she took a job at the* Norwich Bulletin, *which did.*

Specializing in features, Blais wrote many profiles, identified or not, during two decades at The Trenton Times, The Boston Globe, *and* The Miami Herald. *In a 1992 collection,* The Heart is An Instrument: Portraits in Journalism, *she probes the "terrible trust it requires on both sides to go through someone else's truth to get to your own." Her next book, profiling a whole basketball team and winning season for high school girls, earned her a positive "f" beyond freelance–finalist for the 1995 National Book Critics' Circle Award.*

Blais now teaches essay and journal writing at the University of Massachusetts at Amherst. For that, she reads voraciously, noting "I read for a living as much as I write for a living." Russell Baker, Tobias Wolff, and Frank Conroy are required. Blais also offers students drafts of her work, many comments on theirs, and advice that she, at 44, still cherishes: "Work twice as hard as everyone twice your age."

–AK

Madeline Blais, The Arithmetic of Need, *Washington Post Magazine,* June 7, 1992. Reprinted courtesy of the author.

henever I hear talk about all the things that threaten the middle-class way of life, I think of a woman I know who supports herself, a house and a 5-year-old child on take-home pay of $319 a week. The way she figures it, one paycheck each month goes to the mortgage, which is low because it is subsidized by the Farmers Home Administration, two go for day care and the fourth is for food, gasoline, clothes, the phone and other incidentals of just plain living. Life would be extremely tough if there were only 48 weeks in a year, but since there are 52 she has four extra paychecks annually to provide a kind of cushion, not to mention April's harvest in the form of some extremely welcome tax refunds. This year brought $907 from the federal government and $148 from the state. Still and all, there is virtually no decision in her life that is not in some fundamental way driven by the arithmetic of her fate; she is engaged in the constant calculation of dollars and cents balanced against need and desire. She thinks of the practice of thrift as a necessity and also as artistry, a creative force, the ability to get something out of almost nothing.

She limits herself to $50 a week for gas and food. The car she drives is a blue '81 Toyota Tercel SR-5 Deluxe, which she bought used in 1987 for $3,700. She calls it "a poor man's sports car" because it came equipped with air conditioning, a sunroof and a tape deck. These days it has the sagging creakiness of an elderly vehicle and she thinks of it as a town car, useful only for short, predictable distances. Gas usually runs her about $12 a week, for one tank. The $38 that is left over is spent at the grocery store on food and such items as cleaning supplies, toilet paper, stockings. This is the area where economies are most often made and where she feels she can exercise the most ingenuity.

She buys some items in bulk, especially the two 100-pound sacks of unbleached flour she goes through every year and the 25-pound bag of rice that lasts almost a year. She keeps these items under a tight lid in half-size trash cans, and because she has a bug-free kitchen she has never lost a portion to maggots. Cheddar and mozzarella cheeses are also purchased in bulk and frozen in one-pound portions in plastic bags, often shredded. Juice concentrate is purchased frozen in 12-ounce containers, which she thinks are the most economical. Pineapple juice makes a nice poultry marinade. The brand of apple juice she buys is pricey at $1.20 a can but it is vitamin-C enriched and so seems a better choice than some other brands. She likes milk with 2 percent fat; her daughter often adds chocolate syrup made by her mother from a recipe that includes 3 cups sugar, 1½ cups cocoa powder and 2 cups water.

She's a bit of a wizard in the kitchen, and one of her major talents is to make sauces of every sort, from fudge to salsa. She is proudest of her high-protein bread, which she prepares on Sunday and which lasts the entire week. Using the unbleached flour, oat flakes, wheat flakes, powdered milk, soy flour, wheat germ, bran, and leftover rice or couscous, honey (sugar when she's lazy), yeast, one egg per loaf, two tablespoons of butter per loaf, and water, she devotes about five hours to its creation, shepherding the ingredients through their initial mixing, two risings, and of course the hour and a half in the oven when, kissed by heat, it takes on life and shape. It is, in the end, a rich and textured treat, full of heft and character, nothing like the Wonder Bread of her childhood that she used to squish into a gooey ball in seconds flat and pretend was blubber. Once a month, she buys five dozen eggs at 50 cents a dozen wholesale from a farm. Scrambled eggs are frequent dinner fare, sprinkled with nutritional yeast. She waits to buy chicken leg quarters until they go on sale for less than 50 cents a pound; she boils the meat, saving the broth, and sometimes curries it but more often uses it for enchiladas, adding her homemade hot sauce concocted from tomato sauce, chili powder, onions, garlic and jalapeños. She buys fresh vegetables and fruit according to season, and she usually has a bag of frozen peas in the freezer and some canned corn on the shelf. When turkey dogs are priced below a dollar a pound, she buys a package for her daughter. About once a month she will buy a pound or so of porterhouse steak on sale at $2.99 a pound for a special dinner. She never buys junk food of any kind; the only sodas or potato chips to enter her house come free with promotional coupons. She likes coffee and buys the cheapest gourmet kind she can, often pampering herself with a little half-and-half. She doesn't buy wine and she doesn't buy beer, though she usually keeps a gallon of the cheapest vodka ("nine dollars; I think it's called Tolstoy") she can find, and on Friday nights she usually permits herself one drink of vodka accompanied by a cayenne pepper from a stock of frozen cayenne peppers that she grew a few years ago. She eschews most gardening as not cost-effective for her purposes.

All her clothes are secondhand except for socks, underwear and shoes, and these would be too if the used-clothing stores she shops at stocked those items. Once in a while she gets a windfall; when her grandmother was alive, she almost always sent a large check at Christmas, often as much as a thousand dollars. Whenever she gets ahead, she tries to make a long-term investment. Once, six years ago, on her birthday, her grandmother gave her $100, which she spent on six bras that she wears to this day; their life has been prolonged by careful hand-washing and air drying. When she was pregnant, she invested in three pairs of shoes on sale at $30 a pair, pumps with leather uppers, identical except for the colors, which were taupe, black and oxblood. These remain her only dressy shoes. For everyday use she has some boots she bought wholesale at a factory outlet and some sturdy Birkenstock sandals that never wear out. Her favorite secondhand store is run by a woman with exacting standards, who refuses to accept for consignment any garment with so much as a pinprick hole in the fabric or any garment purchased more than three years ago. The pickings tend to be terrific because there is a college nearby and the women students are constantly unloading last year's outfits. Her daughter also wears only secondhand clothes, which, according to the mother, "is probably just as well. I am a lot more philosophical when Eliza gets Magic Marker on a three-dollar dress than I would be on one that cost thirty dollars." She works in an office where her wardrobe of casual, well-cared-for cottons is both practical and appropriate.

The most expensive, calculatedly extravagant thing she ever did in her life was to have her baby. Not the birth itself. Insurance covered that: "I always say Eliza cost the gas to the hospital and a few dollars for prenatal vitamins." But the idea of supporting a child seemed so daunting. Here she was, educated, with a master's degree in linguistics, and the best job she could find was as a stenographer. Most of her skills and passions are not wildly marketable. She quilts, she knits sweaters and mittens, she can do counted cross-stitching. She likes to contra-dance and she knows how to make croissants from scratch. Once she made a fetching flannel knapsack, and she can cut down trees, using either a chain saw or a bow saw. She can deck an attic, rewire lamps and install rheostats. After college, she taught for a while; she has tutored, and at the time she first thought of getting pregnant, she was the cook on a construction crew. She was 35 years old, and the urge to reproduce came on her with the force and clarity of a vision. She remembers asking herself what she wanted to accomplish in the next 10 years, and she knew she wanted to get a regular job and buy a house. She imagined that in that prosperous-burgher scenario her only regret would be if she did not have a child. Single, with no prospects of marriage or even an ongoing partnership ("I never turned down any proposals; I never had any"), she had plenty of male friends, and one in particular suggested himself to her as a suitable candidate to father her child, someone who she thought would accept her condition that she did not want or expect any emotional or financial support. They arranged for a weekend assignation and two weeks later the pregnancy test was positive.

Over the years she has formulated adages to express certain financial realities. One is, "You get poor, you get gutsy." When an acquaintance went through a dramatic weight change recently, she had no compunction about asking her for any clothes she was thinking about discarding. Another is, "It's better to have really nice things secondhand than cheap things firsthand."

Another is, "When you're in bad shape going into the fall, you're in really bad shape because that is traditionally the most expensive time of the year." Precisely because the fall can be so tough, she tries to do all her Christmas shopping in the summer, starting right after Memorial Day. ("Anytime before that," she says, "would be rushing things.") Every year she gets a set of formal photos of her daughter from a place like Sears (usually with a discount coupon). She keeps the 8-by-10 for herself, but the smaller images are distributed to family as their principal gift. For friends she usually makes a jar of her famous cranberry chutney. For her daughter, she gets a combination of new things—a home video or two and a doll, like a Barbie—and homemade items. Two years ago she found a child's vanity table at a tag sale for $15. It was dented and discolored, so she sanded it in secret at night in the cellar, refinished it, and created a ruffled skirt out of some white chiffon she'd gotten on sale. Every Christmas since, at least one item under the tree has been an addition to this ensemble, such as a pillow of matching fabric for her daughter's bed. Christmas is also for gifts of socks and underwear; this past year's had a Little Mermaid theme.

She rarely buys furniture. The sofa with the pullout bed in the living room was acquired during an interval of flushness in 1978. It is gray and brown and beige; "cat furniture," she calls it, because it has been taken over and brought to a state of frayed and friendly ruination by her two cats, Polly and Bari. Her bed came from her childhood room; her daughter sleeps on a mattress and box spring covered with a comforter she made in college out of two sheets with a Cotswold floral design sewn together and stuffed with polyester batting. She bought her knives and forks when she was living at home and had her first job in 1973. Her plates used to belong to her mother; they are Syracuse china. The dining room table is a wobbly metal affair with a Formica top borrowed from a friend, which she wishes could be replaced by the handsome mahogany trestle table her father uses as a kind of bin for his paints and tools. Her parents help out a little. Last year they offered to replace her Cuisinart as a Christmas gift, a lucky break because this is an appliance she uses almost daily. Her brother and his wife are fairly well off and they are hooked on the latest gadgets; as a result she has inherited two televisions, one 13-inch and one 18-inch, two VCRs and an answering machine. ("They go through technology the way those college girls go through clothes.")

Every year she composes a wish list of miscellaneous items that she would like to get. The money for these comes from what she calls the "floating aspect" of her finances. By this she means the four "extra" paychecks a year, as well as the small amount of extra cash she has on hand during the weeks when her check goes to day care, an expense of $225 twice a month. (She gets a slight break from the day-care center, saving $75 a month in exchange for word processing for bulletins and for running the annual Mother's Day bake sale at which her blueberry buckle is a cash cow.) Her monthly mortgage bill of $288 is so low because she is part of a federal program in which her day-care expenses qualify her for a discounted payment. When her daughter starts at public school, the mortgage payments will rise accordingly. She helped build the house she lives in. It is on a wooded acre and the land is the jewel. The dwelling itself is only a modest 960 square feet and 1½ stories tall, with the two bedrooms on the second floor using the roof as the ceiling and an open floor plan downstairs that includes a walk-in "two fanny" kitchen ("and the two fannies better like each other").

Her phone bill is about $30 a month; electricity about $40. Heat comes from a wood stove. She usually goes through three cords a winter at $100 a cord. She gets her hair cut professionally twice a year; her daughter gets hers done at the same time at a bargain rate for kids, a dollar for each year they are old. She does very little dry cleaning, usually one or two items a year, her winter parka and her white wool serape. She's been seeing a man lately, and he's the source of any video rentals, beer, wine and ice cream in her life. Her daughter earns pocket money by collecting recyclables from friends and neighbors, organizing them and accompanying her mother to the store where they are returned. The money is all hers; recently she was able to get a brand-new Belle doll from *Beauty and the Beast* and a brand-new Eric doll from *The Little Mermaid.*

The mother has fun composing her yearly wish list. One time it included a "nice tent, down sleeping bag, ultrasonic humidifier and cross-country skis." This year, she thought about including a rotor for her TV antenna but because she has her boyfriend, this item has less urgency than it once did. She has a friend who did some handyman work for her two years ago to whom she still owes $87; the debt embarrasses her, and she hopes to erase it this year.

About a year ago, when reviewing her job description at work, she realized that given the scope of her duties she could argue that she really was not a Grade 10 Steno Two but a Grade 11 Clerk Three. She filed a host of forms requesting a job review in late June of last year and in January she was rewarded with a promotion, resulting in a pay raise of $15 take-home a week and a back check for $415. This is the ceiling for how high she can go in this job. She used the back check to pay for car insurance and a secondhand gray lightweight business jacket that cost $18 and a used earring-and-necklace set of coral and other tropical hues, flattering to her orange-toned freckled skin. She thinks of herself as living on the edge, and although she hardly expects it to disappear, she enjoyed a few heady moments thinking that at least it had become a little wider. But then her health-care provider announced that visits to the doctor would no longer be free but instead would require a $10 co-payment and she got strep and her daughter had an ear infection, and suddenly the edge, which she dreams of turning into a prairie, once again felt like a precipice, high and narrow with a sheer drop on both sides.

Gary Smith

Crime and Punishment

Gary Smith, one of the most respected sports writers in the country, knows that the game isn't over even when the whistle blows. "Sports, having somehow become the medium through which Americans derive their strongest sense of community, has become the stage where all the great moral issues have to be played out," he asserts. What a cast he covers! Athletes and coaches, parents and teachers, presidents and trustees, con artists and tycoons, heroes and anti-heroes, backers and fans, cynics and idealists.

Whatever the topic—a coach fighting cancer, Muhammed Ali's entourage, a Crow Indian basketball player, or Magic Johnson's comeback—Smith shows us the big picture, directs us to the human issues. Writing from a complex vision of sports and often with a deep sympathy for his subjects, Smith gets us to read long and think longer.

The Richie Parker story followed from a friend's tip. The more Smith looked at the facts, the more Parker seemed to be a force field. Then the cesium analogy— checked out with experts—made the stories fall into place. Of course, structuring stories in ways unusual and amazing and effective—that's standard procedure for Smith. He says luck was with him, however, when Jill Agostino stepped forward; that gave the story balance. Letting readers see the complexities of all the characters, Smith walked a fine line, refusing to come down on any side. Maybe that's why his readers didn't respond with the usual "nice story" comments. Instead, they kept talking in round-table discussions, taking the story apart, analyzing and arguing moral positions, wanting to stay involved.

Smith remembers school as a blur because he went to work so young. Born in 1953, he started with the Wilmington News Journal *at 16 and by 19 was full time at the* Philadelphia Daily News *while majoring in English at La Salle University. Next he wrote for* The New York Daily News *and* Inside Sports, *then for* Sports Illustrated *starting in 1982, becoming senior writer in 1990. That's a lot of years doing what he calls, "exercising the muscle."*

Now Smith lives in Charleston, South Carolina, reads philosophical writers like Nietzsche and Camus and Milan Kundera, and goes on the road to write long features. Always searching for new players to talk to, always alert to their mixed motivations, Gary Smith helps us understand that great morality play we call sports.

—CM

Gary Smith, Crime and Punishment, *Sports Illustrated,* June 24, 1996. Reprinted courtesy of the author.

ONE

Here is a man. Barely a man; he just ran out of adolescence. He stands alone, 2,000 miles from home, beside a swimming pool, in a stucco-walled apartment complex, in a city built on an American desert.

SETON HALL CHANCELLOR THOMAS R. PETERSON buckled under to intense pressure from media and alumni yesterday when he denied admission to star basketball recruit and admitted sex felon Richie Parker.

—NEW YORK POST, *Jan. 24, 1995*

It's too hot to run. But he must run. He strips to his trunks. He steps into the pool. His body leans forward.

THE UNIVERSITY OF UTAH CEASED ITS RECRUITING of former Manhattan Center basketball star Richie Parker in light of a barrage of media criticism and pressure from the university president regarding Parker's sexual abuse conviction.

—NEW YORK NEWSDAY, *May 6, 1995*

His hands ball up. His left elbow draws back, pushing against the water. Slowly his foot begins to rise from the floor of the pool.

GEORGE WASHINGTON UNIVERSITY OFFICIALS informed high school basketball star Richie Parker yesterday they "regrettably" would stop recruiting him and blamed "unbalanced publicity" for a wave of criticism that hit the school for pursuing the youth, who had pleaded guilty to a sexual assault.

—THE WASHINGTON POST, *June 30, 1995*

His foot gradually descends to the bottom of the pool. His other foot begins to push off. His shoulders tighten. The water pushes back.

RICHIE PARKER WILL NEVER WEAR a UTEP basketball uniform. UTEP has bowed out of its recruitment of the controversial basketball player, athletic director John Thompson announced Friday.

—EL PASO HERALD-POST, *Feb. 24, 1996*

His knee slowly lifts again. His arms silently pump.

USC ON WEDNESDAY TERMINATED its recruitment of former New York City All-America point guard Richie Parker, a convicted sex offender. The decision came after . . . two days of sometimes heated exchanges among athletic department personnel.

—ORANGE COUNTY REGISTER, *March 28, 1996*

He climbs out finally and pants for air, in the desert that once was the bottom of an ocean.

TWO

Here is a periodic table. It's the one you would see near the blackboard in any high school chemistry class, a listing of the 109 elements according to atomic number. Why is it being inflicted on you here, in a sports magazine? *Patience.* Remember, this is a story about higher education.

Near the lower lefthand corner of the chart is an element named cesium. Among its own—the metals surrounding it in the chart, such as sodium and potassium—cesium is a quiet, unassuming element. But because it has just one electron on its outer shell, one electron aching to leap to any atom that is lacking a full outer shell of electrons, cesium is a bomb in a suitcase when it leaves its neighborhood. On contact with oxygen, cesium will cause an explosion. Introduce it to chlorine, fluorine, iodine or bromine and look out! Almost everywhere it goes, trying to rid itself of the baggage of that one electron, another eruption occurs, and only those who understand what cannot be seen can make any sense of it at all.

THREE

Here is an assistant principal. She works at Manhattan Center, the East Harlem high school Richie Parker once attended. Teenagers deposit their leather jackets in Ellen Scheinbach's closet in the morning for safekeeping, come to her at lunchtime for oatmeal cookies and advice. The phone's constantly ringing, teachers are always poking in their heads. "A lunatic asylum!" she calls her office, ambling about with her spectacles dangling from a neck chain. But now there's silence, and it's Richie's mother, Rosita, shuffling on her bad knees, clutching her envelope of articles clipped from the *New York Post* and the *Daily News,* extending them toward the assistant principal and asking her to explain.

Ellen Scheinbach is an authority figure, one of the few Rosita knows. Surely she can explain how *all this* could result from that one day in this building, in January 1994, when Rosita's 6'5" son, a junior then—a well-liked boy known for his silence, his gentle nature and his skill on a basketball court—was walking through these halls, having gone to the nurse's office with a sprained ankle and having found the nurse not there, was returning to class when he paused . . . and turned. And headed toward the bottom of a stairwell in the back of the school, where he and a schoolmate, Leslie Francis, soon compelled a 16-year-old freshman girl to perform oral sex on them. And how 15 minutes later, the girl came running up the stairwell, sobbing, and soon thereafter Richie and the other boy were being led away in handcuffs. And how from that moment on, virtually everywhere Richie would turn to rid himself of the baggage of those 15 minutes, another explosion would occur. How careers would be smashed, men fired, dreams destroyed. How some relationships would splinter and others almost spontaneously be fused. How secrets would burst from hidden places, and rage and fear would tremble in the air behind her lean, quiet son. The assistant principal can explain all this to Rosita, can't she?

Ellen throws up her arms. The incongruity of it all still confounds her. Richie Parker? Richie didn't drink. Richie didn't curse. Richie didn't get into arguments or fights; he had never even gotten detention. She knew lots of kids who would play peek-a-boo with a toddler in the bleachers for a few minutes, but Richie was the only one she knew who would do it for an hour. The only time she had ever seen him exert his will—to *force* any issue—was on a basketball court, and even there he did it so softly, so smoothly, that she would be startled to learn at the end of a game that he had scored 35 points. He would be rated one of America's top 50 high school seniors in 1995, a notch or two below Georgia Tech signee Stephon Marbury in New York's schoolboy hierarchy.

Two investigations—one conducted by a George Washington University lawyer and another by the lawyer of the stairwell victim, not to mention the searchlight sweep of Richie's life by the media—failed to turn up a single thread that would indicate that those 15 minutes in the stairwell were part of a larger pattern. Richie himself had insisted on his innocence at first, but eventually he pleaded guilty when the charges were lowered from first-degree sodomy to first-degree sexual abuse in January 1995. His sentence was five years of probation. So now Rosita's standing on the other side of Ellen's desk, holding a half-dozen full-back-page pictures of her son under screaming SEX FELON headlines, asking her what the world has come to that one rotten act by a 17-year-old could take on such monstrous proportions and why Seton Hall has just reneged on its promise of a scholarship for Richie as long as he didn't get a prison sentence . . . and it's only the beginning, because now the great American morality play is ready to hit the road, with actors and actresses all across the land raring to perform their roles, eager to savage or salvage the teenager from 110th Street in Manhattan—often knowing nothing more of him than his name. Ellen keeps shaking her head and blinking. Sports, having somehow become the medium through which Americans derive their strongest sense of community, has become the stage where all the great moral issues have to be played out, often rough and ugly, right alongside the games.

Ellen had tried to protect Richie from that. She had tried to smuggle him out when the media surrounded her school. She sat beside him at games when he could no longer play, to shield him from the media's popping cameras and questions. She went to Seton Hall and told administrators that she would trust Richie with her daughter, if she had one. But it was hopeless. In the same way that cesium needs to rid itself of that one dangling electron on its outer shell, Richie needed to take his sin to a university, to one of America's last "pure" places, and have it absolved so he could find his way to the promised land, the NBA. In the same way that fluorine longs for that extra electron to complete itself, the universities and their coaches were drawn to the basketball player who could enhance their profile, increase their alumni contributions and TV revenues. And the mutual attraction would keep causing explosions, hurling Richie and yet another university far apart, and Rosita would keep returning to Ellen, her eyes filling with tears. Hasn't her son, she would ask, done everything demanded of him?

Yes, Rosita, yes, he fulfilled the requirements of the criminal justice system and of the out-of-court settlement of the victim's civil lawsuit. He had met monthly with his probation officer, met regularly with a counselor, made both a private and a public apology to the victim, an acknowledgment that regardless of the details of the incident, he had done something profoundly wrong in that stairwell. He had promised to speak out against sexual abuse and to make financial restitution to the victim with a percentage of any money he might generate one day in the NBA. He had earned A's and B's at Manhattan Outreach Center, the school he was sent to in the wake of the court ruling, met NCAA qualifications on his fourth try with an SAT score of 830 and enrolled at Mesa (Ariz.) Community College, which refused to let him play ball but allowed him to be a student. And, yes, both the victim and her lawyer had requested that the country's media and universities let him move on. "He's rare among people who've committed a sexual offence," says Michael Feldman of Jacoby & Meyers, the victim's attorney. "He admitted that he did something wrong and committed to help the victim. How does it assist women to refuse him an opportunity now?"

"We believe Richie is truly sorry," the girl's father had told the *Daily News*. "We're religious people who believe in redemption. We don't believe in third chances. We do believe in second chances."

So how can Ellen explain to the 49-year-old woman with the envelope full of news clippings that the second chance, the fresh start, the comeback, the stuff of magazine covers and made-for-television movies, the mother's milk that immigrant America was nursed on and cannot—to its everlasting credit and eternal confusion—seem to wean itself from, has been denied to her son?

"What can I do?" Ellen cries. "I can't get the reporter from the *New York Post* fired. I can't speak to women's groups who are saying he shouldn't have the right to go to college and play basketball. What *is* a women's group, anyway? I know plenty of women, but what's a women's group? I can't call [Georgetown coach] John Thompson and tell him to give Richie a chance—you think he's going to listen to some little old Jewish lady? So I'm just left with this horrible frustration. It's like trying to comfort the survivor of a plane wreck when Rosita comes here. There's nothing I can do.

"He was 17 when this happened. For 15 minutes of rotten judgment, he's been crucified! These women's groups are talking about O.J. Simpson and Mike Tyson, and they're using Richie's name. When teachers here heard what he was accused of, they said, 'Are you kidding?' This is a kid who always tried to fade into the background, who wouldn't push back if you pushed him. Even when he wanted something, he'd just stand there and wait till you *asked* what he wanted. Look, I don't know what happened in that stairwell, but if he did it, he must've had a brain lesion. This kid is not a threat.

"If he were white, would this story have been written this way? But no, he fit the perfect stereotype. He has no money, and he's a black male teenager, so they could have a field day. What do people want—for him to fail, so he's out on a street corner? Are they saying you can never redeem yourself? If he wanted to be a doctor instead of a basketball payer, would they say, 'You can't take biochemistry class'? Basketball is his talent, and while he's on probation he's entitled to play that the same way he'd be entitled to be a musician or an artist. Everyone thinks the NCAA is so macho. I've never seen so many wimpy men in my life."

Once, just once in the 2½ years of watching everything around Richie go to pieces, has Ellen feared that he might go to pieces too. She had never seen him cry, never heard him blame anyone else, never sensed a chip on his shoulder. But when it was clear that the board of education was about to suspend him from Manhattan Center in the middle of his senior season and that the media swirl was sucking down his teammates too, he came to her office with his mother and read his letter of resignation from the team. When he finished, he finally broke down and clutched his mother. "If not for you," he sobbed to her, "I don't think I could make it."

In the end, Ellen decides, perhaps there isn't much she can do to help Rosita, but there's something Rosita has done to help her. "I've learned a lot from her," says Ellen. "I've learned that no matter how frustrated and upset you get, you just keep turning to your kid and saying, 'I love you, and no matter what happens, there's one place for you that's safe.' When my son has a problem now I just try to hug him and say, 'Whatever decision you make I'll stand by you.' Because *it works*. I've seen it work. It saved Richie Parker."

FOUR

Here is a copy editor on the sports desk of a major city newspaper. She's smart, and she's funny, and if an office pushup contest or footrace suddenly breaks out, hopefully after deadline, she's the one you want to put your money on. Of course, because she's a woman, the sensitive stories go to Jill Agostino for editing. Anguish? That's a Jill piece. Morality issue? Absolutely Agostino. Not that it's ever actually stated in a sports department that men are bereft in those areas. It's just sort of understood.

So she gets the Richie Parker stories to polish for *Newsday*. And as she's scanning the words on her computer screen in early 1995, she begins to feel something tightening inside her. It's the old uneasiness, the one she dreads, the one she has no time for here, now, as the clock hands dig toward deadline; the one she might try to run into the ground tomorrow when she's doing her five miles, or scrub away in the quiet of her Long Island apartment, or stow away and convert to fuel someday, something to help flog herself through an extra hour of work when she has to prove her worth to some sexist idiot who dismisses her as a token woman in a man's world, a newspaper sports desk. But not now. Not here. No way.

She begins to sense it here and there between the lines—the implication that Parker is being treated unfairly—and her uneasiness starts to turn to quiet anger. She doesn't sleep much that night, doesn't feel like eating the next day. Another Parker story comes her way a few evenings later, then there's an afternoon drive to work listening to radio talk-show callers chew the issue to death, some of them actually sticking up for the kid, and her quiet anger curdles into a rage that no one knows, no one sees.

The writers like Jill. She's not one of those editors who must tinker with a story to justify their existence. One *Newsday* reporter writes an article that comes right out and says Parker is a good kid who made a mistake and deserves a second chance, and he calls Jill as she's editing it, cheerfully asking her how she likes his piece. There's silence on the phone. And then it erupts from her, something she has never even been able to tell her family.

"I've been raped," says Jill. "I don't agree with you."

"Oh, I didn't. . . . Jill, I'm sorry," he says.

She feels like a jerk for making the reporter feel like a jerk, but it's too late now, the anger's out on the table, and it's not finished. *Mistake?* How can anyone call it that? Leaving your headlights on or forgetting your keys, *that's* a mistake–not humiliating a woman the way Jill had been nearly nine years earlier, at age 22, by a man on a boat on Queechy Lake in upstate New York. She goes into her boss's office, seething at a society where a man like Mike Tyson can walk out of jail a few years after raping a woman and be greeted by a thunderous roar and a paycheck worth millions of dollars, and TV commentators can blather on about all that *Tyson* has been through, as if the perpetrator was the victim and the real victim was yesterday's oatmeal. "I want to write a column," she tells her boss. "People need to know what it's like for the victim. I was raped."

His jaw drops. Well . . . uh . . . sure, Jill, but. . . .

She barely sleeps that night. Her husband, Michael, says that if she's sure she wants to do this, he's behind her. She's sure. She sits on the couch the next day with a red pen, a blue pen and a notepad. The red ink is for *her* pain–the italicized sections interspersed in the column that recount that night on the lake where she swam as a little girl: *"I wanted to throw up every time I smelled the mixture of Grand Marnier and tobacco smoke on his breath as he held me down. . . ."* The blue ink is for Richie Parker: "How often do you think Parker will think about this incident once he's on a college basketball court? For the victim, not a day will go by without that memory. . . . Parker's punishment should last until his victim is able to walk alone up the street, or through a parking lot, or down a dimly lit hallway and feel safe. Until the nightmares cease. Until a day goes by and she doesn't think about the horrible things these boys made her do. But it won't."

What are you doing? a voice inside her asks when she has finished writing. To her, this is not an act of courage, as some would take it. To her, this is Jill Agostino publicly admitting her most private pain just on the chance that it will make some men begin to comprehend how it feels to be violated, how it eats into a woman's life forever, how it can make her hold her breath when a stranger steps into an empty elevator with her, make her want to run when a man rolls down his car window and asks her for directions, make her stare into a mirror some days and hate her body because somehow it betrayed her.

She can't surrender to the urge to crumble up the notepad paper, because if she does, the man in the boat wins again, and she can't let him keep winning. He has won too many times, at night when she sits up rigid in bed from nightmares she can never quite recollect–only raw terror and the faint echo of all the world's laughter. He won every time she bought another size 8 blouse for a size 4 body, every time she froze when a colleague she didn't know well threw an arm around her shoulder, every time she couldn't sleep and had to caffeinate and will herself through the next day so that no one, except perhaps her husband, would ever dream that she was anything but the sharp, competitive woman that the world always sees.

Now comes the next agony. She can't let her family find out in a newspaper story. She must call her mother and father and brother and sister and tell them about the rape and why she buried it. She must listen to her mother cry and feel guilty for not protecting her daughter from something she couldn't possibly have protected her from. A few days later the story appears. Seven hundred and fifty thousand readers learn Jill's secret, and countless thousands more–including old boyfriends, old co-workers, old roommates–come across it in the newspapers across the country that run the story. Some of her colleagues are moved to tears by her column. Some confess to her their own buried stories of rape.

The eddies never seem to end. Radio talk shows call her to be a guest and ask her about her rape, and she has to keep reliving the worst moment of her life. The victim's lawyer calls to compliment her story and ask her if she would testify in his client's civil lawsuit against Parker. When that's settled out of court, he asks if she'd consider doing that in another lawsuit in which the jury needs to feel the long ripple of a rape, and she says yes, because how can she refuse to help someone who has endured what she has or allow so many people to keep insinuating that it's the violated woman who is to blame? *Sports Illustrated* calls a year later and asks to interview her, and she has to worry how that will affect the way her colleagues at her new workplace, *The New York Times,* will look at her, worry that *this* is who she is now to people, that is *all* she is. Each new episode will mean another week of barely eating, barely sleeping, a few more nightmares, and 10 or 15 extra miles of running, but she can't back down. She has never met Richie Parker and no doubt never will, but Jill Agostino is paying for his crime, oh, yes, she's paying.

FIVE

Here is an assistant coach from the University of Utah. Once Donny Daniels, too, was a black teenager from a crowded city who lived to play basketball. And so even though he is the 40-year-old father of three, including two daughters, on this spring day in 1995, he is walking into his past when he walks into the Parkers' apartment. He finds Richie just as quiet and respectful as all his sources vowed. He sits in the living room with the 108 basketball trophies that take Rosita hours to dust. He looks into the kitchen where she cooks pots and pans full of baked chicken, ziti, collard greens, banana pudding and sweet-potato pies on Sundays and has half the neighborhood into her house, just like it used to be when she was growing up in North Carolina. He gazes around the home where Rosita and Richie's ever-so-quiet father, Richard, and Richie's two older sisters, Monica and Tanya, who have both attended college, eat and tease each other and laugh.

Donny talks to Rosita, who for years telephoned after Richie to make sure he had gone where he said he was going, who tried to seal her son from all the bad choices blowing around outside the window. No, Donny can't see her running a half-dozen times to the emergency room with high blood pressure at each twist her son's story takes; can't see her bent in half with chest pains six months after Richie's arrest, paramedics rushing through that front door and clamping an oxygen mask over her mouth, driving an IV needle into her arm, pushing a nitro-glycerine pill under her tongue, trying to stave off the heart attack or stroke that's on the verge of occurring as her son watches, even more scared than he was on that long night when he lay awake smelling urine in a New York City jail. He can't see her lying in the hospital, realizing that if she doesn't stop letting the newspaper stories affect her so deeply, they're going to kill her. But listening to the mother and the son, he can feel it.

And it's all that feeling that Donny lets out when the *New York Post* reporter gets a tip and calls him a few days later to ask, "How can Utah consider rewarding a sex felon with a scholarship?" All that feeling from a man who senses that his and his university's integrity is being assaulted. Of course, he has never walked into the *victim's* house and felt what a heart might feel there. "There are two victims here," he tells the reporter. "He doesn't evaporate into the atmosphere. He's not a piece of dirt. He has feelings and emotions. . . . They both made a mistake; they shouldn't have been there. But everyone's worried about the girl. What about him? . . . You don't see her name or picture, but Richie Parker is plastered all over. . . . She probably will get a doctorate and marry a successful guy and live in the Hamptons. . . . Will he ever be able to forget it? . . . Who's hurt more for life?"

Imagine the explosion this quote causes back in Salt Lake City, the ripping apart of molecules. Imagine how rapidly the college president and athletic director must run from that quote, how swiftly Richie's chance to attend Utah vaporizes, how many columns are written citing Richie as the prime example of America's coddling of athletes and Neanderthal treatment of women. Imagine how tightly doors shut to discuss what must be done with Donny.

He is luckier than others will be. He is placed on probation for a year and ordered to attend sensitivity training sessions with a director from the Women's Resource Center on campus. He gets a second chance.

A year later, when a writer from SI calls, Donny says he was wrong for saying what he did but wishes to say nothing more, and his boss, coach Rick Majerus, the most affable of men, seals his lips as well. Better to fence off the area and let the pieces lie where they fell, to be covered by the sediment of time.

SIX

Here is a university president. Here is the picture of Teddy Roosevelt on his office wall. Which is which? Who's who? Mustache. Spectacles. Hair combed back. Eyes atwinkle. Robust body. Bent for bold action. Oh, so *that's* how you tell the two of them apart: Stephen Trachtenberg's the better politician.

He's the man who transformed the University of Hartford and George Washington, the one who gives big-idea speeches and writes ethics essays for books, magazines and newspapers. He knows something about everything. Even chemistry.

Yes, he's going to do it. He's going to give this Parker kid another chance, and he's going to satisfy the alumni and faculty and the women's groups and the media and the talk-show callers, and even the victim. He's going to introduce cesium to fluorine, and–*eureka!*–nothing's going to go *ka-boom!*

And why not? He's a master at problem solving, a genius at persuasion. "He has a tremendous capacity to anticipate a whole variety of outcomes and the implications of those outcomes," says George Washington vice president Bob

Chernak, "and then calculate how to move an issue toward the most favorable one. He's always three steps ahead of you. He's thinking of ideas in his sleep."

Stephen inherited a university with a profound identity crisis, not to mention a 1–27 basketball team, in 1988. In the wake of his brainstorms, applications have nearly doubled, contributions have soared, average SAT scores have rocketed, and the hoops team has become an NCAA tournament fixture. A new challenge? Bully! A fray? Fine! He would wade right into it and convince people he was right, the way he did during the student sit-ins at Boston University back in the 1960s as a bearded associate dean, persuading protesters not to risk a violent confrontation with police. He has built up a tall pile of chips at George Washington, and he's willing to ante up for Richie Parker.

Sure, he's eager to help his basketball team, but it's also something else. Sure, he's the son of one hell of a Brooklyn life insurance salesman, but he's also the son of a social activist, a mother who sent him to summer camps with black kids and wanted him to become a doctor who would treat the poor, not to mention the grandson of a Ukrainian Jew who fled to America for a second chance. His record of helping kids out of deep holes is long. At Hartford he gave a scholarship to a young man with an eighth-grade education who had been convicted on drug-dealing and burglary charges. That man, John Richters—who played no sport—went on to graduate summa cum laude and get a Ph.D. in psychology and now works as a program chief at the National Institutes of Health in the study of chronically antisocial children.

A young deer—that's the image that forms in the university president's head when Richie enters his office in May 1995. Barely audible, Richie expresses contrition and an earnest desire to attend George Washington, and he's so hopeful that he buys a school hat and T-shirt. All the questions march through Stephen's head as Richie walks out of his office. Is it a college's job to mete out more punishment than the legal system does? Perhaps not, but isn't it a university president's job to make sure that a parent doesn't send an 18-year-old daughter to live in a dorm room next door to a sex offender? What if it were *his* daughter? If a sex felon shouldn't get a basketball scholarship, what about an academic scholarship? What about a thief, a mugger, an embezzler? A custodian or a waiter can return to his normal life after the legal system passes judgment, but a gifted basketball player cannot? Pro sports are fine for felons to play, but not college athletics? What kind of message does it send out when a sex offender gets a scholarship? When you remove the emotion from the question . . . but maybe you *shouldn't* remove the emotion from the question. All this confusion, does it signal a society lost in the wilderness . . . or one finally mature enough to look at questions it has always shut its eyes to? His mind gnaws at the bone, at every last bit of gristle. Beneath it all, he can sense what's going on, the vague feeling people are beginning to have that their love of sports—the sense of escape and belonging that they provide—is doubling back on them like some hidden undertow, pulling them all out to sea. It's not the ripest time for redemption.

But he takes a deep breath and begins constructing a master plan. He sends a university lawyer, a woman, to New York City to compile a massive dossier on Richie. If she finds any smudge, besides the stairwell incident, George Washington can retreat—but he keeps checking with her, and she doesn't. Shrewder still, he decides that *he* won't decide Richie's fate; he'll leave that to a blue-ribbon committee, one that he structures as if he were a supplicant at a Hindu shrine, bowing to a dozen different gods, to every possible political correctness: seven blacks and eight whites, seven females and eight males, including a professor of law, an assistant chief of police, a minister, a campus chaplain, an academic coordinator, a faculty clinical psychologist, a director of multicultural student services, a superintendent of schools, two judges, two trustees and three students. "A Noah's Ark committee," he calls it. If the menagerie chooses to accept Richie, Stephen will have him redshirted for a year, ease him into campus life, save him from the jackals waiting at enemy arenas. And then, as the frosting on the cake, even before the committee makes its recommendations on Richie, he offers the victim, a valedictorian of her junior high class, a scholarship when she graduates from high school. A university lawyer warns him that one won't look pretty in a tabloid headline, but Stephen is determined. Win-win for everyone, right?

Do you recall Chernobyl? It all begins to rain down on Stephen Trachtenberg: the *New York Post* reporter, radioactive telephone calls, faxes and letters, scalding editorials, icy questions from the board of trustees, student petitions and condemnation from the faculty senate. Stephen, the father of George Washington University, is being called immoral, a fool, a calculating liar. Even his wife, Francine, in his corner all the way, warns him that he has underestimated what he's up against, that, politically speaking, he has made the wrong call. He's losing sleep. It's usurping his entire day and all of his night. The story moves to *The Washington Post*'s front page—*that's* trouble. If only he could buy enough time for his plan to incubate, for the scores of Richie's last SAT test to arrive and the Noah's Ark committee to see the results of the nearly complete investigation, but no, Stephen looks to one flank, then the other, and sees a remarkable alliance closing in on him. The feminists *and* conservatives, "the forces of the left and the forces of the right," he says, "coming together like the teeth of a vise." Eight years of working 12-hour days to build George Washington's image is being frittered away, and image is money. And he can't even try to persuade the public that he's right—the NCAA gag rule preventing school officials from discussing a recruit has stripped him of his greatest gift. Could he even lose his job over this, if the teeth keep closing? Could he?

One by one, those in his inner circle who admire the risk he has taken, or have simply indulged it, urge him to halt, even as his investigator's reports on Richie keep coming in, convincing him more than ever that it's right to go on. Finally it's just Stephen out there, hanging onto Richie by his fingernails as everything around them shakes. At last, he has to let go. Stephen looks at himself in the mirror. It's not Teddy he sees. It's not the man who could persuade almost anyone of anything. "I gave Richie Parker a moment of hope," he says, the light going out of his eyes, "and then I took it away."

SEVEN

Here is the victim. No, here the victim is not. She has never emerged from the shadows of that stairwell. She will not emerge now. Of her you shall only know this: For months after the incident she endured nightmares and telephoned threats from people who blamed her. She is an excellent student, but her grades dipped, and the taunts from schoolmates forced her to transfer from one high school, then another. She undergoes therapy. As she gets ready for her senior year, her family will not even reveal the borough where her current school is located.

She hopes to become a doctor. Her father is a social worker who deals with abused children, her mother a hospital nurse. Six years ago they and their daughter left Ghana and came to America, looking for another chance.

EIGHT

Here is a number. Such a nice, plump number. Say it: *500*. Let them scoff at Dave Possinger, let them cringe at his intensity, let them ask him, like wise guys, to total up the traffic lights in the towns where he has coached, but this would be proof he could clutch all the way to the coffin: *500*. One more win is all he needs. One more.

And no, this won't be 500 by dint of sheer endurance, a box turtle's milestone. Eighteen years is all it took Dave, an astonishing average of 28 victories a year. He is the best coach you never heard of, a 52-year-old man marooned in the bush country of NAIA and junior college basketball by bad luck and an old whiff of scandal. But it's summer, and the 1995–96 season is just a few months away, and on opening night his Sullivan County (N.Y.) Community College team will no doubt pulverize Dutchess C.C. as it does every year, and he will join that invisible club: *500*.

He has envisioned the moment all summer, even as the man he has just chosen as his assistant coach, Charles Harris, has begun to grow intrigued by the never-ending newspaper accounts of a kid in New York City named Richie Parker. Richie is the last thing on Dave's mind. Dave has just coached his team to the national junior college Division III championship and is loaded to repeat in 1995–96, and he has no reason to think that Richie will end up with him in the bush country, at a low-level community college. Start making contacts and see what's out there, especially for the year after this, is all he has asked of Harris, a likable 40-year-old black man who Dave is sure will make a superb recruiter.

Everywhere Dave goes that summer, even on his vacation in the Philippines, he imagines the magical night that is coming: The limousine his girlfriend is renting to take him to the game. The official hoisting of the national-championship banner, his second in four years at the junior college in Loch Sheldrake, N.Y. Former players converging to congratulate him, a capacity crowd rising to recognize him. The plaque, the ringing speeches, the commemorative T-shirts, the late-night dinner for 100 in the Italian restaurant. "It dominated my thoughts every day," Dave recalls. "Even in places in the Philippines where there was no running water, no electricity, I'd see kids playing basketball and I'd think about 500. It would stand for all the years, all the kids, all the hard work." It would stand for his nine seasons at a New York NAIA school named St. Thomas Aquinas, where his 295–49 record helped make the program the country's winningest of the 1980s, on *any* level—yes, Dean Smith at North Carolina was second to Dave Possinger. It would stand for his four-year run of 133–5 at Sullivan County and ease the pain from the '89 scandal that forced him out after one year at Western Carolina, his one shot as an NCAA Division I coach, even though it was his assistant, not him, who was cited for minor recruiting violations. Perhaps 500 wouldn't mean quite so much if he had a wife and children, but no, it's just him and his basset hound Free Throw, and 500 stands for his life.

A few hours drive south, at a showcase game for unrecruited players, his soon-to-be-named assistant Harris is watching the one obvious jewel on the floor, Richie Parker. It's crazy, thinks Harris, who remembers inmates from the local prison taking classes from Sullivan County when he was enrolled there in the 1970s. "Everyone has something in their closet they're not proud of," Harris says, "and everyone deserves a second chance." A long shot, but what a coup if he could offer the kid the second chance that the four-year colleges wouldn't.

Harris gets clearance, he says later, from Sullivan County's athletic director, Mike McGuire, to have Richie apply to the school–not as a scholarship student but as any normal student would. Searching for a way to contact Richie, Harris calls the *New York Post* reporter. It's like the mouse asking the cat for directions to the cheese.

McGuire says now that if he heard the name Richie Parker, it didn't register. And that he definitely never gave Harris permission–even though Harris had been unofficially approved to go on contract in two months and had already invested countless hours and a few hundred dollars from his own pocket on phone calls and recruiting trips–to present himself to a *New York Post* reporter as a Sullivan County assistant coach and declare that Sullivan County was "committed to working" with Richie Parker.

You know what happens next. You know about the reporter's call to the president, asking if he knows that Sullivan County is recruiting a sex felon. You know about the next day's headlines, the ducking for cover. Richie, of course, will never play at Sullivan County. Harris's fate will hang in the balance for a few months while the school wrings its hands. In October, after he has spent weeks monitoring the players in study hall and working at practices without pay, hoping for the best, Harris is told he won't be hired.

Harris, with head-coaching dreams of his own, is crushed. Dave, who feels responsible for Harris, is devastated. There have been other slights from his superiors at Sullivan County, he feels, but to do this to a well-meaning man trying to give a kid a second chance–how can he go on working there and live with himself? But then, how can he walk out on this team two weeks before the season opener and deprive himself of the Holy Grail: *500*?

Simple, Dave's friends tell him. Win the opener, then quit. What a scene it would be, the man of the hour strolling to the microphone, saying, "Ladies and gentlemen, thank you, *I quit!*" But Dave's conscience won't let him do it. "If I start something," he tells his friends, "I have to finish it."

Five days before the opener, he quits. He can't sleep. A few days later he smirks and tells a reporter, "Your job is to tell me why I shouldn't jump off a building." His team goes on to win the national championship again, without him.

His record hangs there, rolling around the rim—499 wins and 116 losses—but athletic directors look right past him, searching for a younger man. Eight months later he still hasn't even received an interview. He takes a job as a regional director for National Scouting Report, a service designed to help high school kids get—what else?—college scholarships. "But there's still a claw in the back of my throat," he says, "a claw telling me, 'You are a basketball coach.'"

A week after he quits, Dave goes to his dresser drawer. He opens it and stares at what he purchased in the Philippines a few months earlier, and he makes a decision. Damn the math, they can't take it from him. It's there now, glittering in 18-carat gold from a chain around his neck: *500*.

NINE

Here is the girlfriend of the boy who has pleaded guilty to sexual abuse. She's tall and lean, a beautiful girl whose demeanor is so composed that everyone always assumes she's older than she really is, until that day when people are running to her in the hall, telling her to come quickly, something terrible has happened, and Richie's in the principal's office talking so helter-skelter that none of it makes sense, and the police are on their way, and she's nearly in hysterics.

He's the schoolmate Jaywana Bradley fell in love with in 10th grade, the one who taught her to play basketball so well that by her senior year she will be named by the *Daily News* as one of the best schoolgirl players in Manhattan. Who knew, perhaps they would go off together to trumpets, the king and queen of Manhattan hoops moving on, hand in hand, to set up court on a college campus . . . until this.

But what, exactly, *is* this? Jaywana keeps finding herself in bed, crying, wondering. People keep asking her, "You gonna leave Richie?" Some call her a fool if she sticks with him, and a few boys walk right up to her and say, "Why you going out with a rapist?"

She can't quite answer that. Maybe it's because her mother and father believe in Richie, her dad accompanying the Parkers to court hearings. Maybe it's just sitting there in the Parker apartment all those evenings, playing spades with the family and watching TV, feeling that relentless presence of Rosita—like a rock, a magnetic rock. Listening to Rosita talk about the past, telling how her father died when she was one, how her mother died of diabetic complications when she was 13, how her twin sister stepped in front of a car and was killed when they were five, leaving Rosita clutching the sleeve of the coat with which she had tried to yank back her twin. Maybe Jaywana, just like Richie, just keeps absorbing Rosita's relentless message: "Make your life what it's meant to be, and don't let anyone or anything stop you."

Maybe it's two young people pulling closer and closer together the more that forces try to drive them apart. Maybe she's a sucker for that playful, silly Richie, the side he only shows close family and friends. And maybe it comes from holding him, wiping away his tears the way she does when George Washington closes the door on him and she ends up getting the big-time basketball scholarship to Massachusetts that was supposed to be his.

He goes off to Mesa, to the junior college that decides not to let him play basketball, and she goes off to UMass, and they don't see each other for a long while. He has time to sort out what's essential, what he needs, *now,* sooner than he ever dreamed. When they come home for Christmas, he asks her to come over, calls her to his room and asks her to close her eyes. When she opens them, he's on his knee, asking her to marry him, and she says yes. And later, when she asks him when, he says, "As soon as we're done college."

More and more now, Jaywana finds herself daydreaming of a future. There is no city or people there, just her and Richie in a house surrounded by land and trees as far as the eye can see, a place where no one can touch them. Why the two of them against all odds? She can't explain. "I don't know what made me stick through it with him," she says. "All I know is that nothing anybody can ever say or do can pull me apart from him."

TEN

Here is death. Now, wait a minute—no one is going to be foolish enough to blame Richie Parker's 15 minutes in the stairwell or the administration of Mesa Community College or even the media for the death of a coach's father, but every event in life is chained to the next, and how do you ever separate the links?

This was supposed to be the year that Rob Standifer gave his father, Bob, a gift —perhaps the last one—in exchange for the gift his father had given him. All Rob's life his dad had awakened at 3 A.M. and reported to work three hours early at a construction company, logging 12- to 14-hour shifts. It didn't matter how badly his dad felt, with his bad back, his diabetes or his weak heart. Work made his father feel good, and his father had a knack of passing that feeling all around. The lesson Rob took into his bones was the old American one: Outwork everyone and you'll succeed in life.

And it seemed true. As a kid Rob was always the first one on the basketball court as a point of pride, shooting 1,000 shots a day, and sure enough, he found himself playing for the Mesa Community College team that nearly won the junior college title in 1987, finishing third in the national tournament in Hutchinson, Kans. He worked for nothing as a high school assistant and then for next to nothing for five years as an assistant at Mesa, and he was rewarded with the head-coaching job two years ago. He was only 27, but his dream, to coach a major college team, was no longer quite so far away.

The pantry was bare his rookie year, but Mesa went 15–15. Then, doing it his dad's way—his typical off-season day ran from 7 A.M. to 10 at night—he ran the summer league, organized a computerized scouting system, cultivated his high school coaching contacts, recruited at hours when other coaches relaxed, pushed his players through an exhaustive weightlifting program and then nurtured them at night with so many phone calls that his friends called him Ma Bell. He was single and on fire. "I could be a maniac," says Rob, "and I was."

The pantry filled fast. Twice in the summer league in 1995 his players whipped a team with four former Arizona State starters on it, and Rob's target was clear. He was going to take his father and his team back to Hutchinson and this time win the whole damn thing.

Richie? He would sure make things easier. Rob had seen him play in the annual summer tournament at Arizona State, which Richie's New York City club team, Riverside Church, traveled to each year. Just like all the other coaches, Rob was struck by the distance between Richie and the world's image of Richie. Just like all the other coaches, he got that same feeling in the pit of his stomach when he saw a talented high school player—if you didn't get him dunking *for* you, he might soon be dunking *on* you. Besides, Rob knew Ernie Lorch, the Riverside director, and already had taken a few of Lorch's kids at Mesa. And so Rob, too, was drawn in. Mesa would be Richie's safety net, the faraway junior college where he could go to heal himself and play ball if all the Division I scholarship offers went up in smoke.

And because there was so much smoke, and Richie kept hoping and waiting for the next Division I chance, his decision to go to Mesa occurred at the last minute, just a few days before the start of school last August. And because Richie waited, Rob had to wait, and by the time he found out Richie was coming, there was no chance for cool heads to sit and debate this and perhaps construct a plan. Rob told the story of Richie Parker to three women—his mother, his girlfriend, and his girlfriend's mother, and they all agreed with him. "What Richie did was flat wrong," Rob says, "but are you going to be part of the problem or part of the solution?" And he insists—*are you crazy?*—that of course he notified his superiors, two of them, about Richie and his baggage.

But the Mesa athletic director, Allen Benedict, says he was told nothing of Richie's past, that all he got was a 9 P.M. call from Rob telling him that a great player was coming from New York. The next morning, while Richie was at 30,000 feet heading west across the heart of America, the junior college president was on the phone with Benedict, saying "Why did a reporter from the *New York Post* just call me . . . and who is Richie Parker?" And then the National Organization for Women was checking in, and cameras were peering inside the gym for a peek at Richie, and a TV truck was pulling up to Benedict's house. "Whether you do something wrong or not isn't the point sometimes," says Benedict. "It's the perception."

Rob was called in to a meeting less than two weeks before the first practice and forced to quit. Richie called Rob, nearly in tears at what he had wrought.

As for Richie, he could stay, but he couldn't play basketball. College athletics, Mesa president Larry Christiansen reasoned, are like a driver's license—a privilege, not a right. What the westward trip and the open spaces had done for so many others, they couldn't do for Richie Parker.

Richie had to decide, then and there, what was most important in his life. He chose to stay at Mesa, take courses and learn who he was without a basketball. He would work the shot clock at games, like one of those earnest guys in glasses that no one ever notices, and by the end of the year the administrators at Mesa would all say good things about him.

Rob had to tell his father the terrible news. He knew his dad was on the edge of the cliff—doctors had said that if not for the zest that Bob derived from his work, his heart would've likely given way three or four years before–so the son tried to shrug and keep his face a blank, so he wouldn't give his father that nudge. Bob was devastated, but as with all his other pain, he tried to keep it inside. He was bewildered, too. The ethic he had passed on to his only child–out-work everyone and you'll succeed–had failed, been displaced, it seemed, by a new one: Image is everything.

Rob didn't eat for three days after that, unless you count the antacid medication. He wouldn't even show his girlfriend, Danelle Scuzzaro, how badly this hurt.

On the fourth day after he was let go, he picked up a diamond ring at the jeweler's and took Danelle to dinner. Afterward, he dropped to his knee–cesium is the damnedest thing–and asked her to marry him. She said yes, and thank god.

Two weeks later, at 5:15 A.M., he got the call from his mother. His father's heart had stopped, at the age of 61. It might well have happened then anyway. "What happened to me didn't kill him," says Rob, "but it didn't help."

There was only one thing to be said for the timing. All the tears Rob had held back after losing his job could finally come out, and they did . . . again . . . and again . . . and again. . . .

ELEVEN

Wait a moment. What about the reporter from the *New York Post*–isn't he here too? Sure, just a moment, he's still on the telephone. Gosh, look at him, just a kid, wouldn't even pass for 25. Just started at the *Post*, covering high school sports, when suddenly–*whoa!*–he has his teeth into the story of his life, and his incisors are wonderful.

Look at Barry Baum rolling out of bed in his Manhattan apartment and running, literally, to the newsstand at the corner of 79th and Broadway to check if the *Daily News* has scooped him on the Parker story. That has actually happened before, so Barry knows that sinking feeling. See him getting that 10 A.M. call from his editor, groggily picking up the phone–a medic on call in a tabloid war. "So what's goin' on with Parker today?" his editor demands. And Barry says, "I'll let you know," then shakes off the cobwebs and begins working the phones, looking for a tip. He loves this part, the detective work. And the most amazing thing keeps occurring. Because there's such an innocent charm about Barry, people *want* to help him.

Some high school scout or basketball junkie with his ear to the streets keeps slipping him the name of the next university showing interest in Richie, and then Barry plays his role, just as the university administrators and the coaches and the women's groups and the loved ones do. He becomes the Bunsen burner, the heat that agitates the cesium and fluorine molecules into rapid movement, more-violent collision. He leaps to call the university president and the campus women's center to ask that 64-megaton question–"How do you feel about your school recruiting a sex felon?"–and if they say they don't know who Richie Parker is, so they can't comment, he faxes them a pile of his Parker stories, and suddenly they have a comment. And all at once the coach and the athletic director are being called onto the president's carpet, or what's left of it, and then there's a follow-up exclusive story to write when they all abandon Richie, and there's no time to consider all the layers, all the moral nuances, because the editor's on the phone barking, "O.K., hurry, rewrite that for the second edition!"– just like in the movies. And then street vendors are snaking between the cars bottlenecked at the bridges and tunnels leading into the city the next morning, catching drivers' eyes with thick SEX FELON headlines, and every person who contributes his 50 cents confirms the *Post* editor's instincts and becomes another link in the chain.

"There were nights when I couldn't sleep, an adrenaline I had for a long time," says Barry. "I'd lie in bed, realizing I'd come to New York and made an impact on one of the biggest stories of the year."

Hadn't his editor at the *Post* told him, "We're going to put your name in lights," when he hired Barry in August 1994? Wasn't that music to his ears? Even as a little kid in Brooklyn Heights, he had dreamed of busting back-page stories for the New York tabloids. At 15 he talked his way into becoming the Knicks ball boy by rat-tat-tatting 10 letters to the team trainer, and then he parlayed that job into his own cable-TV show in Manhattan, *Courtside with Barry Baum,* by convincing the station of the wonderful access to big-name Knicks that a precocious 16-year-old ball boy had. He appeared on the televised dating show *Love Connection* three times, and when one of his dates sniffed about Barry's making the wrong turn on their evening out, he brought down the house by sniffing back, "Get a load of Miss Rand McNally, never made a wrong turn in her life!"

And then suddenly the kid who grew up calling *New York Post* and *Daily News* columnists with kudos and beg-to-differs is being lauded for his own back-page *Post* scoops on New York radio talk shows, being asked to appear on the all-sports station, WFAN, and invited to speak at a journalism symposium at Madison Square Garden with a poster board full of his Parker stories. Adrenaline, yes, but anguish, too, stuff you don't talk about when you're a guest on WFAN. Because the nasty phone calls to Barry's desk have begun, people hissing, "Leave Richie Parker alone!"

Then, when he's a guest on a radio talk show one day, a caller says, "Don't you see what you're doing? This is a black kid who comes from nowhere, and you're a white guy who probably comes from a lot of money." Barry blinks. "It hit me," he says. "That's true. I've always had everything, and I'd never even thought of the race factor." New York City high school coaches, his contacts, start saying, "C'mon, Barry, back off. What are you trying to prove?" Even his own father, Bruce, finally says, "Leave him alone already, Barry," and that stings.

"That even someone who knew me that well wouldn't realize that I'm just trying to do my job. . . ." he says. "I mean, don't give me credit for keeping Richie Parker out of college, but don't blame me for it either. And the more people tell me to *stop* reporting a story, the more it means it *is* a story, right? But I keep wondering about Richie. All that time, I couldn't talk to him because his lawyer wouldn't let me, so I couldn't feel him. Finally they let me. You know, it changes things once you talk to him. Before that he was an object, and it was easy to write, 'Richie Parker, sex felon,' because I didn't know him. He was the predator and the girl was the victim, right? I talked to him at a Rucker League game last August, and he actually smiled at me. A smile is a big thing.

"Look, I've never had a problem with Richie playing college basketball. It's not the colleges' job to punish him further. He should be allowed to play—but not without students and their parents being notified, maybe by a letter from the university administration. You know, like Megan's Law, notifying people that a sex felon is in their neighborhood. It's funny. It's like *I've* become Megan's Law for these universities. I'm the one who tells them he's coming. It was amazing how quickly it played out with Oral Roberts. I reported that the school was interested, the story breaks across the country, the TV reporters arrive on campus—and the school announces it has already pulled out! It was like the fire trucks coming, and there's no fire, the local residents have already put it out. These universities have no backbone! Every university president I talk to, except for maybe Stephen Trachtenberg, it's like talking to the same guy. Every one of them says, 'I can't believe my coach did this and that isn't what we stand for and blah-blah-blah.' I'm convinced there's only one college president in the United States: He just keeps changing his name!"

One major college coach, off the record, asks Barry what will happen if he takes the risk on Richie. What's Barry supposed to do, lie? He tells the truth, the coach says thank you and backs off, and—*poof!*—the chance is gone, the chemical reaction begun and finished before anyone ever even smelled it occurring. And it begins to dawn on Barry: "Somehow, I'm *in* this story. I'm not just the observer. People are making decisions based on my reporting. There I am, 25 years old and playing the part of deciding if this kid's going to get into college or not, and maybe, if he's good enough, even into the NBA. I have no agenda or angle at all, but he'd probably be playing now if I hadn't called Utah or GW or. . . .

"So where is the line? I've never been taught that line. I keep wondering, Am I doing the right thing? But I shouldn't have to make that choice. I started compiling a list in my mind of all the people whose lives I've affected, the people who have gotten fired, all the universities. And it tears me apart, because the last thing I want to do is hurt anyone. But I know if I stop reporting it and the *Daily News* gets the story, which you know they will, then my editor will call me and say, 'What's goin' on with Parker? What happened? Where are the words?' and what am I going to say? I can't win. So people blame me. It's like *I* was the one in the stairwell."

He stares off at the wall, catches his breath. "And it's not over yet," Barry says. "It's not over until I find out where Richie Parker's going."

TWELVE

One day about a month ago Richie Parker stepped into an airplane in Arizona. The plane rose, and he looked through the window one last time at the desert and flew back across America, with no idea what would happen next. "I've learned I can survive without basketball," he said last month. "I've learned how the real world is and that I'm stronger than I knew I was. There's less fear now. I know myself more. I trust people less, but that doesn't make me sad. Just more aware of things. I can still live a good life." And he said a lot more, but it would be improper to let him do it here, for it might mislead the reader into thinking this was a story about Richie Parker.

This land is vast, and it contains so many kinds of people, and that is its grace. Two weeks ago Gale Stevens Haynes, the 45-year-old provost of the Brooklyn campus of Long Island University—and the black mother of three teenage daughters—offered Richie Parker a basketball scholarship to her Division I school. She didn't pull the offer back when the *New York Post* reporter found out, and Richie accepted it. When asked why she did it, she said, "Unless there's an island that I don't know about, where we send people forever who have done something wrong, then we have to provide pathways for these people so they can rejoin society. If we don't, it can only explode. It can only explode in *all* of our faces."

Chapter

Telling Stories
from Inside

Susan Orlean

Her Town

Susan Orlean is clearly at home, here at The New Yorker. *A petite woman, dressed smartly in black, she sits in her neat, white office and calls hello to fellow writers passing by in the wide, light halls. Like many English majors, she dreamed of just this job when she was reading her favorite writer William Faulkner at the University of Michigan (B.A. in 1976). Getting here required luck, determination, and enthusiasm—as well as a move West to write for* Paper Rose *and* Willamette Week *in Portland, then East to write for the* Boston Phoenix *and* The Boston Globe Magazine, *and freelancing with story after story in* Rolling Stone, Esquire, Vogue, Spy, Mademoiselle, GQ. *Then one day she entered Shangri-la: writing "Talk of the Town."*

Orlean says she has always had an instinct for stories she can connect with— "It's visceral"—just as she has always known that her great theme is the human community. Like a sociologist or an anthropologist, she asks, "How do people come together in groups? What holds them together? Why do they live the way they do?" One of her questions, "What do they do on Saturday night?" became the book, Saturday Night *(1990).*

She advises young writers: "Write what you care about; you can always find out what you don't know." That's what she does, reporting by immersion. "I have the experience." Then comes the struggle to move from the mass of unstructured information to form and purpose. "What did I see and feel? I sit and sit and think and think. It's painful, and no one can help me. It's mystical, and I'm often shocked to see my leads. Then I write from the beginning to the end," she says.

In writing "Her Town," Orlean started from her belief in the importance of small-town newspapers—one of the forces holding communities together—and the reporters who write for them. "Heather is a critical piece in the machinery of how this town works. She's much more important than a big city reporter," says Orlean. Although she thought her treatment of Millerton—a place near her own weekend retreat—was extremely affectionate, not everyone agreed. Why, they wondered, hadn't she been more of a booster? Writing about your own life, she discovered, can be risky. "Your subjects are vulnerable, but so is the writer."

—CM

A day begins in the village of Millerton, New York. A man pauses while shaving and says to his wife, "I think I will run for mayor." Down the road, a cow expires mysteriously. A shopkeeper in town has labor pains.

Susan Orlean, Her Town, *The New Yorker*, September 11, 1995. Reprinted courtesy of the author.

The corn begins to tassel, earlier than usual. The agenda for the village zoning-board meeting is copied, collated, stapled, and stacked. A family, over breakfast, decides to give up farming and sell its land. A mutt gives birth to ten puppies and then abandons them. Someone makes the high-school honor roll. A lawsuit is filed. A guy dies. A barn burns. A car skids. These kinds of things get reported in the town's weekly newspaper, the Millerton *News*. A woman cracks her husband over the head with an inexpensive piece of pottery. This will probably not be reported in the Millerton *News,* unless she kills him. If she does, it will indeed be big news in Millerton, and big news in the Millerton *News*–bigger than some recent stories like "TEENS UNINJURED WHEN CAR CATCHES FIRE AT INTERSECTION" and "RASHES RUNNING RAMPANT DURING BAD IVY SEA-SON" and "KENNETH HANLEY NAMED JIFFY LUBE MANAGER," but less enduring than the Pet Parade (a photo spread of adoptable pets, which runs in every issue of the paper) or the local crime blotter (every issue) or the Seniors Menu at the community center (most issues) or the list of the new books at the library (anytime any new ones come).

The village of Millerton is two hours north of New York City, in the town of Northeast, in the northeast corner of Dutchess County, and is set in the middle of slumpy hills and wavy alfalfa fields and pastureland as soft and rumpled as someone's lap. The houses in the village are solid and modest. Many of them have gardens blooming with fat, old-fashioned, costume-jewelry flowers, like dahlias and peonies and mums. In the village, you can sometimes pick up Manhattan radio stations, but you can also shop on the honor system for tomatoes and honey and pattypan squash that people leave on stands out in their yards. About nine hundred people live in the village and about two thousand more in the surrounding area. They are dairy farmers, prison guards, antique dealers, schoolteachers, organic-vegetable growers, mechanics, store owners. Over-whelmingly, they are Republican. Once, a woman visiting in town gave birth ahead of schedule, and the baby grew up to be the famous Chicago White Sox second baseman Eddie Collins, whose major-league career began in 1906, but other than being the accidental birthplace of a Hall of Famer the village has never rocked the outside world. On the other hand, the people of Millerton have given birth, argued, voted, married, grown things, built things, burned things, and died often enough to fill their own newspaper for the past hundred years.

The reporting staff of the Millerton *News* has usually consisted of one person. The front page of each week's edition features seven or eight stories and two or three photographs. Each story has a byline, and each photograph has a credit. The front page of the June 15th edition carried these stories:

ELEMENTARY STUDENTS LEARN
ABOUT DIVERSITY
by Heather Heaton

MORE ANSWERS NEEDED ABOUT
ASSESSOR'S JOB
by Heather Heaton

Egg Rolls, Bagels
Coming to RR Plaza
by Heather Heaton

Festival Was Just the Berries!
by Heather Heaton

Webutuck Board Addresses
Concerns Raised at Workshop
by Heather Heaton

Doc Bartlett Remembered as
'All-Round Good Man'
by Heather Heaton

Funds Still Needed
for Field Repair
by Heather Heaton

There were also three photographs: one of second graders dressed as leprechauns and fairies; one of a fake thermometer indicating how much money had been raised so far to restore the town's Eddie Collins Memorial Park ballfields; and one of little kids eating the strawberries and ice cream at the Strawberry Festival in the nearby town of Amenia. The shots of the second graders and of the Strawberry Festival were credited to Heather Heaton. This meant that there were nine mentions of Heather Heaton on the front page of the paper—the Millerton equivalent of having your picture appear on the Sony Jumbo-Tron in Times Square. I have been a reader of the Millerton *News* for several years, and that day, somewhere between the berry-festival story and the obituary for Doc Bartlett, I realized that the big news was that someone named Heather Heaton had just become the incarnation of the Millerton *News*.

Recently, I went to Millerton to spend a week with Heather. It was the thick of summer, just after the raspberry season and just as the sweet corn had started to ripen, shortly after the local American Legion post's chicken barbecue and not long before Millerton Days, the annual town celebration, which was dedicated this year to Eddie Collins. I'd thought it might be a week of dog days, but Heather told me that all sorts of things were going on: the elementary-school principal, Steve O'Connell, had resigned unexpectedly; the Millerton Gun Club was testing a new trapshooting machine; McGruff the Crime Dog was going to visit the village swimming pool; a local man had been killed by a train on the railroad tracks south of town; a cold front was about to collide with a warm front and create a gigantic thunderstorm; the author of a book about ponies was coming to speak at Oblong Books & Music, on Main Street; a woman whose family had been dairy farming in Millerton for three generations was submitting a request for rezoning so she could turn part of the farm into a gravel mine; and executive sessions of the village government would continue to be held downstairs in the town hall rather than upstairs, because one of the commissioners had a sore hip. Also, the village clerk had just quit, and the mayor, who owns an accounting practice in town, was refusing to comment on it. Unexpected things would probably happen, too. I've spent many summer weekends near Millerton, and it had always struck me as a tiny, quiet place, but knowing that all these things were happening made it seem to swell and expand like one of those pop-up sponges.

By now, almost everyone in Millerton knows what Heather Heaton looks like, because anyone who appears on Main Street more than a couple of times gets noticed by almost everyone else in town. Heather is leggy, lean, and a little pigeon-toed, and she has a peachy complexion, a scatter of freckles across her nose, and fine brown hair with loose, loopy curls, which she wears pulled back from her face. When she blushes, which is often, she blushes from above her eyebrows all the way down the front of her neck. Her gaze is mild and disarming, and her voice is wobbly and sweet, like Tweety Pie's. The day I met her, she was wearing a long flowered jumper and a cotton top and a pair of beige sling-back sandals. The next day, she wore a pair of cutoff sweatpants and a T-shirt. The day after that, she wore a blouse and a dotted skirt, and after work she was going to be fitted for a firefighter's uniform, because she serves as a volunteer on the squad in Canaan, Connecticut, the town where she lives.

Heather is twenty-two years old. She grew up in Amherst, New Hampshire, which is not much bigger than Millerton, and graduated this May from the University of Connecticut, in Storrs, where she majored in journalism. She had interned at the Hartford *Courant* and had imagined that she would work for a big daily after finishing college, but then one of her professors told her about the opening at the Millerton *News*. She had never been to Millerton until the day she came to be interviewed for the job. She started work in early June. The first few nights, she went back to a room she rents in a farmhouse in Canaan and felt like crying. Since then, she has fallen in love with one of the other Canaan volunteer firefighters, has met a good proportion of the people in Millerton, and has written about sixty front-page stories for the *News*. Her "EGG ROLLS, BAGELS COMING TO RR PLAZA" article is framed and displayed on the counter at the Bagel Café. Heather still hopes to work on a big-city daily someday, but she's afraid she may be spoiled by all the exposure she's getting on the front page of the Millerton *News*. In the meantime, she's getting settled in Millerton. Once, while we were talking in her office, I could hear the rasping of an emergency-services scanner in the background, and I asked her what was being reported. "Bee sting in Staatsburg," she said. "But I really wasn't listening. After all, it's not my town."

The Millerton *News* used to have its offices on Main Street in Millerton. In 1972, the owner of the Lakeville *Journal*, a weekly in Lakeville, Connecticut, which is just a few miles to the east, bought the Millerton *News*. The two papers are now like Siamese twins: they share an office in Lakeville, and their dozen or so inside pages are virtually the same mixture of community announcements, columns, service articles, church news, and advertisements for tractor dealerships, horse farms, and plant nurseries, but the front pages are different, depending on which town the papers are being distributed to.

Though Lakeville and Millerton are only four mile apart, they are not much alike. Lakeville is rich and sleek and full of summer houses; Millerton is more of a working town. They are connected by Route 44: it is Main Street in Lakeville and then Main Street again in Millerton, and, in between, it is a sharp-curved two-lane country road with a view to the north of a huge dairy farm. After the road crosses the Connecticut–New York state line, it passes the Millerton Burger King, a car wash, a fancy restaurant called the New Yorker, and a house that Heather pointed out to me because the woman who lives there displays a collection of dolls on her lawn; Heather says she plans to write a story about her someday.

On the first day of my week with Heather, we drove from Lakeville past the dairy farm and the doll lady's house and into Millerton. Heather has a big brown beater of a Pontiac with bumper stickers lauding her college soccer team. As she drove, Heather told me she had decided against living in Millerton because she wanted to volunteer on the fire and rescue squads wherever she lived, and she felt that if she were on the Millerton squads she wouldn't be able to write about them objectively. Living in the town you cover has its perils. Once, there was a Millerton *News* reporter who lived in the village, and his girlfriend came to visit him, bringing along her pet six-foot-long python. During the visit, the snake got loose and wiggled its way into the walls of the house where the reporter was renting a room, and his landlady became loud and hysterical until the snake was found. The incident gave rise to some local discussion. Not long afterward, the reporter quit and left town.

In Millerton, we stopped to buy out-of-town newspapers at Terni's, a fishing-tackle/newspapers/camping-goods/candy store on Main Street. The day before, Millerton had celebrated Phil Terni Clean-Up Day, in honor of the store's owner, who is famous in town for sweeping up around his store every morning. Heather had subsequently written a front-page feature about the event and had taken a picture of Phil to accompany it. Phil was behind the soda fountain when we went in. The store's counter is made of cool marble, and the wood of the cabinets is old and silky. Years ago, when Millerton still had a milk-processing plant, the farmers would bring their milk cans to town every morning, drop them off, and then head for Terni's to get cigars and newspapers before they went back to their farms. Now the milk-processing plant has been converted into an apartment building, and some of the grandchildren of the dairy farmers work at Hipotronics, a small electronics plant that is just outside the town, beside fields of sweet corn and hay. "Nice article, Heather," Phil said. "You know, you wrote every single article in that paper."

"I know," she said. "I'm supposed to. Hey, I hope you sold a lot of them."

"Sold out," he said. "I'll order more today."

A few doors down from Terni's is Oblong Books. One of the owners of Oblong, Holly Nelson, is the head of the town planning board. Up the street is an appliance store called Campbell & Keeler; Heather planned to call Jimmy Campbell, one of the owners, about a story she was going to write on the dangers of lightning. Campbell was also one of the organizers behind Millerton Days, so she'd be in touch with him about that, too. Heather told me that not long after she started reporting in Millerton, she called a village board member named Glen White,

and then called a schoolteacher named Glen White, and was about to call someone named Glen White about a third story when she realized that there weren't
three men named Glen White–there was one Glen White who was involved in
three different things. To some people, this state of affairs is what makes a small
town seem monotonous, but to others it is what makes a place seem anchored
and secure, even as it bumps around and changes. In small towns like Millerton,
the same people pop up over and over in slightly different positions, but they
always stay tied to the same deep place, like buoys.

The week begins at Millerton *News* on Thursdays, when Heather and the staff
of the Lakeville *Journal*–Charlotte Reid, Marsden Epworth, and Tim Fitzmaurice
–meet with David Parker and Kathryn Boughton, the editor and managing editor
of both papers, to talk about their stories for the upcoming issue. That Thursday,
Heather told David she was working on the O'Connell resignation, the Scoland
Farm gravel-mine hearing, and the story about safety precautions during electri-
cal storms. She also said that she was hoping to borrow a cache of Eddie Collins
photographs for a pre–Millerton Days feature, but added that the local man who
had most of the Collins memorabilia didn't seem eager to lend the photographs
to the paper. She said she'd keep trying.

"Great," David said. "What else?"

"Well, as soon as I get enough information, I want to do that big story about
how Dutchess County is changing."

"Your 'dying farmers' story?" Kathryn Boughton asked.

"I changed the description of it on my list," Heather said, glancing up at
Kathryn. "I didn't actually mean 'dying farmers.' I meant 'dying farms.'"

Over the next few days, Heather and I drove from Lakeville to Millerton, to
Amenia, and back to Millerton, to the elementary school, to the Gun Club, to
Terni's for papers, to the sheriff's substation in Amenia for the weekly crime
report, back to Lakeville, back to Millerton, to the Burger King for lunch, to the
town hall, to the village hall, around the fields and the farms, back and forth
through the center of Millerton–around the bend in the road where the low, flat-
front buildings of the village huddle–and to the ends of town, where the buildings thin out and finally disappear. Covering a town keeps you busy. At the
elementary school, Steve O'Connell was packing to leave. The school is perched
on a bald gray hill, and in the summer stillness it felt a little forlorn. Steve was in
a great mood because of his new job, in Westchester County. "I read the description of your new school," Heather said to him. "It sounds like a country club."

"Well it's gorgeous," he said. "It's gorgeous, Heather. I'll tell you all about it,
because I know you're not from New York. I know I'm talking fast, but that's the
kind of guy I am." At the end of the interview, Heather took half a dozen pictures,
because she suspected that the story would end up as her lead.

The next stop was the village pool, to cover McGruff the Crime Dog's presentation. Angela White, who is married to Glen White and is the Millerton recreation director, was waiting, with an unhappy look on her face. "I spoke to
McGruff this morning, Heather," she said. "He cancelled. He said it was so hot
yesterday that he almost passed out. I thought there was a fan in his costume, but
I guess I was thinking of Smokey Bear." She said he had promised to reschedule,

but meanwhile there would be no "MCGRUFF COMES TO TELL HOW TO PRE-VENT CRIME"—at least, not until the following week.

"I think I'll just take pictures of the kids swimming," Heather said. "The only trouble is, I have a lot of pictures of cute little kids this week."

The days had a jerky rhythm. After the cancelled McGruff appearance was a stop at the town hall to get information on the Scoland Farm rezoning. It was a local tale without whimsy: an old farm, a fire that destroyed barns and silos, a son killed in a car accident, a family belt-tightening, a petition to mine gravel from dairy land. We went to the pig races at the agricultural fair, in Goshen, where the master of ceremonies announced the contestants as Roseanne Boar, Tammy Swinette, and Magnum P.I.G. Back at the office, after Heather called the medical examiner about the outcome of the autopsy of the man killed by the train, she explained the small-town rule on obituaries: "Everyone is an avid *something*. An avid gardener, an avid walker. Charlotte told me we once had someone who was an avid coupon clipper." Another rule: If you crop the Pet Parade photo so that the animal's ears poke out of the frame of the picture, the pet will be adopted more quickly. Everyone at the paper got distracted for a while, listening to reports on the scanner about an ex-convict engaged in a gun battle with a local deputy sheriff. Heather called several appliance stores to catch up on her electrical-storm story. And after that she drove to the Gun Club, where three chubby old men smoking Tiparillos were shouting a conversation—"His goddam blower went out!" and "I don't know what the hell he paid for it!" and "Well, he's tougher than whalebone!" —and firing shotguns at neon-orange clay disks. Heather chatted with them, men-tioning the fact that she wouldn't be able to come to the Gun Club clambake. The men looked sad for a moment, then resumed shooting. One of them cocked a thumb at the trap and said, "You girls shoot? Oh, no, you're reporters."

"Tell me about your gun," Heather said.

He patted it and said, "Darling, it's a 12-gauge Browning."

"Nice," Heather said. "How do you spell that? Like food brownie?"

"Exactly," the man said. "You're learning."

Near the end of my visit, Heather went to talk to a shiny-faced young man named Todd Clinton, who was on the organizing committee for Millerton Days. Todd is a local banker, a Lions Club member, the treasurer of the volunteer fire squad, a Chamber of Commerce vice-president, and the husband of the woman who owns the new seamstress shop on Main Street. He was in his office, at the Salisbury Bank & Trust Company, and he had a lot of information for Heather about Millerton Days. "We're doing snow cones and cotton candy," he said. "There will be clowns. And fifty per cent of the proceeds are going to the Eddie Collins ballfield restoration. We've hired a Mickey and Minnie—Wait, don't say that. Say, 'There will be a cute mouse couple.' We don't want to get in trouble with copyright people at Disney." Heather scribbled. Todd called his secretary to find out who was lending the freezers to store the ice for the snow cones. She told him that it was Jimmy Campbell, of Campbell & Keeler. Todd said one of the local restaurants would be donating tablecloths, but that there weren't enough tables yet for the Millerton Days clambake. Heather said, "I could put in 'Please call Todd if you have tables.'"

"Great," Todd said. "Because it's a little bit of an issue with the tables. Oh, and for the antique-tractor show you can put in that anyone interested in showing their tractor can call me."

Heather said, "Sounds like I have it all. I have just one question. Will the clowns be free?"

Todd nodded, and said, "Absolutely free."

It was all there in the Millerton *News* the next week: "O'CONNELL LEAVES FOR POST AT ARDSLEY MIDDLE SCHOOL," and "STORM CLOUDS REQUIRE PRECAUTIONS TO PROTECT HEALTH AND PROPERTY" and "MAUREEN BONDS ENDS WORK AS VILLAGE CLERK" and "PREPARATIONS PICK UP FOR MILLERTON DAYS," and a late-breaking story about a lawsuit filed against the town board of Amenia. A few stories had evaporated, and Heather had saved a few others for a later week. It turned out that the man who had squirrelled away all the Eddie Collins memorabilia died over the weekend, and the paper had been able to get the pictures for the special Eddie Collins section from his widow. His avidity for local history was noted in his obituary, which also ran that week. By then, I had left Millerton and was back in Manhattan. Heather sent me the paper, and when I had read it I called her. I could hear the hum of the newspaper office in the background. We talked for a while, and then she said she had to go, because she was expecting another busy week.

Dennis Covington

Serpents and the Spirit

Dennis Covington admits he's addicted to danger. "In 1983, I decided I wanted to go to a war, and the nearest one was in El Salvador. Journalism seemed the logical means," he says. So he borrowed a thousand dollars and, though he had never written a word for a newspaper, talked an editor into giving him his press credentials. There he found "the antidote for a conventional life": fear. Since then, he's covered disasters, both natural and man-made. His stories often appear in The New York Times.

"Serpents and the Spirit," published in the Los Angeles Times Magazine, *condenses his book about snake handlers,* Salvation on Sand Mountain. *After covering the trial of a snake handler, Covington had planned to write a piece of creative nonfiction in the third person. But something happened—maybe that addiction. "I became one of the handlers, and their stories and mine intertwined," he says. "Opening my own life to the reader, as I had opened the handlers' lives, was the greatest risk I took. I still pay for it in ways too numerous to mention. . . ." But as he also explains, "I have long been aware that writing of any sort is risky business."*

Before becoming a journalist, Covington wrote fiction, earning a Master of Fine Arts from the Iowa Writers' Workshop in 1974. Now he writes in many genres: short stories, articles and essays for magazines and newspapers, and novels, among them Lizard, *a prize-winning young adult novel that became a play. He says his writing has been influenced by some Southerners, among them Flannery O'Connor, Reynolds Price, Peter Taylor; by some short story writers, Raymond Carver and John Cheever; by some Russian realists, Gogol, Turgenev, and Chekhov; and by nonfiction. "Reading Michael Herr's* Dispatches *was a revelation," he says. "I understood then that nonfiction could transport the reader in the same way fiction did." Covington's writing about snake handlers does just that.* Salvation on Sand Mountain *was a finalist for the National Book Award in 1995.*

Currently, he is working on more books, a memoir with his wife, novelist Vicki Covington, and a work of nonfiction, enticingly titled Redneck Riviera. *He also teaches writing, all kinds, at the University of Alabama in Birmingham. There he advises his students, "Just tell the story."*

—CM

Dennis Covington, Serpents and the Spirit, *Los Angeles Times Magazine*, January 22, 1995. Excerpted from *Salvation on Sand Mountain*, Text © 1995 by Dennis Covington. Reprinted by permission of Addison-Wesley Longman, Inc.

I t's hot in here, ain't it?" Preacher Carl Porter was standing in the pulpit at the Church of Jesus with Signs Following in Scottsboro, Alabama. His audience, a congregation of about a dozen men and women in the tiny church, knew he wasn't talking about the temperature. But I thought he was.

Brother Carl had taken for his text the story of Pentecost, when the Holy Ghost swept over the apostles and they "began to speak with other tongues." He opened his Bible and read from Acts, Chapter 2, then he looked up, over glasses that had a tendency to slip to the end of his nose. "This wasn't just something that happened to the apostles," he said. He ducked to one side of the pulpit and came up bobbing. "Jesus sent the Holy Ghost for *us,*" he shouted. "I can feel it all over me right now. Woo!" He did a little hopping dance on one foot. "Woo! I just love it when it gets in my hair."

The congregation was on its feet now, hands outstretched, amen-ing and praising God. Brother Carl took out a handkerchief and wiped his forehead.

"Whew," he said, "I'm glad I'm His, aren't you?"

"Amen!" the congregation answered. "Thank God!"

"I wouldn't have no other God. No, sir. I want the real thing. And let me tell you, this thing is real."

He opened his Bible again, this time to Mark 16. "It was after they crucified Him," he said, "and the women went to the grave. You know what He said, don't you?"

"Amen!" They all knew.

"He said, 'And these signs shall follow them that believe; In my name shall they cast out devils; they shall speak with new tongues; They shall take up serpents; and if they drink any deadly thing, it shall not hurt them . . .'"

Brother Carl lay his Bible on the pulpit in triumph and took a hard look at the wooden box, finely joined, that rested on the altar. He leaned over and tapped it. The dry rattling that arose seemed to satisfy him. He did a stutter step. He shuddered. He shook. He praised and shouted and prayed. When he finally opened the box and lifted out a canebrake rattlesnake, we were all singing "Prayer Bells From Heaven."

The snake was fat and desultory, a yellowish gray. After holding it up, Brother Carl passed it to one of the faithful and took out a copperhead that had almost finished shedding its skin. In the overhead light, it flashed bronze and gold. He let the snake fall to his side and then lifted it up again. This time, he held it high above his head, draped over his forearm and stretched across the tips of his fingers. It was as though he were holding aloft a fine gold chain, some elegant piece of filigree. When the snaked moved in and out of Brother Carl's fingers, bits of shed skin fell to the floor. It appeared to be in the process of reinventing itself, forging a new self out of the old.

After a few minutes, the snake was put back into the box, and the service went on. One woman was anointed with oil, another spoke in tongues. But it was the image of the copperhead, slowly winding through Brother Carl's hands, that I couldn't shake. It was March 1992, and it was the first time I'd ever seen a snake at church.

I grew up in East Lake, an urban residential neighborhood of Birmingham, Ala. My family attended a small Methodist church there. Occasionally we'd get preachers from what we thought of as the sticks. They usually seemed a little out of place in our neighborhood, where the families of grocers and plumbers and office workers tried to secure a hold on middle-class respectability. These preachers would attempt to liven up the services by shouting till they were hoarse. Sometimes they resorted to bolder tactics. In the middle of a sermon, for instance, Brother Jack Dillard, my favorite, would suddenly be so overcome by the Spirit, he would run down to the piano and start banging away on it. He could not, in fact, play the piano, but that didn't seem to matter.

Of course, all of us teen-agers got saved in that church during Brother Dillard's tenure, some of us multiple times. The record was held by a girl named Frances Fuller, who never passed up an opportunity to rush to the altar. She occasionally had a seizure halfway there, though, and someone would have to run to the kitchen to find a spoon to put in her mouth while the choir sang "All to Jesus I Surrender."

Those days were filled with desperate innocence and with a spiritual light that I would later miss. If my experience in that church did nothing else for me, it accustomed me to strange outpourings of the Spirit and gave me a tender regard for voices crying in the wilderness. I believe it also put me in touch with a rough-cut and reckless side of myself, locked way back somewhere in my cell memory, a cultural legacy I knew nothing about at the time.

Growing up in East Lake, where people were trying so hard to escape their humble pasts, I had come of age not knowing much about my family history. As far as I was concerned, we went back only two generations, to my grandparents. It was only later that I discovered that the Covingtons had not always lived in Birmingham—that at some point, we, too, had come down from the mountains, and that those wide-eyed, perspiring preachers of my childhood were, in a way, kin to me. In retrospect, I believe that my religious education was pointing me all along toward an ultimate rendezvous with people who took up serpents.

Six months after my first visit, I was feeling comfortable among the handlers, and they had begun to call me Brother Dennis. They knew I had decided to write a book about them. They seemed to want to show me something. And I was ready to be shown.

At my regular church, urban Southern Baptist, I was beginning to get restless. I'd occasionally want to put my hands up in the air. I didn't. But sometimes I'd tap my feet during the choir's anthem or mumble an amen or two. I was pretty much obsessed with snake handling, though I had not, in fact, handled one myself.

Just before Labor Day, at an outdoor service, Brother Carl invited me to a "homecoming" in Jolo, W. Va. "It's a 10-hour drive," he said. "But you'll miss some good services if you don't go. They always have a lot of serpents in Jolo."

Brother Carl had become something like my spiritual guide by then. It had never come up between us before, but I knew what was on the tip of his tongue: Maybe I'd take up a serpent in Jolo.

The Jolo church turned out to be a small frame building perched on the edge of a ravine in the southwest corner of West Virginia. When I arrived, with photographers Melissa Springer and Jim Neel, the Friday night service was in full swing. The Jolo preacher, Bob Elkins, a marionette of a man with thick glasses and the remains of a pompadour, was flailing his arms. "People today, they want to look around and see what the other fellow's doing," he preached. "Honey, I'll tell you what, you get the other fellow in your eye, and you'll both go to hell." And he hopped back across the platform on one foot while the congregation amen'd.

Sermons at snake-handling churches are short but numerous. Nobody ever uses notes, preferring to let the Spirit move. After Brother Bob spoke, a visiting evangelist took the pulpit, and after that, Carl Porter preached. Nothing in his demeanor hinted of his peculiar power behind the pulpit. He looked like a barber, or someone's favorite uncle. Watching him make his way tentatively to the front of the church, you would never have suspected that the Spirit of God regularly moved upon him or that he handled rattlesnakes.

"This thing is good," he said, when he finally took his place at the microphone. By *thing*, he meant it all—the Bible, the serpent handling, the Holy Ghost. He held the Bible aloft. "With the word of God," he said, "you can put that devil to flight."

"Amen! Thank God!"

"It'll make him put his tail between his legs and run like a scalded dog." And he started hopping and convulsing like it was him, instead of the devil, being put to flight. "This thing is real," he shouted.

"*Amen! Thank God!*"

"There's a hedge," said Brother Carl, and he threw his arms out as though to describe its arc. "That hedge is Jesus.

"And let me tell you, if we break that hedge, we'll get serpent bit." He was pointing straight into the congregation now, crouched and red-faced. "You can leave this world, and honey, it don't take you long to do it."

"*Amen!*" The West Virginians knew how long it'd take. The year before, one of their members, Ray Johnson, had died after being bitten by a rattlesnake during a service at the church.

Carl finished it with a flourish. "We better know who our Savior is."

"*Oh, yes!*" they said. "*We do!*"

I was sweating and expectant by then, lifted on the general surge. I could tell something was about to break loose. Sister Lydia Hollins, Jolo's bird-like organist, was singing in a voice as raw and tortured as Janis Joplin's: "*Everything's gonna be all right!*" Brother Timmy McCoy, who worked in produce at Kroger's in Richlands, Va., started dancing down the aisle. Timmy was dressed in a ruffled yellow shirt, a vest, and pointy-toed shoes—the Liberace of snake handling, I thought.

Close on Timmy's heels came another couple, Ray McAllister and his wife, Gracie. Gray-haired, in a pink jersey and flower-print skirt, she seemed the least likely person in the world to pick up a rattlesnake, but in the midst of her dancing, she suddenly veered toward one of the serpent boxes on the altar. Unclasping its lid, she took out a 2½-foot canebrake rattlesnake and held it up with both hands. Then she turned a slow circle with the snake outstretched, her face transfigured. Handlers talk about receiving the Holy Ghost. But when the Holy Ghost is fully upon someone like Gracie McAllister, the expression on her face reads exactly the opposite, as though someone, or something, was being violently taken away from her.

By the time Gracie passed the snake to her husband, Ray, a half dozen more of the faithful had begun lifting snakes from the other boxes. They were shouting and praying out loud. Some were speaking in tongues. I came to the front then, banging a tambourine against my leg. Brother Carl was there, smiling at me. He held a four-foot black timber rattler, and I saw him stroke its chin.

To my left, a man named Dewey Chafin took up three rattlesnakes at the same time. One of his thumbs was still bandaged from a copperhead bite he'd received a few weeks before. A few feet away from Dewey, young Jeffrey Hagerman grasped a snake in either hand and hopped joyfully, while his wide-eyed children, one in pajamas, watched from a nearby pew. I saw Brother Charles McGlocklin hold six snakes in a row by their tails, smoothing them out as though he were straightening a rack of ties.

For 20 minutes, the action was wild and fast, and the music ground on like some wacko, amphetamine dirge. Sister Lydia's voice was like ripping cloth: *"Everything's gonna be all right."* Sure it is, I thought. The Holy Ghost seemed to have descended like a hurricane, and we were all in danger of being swept away.

But right at that moment, when it seemed the frenzy could no longer be contained, the lunatic music stopped and everything seemed to go into slow motion. We'd reached the eye of the storm. The air seemed brighter than it had been before. Soothing. Clarifying. It was as though a thin, light oil had been poured down on us all.

I'd had this feeling before, under fire, as a journalist covering the war in El Salvador. It was an adrenaline rush. I felt as if I were in an element other than air. The people around me were illuminated. Their faces were filled with light. And it was as though nothing could happen to any of us that would harm us. We seemed invulnerable, forever alive.

Then the music intruded again, slower, more stately this time, and without any other signal, the handlers started returning the snakes to their boxes. Suddenly, I was seized by the desire to testify. I seemed to have no control over my legs or my mouth. I stalked out in front of the congregation and, in what sounded to me like an unnaturally loud and guttural voice, announced that the Holy Ghost had led me to West Virginia to document these events. I was astonished at myself afterward. Appalled is not too strong a word. At the moment, though, the words not only seemed right but inevitable.

"This thing is real," I told Brother Carl after the service.

"That's right," Carl said, pounding me on the back and looking sideways into my face, inquisitively, the way a physician studies a patient's eyes to see how the pupils are responding to light.

Driving to a motel that night, Jim and Melissa and I posed all kinds of questions to one another. Among us, we had been to scores of services by now, and we had seen similar displays of snake handling, but not this close up. Why didn't more people get bitten? Jim thought there was a technique to it. Most of the time, the handlers held the serpents very lightly, right in the middle. The snakes seemed balanced, unable to strike. But tonight blew that theory. The handlers had just grabbed them any way they could. Maybe loud music disoriented the snakes? But snakes don't have ears. Surely they felt vibrations? But what about the times when there wasn't any music, when everything was still? Something extraordinary had happened, we decided, a sort of group hypnosis, group hysteria.

"Of course"–and here I paused, not because I knew how Jim and Melissa would take this, but because I, too, was surprised by my thinking it–"it could also have had something to do with the presence of the Holy Ghost."

Jim looked at me. "That's what I thought you'd say," he said.

I can tell you the exact moment I decided to take a closer look at my family history. It was New Year's Eve, 1992, at Brother Carl's home church in Kingston, Ga. My wife, Vicki, had been to a snake-handling church before, but this was the first time we brought our daughters, Ashley, then 7, and Laura, then 5. The moment occurred when the music got cranked up and the snakes started coming out of the boxes. Laura took one look at Brother Junior McCormick, dancing in front of the pulpit with two rattlesnakes draped across his shoulders, and decided to spend some time outside in our van. Ashley, though, was transfixed. "Cool," she exclaimed over the uproar. She was clapping her hands and stomping her feet. The snakes didn't faze her one bit.

Ashley has the Covington long arms and the Covington chin. The sight of her, so clearly at home in the chaos of a snake-handling service, made me think of this thing called cell memory. *Could we actually be kin to these people?*

The next day, when we got back to Birmingham, I dug out a green "family history" binder my father had left me when he died. The details were slim, especially when it came to the Covingtons, my father's paternal forebears. But on his mother's side, there was more information. I discovered that my great-great-grandfather, Benjamin Franklin Lea, had been a Confederate soldier, and that after the war, he had become a Methodist circuit rider in northeastern Alabama, on the cusp of what would soon become snake-handling country.

It was like closing in on the resolution of a mystery. I had no reason to believe that my great-great-grandfather took up serpents, but my reading in the history of American religion suggested that he might have been a precursor to those who eventually did. In 1870, about the time Benjamin Franklin Lea would have begun his ministry, Methodism was in the sway of the Holiness movement, a belief that after salvation, or "new birth," there occurred a second act of grace, the "baptism of the Holy Spirit." For John Wesley, the founder of Methodism, the result of this second baptism, whether immediate or gradual, was supposed to be moral purification. But over time, for many believers anyway, the phrase also came to mean an imbuing of power from on high, spiritual "gifts": healing, prophecy, casting out devils, speaking in tongues. Out of Holiness came Pentecostalism, and in 1910, out of the Holiness-Pentecostal belief in spiritual gifts came those who took up serpents. Whether we were blood-related or not, the handlers and the Covingtons at least shared the same spiritual ancestry.

At about the time I came to this realization, a librarian in the Southern Collection of the Birmingham Public Library handed me a clip file containing, among other pieces, an Associated Press article from 1953, datelined Florence, Ala.: "Snake Handling Brothers Fined $20 and Costs." Three brothers–Allen, Mansel and George Covington–had been arrested, jailed and fined for bringing a rattlesnake into a rural church. "We felt we were obeying the spirit of the Lord," George Covington testified.

And there was more. Two years later, Mansel Covington and his sister, Anna Marie, were bitten by rattlesnakes during a service in Savannah, Tenn. Both were under a suspended sentence for snake handling at the time. Mansel was forced into treatment; his sister died.

As it turned out, there had been seven children in this family of Covington snake handlers. I tracked down one of them, Edna, 80, who still lived in Savannah. "My brothers got into snake handling at outdoor camp meetings," she said. "They were just fooling around. They didn't keep busy enough."

When Anna Marie was bitten and died at the end of a two-week revival in 1956, Edna, a nurse, was working the night shift at the VA hospital in Louisville. She didn't see any reason to rush back to Savannah, since Anna Marie was already dead. But George insisted she leave work and drive all night to get back. George said he and his brothers were going to raise Anna Marie from the dead through prayer, and he wanted Edna to be there to check her sister's vital signs.

"There was a big full moon that night," Edna said.

I left Edna's house with that image in my head: a woman driving all night under a full moon so that she could check her dead sister's vital signs while their brothers attempted to pray her back to life.

When I told Carl Porter that I might have run across some handlers in my family tree, he seemed amused but not suprised. Brother Carl came from a family of Alabama sharecroppers. He knew even less about his ancestors than I knew about mine. Unlike me, though, Carl seemed to have an intuitive grasp of the sort of people they were, and he had accepted it as the natural order of things. I was a city boy still trying to make sense of the notes in my father's green binder. My journey with the snake handlers had become not so much a linear progression through time as a falling through levels of complacency toward some hard understanding of who I was. I did not know where or when I would arrive at my destination. All I knew for certain was that the snakes would be waiting for me there.

When the time came, I didn't stop to think about it. I just gave in. I stepped forward and took the rattlesnake Brother Carl held toward me with both hands.

Just a few minutes before, I had watched him lay the snake down–a yellow-phase timber rattlesnake–and tread barefoot on it from tail to head, as though he were walking on a tightrope. "Who knows what this snake is thinking?" Carl had shouted. "God knows. God understands the mind of this snake."

It was more than a year after I first heard Carl Porter preach in Scottsboro. In that time, he had taught me about serpent handling from the inside out. He'd encouraged me to read the New Testament straight through, something I'd never done before. I had even considered asking him to baptize me in the Tennessee River. On this day, when he walked into the Old Rock Holiness Church in Macedonia, Ala., he was carrying the biggest rattlesnake I'd ever seen. "He's never been in church before," Carl told me. Then he tapped the screen until the snake started rattling: "Got your name on him," he said, and smiled.

It's not true that you become used to the noise and confusion of a snake-handling Holiness service. On the contrary, you become enmeshed in it. It is theater at its most intricate—improvisational, spiritual jazz. The more you experience it, the more attentive you are to the shifts in the surface and the dark shoals underneath. For every outward sign, there is a spiritual equivalent. The more faith you expend, the more power is released. It's an inexhaustible, eternally renewable energy source. It's the only power some of these people have.

The longer you witness it, unless you just don't get into the spontaneous and unexpected, the more you become a part of it. I did, and that night the handlers could tell. They knew before I did what was going to happen. They saw me angling in. They made room for me in front of the deacons' bench.

Carl's eyes were saying, "You." But he was embarrassed. The snake was all he had, his eyes also seemed to say. But as low as it was, as repulsive, if I took it, I'd be possessing the sacred. Nothing was required of me except obedience. Nothing had to be given up except my own will. This was the moment.

I turned to face the congregation and lifted the rattlesnake up toward the light. It was moving like it wanted to get even higher, to climb out of that church and into the air. And it was exactly as the handlers had told me. I felt no fear. The snake seemed to be an extension of myself. And suddenly, there seemed to be nothing in the room but me and the snake. Everything else had disappeared. Carl, the congregation, all gone, all faded to white. I could not hear the ear-splitting music. The air was silent and still and filled with a strong, even light. And I realized that I, too, was fading into white. I was losing myself by degrees. The snake would be the last to go, and all I would see was the way its scales shimmered one last time in the light, and the way its head moved from side to side, searching for a way out.

I knew then why the handlers took up serpents. There is power in the act of disappearing; there is victory in the loss of self. It must be close to our conception of paradise, what it's like before you're born or after you die.

I came back in stages, first with the recognition that the shouting I had begun to hear was coming from my own mouth. Then I realized I was holding a rattlesnake, and the church rushed back with all its clamor, heat and smell. I remembered Carl and turned toward where I thought he might be. I lowered the snake to waist level. It was an enormous animal, heavy and firm. The scales on its side were as rough as calluses. I could feel its muscles rippling beneath the skin. I was aware it was not a part of me now, and that I couldn't predict what it might do. I extended it toward Carl. He took it from me, stepped to the side and handed it off again.

I took another snake in my hand. It was much smaller than the first, but angrier, and fear had started to come back to me. I couldn't seem to steer it away from my belt line. I studied it, as if seeing it for the first time, and then handed it back to one of the faithful. It curled, rattling furiously, as I walked out the side door of the church and onto the steps. Bobbie Sue Thompson, the woman who had first invited me to a snake-handling service almost a year earlier, was clutching her throat and leaning against the green shingles of the church.

"Jesus!" she said. "Jesus! Jesus!"

I thought at first that she was in terrible pain, but then I realized she wasn't. "Yes. I know," I said. "Jesus."

Endings are the most important part of stories. They grow inevitably from the stories themselves. The ending of a story only seems inevitable, though, after it's over and you're looking back, as I am now.

The ending of this story came in December 1993, when Vicki, Melissa and I attended a wedding and then a regular evening worship service at Carl Porter's home church in Kingston, Ga. For almost two years, I had been drawn by chance and inclination into a close relationship with the handlers. I had come to admire them and to respect their faith. I had taken up serpents; I had even begun to envision myself preaching out of my car with a Bible, a truckload of serpents and a megaphone. I had wondered what it would be like to hand rattlesnakes to my wife and daughters. I had imagined getting bitten and surviving. I had imagined getting bitten and not surviving. I thought about what my last words would be. It sounds funny now. It wasn't always funny at the time.

That night in Kingston, I knew I wasn't going to handle. I didn't feel the craving. Instead, as I thumbed through my Bible, I felt something similar, but oddly reversed, as though the urge was not to step off the ledge, but to step up onto it. It was a calm and secure impression of well-being that kept building, but I didn't know toward what, until Brother Carl stopped in the aisle, pushed his glasses up on the bridge of his nose, and said, "Are you gonna preach tonight?"

I don't know if I surprised Carl, but I definitely surprised myself: I shrugged and told him yes.

It's difficult for me to recall now the sequence of events or the words. I remember that the service began in customary fashion and that the snakes came out early. When Brother Carl began to preach, he walked down into the congregation, citing Scripture from memory as he descended. "You can't do both!" he shouted. "You can't walk in the flesh and walk in the Spirit."

Melissa was following him unobtrusively with her camera. She wasn't using a flash, and she was dressed in a style befitting a Holiness woman—an ankle-length black dress, uncut and unadorned hair, a blouse buttoned modestly at the neck. But there was one thing about herself that she could not disguise. Her husband and children weren't by her side. She was 150 miles from home on a Saturday night, and she was at work.

At one point, Carl looked up and came face to face with Melissa. He suddenly seemed not to know her. His customary bashfulness gave way to a humor I can only describe as sexual discomfort. It was as though her camera had caught him naked. His cheeks reddened. His jaw set. He pointed his finger in Melissa's face, and the sermon that suddenly poured out of his mouth was a diatribe about the necessity for women to stay in their place.

"It's not godly for a woman to do a man's job," he said. "To wear a man's pants. Or to cut her hair like a man does his."

Melissa kept on working, bobbing to get the best shots.

"A woman's got to stay in her place!" Carl shouted. "God made her for a help-mate to man. It wasn't intended for her to have a life of her own." I could feel

Vicki stiffen beside me. I was embarrassed, for Melissa's sake, for Vicki's, but mainly for my own. Carl had always been so gentle and encouraging. He *knew* better than this.

I thought the sermon would never end. But finally, Carl seemed to come to his senses. I wondered if he would remember everything that he had said. He stepped back toward the pulpit, then turned and came up short, as if he had just remembered an unpleasantness. "Brother Dennis," he said into the microphone. "Why don't you come up here and preach?"

I took a deep breath and glanced at Vicki. When I stepped up onto the platform, I looked once at the congregation. They were hushed and attentive, even the teen-age boys with slicked-back hair and unbuttoned shirts. I took the microphone from its stand and slung the cord out so that I'd have slack to move around.

I went to each of the brethren on the deacons' bench and shook their hands, down the line, until I came face to face with Carl. He was sitting in a folding metal chair with his hands on his knees, a man who had been generous and fatherly to me and recommended me to his congregation. I couldn't help but smile at him. What was about to happen had been ordained. I think we both knew it. I think we were both savoring that fact.

"I love to testify," I said into the microphone, "but I've never preached before. I just want you to know that I submit myself to your authority, Brother Carl. And if I step out of the Word, I want you to tell me."

The choice of text was simple—the chapter the handlers believed so deeply, they risked their lives to confirm it. "Let's look at Mark 16," I said.

"Amen!" Carl replied. He was pulling for me.

"It was after they had crucified Jesus," I said, "and some of the women who had stayed with him through it all came down to the tomb to anoint his body with spices. Am I in the Word?" I looked over to Brother Carl.

"You're in the Word," Carl said.

"Amen!" the congregation answered.

"But the stone had been rolled away from the tomb," I said, "and a man in white, an angel, was sitting there, and the angel said to the women: 'He's not here. He's risen.' Am I in the Word?"

"Amen!" Carl said. "You're in the Word."

"I'm in the Word," I repeated, and I moved along the platform like I'd seen Carl do so many times. "And who did Jesus appear to first after his Resurrection?"

"The eleven," Carl said.

I turned back to him. "No. He didn't appear first to the eleven." And I walked slowly across the platform again. "He appeared first to Mary Magdalene," I said, and I drove each word forward with my finger. "A woman out of whom he had cast seven devils."

There was no amen.

I whirled back around and faced the congregation again. "The angel had told her to tell the disciples that Jesus was risen, but she was afraid, and she didn't do it. So Jesus himself appeared to her, and when she told the disciples that he had risen, none of the men believed her."

I knew I was in the Word now. It was close to the feeling I'd had when I'd handled. "Mary Magdalane was the first person to spread the news of the risen

Christ," I shouted. "She was the first evangelist, and men didn't even believe her. So when we start talking about a woman's place, we better add that a woman's place is to preach the gospel of Jesus Christ. In Him there is no male or female, no Greek or Jew." And I spun on Carl. "Am I in the Word?"

"No," Carl said. "You're not in the Word."

"Are you telling me I'm out of the Word?"

"Yes, you're out of the Word." He smiled. It was a smile of enormous satisfaction and relief. At last we had reached the end of our story, his eyes seemed to say.

I looked back at the congregation. No help there. I'd never heard the place so quiet.

"Well, if I'm out of the Word," I said, "I'd better stop preaching." My heart was beating fast, and I could feel the blood in my cheeks. I put the microphone back in its stand and walked slowly off the platform and down the aisle.

Before we left that night, Carl smiled and bobbed at us, as he usually did. "We appreciate you and love you, Brother Dennis. You and Sister Vicki and Melissa," he said.

It was as though nothing had happened, but, of course, everything had. I knew it would never be the same with the handlers. I had found my people. But I had also discovered that I couldn't be one of them after all. Knowing where you come from is one thing, but it's suicide to stay there. A writing teacher of mine once told me to live in his house as long as I could. He didn't mean his actual house but the house of fiction he'd made. The only thing he asked was that when I left, I'd leave for good, that I'd burn the house down. That was exceptionally good advice, and I believe Carl Porter gave me that same advice that night in Kingston. I think he knew what he was doing in releasing me back to the wider world.

It's sad, in a way. I wish I could assure Brother Carl and all the others that we will still be friends. But I won't be taking up serpents anymore. I refuse to be a witness to suicide, particularly my own. I have two daughters to raise and a vocation in the world.

Driving home that night, on the highway from Kingston to Birmingham, we crossed the mountains twice: once as we entered Alabama and then again at 50 miles north of Birmingham. Those last miles into the city were lonely and dark, but gradually the suburbs and towns became increasingly familiar, until I realized that the elevated highway would take us right above East Lake, the old neighborhood where I had grown up not knowing who my people were. The traffic began to pick up. First, there were the tractor-trailer rigs, and then the vans with children asleep in the back. Soon enough, we were being led back into the city, toward home, by a river of light.

Patricia Smith

To Keep Their Memories Alive

As poet and performance artist, Patricia Smith struggles "to step inside stories and live them." As columnist for The Boston Globe, *she also tries to draw tone, rhythm, and emotion from workaday reporting: court transcripts, a pile of stats, press conference sound bites. "I always believe it's possible," she says.*

Smith's background is nontraditional: "no J-school, no internship at small but earnest newspapers, no pounding of those damnable 'rules' into a young and pliable noggin." After one year of college, she dropped out and began typing at The Chicago Daily News *part-time while pestering editors there full-time ("I can write, I can write!"). When the "sister"* Sun-Times *hired her as an entertainment writer, Smith settled in for 13 years. "Some people just aren't meant to spend their time in the classroom," she says now. "I never saw the sense in listening to other people talk about what I should have been doing."*

In "To Keep Their Memories Alive," Smith wanted readers right beside her at the Vietnam Memorial, sounding aloud Massachusetts names etched there. "Each man stood up to take his place, once his name was called," she recounts. "He was alive; he was vital." When readers happened upon names of friends or family, she knew her approach was right–and worth fighting for. Though, at 40, Smith advised colleagues to "forget about your editor's weak heart," she tended to hers. Five minutes after she filed "Memories" from home, an editor called to ask: "Can we do this?" And Smith convinced him that, yes, a newspaper could publish a "virtually verbless story without a nut graph" and still survive.

Besides defending poems, Smith often performs them, roaming from Europe to the Caribbean, Osaka to Bahia. She's been declared individual champ an unprecedented four times at the National Poetry Slam, where poets are judged on content and delivery. Derek Walcott, a Nobel Prize winner, produced Smith's one-woman show, and the Sundance Film Festival screened her poetry performance. Bop Thunderous, *a book recalling her coverage of South Africa's elections, will soon join three collections of poems.*

Poetry follows Smith to the newsroom, where she often heads "beyond first-person to the poetic middle ground." There, she advises, "your presence in the mix actually improves your story." There, she insists, you can pursue accuracy, originality, and effect in journalism as well as poetry.

–AK

Patricia Smith, To Keep Their Memories Alive, *The Boston Globe,* May 29, 1995.
Reprinted courtesy of *The Boston Globe.*

SAY THE NAMES ALOUD. Dennis Michael Higgins. Thomas MacMillan. Arthur Francis Bartlett. Raymond Roland LaPointe. Stephen Hinckley. Robert Carl Foley. Gregory Chalmers Davis. James Harold McMahon. James Kevin O'Leary. Joseph Elwin Nimiroski. Edward James Wolfendale. Richard Brian Murphy. John Andrew Barnes 3d. Jeffrey Philip Myers. Richard John Vasconcellos.

Give voice to their memories. James Francis Hubisz. Richard B. Fitzgibbon Jr. Michael Paul Minehan. Thomas James Burke. Gerald Francis Young. Thomas Richard Moore Jr. Craig Houston Waterman. Paul James Gorman. Paul Joseph Hughes. Gerald Arthur Letendre. Peter Moskos. John Richard Houlihan. Dennis John Mannion.

Our fathers, sons, brothers from Petersham, Gloucester, Norwood, Falmouth, Roxbury, Wallaston, Buzzards Bay. Paul Dennis Fleming. William Correia Medeiros. William Lawrence Bonnell. David Alfred McAfee. Stephen Francis Kostanski. Paul David Berthiaume. John Henry McCarthy. James Leonard Melvin. David Lee Owens. Neil Robert Burnham. Joseph Adelbert Merrill. Barry Lowe. Robert Paul Marsden. Lawrence Thomas Borden. Robert John McCarthy.

Pulled into the teeth of Vietnam. Anthony Guy Velardo. Dana E. Brann. Richard John Nashawaty. John Michael Nealon. Paul Thomas Looney. Peter Mary Nee. Harold Barnett Nelson. Richard Joseph Bois. Vincent Burke Lee. John Edward White. Micheal John Laderoute. Wayne Paul Newcomb. Alan Wayne Berry. Richard L. Norton. Paul George Bellino. Russell Willis Noyes. Philip Anthony O'Brien. Frank Thomas Kreseskie Jr. Dale Adams Blake.

Sing their names into the open air. Ronald Lee Bumpus. Glenn Alfred Menowsky. Richard John Borovick. Thomas Edward O'Neill Jr. Charles Dennis Bartlett. Bruce James Kennedy. James Michael Barry. John Leo Murdock. George Alfred Odiorne. Fidele Joseph Bastarache. James Francis Murray. James Clifton Offley. William F. Thompson Jr. Robert James Bergeron. James Costa Maiato Jr. John Joseph Mailloux. Michael T. Guzzetti Jr. Arthur Patrick Murphy Jr.

Sing their names into the open air. Theodore A. Thompson Jr. George Francis Barry Jr. Kenneth Richard Johnson. Vincent Antonio Mottola. Patrick Joseph Kelly Jr. Ronnie Gordon Vaughan. Thomas Edward Murray. Timothy Lawrence Vicalvi. Gerald Francis McDonald. Carl Daniel Wakefield. Walter William Morgan. Patrick Michael Lorditch. Kevin Barry Hardiman. Joseph Robert Wallen. Daniel Francis Lynch Jr.

Bring them home for the moment. Donald Alfred Wilkinson. Edward Charles McCarthy. Arthur Paul Williams. Robert William McCluskey. Laurence Oliver Woodson. Mark Michael McLaughlin. Jerry Lenwood Thompson. Michael John Medeiros. John F. Lazarovich Jr. Douglas Allen Young. Sidney Daniel Lane Jr. Norman William Grant Jr. Andre Roland Latessa. John Francis Bettencourt. Harry William Wallace.

Turn the loss to music. Say the names. Robert Griffin. Brian Richard Kelly. Jimmy Lee Thompson. Gary Richard Guest. Patrick Kevin Burke. Joseph Guilmette Jr. Christopher John Bean. William Francis Gunset. Ronald Williams. Wayne Douglas Hamel. Alfred Lacy Williams. Ralph Gerald Hamlin Jr. Francois

Josephi Builaert. John William Hanscom. Gary Joseph Webb. Robert Schrack Matern. John Daniel Harrington. Jan Krawczyk. Christopher Robert Hartley.

No room here to hold them all. Douglas Robert Mohrmann. John Joseph Hayden Jr. Dennis James Brault. Alfred L. Jasnocha Jr. Bruce William Monska. Roy John Henderson. Bruce Edwin Jones. Richard Stephen Moxley. Thomas Daniel Latanowich. John Joseph Kenney. Stephen Michael Henry. Robert Micharl Hurd. David Paul Ingersoll. Anthony Edward Kupka. Joseph Thomas Hunt. Lawrence Graham Leigh Jr.

But if we look in our hearts . . . William Francis Joyce. Kenneth Russell Joyner. Thomas Joseph Kane. William Francis McCarthy. Richard W. Hellard Jr. Gregory Patrick Kent. Paul McEachron. Richard Norman Brusco. Lawrence Frederick Beals. Peter Frank Kristof. Dudley Norman Jordan. Arthur Leroy Brown Sr. Cleaveland Floyd Bridgman. George Arthur Kyricos. George Donald Lacus Jr. Bruce Ellsworth Jason. Franklin George Hazzard. William Clive Laidlaw. Michael James Monahan. Willard J. Bouchard Jr.

. . . and they are not there . . . Walter Stephan Mooney. James Philip Hickey. John David Lawson. Thomas John Brennan. Rudolph H. Lefebvre Jr. Dennis Guy Benson. Francis John Muraco. Thomas Evans Bennett. Paul Francis McNally. Gregory William Beecy. James Brian McGarry. David Peter Bedrosian. Patrick John Muraca. William Alexis Beaubien. Daniel Wilder Kent. Robert Everett Moore.

. . . then they are truly lost.

Bill Tonelli

The Amazing Story
of the Tonelli Family in America

As a young man, Bill Tonelli sat at the corner of 15th and Moore in South Philly and earned what he calls a "Ph.D. of the pavement." His more formal education came in 1975, with a journalism degree from Temple University. Before prospering as executive editor at Philadelphia Magazine *and now articles editor at* Esquire, *Tonelli won awards at trade weeklies and struggled as a freelancer.*

Then, at 38, still phobic about driving, he rented a Buick and logged 12,000 miles en route to his first book, a much longer version of "The Amazing Story." His theme? Culture, ethnicity, family, tomato sauce. His strategy? "I put myself in comical situations and then told how I got there and how I got out."

Like New World explorers writing letters from the edge, Tonelli assumed a style of reportage so old as to be new. Taking notes by hand, he recorded everything– what he calls "the purest journalism" in an era of bits and bites. He determinedly sought every Tonelli in America and granted each one whom he met at least a paragraph. "Sure, the concept is a gimmick," he concedes, "but the writing isn't."

Such completeness is extravagant, much like Tonelli himself. He delivers a spill-it-all style that most editors, including he himself, might not tolerate. In one paragraph, he roams from Aunt Jo's kitchen kibitzing to historian Barbara Tuchman's familiar philosophizing. The result draws chuckles–even from the author. "I think I'm hilarious," he insists. An editor ever editing, he revises that: "Well, let's say this: I crack me up."

Getting humor on the page was anything but funny. Tonelli now calls the book a "ball-breaker," and here's why. To finish, he wrote after work: three hours a night, 5,000 words a week, one summer long. ("It's a grind," he admits. "But if you wait for inspiration, you'll wait your life away.") He even resisted reading magazines. ("It pollutes you.") Instead, he turned into a plodder, and rewrote. Then, he awaited feedback.

"As a writer, you take the risk that what you're writing is really bad and will be ridiculed or, worse, ignored." And that *he fought. "I don't want to be bored, and I don't want to be boring. That's the biggest sin for a writer: to be dull. What's dull?" he asks. "When I stop reading."*

–AK

Bill Tonelli, The Amazing Story of the Tonelli Family in America, *Los Angeles Times Magazine,* April 17, 1994. Excerpted from *The Amazing Story of the Tonelli Family in America,* © 1994 Bill Tonelli. Reprinted by permission of Addison-Wesley Longman, Inc.

Once upon a time, I had the luck to open a piece of junk mail that changed the world.

Not *your* world, maybe, but mine, though even I didn't know it at the time. At the time, all I knew was that I was about to become a $27.95 sucker, thanks to an irredeemably cheesy appeal that began:

Dear Friend,

As you may already know, we have been doing some work relating to people who have the same last name as you do. Finally, after months of work, my new book, "The Amazing Story of the Tonellis in America," is ready for printing, and you are in it!

We have spent a great deal of effort and thousands of dollars . . . and have located almost every Tonelli family in the United States. My new book features this valuable and extensive directory of Tonellis living in America. . . .

Due to the uniqueness of the Tonelli name and the small Tonelli population in the U.S., it is economically impossible to produce extra copies after our scheduled publishing date. This is the first edition of the book, and it is certain to be quite a rare and valuable acquisition.

I believe this is the only book of its kind in the entire world, and you will want to have your own copy. . . .

Would you fall for that? Look, *I* knew I was making an idiotic mail-order *acquisition*–it was practically a Thighmaster. And when the burgundy leatherette-bound, gold-embossed volume arrived, it was bad, but no worse than I expected–with a spurious Tonelli coat of arms (crossed goats over a bed of linguini), some very generic advice on how to hang yourself from your family tree and, the only part I cared about, the complete directory of Tonellis in America.

Amazing. A Tonelli in Texas! A Tonelli named Abner! And, to my chagrin, only *two* Dr. Tonellis in the whole frigging country. It went on and on that way, page after page–roughly 350 Tonelli households in 22 states, a thousand or so individuals, .002% of the American population, give or take. The book listed only names and addresses, but for some reason I was spellbound; reading it had the same effect as staring at a map: uncompromisingly quotidian at first but capable of sucking you into a dream state.

And, in fact, for months after, the giddy-dread sensation of reading the junk-mail book lurked in my thoughts, undigested, unabsorbed, floating to the fore at odd times. Once, while riding through New England, I flashed on the memory that a great many Tonellis were listed in Massachusetts. There in the front seat, intoxicated by velocity, a vagrant urge seized me: Wouldn't it be something to get a car and, using the junk-mail book as my guide, drive around the country to shake the hand of every Tonelli in America? I saw myself steering confidently up to the grassy borders of countless anonymous suburban tracts, leaving the engine on, hopping out, ringing the bell and extending a paw of kinship past the half-opened storm door to the astonished resident. (*"You're who? Wait–let me get the camcorder!"*) Then I'd race back to my wheels and peel out to my next visitation. Crazy! The obvious impediments to such a spree–I hated driving, plus the trip would require a luxurious amount of time and money—didn't occur to me because I *knew* I'd never actually do it.

Until, of course, I *did* it.

"C'mon, I have to hug you if you're a Tonelli," says Denise, wife of Rick Tonelli, who's not home from his auto-repair shop yet. I have just made my way down a country lane near Lithonia, Ga., and turned in at a rustic-looking mailbox bearing my last name. Funny to see it way out here, within sight of Stone Mountain.

Denise is effusive and bubbly, just the opposite of Rick, who comes home and tells me, once we're settled in the living room, "See, I'm just the opposite of you. I've *never* been interested in my family history."

"And I don't understand that," Denise says. "I'm a Heinz 57—Jewish-German is my strongest suit—but if I was Italian, I would want to know *so much*. Like his mother's father, he came over here and moved to *Mississippi*. To be a *farmer*. Trying to speak English with an *Italian-Southern accent*. I *mean!*"

Rick Tonelli's a friendly but taciturn guy, born in Connecticut. His father died at 46, when Rick was 16, which had been the last time Rick saw either Connecticut or any of his extended family there. But a few years ago, Rick was approaching 46 as his son, Craig, was about to turn 16. And Rick started to feel the similarities. So. . . .

"So we went on a trip to Connecticut to see my father's brother, my uncle," Rick says. "We call him Lolly, but his name's Alexander. Usually, we'd go to the beach for our vacation. But I really wanted to see my uncle. And it was our best vacation ever."

"We were worried that Craig might rather have gone to the beach," Denise says. "These were people Craig and I had never met. But I knew how much it meant to Rick, and I would have crawled on broken glass to make that trip."

"It seemed so funny," Rick says, "Because we had never been around any Tonellis, and we pull up to my uncle's house, and there are the cars, with plates that say 'TONEL-1' and 'TONEL-2.'"

"You have to understand," Denise says, "on that trip we heard all these things that Rick never knew, and he sat there for two days and listened to his Uncle Lolly tell stories about the old days, and Rick laughed and cried at the same time."

Rick squirms at the mention of crying.

"Yeah," he says offhandedly. "It was a good trip."

"And we were in stitches for two days," Denise says. "And I cried and Rick cried—"

"Yeah," he says, heading her off at the pass, "this uncle of mine is so cool. Anyway, we drove to their town up there, got a motel room, and then we called my uncle and said we were coming by. And when he heard about the motel, he went crazy. 'Whaddya mean, you're in a motel, we have all this room.' Now I hardly knew these people. But the second night, we stayed with them. We even slept in their room."

"Oh, God, remember?" says Denise. "The rosaries?"

"Yeah, I have a great family."

"You're lucky," Denise says.

"Yeah, I can't complain. And our son also loved it."

"Well," Denise says, "he's very proud."

Rick shrugs. "He's more interested in family and that stuff than I am."

"He's proud," Denise says.

"Well," Rick allows, "I am too."

Craig comes in from his job at a convenience store. He's a gregarious kid of the New South, baseball cap on backward, about to join the Air Force.

I ask, "Do you come across many Italian kids at school or anywhere?"

He shakes his head.

"How about Brent?" Denise says.

"Yeah," says Craig. "*He* is. He's my real good friend, too. But I just don't think of him as being *Italian*." Then he grins and turns his cap around, and on the front it says "Italy."

I get to the parking lot (Chip and Dale Section, Row 9) early and ride the monorail to the Magic Kindgom's gate, where Ed Tonelli, a Disney World janitor, and I have agreed to meet. But where is he? Wait a second. There's a three-foot-tall employee in a jumpsuit walking my way. Please, let this be Ed. Imagine, a midget Tonelli. Nope, there he goes.

I've never been to Disney World. When I called from New York to ask Ed if he'd show me around, he agreed in a second but had a request: "Bring me some provolone," he said. "I buy it down here, and it tastes like plastic."

So I'm feeling like a latter-day immigrant, standing outside the gates to the Magic Kingdom with a chunk of stinking cheese in my bag. An hour later, I'm still hanging, so I call Ed's apartment from a pay phone, and he answers. Could I *really* have failed to spot the only man in Disney World in a green "M*A*S*H" T-shirt and shades? OK, so he's on his way back, but I'm pissed, until I see this jolly little guy in oversized, impenetrable black goggles striding toward me. Gotta be Ed. I'm happier already.

"My mother brought me down here to visit for the first time about nine years ago," he tells me. We're in a theme restaurant just inside the gate, having a big breakfast: "Daisy Duck's eggs." "We got hold of one of those cheap package deals. And when I got here, the magic hit me. I got impregnated by that pixie dust. I came back to visit every year after that. Well, some years I missed, but then other years I came twice. I always knew this was my place down here."

Finally, at 37, Ed made the big leap: He applied for a job at Disney World and got one. Back home in Connecticut, he'd roamed from security-guard job to dish-washer job to janitor job. "I took sick days all the time. I had the worst attendance record ever. And here, as of now, I've got 19 months of perfect attendance. I'll never go back to Bridgeport again, not for a funeral or a wedding, not even my own. It's part of my past."

Now breakfast's out of the way, and he's ready to begin the grand tour. We head first to Splash Mountain, which is dear to Ed's heart since part of his duties involve scrubbing the big plastic logs that carry customers down the mountain. (He also cleans one men's bathroom, which he includes on my tour, and a ladies' bathroom and a baby-changing room, which he does not.)

We wait in line, then climb side by side into our bobbing log; in the darkness of the mountain's innards, I hear Ed laughing at every one of the robot animals' jokes, even though he's heard them a thousand times by now. Slowly, we're rising to the peak of the ride's big dramatic drop, but instead of gripping the rail with all his might–like *me*–Ed throws his arms up in the air and braves the final, splashy 50-foot plunge no-hands.

We travel through some kind of pirate thing, then zoom over to Epcot, and all I remember there is a ride through the history of the world as narrated by Walter Cronkite and a walk through a series of pavilions devoted to foreign countries. "Here, let's go this way," Ed says, stepping from Norway into Mexico. "I want to take you through Italy."

In a Georgian-looking building, something called "The American Adventure" is about to begin. A crew of collegiate weenies dressed in colonial and antebellum costumes starts to croon: "This is my country, land of my birth. . . ."

"Hey, Ed," I suggest after about 12 seconds, "why don't we skip this and go somewhere we can talk?"

"No, we have to stay for this," he says urgently. "This is really beneficial. I know you think it's a drag. But since we're cutting it short"–I'd already told him, three hours tops for the whole tour–"I don't want you to miss the best parts."

The show isn't as bad as I expected. It's a lot worse. It's hard to understand the point of making robot actors so lifelike that they're almost human when it's so cheap and easy to use humans in the first place. I'm squirming through a half-hour of the Ben Franklin robot and the Mark Twain robot tossing prefab homespun one-liners back and forth; if I hear the words "freedom" and "liberty" once more I might strangle poor Ed, I think. In the darkness, as the final crescendo of platitude-swapping cranks to life, I scribble in my notebook, *This is f--ing inane!*

I'm carving in the exclamation point when Ed turns to me and says, "Doesn't that make you proud to be an American?" I'm so torn–between thinking that Ed's gone a little goofy on Disney World and thinking that his quest to find a hometown he can love makes him the wisest man I know–that all I can do is nod.

Before I went on the road, I sent a four-page questionnaire to every Tonelli household in the mail-order book and then some, 450 in all. "As you'll see," I wrote in the cover letter, "I'm asking the questions you'd expect–about how you live, your jobs, your eating and social habits, and how much (if at all) you feel your Italian background in your daily life."

I got back more than 200 questionnaires, hired professionals to crunch the numbers, and here are some highlights:

Only a little more than half (53.3%) of the Tonelli Nation is of full Italian ancestry. As it turns out, I could use lots of my interviews as research for a book about German-Americans. Of respondents under 30 years of age, almost three-quarters have only one Italian parent.

Most responding Tonellis (52.3%) are the grandchildren of immigrants. And most Tonelli ancestors came from north-central Italy, above Rome.

Most (57.4%) did not marry someone of Italian ancestry. Of course, since many of them are not of full Italian ancestry themselves, their choice of mate doesn't even represent intermarriage. Sociologists say that endogamy–marriage to someone of your own group–is the most important indicator of strong ethnic identity.

Forty percent of Tonellis speak a few words of Italian, 24.1% speak none at all and 16.6% speak it fluently.

Most (72.9%) thought *The Godfather* was the best of the Godfather movies; 8.5% voted for *II,* and only 2.5% went for *III.* (Scary to note that 2.5% of Tonellis are insane.)

When Tonellis serve tomato sauce, 67.3% make it themselves, 27.6% open a jar and 4.5% do both. About 80% of Northeasterners make it themselves, compared with 42.1% of Westerners. And 75.5% of Tonellis of Italian-only ancestry go homemade, compared with 58.1% of those of mixed ancestry.

Because I don't really trust myself around numbers, I commissioned Dr. Richard D. Alba, a professor of sociology at the State University of New York, Albany, and a respected authority on ethnicity, to analyze the Tonelli Nation census. In the "near future," he wrote, the fourth generation will begin to define the majority of Tonellis in America, "an important transition, because the fourth generation has little or no contact with the immigrants and thus is missing a set of experiences that can help to sustain a strong ethnic identity."

Even now, according to Dr. Alba, "the ethnic dynamics visible in the demographic data for the Tonellis lend themselves to a 'soft' form of ethnicity. . . . Signs of ethnicity tend to be muted and to be kinds that, like food, can be appreciated by, or at least do not give offense to, those who do not share one's background."

In other words, we Tonellis have never been less Italian than we are right now, and we'll never be even *this* Italian ever again. The "us" and "them" mentality goes, but with it goes the idea that anything more meaningful than macaroni holds us together. And that's true not just for Tonellis but for all Italian-Americans, and I'm sure for every other kind of hyphenated American, too. You're going to miss us Tonellis when we're gone. You're going to wish you had been nicer to us when you had the chance.

I'm in a living room in Escondido, just outside San Diego, listening to a burly, thick-fingered exterminator play a delicate, lyrical, sentimental melody on his piano. He composed it, and his wife and I applaud when he finishes. Then Beatrice and Mike Tonelli and I sit at the kitchen table.

Beatrice: I came out here from the Bronx on vacation when I was 18, with my mom. We took the train from New York, came to San Diego and stayed at Mike's parents' house–my aunt and uncle's. And Mike and I met and fell in love, and I went back home and told my father I was moving to California, and we got married. Married for 18 years.

Me: Was anybody upset about it?

Beatrice: Oh, we had a lot of . . . *your* parents more than mine.

Mike: My dad, he was all against it. My parents didn't want us in their house *at all.*

Me: How exactly did it happen?

Mike: When they came out to visit, my dad told me to show my cousin around town. So I did. And we fell in love.

Me: But didn't it occur to you that there would be trouble?

Mike: Sure it did.

Beatrice: Yeah, it did, but it didn't stop us.

Me: How did your father find out?

Mike: He caught me writing her a letter. He grabbed it and read it, and, oh boy, was he mad. Sheee. Plus, she started crying at the train when they left. So my dad and mother and her mother kinda went, "Well, what's goin' on *here*?" My dad told me, "You can't marry your *sister.*" I said, "She's not my sister," but he said, "She might as well be, she's my brother's daughter." Then my dad said, "Oh, she's not gonna come back and marry you anyway. You have nothing to offer." And I was so tired of hearing that from him– "She's got a good education and good job out there, she's not coming"–so I said, "What do you mean, Dad? What about this? [Re-enacting the nonverbal part of their exchange, Mike looks down at his lap, so I do, too, and then we're both staring at his crotch, which is pumping up and down on the chair.] Oooh, he almost sent me flying. *"You talkin' about my brother's daughter?!"* I said, "Yeah, I got plenty to offer, Dad." He was really pissed.

Me: How did you break the news?

Beatrice: On the train home, I told my mother that we had fallen in love and I wanted to come back to California.

Me: Was she mad?

Beatrice: I'll tell you, my mom was upset when I was going out with this Puerto Rican guy. She grabbed a kitchen knife and told him, "Your name is on this. If I see you with my daughter again, this is going right through you." So she wasn't that radical about Mike.

Mike: She said she wouldn't have married me if the priest back there hadn't OK'd it.

Beatrice: Well, I had to be married in church.

Mike: But I didn't think the priest would OK it.

Beatrice: Fooled you, ha-ha.

Mike: And a year later, my father said it was the best thing that ever happened to me. And at the time they had told me they'd rather see me marry a black person.

Mike and Bea saw a geneticist before they married, and he gave them the OK to have kids. They have two daughters, Ginette, who's 16, and Sabrina, 12.

As I'm packing to go, Mike says, "Yeah, Italian is the only nationality there is. And if there were more of us, this would be a better country. I only wish I was pure Italian. My mother's German. I don't even *tell* people I'm half German."

Then, as I'm walking out the door, Beatrice says, "Oh wait–did I tell you both my dad's parents were Tonellis?"

"Mine too!" says Mike.

The woman at the Frontier Airlines office in Fairbanks, Alaska, suggests I get to the airport an hour early, even though the departure area is an office the size of a restroom and the plane is parked right outside the door. They just want you to get in a full hour of dread before you take off. A minute before we board, a Pizza Hut guy rushes into the office. "Hey, you barely made it," says a man who takes delivery of one large pizza. I assume he's going to eat it on the flight, but instead he belts it into the seat next to his. I knew Allakaket was *out there*, but until I witnessed how you get a pizza delivered, I had no idea.

I hate these little airplanes. I hate any plane where you can sit in the tail and still read the dials on the dashboard. As soon as we're high, I open my eyes and see black land, white snow, frozen lakes and rivers and miles of jagged mountaintops—no roads, no buildings, nothing human. After 15 minutes, we run out of land, too, and the rest of the hour it's solid white outside. We start our descent, and I can't see anything down there. We hit the ground, and I *still* can't see anything. Wait—there's a barn. I few log cabins almost totally buried in snow. Some people on snowmobiles.

"Who are you waiting for?" an Indian woman asks me.

"Stanford Tonelli," I say.

"Stan's out running his dogs. I'm Annie. Come with me." At this point I would normally think to ask, *"Annie who?"* but instead I grab my bags, climb behind her on the snowmobile saddle, and off we zoom over a path of solid, bumpy snow that winds past the scattering of log cabins that makes up the village of Allakaket, population about 200 Athabascan Indians. I'd have a million impressions to report now were it not that all my concentration is in my knees and ankles, which are squeezing dents into the snowmobile, trying to keep me from bouncing off into the void.

A few months back, Stan had been the first Tonelli to call in response to the questionnaire. He had some weird news to report: "I'm not really a Tonelli. I don't know if my father was Mexican or Italian or whatever, but he fought in the South Pacific during World War II and got malaria. Now, this is more or less how I understand the story from my second cousin. Anyway, he almost died from the malaria, except an Italian corpsman named Tonelli saved his life. And my father was so grateful he changed his name to Tonelli. I don't know if it's true, but that's what they tell me."

Stanford said he was born in Northern California in 1957, and his dad took off when Stan was small, leaving Stan's mother to raise their three sons alone. I asked how he ended up in Alaska, and he said, "I had trouble dealing with people. No. I didn't have trouble. I just don't *like* people. I like peace and quiet."

Despite the shadowy circumstances by which he acquired the Tonelli name, he welcomes my visit.

My corner of Stan and Annie's one-room cabin is homey and A-OK, near the wood stove, with a curtain around the bed, a reading lamp and several small toys (the bed belongs to 8-year-old Justin). The whole cabin is maybe 20 by 20 and also holds Stan and Annie's big bed, a sofa, a kitchen table, some chairs, cabinets, the stove, two TVs, a Nintendo and VCR and a deep freeze.

Once I'm settled in, Annie and I go outside to wait for Stan. On their little piece of Alaska, there's an outhouse, a shed and an oil drum, around which, half buried by snow, I can make out a few disconnected animal heads, forelegs and tails, and some scraps of gray fur—spare parts. Improbably, there's also a street light.

Suddenly the profound Alaska silence is broken by weird noises, something between barking and screaming bloody murder. I look down the path, away from the village, and see these dogs, smaller and scrappier than I pictured, dragging a sleigh through the snow, and standing heroically at the helm is Stanford: Tonelli of the North.

Stan and I say our hellos and how-was-the-trips and all that. He's a lean, quiet, good-looking guy, mid-30s. He asks if I saw any caribou herds as I flew in, and I say no, but the truth is that it never occurred to me to look.

After Justin comes home and we polish off a meatloaf, Stan's friend and neighbor Philip drops by, and we men crack a half-gallon of Canadian Mist. The whole idea of my being here amuses Philip, I can tell. When the subject turns to New York, he asks, "Hey, Bill, tell me—did you ever sit in on a Mafia meeting?"

Justin wants to go to the high school basketball game tonight, so the three of us pile on Stan's snowmobile and we're off. Stan deposits us at the gym, and Justin immediately disappears with his school buddies, leaving me alone on the bleachers, the object, I suddenly realize, of sizable curiosity. One little kid, maybe 4 years old, stops dead in her tracks, astonished, when she sees me, then she cracks up laughing. Another one races by, touches my hand and keeps running. It's like I'm suddenly on the wrong end of a National Geographic TV special.

The basketball game ends, and Justin and I go outside to wait for Stan. The darkness deepens; my thoughts, naturally, run to calamity: What if Stan forgot us? In my mind, it's *McCabe and Mrs. Miller* time; one false step, and you're permafrost. So I pull Justin out of his group of buddies and tell him we're going to a house maybe 50 yards away to call Stanford at home. Like any kid, he's willing to go along obediently with whatever foolishness an adult suggests. We walk maybe 20 steps into the night when I look down at him, and it hits me like an electric shock: *I grabbed the wrong kid.*

Well, look, I've known him for all of three hours at this point. Plus he's bundled up in a hat that covers half his face. Plus, to my eyes these Athabascans look more alike than not. I see it all in a flash: Millions of miles from home and reliable legal counsel, in the middle of the most alien environment I've ever known, I have just kidnaped a small boy.

OK, as it turns out I did *not* grab the wrong kid. We make it to a telephone, call Stan, and he comes to fetch us straightaway. As we pull up to the cabin, I notice that the street lamp is broken.

"Hey, Stan," I say, "your light's out."

"I know," he says nonchalantly as he dismounts. "I shot it."

What next? When I settle down to sleep, from outside the curtain around my bed Stan says, "Uh, Bill, if you hear any noise during the night and it's a bear, the gun's over here." Got it, Stan. If I hear a bear, I'll shoot myself.

The next day, Stan remembers he has something he wanted to show me. His mother recently sent him photocopies of long, handwritten letters from a woman in San Diego, the histories of three Mexican-American sisters born between 1878 and 1900. One of them, Adelaide Rodriguez, took as her third husband a man named Arthur R. Ybarra. Their son Jerome was Stan's father. In the course of the letters, without explanation, Jerome's last name changes from Ybarra to Tonelli. It's a weird document, but it's all Stan has to explain who his mysterious father was, who Stan himself might be. I think that the main reason Stan invited me up here was that he thought I might have some clues to share. But I don't, except for a few pages I tore out of the San Diego phone book, the pages that list column after column of Ybarras. So I hand them over.

A little later, we decide to ride up to Graveyard Lake, to see about getting some ducks or maybe a moose. As we walk past his dogs, Stan points to one and says, "I'm gonna have to kill him."

"Gee, how come?" I ask.

"He isn't working hard enough pulling the sled. He isn't giving 100%. He's not worth the food I'm feeding him."

"Why doesn't he work harder?" I ask.

"I don't know," Stan replies. "Bloodlines."

On the corridor wall of my cheap Des Moines motel there's a faded "Lounge" sign pointing down a shadowy flight of stairs. At the bottom of the steps, I find a door, and behind it there's a room with a jukebox and two pool tables; it's like somebody turned his grandparents' basement into a cocktail lounge. There's a gorgeous, sassy Ethiopian bartender, obviously on very familiar terms with her cast of regulars: Gary, the 50-ish wise guy; Chester, the mild and laconic, prematurely bald guy; Donny, the spry, silver-haired grandmother in peppy sportswear.

I'm the silent, unknown presence at the end of the bar until two more women come in, and one of them, feeling frisky, puts some Patsy Cline on the box and asks me to dance. "Sure," I say, and before long somebody asks why I'm in town, and I tell the truth. It strikes everybody funny for about a minute. Then a noisy group enters, including a woman named Janet, whom everyone seems to know.

Chester leans over from the next stool and tells me, "That's Janet Tonelli."

My dance partner extends an invitation to see Mt. Rushmore.

"You should go," Chester says. "You can see *George* Tonelli."

Now somebody is at the jukebox, and "All Shook Up" comes on.

"Elvis Tonelli," Chester announces.

It's still dark when I leave Des Moines for Anamosa, Iowa, where Bob Tonelli pays the price for his crime. I have already met Bob's half-sister Carmella, in a federal prison camp in Texas (cocaine); his cousin Mike, who also did time at Anamosa (armed robbery), and another cousin, Albert, Mike's brother, who went to prison for willful injury. When I introduced myself to Bob's elderly father, Charlie, I told him I was going to see his son in prison. "Yeah, get him out of there," the old man told me. "He's a good boy."

To get to the narrow, airless conference room where Bob will tell his tale, I pass through two grim sets of barred thresholds. "As I remember it, it happened at approximately 11:15, 11:30 at night," Bob begins. "I laid him down on the floor to change his diaper, and I went into the other room to get the diaper and baby wipes.

"When I came back, he had pooped on the floor, so I cleaned him up and cleaned the poop. Then I tossed him onto the–the papers say I hurled him, that was his mother's mother's word. I wouldn't so much say that I hurled him, but I tossed him on the couch. By no means did I mean for this to happen. I can't really tell you how much force was involved, but he hit an ashtray. He hit his head on an ashtray. Then he got up, and he walked around the room once, and then he fell down and went into convulsions.

"And I called 911. Then I called his mother, who was my girlfriend at the time. And I tried to get him to breathe. He was breathing, but he was breathing hard, and he, uh. . . . I was trying to give him CPR. His mother got there, and she called the ambulance. She had to look up the number in the phone book.

"And then, the ambulance got there and took him to the hospital. She called me from the hospital and said, 'Did he hit his head?' And I said, 'Yeah.' Then she said, 'Well, he's in a coma.' He went on for a day and a half. She called and said, 'He moves, he opens his eyes when I call his name.'

"But then the day after that, the sheriff showed up at my house, and he said the baby had just died.

"If I could change things, I'd rather I was dead than that little child. I wake up at night . . . sweating. . . . I guess you'd have to go through it yourself. But it's bad thoughts, bad dreams. Bad dreams. Oh . . . I don't know. . . ."

Silence.

Since I first learned of Bob, I'd been looking forward, in a blackish way, to meeting the most notorious Tonelli in the world. Now here I am, having just encouraged a soft-voiced, visibly shaken 22-year-old to describe the bleakest moment any living being can imagine. I feel sick, and we still have a few minutes left.

I ask, "What would you be doing if none of this had happened?"

"I'd probably be in my own apartment," he says, "close enough to my dad's house so I could go over there to visit him."

Heading east from Anamosa, only one thing occurs to me: Tough times make tight families.

Do I or do I not pay a visit to Alexander Tonelli in Connecticut? On the one hand, by now I've had enough Tonellis. I want it to be over. On the other hand, Alexander is the uncle to whom Rick Tonelli of Lithonia, Ga., paid that emotionally charged visit a few years back.

I pull off the highway and call, and he's home and sounding hesitant. But if I hurry. . . . I zoom over and into the driveway, which is just as Rick described it, two cars sticking out of the garage, "TONEL-1" and "TONEL-2."

"Yeah, Rick called me on the phone and said they were going to take a trip, and I said, 'Well, come on up,'" Alexander, Uncle Lolly, says. He's 78, a retired gun-stock maker, sitting in his dining room. "And he was tickled pink when he got here. I hadn't talked to him or seen him for 30 years, since his father died. In fact, he had to say his name twice on the phone; it caught me off-balance. I wasn't expecting him. And then he came over, and we reminisced, and he met all my kids and their families—I've got seven grandchildren—and he met so many people in such a little bit of time. We took him to see the house where he used to live. He was only about 6 years old when they moved. His father, my brother, moved away right after our mother died. He said, 'Well, I don't have anybody here. . . .'"

I ask him, "What do you think the trip meant to Rick?"

"That's a good question. But there really isn't much I can tell you," he says with a shrug. "It was a pretty short stay."

Anyway, that's how it went for two solid months on the road with the Tonelli Nation.

I know it was just a trip in a car, meeting ordinary people, but it feels like a miracle happened to me. I met more Tonellis than I ever thought I'd meet, in more places than I ever thought I'd see. To be honest, all that traveling unhinged me, like an out-of-body experience, but I learned a lot, too.

OK, let's get it over with. Here's what I learned:

There really are Tonellis all over America.

Which, granted, I already had cause to believe, but now I *know*.

They really were happy to see me.

I know, partly because it's flattering to be the object of someone's curiosity for *any* reason. But my visits touched something genuine in these people, I could tell, some desire to connect with history or blood or experience. Their imaginations, like mine, were stirred by the vast mystery that there could be so many of us, in so many different forms.

But they really don't think much about their ancestry.

The tie has been severed; no aspect of their lives speaks to their sense of themselves as creatures of history. They (or somebody before them) made a crucial transfer. They stepped out of the story of their blood and into that of their country. They're *Americans,* and that's why their ancestors came here in the first place, I guess. Those brave old greaseballs in the great beyond should be happy; they wouldn't be able to recognize or even speak to their own flesh and blood.

The thought that comes to mind is that histories end in America–that for America to succeed, ethnic identity has to go out the window. This country isn't dedicated to blood or even to shared memories; it's dedicated to a proposition. The bonds of family and kinship, which have proved their savage power since before history *started*, have to be dissolved for this country to succeed.

So, do you see how America happened? It's like algebra:

Ethnicity equals history.

History equals memory.

America equals amnesia.

And that's what's amazing about the story of the Tonelli family in America: For the good of mankind, we had to try to obliterate centuries' worth of memory in just two or three generations. And we did it. We forgot so well, we don't even remember forgetting. Now we're fit to live nowhere but here.

That's probably what's amazing about *your* family, too. (Go ahead, say it–*Ich bin ein Tonelli!*)

So, that's all of it, my only true story. I drove 12,000 miles in two months without killing anybody! As I met Tonellis, I felt as though I could claim them, and as I claimed Tonellis, I claimed America, too. Everything finally all came together. It really was a hell of a trip.

Lisa Grunwald

Betrayed: A Story of Two Wives and Many Lives

When Lisa Grunwald was falsely fingered as Anonymous, author of the trendy political novel, Primary Colors, *she got a rush from her 15 minutes of fame. "I was up, I was hot, I was down, I was out," she wrote. Then, valuing writing over writers, she composed an elegant antimetabole: "I would rather have someone know a book I'd written and forget my name than know my name and forget the book."*

Grunwald has been writing for magazines since 1981. She has profiled writers and actors, reviewed fashion shows and best-sellers, written stories about war and obesity and high school, but not in the first person. "I normally don't think much of a writer inserting herself into a piece–it's an easy way out and often irrelevant," she says. "Why do we need to know how the reporter feels?" When Grunwald drew the adultery assignment for Esquire's *issue on the American wife, however, her rules ran aground.*

Here she was, a newly married 29-year-old, waiting for the phone so she could listen to a female voice tell her about the great trip of adultery versus the boring trap of marriage. Creepy. Here was Anonymous (there's that word again), perhaps inventing her hot tales, perhaps tricking Grunwald into perpetrating a fraud. When Susan vaporized, Grunwald started over in the first person and on deadline. She confessed to being fooled but also asked some heavy questions, exploding the simple Q and A assumptions of journalism, revealing a narrative sensibility as sophisticated and self-conscious as a novelist's.

And a novelist she is, having written three so far: Summer, The Theory of Everything, *and* New Year's Eve. *Now she's reading correspondence by the pound for a project with her husband, Stephen J. Adler–a history of 20th-century America told through letters. Some are by ordinary folks, some by her favorite writers– Fitzgerald and Faulkner and E. B. White. Tom Wolfe, Ron Rosenbaum, Anne Tyler, Philip Roth, and Robert Caro also keep her buying books.*

Grunwald appreciates her education. At a girls school in Manhattan, she says, she gained "a great, lasting love of learning as well as tools for studying and writing." Then at Harvard she learned "a great, but not-lasting love of partying." Since the party ended, she's worked at Avenue *magazine, as writer and editor at* Esquire, *and now as contributing editor at* Life.

Though it's risky, she signs all of her stories.

–CM

I sat down. I was there first. I had the aisle seat, and I was doing some reading for work, and I glanced up, and he was coming to the seat, and I thought, *Hmmm.* He sat down and nodded hello, and I just nodded and went back to reading, but I guess I immediately became aware that he was attractive. He was my kind of man. He was a man of substance, and I don't necessarily mean material substance. But you could just look right away and know there was something there.

"Anyway, we started talking around the time the flight attendants began serving drinks. We talked very easily. I'll call him Tim. He told me he lived in L.A., and I told him that I was just going for work. He's in the business of banking, and we spent time talking about that. He's recently divorced, and I let him know right away I was married. Anyway, it was really a very easy, very pleasant conversation. There weren't awkward moments of silence. It flowed. And of course my thoughts turned into fantasy. And when it was time to fasten our seat belts, he offered to drive me to my hotel, and I accepted. And lo and behold, he had a car and a driver.

"On the way to the hotel, he said he'd like to see me again, and how did I feel about it? And I said, 'Well, I am married.' I never give anybody the impression that this is something I do. It's just not good business. So I was somewhat coy and reluctant. And I gave him the opportunity to be somewhat persuasive, and of course I told him that I wasn't sure what my schedule would be, or how much free time I was really going to have. He wanted to go and get a bite right then, and I said that was out of the question because I really had to do some work. I really did, and also it's not my style. It may sound funny—here's this person having all these affairs—but I don't jump into these things. I don't, as a rule, have one-night stands. I really do have to be interested in the guy. So we made some tentative plans for the following night, but of course I knew that I was going to keep them.

"Part of the excitement for me is being pursued, being seduced. Because I think no matter how great a marriage is, that's one of the elements that sort of fades away. Your husband doesn't really pursue you and seduce you. I mean, maybe some do. But I would think that as time goes by, it's more like, *Okay, I'll meet you at the bed in twenty minutes.* Sex becomes the thing you do before you go to sleep."

This is a story about betrayal. I didn't know it would be about betrayal when I started. When I started, I thought it would be about adultery, which is in some ways a far less complicated idea. Adultery is the product of fire, deceit, and conscious choice; betrayal is its ash. When I started, I didn't understand the unshakable nature of that relationship.

Some of my best friends are adulteresses. Last summer, inexplicably, they all started running amok. Over long-distance phone lines and melting iced coffee, I heard about neglect, indifference, temptation, sleeplessness, passion, lust, self-image, newness, first kisses, long looks, repercussions, and denouements. In other words: girl talk.

I decided that the myth of female fidelity was principally a male myth.

"Look to thy wife; observe her well." That was how Iago told Othello to think twice about Desdemona. I wanted to write an article that would update his refrain.

My friends' stories were perfect—except that they were my friends'—and so I set about trying to find a woman whose anonymity I could protect. I looked for about a month, but I found no one willing to risk it. Finally I did what millions of people have done when the hope of meeting the right person through chance or through friends dries up: I placed an ad in the personals. The ad said:

HAD AN AFFAIR?
I AM INTERVIEWING WOMEN WHO HAVE
FOR AN ARTICLE ABOUT ADULTERY.
USE A FAKE NAME IF YOU LIKE
AND CALL LISA GRUNWALD
AT ESQUIRE MAGAZINE.

The ad ran only one time, for one week. More than seventy women answered it. At a certain point, my assistant and I simply stopped counting the calls.

Most of the women were guilty, confessional, speaking in hushed tones from noisy places. They seemed to be anguished by something that they could neither understand nor control. Others were brash and bitter. The first one, in fact, was furious, all her rage and her years of invisibility hissing out at me. "I hope the bastard finds out," she said when I asked her about her husband. I could picture her sitting in hotel bars, looking for interest and revenge.

"I was a virgin when I got married," another one said, "and I just didn't want to die without having fucked someone else."

Their voices formed a strange chorus:

"I did it because I was lonely."

"I did it because I was bored."

"I did it to make myself feel more attractive."

"All my girlfriends have had affairs."

"Everyone needs attention, and I didn't get that too often."

"When the realities of marriage come into play, the fantasies come into play."

"I wore my regular clothes, but I had painted my toenails the night before. My husband said he liked how it looked. God, I felt guilty. I still do."

"It was lust. It was pure lust. It was great. I've never once regretted it."

"I didn't really look up to him, but boy, he was great in bed."

"I'm calling you from a pay phone. You're the first person I've ever talked to about this."

One woman was a lesbian. Two more were married to gay men. Several had found out their husbands were cheating. Some were married to alcoholics; one had been beaten; ten were divorced. Most of them were in their twenties or fifties. None of them sounded like my friends. They were either too gleeful or too penitent, and I thought that their ages and backgrounds would make them seem too safely distant from our readers' lives.

Susan was the twenty-first caller, and she was neither guilty nor angry. She was articulate and sophisticated. When I asked her difficult questions, she gave me simple answers. Her voice was clipped and efficient, and she chose her words deliberately.

She said she was in her mid-thirties and had gone to an Ivy League college. She worked, but would only describe her profession as doctor, lawyer, or banker. She had been married for ten years, she said, and lived with her husband and daughter on the Upper West Side of Manhattan. She told me that for the last eight years, she had had what she called serial affairs. What that meant was that she had traveled a lot on business, and several times a year she would have an out-of-town fling. Her husband knew nothing about this. There was no reason why he should, she said. She said that she had a great marriage.

She told me that she'd kept journals ever since the first affair she'd had, in Rome. Eight years of journals.

She told me her husband subscribed to *Esquire*. That was striking, too. "To be honest," she said, "when I saw the ad, I did have a fantasy of my husband reading about my exploits in a magazine. You know: He'd know, but he wouldn't know." It was clear from the way she had said it that she deeply relished the danger.

There was something else she said that made me think she was perfect for the story. "To me," she said, "what I do is the same thing that men have done for so long. If I know I'm not going to get emotionally involved, and I know that I love my husband, then what's the harm? It's not as if I fall in love with these guys. It's strictly physical. My husband doesn't know, and it's not hurting him."

This is the one, I started thinking, already wondering, as I scribbled notes, when she would talk to me again, when she would trust me, when I could meet her in person. Our readers would not dismiss her, I thought. She could have been any one of their wives.

So our game began.

"I think I might like to talk to you again," I said, as casually as possible. "Would that be all right with you?"

Susan said, "Oh, yes. Do you think you might want to put me in the article?"

I told her I didn't know yet and that we'd need to talk some more. I said I had assumed I'd need to write a composite portrait, but that if I found one woman who was really willing to give me a lot of time, one woman whose story was really interesting, I might want to make her the sole focus of the article.

"I'd have no problem giving you time."

"Great," I said. "When can I call you?"

"Oh, no. It's not good if you call me," she said. "I'll call you again tomorrow."

There aren't that many times in life when something extraordinary is handed to you, and though by anyone's standards I am a very lucky person, some bad things have happened to me—enough so that I tend to be suspicious of great good fortune. But I am at heart a reluctant skeptic, and eventually trust and hope always win out, the sense that maybe I'm going to get a break after all. I felt that way when I met my husband. I felt that way when I got my present job. I felt that way about Susan too. I'd done nothing to deserve the great luck of meeting a woman whose fantasies and secrets fit my journalistic needs so well. She probably wouldn't call back, I thought, but I knew that if she did, then I would try to make the most of it.

She didn't phone until 4:00 the next day.
  "I'm glad you called," I told her.
  "Did you think I wouldn't?"
  "I didn't know."
  She explained that she worked half days and was usually free by 4:00, but that the best time to talk would be 6:00 or 7:00, when her daughter was eating dinner and her husband was still at work.
  It is legal in New York State to record telephone conversations without asking permission. But in that brief phone call, Susan asked that I not tape her. She said she didn't want anyone but me to listen to what she was going to say. She also said that she'd never talked about her affairs to anyone.

My study at home is a shadowy room, dark and a little spooky, with only one lamp, which sits on the desk. I waited there at 7:00 on the evening of September 13, my word processor up and running with an empty file labeled SUSAN, the cursor blinking, a soda before me, a cigarette burning. I watched the phone.
  When it rang, and Susan started talking, I took notes on the computer, the phone jammed against my left shoulder, and for the next two months, as we spoke several times a week, my back always hurt a little from that posture, and my evenings belonged neither to me nor to my husband. If she said the best time to talk was 7:00, then we talked at 7:00.
  How much detail would I want, she asked as our first long interview began.
  "Everything," I said.
  "Everything?"
  "Sure."
  "Because this can get pretty graphic," she warned me.
  "Graphic is good," I told her.
  Her voice was the voice of a sixth-grade homeroom teacher. She had a beige-stockings-type of voice, a voice that said rules and neatness, politeness, control, and self-effacement. It was hard to believe that her idea of graphic wouldn't be my idea of euphemism.
  "Well, it'll be easier if you ask me questions," she said. "I'll answer everything. Anything. But it's hard to know what level of detail you're really looking for."
  She did answer everything. Anything. I turned into a confessor, a shrink, sitting in my dark office, asking sexual questions in a clinical tone. I offered quiet acknowledgments as she struggled to give precise answers, as if the things she was describing didn't concern the one part of life that in my experience had always been blissfully free of a need for precision.
  "Did you compare your lovers' bodies with your husband's?" I asked.
  "Yes, and I wrote a lot about the differences in my journal."
  "Like what?"

"I would take notes on the way different men had their orgasms—just the craziest sorts of things."

"Like what?"

"The amount of noise they made, were they grunters, were they moaners, were they silent, how different men tasted, the different things they said, how somebody curved to the left or somebody had this odd shape."

We talked for half an hour about the night of her first affair. "I remember one thing that struck me," she said. "He wasn't circumcised. And that's something I'd never seen in a person. And this stands out, when I think back."

"Did you like that?"

"It was exciting."

"Why?"

"I was doing something forbidden. He was somebody new. It was great."

He had insisted that she undress first; she had had some trouble undoing his tie. Her small recollections, her awkward details, made me imagine everything, even the things that she didn't describe.

She told me about her schedule of travel, her upper-middle-class childhood, her social life. She talked about her secrecy. "If someone tells an off-color joke in my office," she said, "they make apologies to me. They really consider me prim and proper. If they only knew."

She told me about her summer house on the Cape, her charities in New York. She was wealthy. She owned a fur coat. She had a maid and a cook.

Not until the end of our talk did I ask her how she felt about her husband, believing that the reminder of him might make her feel guilty, might risk her trust.

How can a journalist not admit that an interview is a seduction? *Tell me tell me tell me,* you think. *Tell me before you realize that you're telling me. Just tell me.* You're a teenage guy at a drive-in. You know only that you want to score, and you don't really know what you'll feel afterward.

It is a measure of the naiveté I brought to this story that I believed I was the seducer and that to ask Susan about her husband would be like asking the girl at the drive-in what her parents thought about sex.

She didn't seem to finch.

"My husband's very bright," she said. "I think he's very attractive. I find him attractive, and I think women do; most of my female friends do. He dresses well, he's well read, he has a very dry sense of humor. One of the things that I love about him is that he's the same no matter who he's with."

I asked her if she'd ever be in danger of falling in love with another man.

"There have been guys I thought I could fall in love with," she said, "but there's never been danger. I absolutely adore my husband."

I asked her if he had been faithful.

"He's never had an affair," she said. "He's not the type. Of course, well, he thinks *I'm* not the type. But I've become sort of an expert, and I'd pick up on it. I'm a caller. I call him. And the reverse isn't true. He's always been home, always where he's supposed to be. Which is kind of nice; I'd kill him if he had an affair. I guess I do feel the way men say they feel. I know there's nothing emotional when

I have an affair, and it doesn't mean I love my husband any less, and if he were to have an affair, I wouldn't know what that meant."

I asked her if he was bad in bed.

She said that their sex life was wonderful.

What emerged, even in that first week, was the sense of an adulteress utterly different from what the word conjured. She didn't seem to be looking for love, or looking for Mr. Goodbar. She wasn't the vengeful type either, it seemed: the type with the painted nails and the brittle hair, and the need coming off her along with the perfume. Nor was she thy neighbor's wife, the only one who wouldn't reach for a coverup when she climbed out of a pool. If she was like anyone I'd heard or read about, then she was probably like Madame Bovary, with the same cool deliberateness, and the same need for excitement, and the same secret contempt for men.

"I had made plans with Tim for my second night in L.A., and he picked me up at my hotel. It's interesting when you go out with a man and it's his city; he will always—well, very often—he'll go someplace where they fuss over him. Well, Tim was known at Spago, and we were properly seated, and I of course made as if I was properly impressed with the fact that he was properly greeted.

"He asked me in the course of dinner if I had ever had an affair. And of course I looked down and said no. And he said, 'I'm flattered.' I said, 'Why? We're not in bed. We're at a table at Spago. You're a very interesting man, but I love my husband very much.' And he said, 'Well, you're having dinner with me. Your husband certainly wouldn't be happy about that.' I said, 'Well, I think he'd be a little less happy if we were in bed. After all, maybe we're having dinner because I think you're a prospective client.' That brought a little furrow to his brow, and then I assured him that I had absolutely no business interest in him at all.

"He wanted to know if we could get together Tuesday night, and I told him I didn't think it was possible, but I'd probably be going back and forth over the next month, and that I wasn't opposed to seeing him again.

"He drove me back to the hotel and asked me if it would be all right if he kissed me goodnight. And I said, 'Well, that seems fairly harmless.' And so we kissed—not a wonderful wet sloppy kiss, but a sort of lips-parted sort of kiss, and I left.

"I'll definitely see him next weekend. I find myself very attracted to him. It's new, and the newness is just very exciting for me. He's in really good shape. He's slim. I imagine he's a very slow lover, and the reason I imagine that is because of the way he ate his dinner, the way he drank his wine, the way he moved—very graceful. Long legs. He's really tall. He's got very long fingers. Probably a good omen. I've always wondered: Do other women, when they're dating someone, do they worry about that? Do you?"

I had been married about a year and a half when Susan and I began our conversations. She asked me about myself and my marriage many times in the course of our talks. Sometimes I didn't answer her, and sometimes I answered her honestly, and sometimes I answered her in ways that were designed to elicit more trust and more confessions. I would tell her that no, I hadn't had an affair and didn't think I ever would, but then I'd say something like, "But of course I've only been married a year"–as if I believed that my romanticism was a passing phase and not, as is really the case, a piece of my personality as unchangeable as my fears and my curiosity about people.

I frankly cannot remember everything I said to her, because I was typing her words, not my own, and when I look at the transcripts now, I see some of *her* questions–How often do you and your husband make love? How many men have you slept with? Is your husband the best lover you've ever had? Do you like wearing fancy lingerie? Do you fantasize about other men?–and I shudder a little at the memory of believing that I was the one doing the manipulating.

At the time she asked these questions, I believed that she was looking for reassurance and, in fact, for a safe female friend. I thought that she was lonely, in the way that people who tell lies sometimes are. "It's wonderful to talk about this stuff," she said once. "You know, aside from the men I've slept with, there's really only one other person who knows. That's you."

Often she asked me, flatly, how I felt about what she was doing. Generally I told her that I didn't know what I felt, which was rarely true, or that what I felt was irrelevant, which was–and had to be–true. I told her the article I planned to write would not be a judgment of her, but a history. I believed that if there was any judgment involved, it would be a tacit indictment of men like Susan's husband, men who lacked the imagination to see what was possible.

The ground rules developed as we went along. I was not to have her phone number, and not to tape our talks. She was not to harbor second thoughts, or change her mind without warning me. "I'll never just disappear," she said once. "If I want to stop, I'll tell you."

Fairly early on, I told her that if she was going to be the sole focus of the article I then intended to write, I would have to meet her at some point, have to know her real name, her job, have to see her journals and any kind of proof she could offer that she wasn't lying to me. "Your worst nightmare is that I'd print all this without disguising your identity," I said. "My worst nightmare is that you're pulling some elaborate hoax, and when the article is published, it'll turn out that you work for some other magazine, and you'll come forward and say how easy it is to manipulate the press."

She laughed but said she understood. She said she would tell me her real name when we met. "I trust you," she said. "I'm very good about people. But I'll still want to look you in the eye before I tell you."

I tried in several different ways to push her for this meeting. She had told me once that she'd had a fling with a model she later learned had posed in an issue of *Playgirl*. She'd never seen the issue, she'd said, and when I'd asked her why she hadn't just called for a back issue, she'd said, "Right, and where would I have them send it?" So I'd gotten a copy of the magazine, and I kept saying I would give it to her when we had our meeting.

She never took the bait. She was happy I'd gotten the magazine, but she insisted that she didn't want to meet until our talks were over. "I think it'll be harder for me to talk to you once I've met you," she explained. I said that I understood, and I did. Meeting me might finally make what she was doing seem too real.

She agreed that she would try, as hard as possible, not to let the prospect of the story in *Esquire* influence her actions. When we talked of this, she had just met Tim—the man who had picked her up on the plane to L.A.—and I said, "Listen, the rule is: The experience shapes the story; the story doesn't shape the experience. If you're going to sleep with Tim, that's fine. Just don't sleep with him on my account."

As far as her anonymity went, I swore that no one would ever know her real name. We also agreed that for the purposes of our conversation, she should make no effort to disguise the truth. We said that, later, before I wrote the piece, we would sit down together and disguise what needed to be disguised.* I would have no problem, I said, distorting her profession or age or number of children or years married—even the city where she lived could be changed. The point of my piece was to tell men about an American wife who was having an affair. It was not to destroy a marriage.

She agreed that it would be too confusing for her to try to keep made-up stories straight.

"I called Tim when I got back to L.A. He was happy to hear from me. He picked me up at my hotel. I met him downstairs. There was great excitement on my part. But I had decided that I was not going to sleep with him that night for a couple of reasons. One, I had to be up really early the next morning. Two, I think I told you I love being pursued, being seduced. And I also at that point knew that there would be one more trip out to the coast within the next week to ten days and I'd probably have more time. So it gave me an opportunity to play a little hard to get.

"He took me to this very romantic restaurant in the Valley, maybe an hour out of L.A., and we had just a really lovely dinner. One of his interests is yoga, and he very slyly indicated to me that he's a master of a certain kind of yoga, and it's called tantric. I said I'd done hatha-yoga. I said, 'What's tantric?' And he said, 'Oh, well, in time you'll know.' It clearly had something to do with sexuality.

"Anyway, we finished dinner I guess at about eleven, and he stopped as we were driving back to show me a vista, and I sort of felt like a teenager parking on Mulholland Drive, and we were necking, and I assured him that I was not going to sleep with him. And of course he was confident that I was, but I, in fact, knew I wasn't. And it was very, very exciting for me. It's been a while since I've been in that situation with somebody new. He kissed pretty passionately. And I sort of put myself in the position of resisting such an overtly passionate kiss, but slowly giving in to the moment."

"Do you act like it's the first time you're having an affair?"

"In a sense it is. It's the first time I'm with him."

"But do you say, 'My God, nothing like this has ever happened to me before'?"

---

* *We never did have that conversation, but some of the identifying details in this story have nonetheless been changed.*

"Sure. Which gets him more excited, you know. I think I mentioned that for a man like that, finding a married woman is the next best thing to finding a virgin. Less risk of any kind of repercussion.

"At some point, he touched my breast and of course I pulled away. It's almost funny. Kind of playing a part."

"Do you have different roles?"

"How I act depends on the guy, depends on the situation. It's a different me. I think in this situation I'm probably more like people would expect me to be—sort of Doris Day-ish."

"Do you have any fantasies you've never told me about?" I asked my husband one night.

"About other women, you mean?" he asked.

"No. About sex in general," I said. "Anything you've been wanting to try?"

"You must have talked to Susan today."

"I don't want you to get bored," I said.

"Unbeknownst to him, my husband had the benefit of our conversation last night," Susan said to me.

"Mine did, too," I told her.

"Don't have an affair," my husband said to me another night, after I had been reading the transcripts.

"I'll never have an affair," I said, and then watched him, after he'd fallen asleep, and tried to imagine what it would take.

Susan had said that she and her husband made love three or four times a week. She said they had pet names for each other, that they didn't argue. They looked into each other's eyes a lot, she said; they touched a lot. She said that he was successful, but that he had always put the family first. She said he was bright and generous, that she had never been able to imagine being in love with anyone else.

When she talked about her husband, she was talking about my husband. It was impossible, listening to her, not to look for the telling answer, the crucial distinction that would separate him from my husband, and thus separate Susan from me. I asked questions designed to find that distinction, wanting to feel safe, as if adultery, like disease, was something that happened to you, that was visited upon you, that was beyond your control.

I asked her if she'd ever felt there was something wrong with her marriage.

"Look, obviously with somebody who has affairs, it's difficult to make an argument that there's nothing wrong with the marriage," she said. "And it's difficult for me to be at peace with myself and convince myself that there's nothing wrong. I'm sure it's going to be impossible to get that message across to you. In a perfect world, it's certainly not right. I don't think what I do is particularly moral. But the bottom line is, I've seen or known my husband's male friends who routinely have these casual flings, and other than that, they're very loving, and wonderful husbands, and good fathers. The bottom line is, I find it tremendously exciting to be with someone new. You know, that moment when we're both getting undressed for the first time—that's indescribable.

"I love my husband," she said. "I love making love with him. What I believe—maybe I'm completely off the wall—but I think that there are a lot of married people who, if you gave them a circumstance where they were sure that nothing bad would happen and they found some person in another place who was just terribly exciting to them, I think that you would be amazed at how many people would want to have the quick affair and then fly back home to their spouse. Now, if I had two hours left on this earth to make love to somebody, it would unquestionably be my husband. But it's different for me when I'm with somebody else."

The mechanics of her life were a constant revelation to me.

"I should write a book about how to have a safe affair," she joked one evening. She was right.

She said that she'd gotten a second diaphragm, so that her husband would never notice if the first one was gone when she was away.

For the same reason, she said, she never packed fancy lingerie, although wearing it with new men was one of her pleasures, part of her fantasy of herself. Instead, she would buy new panties or camisoles in other cities, and she would throw them away when she left. "So it's fifty dollars," she said. "So what?" She wouldn't leave them in her hotel room, though. Maids might find them and forward them. She would throw them out at the airport, or in a garbage can on the street.

She never used her real name.

She never said where she worked.

She never let anyone see her wallet.

She would call her husband at her usual time, no matter where she was. Sometimes, if she knew she was going to spend the night elsewhere, she would tell the front desk at her hotel not to put through her calls. If she called home from a man's apartment, she used her corporate phone card, so her number couldn't be traced, and so her husband couldn't see the bill.

There had been only one time, she said, when she'd had a close call—the one time that she'd had an affair in familiar surroundings. It had taken place on Cape Cod, she said, when her husband had been away and she had gone to their summer home alone. She had spent an afternoon with a neighbor whom she'd been seeing. They had necked on the beach, she said, then made love in the outdoor shower. They had come back to the porch, and he had put on his clothes and left.

He had been gone for what seemed like a minute, she said, when she heard a car pull up in the driveway and figured that he had forgotten something.

"Well, it's the husband," she said. "So they literally could have hit each other with their cars. That was a miracle. The awkward part about it for me now is my husband comes in and announces that he's incredibly horny. He grabs me by the hand, takes me into the bedroom, and he wants to make love. And he gets undressed. Now what do I do? This guy has just come inside me. I go into the bathroom. My husband comes in with me. I start to feel paranoid—I'm thinking,

He's not letting me out of his sight. But we get into bed, and he's kissing me and, as happens from time to time, he wants to go down on me. And I just think, *God, what am I going to do?* Because I just know that he's going to taste something, he's going to see something. On the other hand, I don't want to say no because I don't want to do anything that wouldn't be natural. And I'm thinking I should tell him.

"But he goes down on me, and I'm lying there, and I'm, God, and you know, he's not saying anything, and at one point he does pop up his head and says, 'Gee, you're really wet.' And I say, 'Well, you know, you've been away.' And I guess I realized that he didn't know, and it was okay. I was still incredibly nervous. God, I felt really bad that he's down there doing that, and some other guy's semen is there.

"At some point I just pulled him up and said, 'I want you inside me.' It's one of the only times I can ever remember faking an orgasm. But afterward, an interesting thing happened. I began to find it exciting.

"I still think about it a lot. And sometimes when I think about it, I get excited. There he was. I can't tell you how many times I've been by myself taking a bath or something and just started laughing."

I told a colleague about this.

"She's sick," he said immediately.

"She's what?"

"She's sick."

"You wouldn't say that is she were a man," I said. "You wouldn't say that if she were some guy who'd scored with two women in one day."

"Well, why is she telling you all this, then?"

"Hey, why does *anyone* talk to the press?"

"She's crazy," he said.

I believed that his reaction reflected the threatened feelings that most men would have–and that that had been the point of writing the story in the first place.

As the weeks passed, though, I couldn't help brooding about what he had said –and rereading the transcript. I kept asking Susan whether she felt contempt for her husband, and she kept saying that that wasn't it. I asked her how she could say that what she felt for her husband was love.

"Because it is!" she said. "Because I adore him!"

Again and again, I asked her what it was about the beach scene that was so exciting to her. I was hoping that she would offer an explanation that would have some emotional logic to it, something that wouldn't set her apart as monstrous or crazy.

"I'm not turned on by the fact that he could have run into my lover in the driveway. I shudder at that," she said. "The thing that turns me on when I think about it is making love to him immediately thereafter. I mean, I just find that incredibly erotic. The mingling of the two. Maybe it's a way of combining the lust I feel for a lover with making love to my husband."

"The lust carries over?" I asked.

"Oh, definitely," she said. *"Definitely."*

She told me about another lover who'd liked to talk about her husband when he made love to her. "He'd say, 'I bet he doesn't do this to you,'" she told me. "'I bet he doesn't fuck you like this.' I was definitely turned on by that. I realize that when I'm with a lover, I think a lot about my husband, and when I'm with my husband, I think a lot about the lovers."

Listening to her, I began to believe that duplicity wasn't her true turn-on. I began to believe that *doubleness* was. The difference was not just semantic. It seemed to define the way she could do what she did, want what she wanted, have what she had.

What she had and wanted were two sets of hopes, two sets of memories, two sets of dreams, feelings, and regrets.

She wasn't crazy, I thought. She was greedy. It seemed that the glorious normalness of life had never been glorious to her. She'd imported the men to give her life danger. Without it, her life would have lacked an edge.

Perhaps she was, I thought, a symbol of the hungry decade in which nothing had ever been enough, in which all that anyone wanted was *more.*

"We went to Tim's apartment outside L.A. And we started to neck and grope, as it were. And at a certain point he took my hand and put it on his crotch, and I said, 'You know, I'm not sure that this is right for me.' What I had anticipated—what I had fantasized about—was him just not taking no for an answer, and sort of eventually forcing himself on me, and me getting so excited that I'd have to 'give in.' Well, he said, 'What do you mean, why are you seeing me, why are you sitting here with me necking?' There was some great anger there for a minute. He said, 'Aren't you excited?' So I said, 'Well, sure I'm excited, but I'm also married.' And he said, 'Well, then you shouldn't be in this apartment doing what you're doing unless you want to go to bed with me.' And I sort of sat back on the couch and 'thought,' and there was this little bit of anger in him, and then he put his hand under my dress. And I sort of stopped him and then, unfortunately, he sat up and said, 'Look, I'm not a high school kid, I'm a grown man, I don't play games, I don't want to play games. I understand you completely.' He said, 'You've never had an affair, and you want me to take the responsibility of either talking you into it or forcing you into it.' And he said, 'I'm not going to do that. You're probably looking for something you don't get at home. You're probably looking for some rough sex, and I'm not going to oblige you, but I will take you back to your hotel, and I want you to think about it, and if you want to come back tomorrow and you want to sleep with me, we'll do that, and you'll have everything you want and more than you ever thought possible.'

"Well, the best-laid plans and all that stuff. Now, I couldn't say, 'I was only kidding, I was only trying to get you to force yourself on me.' So I said, 'Okay, I'll think,' and he drove me back. I went upstairs, slammed my door, and screamed."

By the time Susan told me about that evening with Tim, we had been talking to each other for more than a month, and I was getting restless. I knew I had a story, and I wanted to meet her and get on with the writing.

After five weeks, I had asked her every question I could think of, many of them more than once. She had told me about her father and mother, her years in high school and college, her favorite music, books, and movies. She had told me that she was a lawyer, and she'd told me what she said was her real first name.

She had asked me to guess what she looked like, and she'd guessed what I looked like, too. Then we'd told each other how well we'd done. We had talked about her favorite stores, her favorite designers, colors, fabrics. She had told me about being pregnant, being a mother, a wife, a friend. We had attempted a chronology of all her infidelities, and I'd heard the stories, short or long, of at least eight of them.

Finally, near the end of October, she said that we could meet sometime in the second week of November. Her husband would be out of town, she said. We could meet first in a coffee shop—she still wanted to look me in the eye, she said—and then, assuming she trusted me, we could go to her apartment and have the place to ourselves.

She wanted to know if I would want to look around there, and of course I said I would. She said she imagined that she would let me have the run of the place, look through her drawers and closets, study the photo albums and the wallpaper and the light fixture that hung over the bed. I told her that what I wanted most was to have time with her journals. She said that that would be fine, and then she told me, with great relish, about her next night with Tim.

"During the day, I worked, did my thing. He picked me up and we went back to his apartment. He opened a bottle of wine, and we were in the kitchen, and we were kissing, and he was saying that he was glad that I went home the previous night because he now knew this was what I wanted to do. He was making pasta, and I helped, and there would be these moments of kissing and touching, and he was making a big bowl of fusilli with all sorts of vegetables, something good at room temperature, he said, so we could eat it as we wanted. He guided me to the sofa, and he began to tell me about tantric yoga. He has shelves full of literature, and he is a tantric master or yogi or whatever, and he told me that one of the things that they practice is prolonged sexual excitement. And in the case of the male, the ability to maintain an erection for great periods of time without ejaculating.

"Anyway . . . he decided that he thought we should go into the bedroom and get comfortable. And he was very gentle, you know, in his touching. So we got in the middle of the bed and assumed a lotus position and he had me get on top of him. I was very curious about it, and I also thought it was sort of silly. I mean, frankly, I wanted to be on my back with my legs up. But it turned out to be really, really stimulating, and we got into this rocking rhythm, and it just went on and on. I came about three times. He didn't come. And he stopped, and he had me turn around, still sitting on top of him, and he told me that that would feel different, and it did feel different. I mean, I didn't have to be a yogi to know that.

"Anyway, we stopped, and now came the part that as I look back says that I must have been out of my mind. He asked me if I'd ever been tied up, and of course I said no. And my heart started racing, because he was in fact a stranger.

And he took out these really thick, luxurious sashes, like from heavy drapes, and he said, 'Well, why don't you let me tie you up?' and 'Nothing bad will happen to you.' He basically gave me this spiel about how it's good to give yourself completely and this is a way of doing it. And I was feeling pretty good, and so I agreed. He assured me that he had no intention of hitting me, whipping me, or anything like that. But of course there was the danger, and in fact, after I was tied up, he said that in tantric there is the principle of yin and yang. He said, 'You know, you need to have the extreme pleasure on one hand and the occasional bit of pain on the other,' and I said, 'Whoa. I'm not interested in any S-and-M scene here.' He said, 'This is not going to be any S-and-M scene. I just want you to consider the fact that you're at my disposal for a while.'

He got some feathers and he began tickling me. All over. Long, plumy kind of feathers. And that was fun, that was really wonderful. Then out of the blue he pinched one of my nipples, pretty hard, and of course I reacted, and he stopped. It was only for a second, and he said, 'That's what I mean by the yin and yang.' So I said, 'Well, how 'bout some old-fashioned sex?' And he said, 'You don't understand, you are at my disposal.' I actually at that point got a little concerned, because now he said, 'Listen, you played your little games, and now it's my turn.' Intellectually of course I said to myself, 'Well, he's got a point.' Nevertheless. Well, then he went down on me, and his tongue was now the feather. Really, really teasing. Then he sort of stopped and got on top of me, and we had pretty vigorous intercourse. And again he didn't come. And I told him, you know, 'I want you to come, part of the excitement for me is you coming.' He said, well, he'd come when he wanted to. I said, 'You mean you can only come once, is that the problem?' I thought I'd use a little child psychology. Anyway, that didn't work. I will tell you that it was a long, long time, and the guy just wasn't even breathing hard. I mean, you know, intercourse with most guys can be anywhere from a couple of minutes to fifteen minutes. I mean, this really lasted half an hour. I wanted him to stop. It got boring after a while.

"Then he went to his closet, and he came out with a minicam, and I went *crazy.* He said, 'Listen, I'm going to tape us and I'm going to give you the tape. You'll be happy you have it.' I said, 'Look, I don't want it, I don't need it, I don't care about it.' He said, 'I'm not going to keep it.' And he taped us. And he gave the tape to me. I've got it. I put it in the safe-deposit box. The whole thing was exciting, but it was frightening. He obviously knows how to take someone to the edge. I guess the bottom line is, I got more than I bargained for. I won't call him again."

"You know," Susan said, "maybe I do have an exhibitionist streak."

"Yes?" I said.

"You know, that my husband will be reading about me. That he'll know but he won't know. I mean, one of the reasons I called in the first place was the fact it was *Esquire* and my husband reads it religiously, and I imagined him reading this article. I certainly had no idea that it might be an article in which I would be contributing so much, but as it developed, it became, you know—believe me, I sit and fantasize about him lying back on the sofa and reading it, and me reading something else, or whatever. And then he pops his head up and reads me some particularly interesting paragraph. I guess in a way it's the next best thing. In a way I'm having my cake and eating it too—his knowing about it and not knowing about it.

"Don't think that the thought didn't cross my mind to let you see the tape."

"You mean the tape of you and Tim?" I asked.

"I figured in fantasy it would be great," she said, "but in reality it will never see the daylight."

"Well, that certainly would be proof," I said, laughing.

"That's one bit of proof that will be tough to get out of me. Only because of modesty. Nothing else."

"That's fine," I said.

A few days later she said, "I've thought about leaving you alone in my apartment. I've thought about leaving the tape for you. I don't know what to make of this, but I find that whole idea exciting. Maybe it's the danger factor. I have very mixed feelings about it. I toyed with the idea of leaving it in the bedroom."

I thought it was true that if I saw even five seconds of the tape, and also saw a photograph of her husband, I would be able to print her story without equivocation. "Well," I said, "you could always leave it and leave me alone for a while, and you'd never know if I looked at it or not."

She laughed. "One thing I know and one thing you know is that you'll look at it."

"How do you know?" I asked.

"Because I know I would look at it."

"It's not important," I told her.

She paused. "Knowing me as well as you've learned to know me," she finally said, "do you think I'm going to leave the tape or not?"

"I think you want to," I said, "but you don't want me to think you want to."

"That's pretty accurate," she said. "I do want to leave it. Now, this may sound silly, but I do have a certain amount of modesty, and what I'm having trouble with is you just throwing this into the VCR and you just seeing something like that. It's going to sound off-the-wall, but somehow, had I known you for a longer period of time in a different way—for instance, I have friends, and we go to the same health club, we undress in front of each other. I thought about that, and I thought I somehow wanted to break the ice. I thought about going with you to my health club, so you would sort of see me."

"It's not that big a deal," I said. "If it makes you uncomfortable, I understand."

"But do you see what I'm saying?"

"I think so," I said.

"I thought we could just meet for lunch," she continued. "I could take you shopping. We can go to Bergdorf's. You can come into the dressing room and give me your opinion. I'll be getting in and out of clothes."

"That's fine," I said, not thinking it was, but not knowing quite how to tell her so.

"All right," she said. "The tape will be out. It's going to be quite an eyeful. I just want you to be prepared."

She told me she wouldn't be able to talk to me for the rest of the week, that she was going back to L.A. that weekend.

The conversation did not sit right. For weeks I had managed to tell myself that she wasn't a crazy person, that a man in the same role would not seem nuts. But we'd clearly entered the Kinky Zone, and I had no wish to be there. It began to hit me that I had not only agreed to watch her get naked, but that I'd be going to the apartment of a woman whose true identity I didn't know, and couldn't check against a job or an address. Apart from anything else, that suddenly seemed dangerous and stupid.

She called the office at 4:00 on the following Tuesday. I told her that I'd been thinking about our last conversation, and that I didn't feel comfortable about the Bergdorf's thing. I told her it wasn't that necessary for me to see the tape. I also told her I wanted to know her name before I went to her apartment. I said, "If you don't want to tell me on the phone, that's fine. You can tell me when we have coffee, and we can go to your place the next day." The tone of her voice didn't change at all. She said that she'd call again the next day.

She didn't call on Wednesday, but I didn't think much about it. True, she had always been punctual, but I figured she felt rejected, and she would want to make me worry and want her before she called again.

On Thursday she didn't call either, and my calm was replaced by a sense of wild need.

A week passed. *Enough*, I thought. *You've punished me enough.* I placed another ad in the personals:

> DESPERATELY SEEKING "SUSAN."
> THE STORY NEEDS AN ENDING,
> ONE WAY OR ANOTHER. PLEASE CALL.

No one answered the ad.

For two weeks, I sat by the phone each day at 4:00, and sometimes when it rang I called out *Please* before I picked it up. Then I decided to find her.

She had let her husband's first name slip out at one point, and she'd said, many times, that he subscribed to *Esquire*. I called the subscription department and asked for a printout of all subscribers who lived in the three zip codes that covered the neighborhood where she'd said they lived.

The subscriber labels arrived a week later. I shut the door to read through them so no one would walk in and see the name I was circling. Only four men had his name or first initial. One of them had an unlisted phone number. The other three didn't check out.

She had told me that she was a lawyer, and she had told me the kind of lawyer she was, and that she worked downtown. Martindale-Hubbell is a multivolume listing of virtually every legal partner and associate practicing in America. For a week, I spent my evenings pouring over the three-thousand-page volume that includes New York City. I read through column after column of names in tiny type, the thin, Bible-like pages fluttering as I turned them. I looked for anyone with the first name she'd told me was her real name: There were about a thousand. Then I looked for the right age: There were about fifty. An Ivy League school: There were three. A downtown office: There were none.

Weeks passed. In January, Alan Abel, a self-described media hoaxter, revealed that he had put a woman up to claiming she'd won the New York lottery. His point, he explained, was to show how easy it was to fool the press. I decided that Susan had done the same thing. Then I reread the transcripts again, and I was drawn back into believing her, and believing in our relationship. *I know it was real,* I thought. *I didn't make all this up,* I thought.

Finally, I called *Playgirl* magazine, and I asked how to get in touch with the model Susan said she had slept with. Two days later the model himself called back. I thanked him profusely. I told him my problem. He was thoughtful, un-ruffled, perfectly clear. He said he'd quit the pickup scene six or seven years ago. He said in any case he couldn't remember ever dating a woman from New York. I said he might not have met her in New York; that it could have been California, Florida, anywhere. "No," he said, seemingly neither suprised nor intrigued by the prospect of being included in some woman's fantasy life, "that just doesn't sound like anything I've done."

The last thing I did was read through four weeks of *New York Times* obits. There was no one remotely like her.

I tried to be philosophical. I tried to think that just because she'd obviously lied about some details, it didn't mean that she'd lied about everything. But I was stung even by the little lies, and that, I realized, was just the point. I understood that if she could have lied about the little things, she could have lied about the big things. The relationship that we'd had on the phone hadn't left any room for lies at all.

How could she have made all this up? I looked for inconsistencies. In fifty pages of single-spaced transcript, she'd only made one mistake: She had used two different pseudonyms to describe one particular lover. Big deal. I write fiction. When all this happened, I was finishing a novel I'd been working on for four years, and I couldn't have told you, if you'd paid me, what my characters were wearing from one scene to another, or what they'd said in bed on page 15 versus page 150.

The sting became an ache. The ache was made up of mystery, self-loathing, embarrassment, hatred, sanctimony, disbelief, and anger. The ache is the ache of betrayal.

I am left with her voice. I would know her voice in any crowd, on any day, in any country. I still listen for it in restaurants, on street corners, in clothing stores. Even after all the fruitless checking, the seeming contradictions, and the appar-ent lies, I still cannot believe that what she told me wasn't true. I would still find it more plausible to learn that she'd been hit by a bus than that she'd made the whole thing up.

If this was a hoax or practical joke, then it was far beyond any definition of humor that I have ever heard. If this was invention, then it was pathology. But if it was principally true—if she is out there, and real, and reading this—then she has won, and she knows it. She has gotten away with having both her fantasy and her secrecy. She has given nothing up. If she is out there, then she will sit in her living room some evening, watching and waiting while her husband reads this article. And just as she planned it all along, she will allow herself an inward grin at the thought that he knows but he doesn't know, and the thought that I know but I don't know.

Tim Rogers

Gen X, Lies, and Videotape

*Humor columnist Tim Rogers is provocative, in print and in person. Part is atti-
tude. As* The Met's *major general editor, he keeps his tongue firmly in cheek about
the Dallas alternative-alternative weekly ("where printing swear words equals
good journalism").*

*Rogers regularly tackles topics most columnists won't: masturbation, overrated
cybersmut, dinner in a topless bar—all in all, a syndicator's nightmare. Indeed,
with pay so low, he often resolves to write only for himself. ("We're real cheesy. We
write what interests us. We hope that a couple of other people are interested too.")
But part is affectation. ("I'm too deep to make any sense.") So he applauds Strunk
& White and* The Wall Street Journal *as he rails, really rails, against TV, sloppy
'zines, even ("clueless") compatriots.*

*Rogers works as frenetically as he speaks. He writes some longer pieces, such as
"Gen X, Lies, and Videotape," unconventionally fast, relying on very few traditional interviews. He struggles for focus. ("I suddenly discover that my fingernails
need to be cut, but even when I'm clipping my nails, I'm working.") Yet he works
without an outline. ("Maybe that's a lie. You might want to know where you're
going even if you don't know exactly which roads you'll take.")*

*At 24, as assistant editor for a trade magazine, Rogers began "Gen X" on
assignment for his alma mater, the University of Notre Dame. After fuming
through three weeks of research, Rogers flooded his headphones with Chopin
sonatas, wrote overnight, and e-mailed at dawn. He waited, waited, waited as
doubts set in. Then the editors, his former professors, killed it—a first for Rogers.
Why? ("Not enough heft.") Undiplomatic to quote editor e-mail? ("Kind of cocky.")
Undaunted, Rogers took the story, added a twist, and pitched it to* The Met. *On
publication, he sent the still-anonymous editor at Notre Dame five copies. ("Basically, kiss my ass.")*

*Rogers is not always so irreverent. He recalls one course en route to graduation
in 1992 where he learned that every word counts. His professor failed any paper
that relied on "to be" verbs. ("Silly, stupid. . . . It worked.") So Rogers still believes
writers can learn from every prof, every class, every story. ("That's sexy.")*

—AK

I am not going to tell you anything you haven't heard 100 times already. It's
too late for that. The entire electromagnetic spectrum has been flooded
with it. Electrons everywhere are vibrating this very instant, buzzing anx-

---

Tim Rogers, Gen X, Lies, and Videotape, *The Met*, November 23–December 1, 1994.
Reprinted courtesy of the author, *The* (Dallas) *Met's* major general editor.

iously with more of the same. Just click on the radio. Turn on the television. Boot up your computer. Thumb through a newspaper. Open a magazine. You'll see.

On August 12, a co-worker appeared at my cubicle with an urgent question: "When were you born?" she asked.

I knew what was going to come next. Up in Saugerties, New York, they were putting on a big show.

"May 5, 1970," I said. "Why?"

"You weren't even born when they had the first Woodstock!"

"You know," I told her, "I missed the 40 days and nights in the desert, too."

A polling posse was formed, and after a few minutes of research, they discovered I was the only person in an office of 30 people whose gametes had yet to meet by 1969. Co-workers gathered at my cubicle and gawked.

It turned out none of them had been there, either, but they *could* have been. One person actually hit some of the traffic that was crawling toward the gig. Another had a chance to go, had a friend who had tickets, but she turned down the chance because she heard it was going to rain that weekend. She didn't want to get wet. But none of them was actually there.

At least not in person. While one inconvenience or another kept them from attending, their memories somehow made it. For the group of boomers I work with, Woodstock was a defining, unifying moment. They all seem to think they ran naked through Max's farm. They all act as if they rolled in the mud and took a free hit of brown acid.

Scattered before you are newspaper clippings, Xerox copies, miniature audio-cassette tapes, magazines, books, and printouts of downloaded articles. Here and there you have underlined sections with a blue ballpoint pen. There is coffee, too. With milk and sugar. And what used to be a plate of cheese fries with ranch dressing and jalapeños. *One Step Ahead of the Spider* by MC 900 Ft. Jesus spins on the CD player. If you smoked, there'd be an ashtray filled with Camel butts, but you don't smoke.

This is what happens when you one day find E-mail waiting for you from an editor at a magazine. "Here's the story idea," said the letter, "something I know little about: the twentysomething generation . . . Generation X. Who are these people? What are their problems, concerns, hopes, dilemmas? What sets them apart from other generations?

"I assume you'll be dealing with jobs and family matters and societal trends. I guess there are books on the topic (*Generation X*) and movies (*Reality Bites*). From what I gather, you're part of all this—as are an awful lot of our readers."

Here is where the trouble starts. Someone has gathered that you are "part of all this."

But you are part of it like a Confederate private at Antietam is part of the Civil War. If a passerby walks up to the private as he loads his musket and asks how the war is going, the private could only venture a guess. He probably doesn't even know how the battle is going, much less the whole war. A better question for the private would be: "What does gunpowder smell like?"

So for months you collect references. You keep your eyes and ears open. You talk to people. And then you have stacks and stacks of it.

I wasn't sure how to handle those co-workers. Somehow they made me angry. Their attitude suggested I lacked a certain necessary experience without which I could never fully understand or even appreciate the world around me.

"We were *there*, man. The whole country was there. Peace. Love, Unity. Jimi Hendrix. We were the Woodstock Nation. We know things."

"And, so? I am the walrus. What's the point?"

When you get down to it, I suppose I felt jealous the day my co-workers found me out. My generation has yet to have its defining moment. We haven't had a real humdinger of a war to get us going. Saddam Hussein isn't Hitler. We haven't had to worry about the bomb. Iran Contra isn't Watergate. Gameboy isn't even the Hula-Hoop.

The only thing keeping us together really forces us apart: television. We were the first generation to grow up on TV—not on it as in *broadcast*, but on it as in *addicted*. We share *Seinfeld* and *Beavis and Butt-head* like junkies share needles, but we don't have to meet each other to do it. We kick back in our stalls and have it all fed directly to us, fattening our brains like veal, giving us the ability to crack inside jokes. "Are you the master of your domain?" Or with T-shirts pulled over our heads: "I am Cornholio. Are you threatening me?"

Music molded the identity of those before us. The medium demanded that people gather. They flocked to a farm to share and listen and dance. They copulated in front of one another.

Now TV defines us. It forces us indoors. It makes us sit still. Separated and solitary, we copulate with ourselves.

The one thing we share, after spending more time in front of the tube than in the classroom, is a high tolerance for discontinuity. We love the jump cut.

I call Bob and get this: "Hi, this is Bob. You've reached my pager. If you enter the phone number you're calling from, I'll get back to you as soon as possible." So I do. And wait.

Two minutes pass. Then the phone rings. Bob is calling from his car phone. He is on his way to a meeting at 8 o'clock in the evening. Over the static, I can hear Bob's car stereo and the sound of traffic.

"Bob. Thanks for calling me back. Listen, if you've got a sec, I need to ask you a few questions for something I'm working on."

Bob Johnson (whose name has been changed) is a 24-year-old sales manager. He graduated college in 1992 with a political science degree. He recently abandoned his juicer, with which he extracted the vital essence of carrots to give him energy, and now firmly believes in neural linguistic programming. He is reading *Selling the Dream*, by Guy Kawasaki, the second book he's ever read that wasn't assigned to him, and he calls himself, with all sincerity, a "turbo entrepreneur."

"Bob," I ask, "what are your concerns?"

"I don't have any concerns," he says. I can tell by the sound of his voice that he is driving fast, perhaps forcing other cars off the road. "I can't afford to have any concerns. I'm too busy to have concerns. A turbo entrepreneur doesn't have concerns; you just have challenges to overcome."

"Yes, I see your point. Is it money that drives you? What would you do if you weren't a turbo entrepreneur?"

"I don't do it for the money; I do it for the jazz. I'd be selling pencils on the side of the street, I guess. You could put me anywhere, man. I could create something anywhere, because I'm a *salesman.* I sell things, I sell ideas, I sell concepts, I sell a dream. That's my biggest thing: I can sell the dream."

"I believe you," I tell him. "How about religion? Are you a fan of the vengeful, Old Testament God, or the forgiving, New Testament one?"

"I'm a spiritual person," Bob says, probably running stop signs. "I'm into free thought. There's a god within all of us. There's a power within all of us. Some people choose to find that power by going to church, some people find it through yoga, some people find it through medication. I believe in all that. I'm just very spiritual, very into energy and karma."

"One last thing: When do you plan to get married? Will that fit into your schedule?"

"Family will always be secondary. It's not going to be my *primary* concern. It will never be my primary concern. Not to say that it won't be an *equal . . . equal* focus. It could be equal to my career, but family will never take precedence at this point.

"Who knows? I may change. I may fall in love and turn to mush. Women are an evil, uncontrollable, unforeseen power."

Staring at all the stacks of magazines and newspaper clippings with their blue underlined passages, you have a revelation: Editors everywhere do a lot of gathering that someone is "part of all this" and then ask them to write about it. There is white space to fill, electrons to vibrate, images to make.

In 1987, an editor at *The New York Times Magazine* thought Bruce Weber was part of it and assigned him a cover story. More recently, an editor at Times Books/Random House thought David Lipsky and Alexander Abrams were part of it and gave them a contract to write a book in which they quoted Weber. Then, an editor at *Harper's Magazine* figured they were all part of it, because she excerpted the part of the book containing the Weber quote in last July's issue.

The whole parasitic process wound up getting Weber's words about your generation underlined before you in blue: "The author found his subjects to be 'determined, career-minded, [and] fiercely self-reliant.' As he summarized his many interviews, 'They are planners. They look ahead with certainty. They have priorities.'"

That was in 1987. Three short years later, an editor at *Time* thought David Gross and Scott Sophronia were part of all this, forcing the two writers to come up with a new, fresh angle. They decided to go with this: ". . . while recruiters are trying to woo young workers, a generation is out planning its escape from the 9-to-5 routine." And ". . . the young work force is considered overly sensitive at best and lazy at worst."

More and more people were considered part of all this. Douglas Coupland gave us the book (and term) *Generation X*. Richard Linklater gave us *Slacker* (another catchy term). Less inspired folks filled space with *True Romance* and *Reality Bites.*

Then the book *13th Gen* showed up on bookstore shelves, explaining how your peers were getting a bad rap. On January 4, 1993, *The New Republic* chimed in with "The 20 Something Myth" cover. *Newsweek,* this year, agreed with its stunningly original "Myth of Generation X" cover. New figures, just in, painted a completely different picture. Fresh insight abounded.

So, if you have it all straight, it went like this: You were ready to go get 'em, strap on a tie, and join the work force. You changed your mind, got lazy, and either gave up or settled for a McJob. No, wait a minute, those numbers were wrong; now you're going to do just fine.

All you can do after wading through the collected wisdom is take a break from the stacks and stacks. Thankfully, your roommates are awake at 4 in the morning, playing PGA European Tour for Sega. They do not have jobs that require regular sleep. One roommate is unemployed, but he had an interview with a tissue transplant center this week for a position as an organ harvester (really, no kidding). Another waits tables and plays guitar in a rock-and-roll band. The third is the would-be harvester's girlfriend, who goes to dance school and also waits tables.

No one plays well, and scores run high for this round of late-night golf. Despite the numbers, everyone seems to be doing just fine.

I call Loren at the restaurant where he works in Portland, Oregon. I can hear music, people talking, and plates clinking together.

"Loren. This is Tim Rogers." I have not talked to Loren in a year, and it takes him a second to put it all together.

"Hey! Tim! What's up, buddy?"

"I'm working on a story, and I need to ask you some questions. Can you talk for a few minutes?"

Loren Barr is the 24-year-old dishwasher for Dots Cafe. I graduated from high school with him, then he moved to Portland to attend Reed College. He studied art, but hasn't graduated yet, because he still needs to finish two PE credits. Loren also reads anything he can get his hands on, which, right now, is *The Great Shark Hunt,* by Hunter S. Thompson. He once kidnapped a weathervane that looked like a weasel from a randomly chosen house and delivered a series of ransom notes, over a period of months, to the address. He then returned the weathervane unharmed. I was with him at the time. The entire family to whom the weasel belonged was seated around a picnic table and watched in bewilderment as Loren popped over their backyard fence and stuck it atop its pole. When I explain that I'm writing a story about Generation X, Loren says, "Well, shit, I'm your poster boy, man. Ask away."

"First off, why do you wash dishes?"

"I don't have to be in charge of anybody else. I just do my own thing. I don't want to be in that position of power. . . . It's corrupting or something–you can write that. That would suck to have to tell people what to do."

"So you're afraid of responsibility?"

"It's not that I don't want responsibility; I just don't want responsibility over other people. And that's good for dishwashing, because you just do your job. You know, just wash the dishes. Kind of take away all this dirt, and render cleanliness. Confer cleanliness on the world. It leaves my mind free to wander and think thoughts while I'm doing repetitive tasks."

"You suppose you'll go on rendering cleanliness forever? Or is there a master plan?" I ask.

"Oh, I guess to just keep maintaining. I won't wash dishes forever. I think change will come, but I have faith in the power of fate to move me. I'm not going to try to force plans that are doomed to failure anyway and then be disappointed."

"Is that your biggest concern, your fear, that fate might not come through?"

"I suppose my biggest fear in life is . . . uh . . . I don't know. I guess just general loss of dreams. Are you going to use my real name in this thing?"

You finish the thing as the sun comes up. The coffee is gone, and your room-mates have all gone to sleep. You can hear footsteps of the couple that lives on the second floor of your duplex as they get ready for work. You run the spell check, do one last word count, and E-mail it off to the editor at the magazine.

And you wait. Several days pass. You begin to wonder what's happening on the other end. Finally, you get this message:

"Your piece on Generation X has been passed around among the editors, and I'm afraid the response is not good. I hate bearing bad news, but it goes with all the joys of this job.

"The main problem, we agree, is that the essay is simply thin. We read a lot but come no closer to any kind of understanding as to what Generation X is. Perhaps that is your major point, but it'd be nice to at least learn what some of the characteristics are, why this generation has been singled out, who cares, what does it mean, and then go into exceptions or people saying they don't fit. You mention, for example, all the collecting you do, but then we see no evidence of that collecting—what was said.

"That's the main thing: The reader really learns nothing. But in addition, it seems your theme is that the whole thing was a media creation, and now here we are mimicking the media who created something out of nothing.

"It's also a little puzzling to start a story telling the reader he/she won't hear anything they haven't heard already.

"Anyway, I did like parts, and you had some good lines, but we all agreed the piece lacked the substance and heft we were looking for. Perhaps it is an impossible story. . . ."

I hope you'll forgive me; now you've heard it 101 times.

Like everyone else with power over a few electrons and an editor who thinks he's "part of this," I've contributed the only thing I could: a caricature. I've simplified some things and ignored others. (What about sex and AIDS? What about education? Where are the women's voices?) By searching the ends of the gumption spectrum for interview subjects, I've exaggerated the rest. Objectivity and authoritative analysis are merely magic tricks.

Don't worry. Editors and publishers and producers and moviemakers everywhere are this very instant staring into the media maw, facing deadlines. They'll pick up the phone or hack out an E-mail and get in touch with someone who has something to say. Even this will survive a kill. And more will follow.

You'll see.

Wheel Life

Jay Searcy says, "My interest in writing began when I was delivering morning papers house to house as a kid. I would open my bundle of Knoxville Journals, *load my shoulder bag, then sit under a street light in the predawn darkness and read bylines from all over the world." What a life those sports writers led: Jack Hand, covering the Olympics in Tokyo, Red Smith and Arthur Daly, riding trains all over the country with baseball teams.*

Searcy left college to take a newspaper job, learning by writing, and has been a sports writer or editor some 40 years now. "Sports writing includes the whole spectrum: victory, tragedy, metro, obits, even the police beat, but best, even better than the travel, are the great people you meet," he says. He won prize after prize, moving from the Oak Ridger *and the* Chattanooga Times *to* The New York Times− *until he was hired away to be executive sports editor at* The Philadelphia Inquirer. *But editing without writing was no fun, so since 1986 he has been senior writer at* The Inquirer, *covering boxing ("a scum sport but still the ticket out of the ghetto") and horse racing.*

The inspiration for "Wheel Life," written in his fifties, was his nephew's tales of the road. He says his challenge was "to take a subject that, on the surface, appears dry and common and try to make it come alive with grand detail. The risk is in overlooking the detail, or not knowing where it lies. Detail has to be used skillfully, thoughtfully. Risk takers need editors who will allow them, encourage them, to reach−and to tell them when they miss." The trip, he says, almost demanded a diary format, "a great vehicle for disparate detail." Another challenge, however, was the confinement; all that time in the cab meant little time to talk with other truckers. So he researched the trucking industry before he left, brought a list of interesting people to contact along the way, and reread his favorite book, Steinbeck's Travels with Charley.

Searcy grew up in Oak Ridge, Tennessee, attending school inside guarded fences and locked gates; his parents were working on the Manhattan Project−though they didn't know what that meant at the time. Now he's thinking about retirement and writing a book about growing up in "Atomic City."

−CM

I t is 10:15 on a Sunday morning, cheerless and chilling. Rod Stewart is singing above the static on AM radio. The CB radio is squawking but getting no attention from the truck driver, 39-year-old Steve Daffron, who is

Jay Searcy, Wheel Life, *Inquirer Magazine*, July 21, 1991. Reprinted courtesy of *The Philadelphia Inquirer.*

working his way through Chattanooga church traffic toward Interstate 24, air brakes hissing, gears groaning. It is the beginning of another routine 12-hour workday for Steve, a 6-foot-1, 256-pound former college fullback and one of the few truck drivers in the world with a college degree.

We are sitting high up in the cab of a brilliant cherry-red, $70,000 Peterbilt tractor, he in a cushioned, air-ride, custom-made seat, me beside him in a jar-ring, unforgiving, rarely used straight-back stump-of-a-seat that magnifies every bump. We are pulling a glistening 48-foot, silver-and-blue aluminum trailer filled with 16 tons of hospital supplies. Not long ago Steve pulled a load of cadavers to Atlanta. Today it's sheets, blankets, pajamas and gowns—to be delivered to a Mundelein, Ill., warehouse in 24 hours.

I am here with special permission to witness the wild and colorful lifestyle of the trucker—often romantically billed as the Last American Cowboy—to check out the truck-stop women, to spy on the bizarre front-seat activity of passing automobiles, to explore the lure and mystery of the open road. The truth about America is out here somewhere in the hearts and minds of these truckers, those running to and those running from. And if it's not right here, then surely it's just down the road.

When we drop this load, we will get directions from central dispatch for our next pickup, which could be at any northern city east of the Mississippi. We should be back at Steve's home terminal in Chattanooga in three or four days, I'm told, after adventures in six or seven states. For Steve, who will drive more than 120,000 miles this year, this trip to Illinois and beyond is just a Sunday drive.

Now he rumbles down the ramp onto the interstate, looking from side to side into six rearview mirrors, takes the last bite of a Snickers bar and washes it down with a swig of Coke. Brunch over, he shifts into an eighth-gear, 58-mile-an-hour cruise, lights a Salem and settles back in his floating chair to listen to the news. We are off to see the wizard.

Once, when he was barely 25 and seemingly indestructible, he would make Chicago in one torrid 13-hour drive, guzzling coffee and popping pills to stay awake, then head off to Denver or someplace with another load. It was not uncommon then for him to drive until his eyes became bleary, until he began to nod or, sometimes, to hallucinate.

One late night, after he had been driving all day, he was speeding down a long grade of interstate when suddenly he saw a woman running ahead in the darkness with a baby in her arms, a blanket streaming along behind them. He locked down his air brakes and wrestled the lumbering 18-wheeler all over the road to keep the trailer from jackknifing, stopping just short of the terrified woman.

But there was no woman. No baby. No streaming blanket. There was only the darkness and the driver's tired, hallucinating mind.

And once he pulled to a stop on a highway to wait for a passing freight train just before the crossing gate dropped. He watched the train pass for several minutes before the driver in a rig behind him knocked on his window to ask what was wrong.

"Nothing's wrong," Steve replied. "I'm just waiting for the train to pass."

There was no train. There were no tracks. There was only the lonesome highway and his weariness.

But all that was long ago, when he owned his own rig and raced across America on the seat of his pants in search of adventure and money enough to make his truck payments, stopping only for coffee and cheeseburgers and to pee on his back tires somewhere along an interstate.

Those were the good-ol'-boy '70s, when the truckers' image was that of unshaven, tattooed, swaggering, macho men whose white beer bellies winked from beneath food-stained T-shirts, who wore grease in their hair and under their fingernails, blazed a path across the country with their air horns, and intimidated four-wheel America with tailgating arrogance. They popped pills, smoked dope and told stories about their women, who were waiting for them just down the road.

An accurate picture?

"Pretty accurate," Steve estimates. "I'd say at least 60 percent were doing drugs of some kind, and they didn't try to hide it. It was rampant. They'd pour pills out on the table at truck stops and divide them up."

And about the women?

What one must remember about truck drivers, Steve reminds, is that, next to driving, their greatest skill is storytelling. What they lack in real-life adventure, they invent. The only difference between a fairy tale and a trucker's story, they say, is that a fairy tale starts, "Once upon a time," and a trucker's story starts, "Now this ain't no s–."

They are still out here on the highways, these lonesome cowboys, still the backbone of American transportation, still intimidating just by their sheer size and numbers, scratching their hemorrhoids–feared and loathed and cursed by the masses, who see them as a blight on the landscape.

It's hard to tell by their appearance, Steve says, and America won't believe it, but truckers have begun to change. With periodic drug testing now mandatory in the industry, with an alcohol policy twice as tough as that for regular drivers, with companies controlling road speeds by computerized engine governors, with the number of road inspectors quadrupling in just three years, with the strict new national commercial driver's license becoming mandatory early next year, the Last American Cowboy is being reduced to only a whimper of his robust past. He is an endangered species in a turbulently changing industry that has seen more than 10,000 companies fail in the last 10 years, four every working day.

Companies struggling to stay in business are becoming more public-relations conscious, many putting toll-free telephone numbers on their rigs inviting the public to comment on their drivers' performance. Unfit, illegal operators are running out of places to drive, forced to conform or leave. Thousands of good drivers are leaving because of poor pay and working conditions that have some of them on the road for weeks at a time. The pay scale for truck drivers has been among the slowest of all industries to rise. Divorce rates are high. Owner/operators, those independent gypsies who represent the soul and spirit of trucking freedom, are being squeezed out by big companies offering big discounts to shippers.

What remains is a highly competitive industry of more than 200,000 companies faced with a massive driver shortage and an increasingly stringent government watchdog.

Stepping out from all this, almost unnoticed, is a new generation of driver, deridingly referred to by old-timers as "Mickey Mice" or "Road scholars"–a gentler, more courteous, better-trained, better-educated class, many wearing the creased uniform of some big trucking firm and a growing 5 percent of whom are women.

My driver is one of the converts. He carries a briefcase and wears the blue pinstriped shirt and blue slacks of Averitt Express, a Tennessee-based carrier that, along with United Parcel Service (UPS), is acknowledged to be among the leaders in establishing a new image for the maligned industry. Last year, Averitt spent $350,000 on "image apparel" for its 2,490 employees, 1,104 of whom are driver/salesmen (they carry business cards and sometimes call on potential customers), and nearly $400,000 for washing a fleet of 839 tractors and 2,044 trailers.

Averitt handpicks its drivers, screens them for drugs, tells them how long to wear their hair (not over the ears or collar) and how much jewelry they can wear (nothing flashy or excessive), and dictates the color of their shoes (black or brown and no sneakers).

It is installing its own defensive driving school, considers tailgating a cardinal sin, and despite the industry's current driver shortage, when driver turnover at many companies is 90 to 100 percent, Averitt has only a 3 percent turnover and a waiting list of applicants.

Steve returned to driving almost two years ago, after 10 years in trucking management, because he wanted to feel the road again. One day he will return to management, he says, "but right now I love driving a truck so much it scares me."

Pulling into a rest area atop Monteagle Mountain, he says, "I have finally realized that no matter how many cars and trucks you pass, you can never get to the head of the line."

What we will see and hear on this trip will be a mixture of the new, the old and the routine. The truck routes, Steve says, are like the streets: "You can find anything you want if you go looking for it."

MONTEAGLE MOUNTAIN, 11:10 A.M., a rest area 50 miles west of Chattanooga–Steve has pulled in here to double-check his log book, which must be in order when we come to our first weigh station (called a chicken coop) at the foot of the mountain. We are safely under the maximum allowed gross weight of 80,000 pounds, but our cargo, equipment and papers are subject to inspection. Stiff penalties–fines, travel suspension and even jail–can result from violations. Drivers are allowed to drive no more than 10 hours a day, 70 hours in any eight-day period, and their total workday cannot exceed 12 hours. Their work record must be kept updated in log books at all times and made available upon request to state inspectors or officials of the U.S. Department of Transportation.

The log-book law is so detested that many believe it is violated 100 percent of the time by 100 percent of the drivers. Most drivers alter their books by no more than a couple of hours, but some keep two logs, one of heavy fiction to show police and another of light fiction for their records.

Let's say you are 50 miles from your drop and your 10 hours are up. If you stop, the receiving company may be closed when you get there and you may be stuck on their lot for hours. Maybe for the weekend. No driver is going to do that.

What if you were a doctor, truckers reason, and you weren't allowed to practice medicine more than 10 hours a day? Or an electrician or a lawyer or a writer or a scientist?

The law, enacted in 1930, long before interstate highways, is now under government review.

MONTEAGLE MOUNTAIN, 11:17 A.M.–We are rolling down the mountain now, a treacherous stretch of Tennessee interstate for big rigs. Seventeen people were killed in accidents along here one year in the mid-'80s, before road improvements were made. Signs warn of the highway's 6 percent grade and advise drivers to shift to a lower gear or risk burning out their brakes. Two emergency ramps are spaced along the steep eastern grade, leading into the mountainside for runaway vehicles. Some truckers have crashed through the end of ramps and soared off the mountainside. But the gears of our 300-horsepower Cummins engine seem hardly to strain as they hold back our 64,640 pounds.

MANCHESTER, TENN., 11:46 A.M.–The line is about 15 trucks long when we reach the Manchester scales, considered the most unforgiving inspection station in Tennessee, if not the country. One pound overweight and it's an automatic $123 fine (plus 3 cents a pound for the first 3 percent over and 5 cents per pound beyond that). And Tennessee's Public Service Commission is the only state regulatory agency that uses drug-sniffing dogs, who may show up at any station at any time. But there is no problem this morning. The attendant in charge is on the telephone when our turn comes to roll across the scales, and he gives us a green light without looking up.

A driver doesn't have to stop to be weighed. The weight on each axle and the gross weight flash before the attendant as the rig crosses the scales. An overweight vehicle, or one with improper licenses displayed, or with suspect equipment, gets a yellow inquiry light or a message on the P.A. system. The driver must then pull aside and take his papers inside for review. In most states, if the trailer is 500 pounds overweight, the driver must reduce the load before he continues. Some illegal drivers, knowing the location of every weigh station, will leave the interstate and drive miles out of their way to dodge inspection. But even that isn't a guarantee. Tennessee agents are equipped with portable scales and may set up shop along any highway at any time.

Like some drivers, a few state agents try to take advantage. Once, in Mississippi, when Steve was hauling a load of strawberries that he knew to be well under the weight limit, he was called inside the chicken coop.

"What's the problem?" Steve asked.

"You're overweight," said the attendant.

"By how much?" Steve questioned.

"You're one case heavy," the attendant replied without a smile.

PICKLE PARK, NEAR MANCHESTER, 12:03 P.M.–Truckers have nicknamed this rest area Pickle Park because it is a notorious hangout for sexual trysts. Prostitutes do most of their business from midnight to 6 A.M. week nights, waiting in their cars and flashing their brake lights to signal when truckers pull in. Homosexuals are known in CB parlance as "good buddies." Women are "beavers," and prostitutes are "eager beavers." They often drum up business over the CB and meet here. The going price for a prostitute is $25, but everything is negotiable. At a few big truck stops ahead, where 50 to 100 drivers may be sleeping in their cabs at any given time, prostitutes known as "lot lizards" go door-to-door. A few work with truck-stop management, accept credit cards and give the driver a receipt marked "fuel."

Many truck stops, fearful of losing business, have hired security and erected fences and installed lighting to help keep prostitutes and drug dealers away. The National Association of Truck Stop Operators (NATSO), with more than 2,000 members, last year launched an anti-drug campaign called Operation Road-block, which offers help to employees who abuse drugs and makes it difficult to use or sell drugs at truck stops. Some truck stops post notices signed by law enforcement officers, warning that undercover agents may be about: "If you're selling, we might be buying, and if you're buying, we might be selling."

THE KENTUCKY STATE LINE, 1:32 P.M.—For every mile a rig travels within a state, it is assessed a fuel-use tax, whether the driver buys fuel in that state or not. With two 163-gallon diesel tanks, Steve will not have to buy fuel on this trip, but when he returns, he must file a report showing the number of miles driven in each state, and his company will be billed accordingly. In Tennessee the tax is 18 cents per gallon used. In Kentucky it's 12 cents, and in Georgia it's 7½ cents. Just outside Chattanooga, I-24 cuts through the northwestern tip of Georgia for four miles, then leads west to Nashville. Georgia will bill Averitt about 6 cents for that great adventure. The fuel-use tax is but one of a long list of fees and taxes assessed the trucking industry, which pays a total of $14.4 billion yearly in taxes. Almost a third of all highway taxes are paid by about 15 million commercial trucks on the road.

A trucker's driver's license from one state is generally recognized by all, but not license tags. That's why you see rigs with a double row of state tags across the back and side. Some shrewd drivers keep driver's licenses from three or four states in their billfolds so that if their reckless driving has cost them their license in one state, they simply use another. The new commercial driver's license system, which requires a 2½-hour road test and a five-hour written test, will keep a national accounting of violations, and next year those violators will be gone.

Steve learned to drive rigs in 1970, parking trailers in terminal lots. No formal training. The state never required him to take a road test. His only road test was for the company employing him. Soon he was making up to $400 a week driving during college breaks and loved it so much he almost quit school to drive full time. His license cost $6.

GLENDALE TRUCK STOP, GLENDALE, KY., 2:57 P.M.—A river of trucks flows constantly in and out of this service center on I-65, 90 minutes south of Louisville. Many truck stops, now a $15 billion-a-year business, are like mini-malls. You can get a diesel fill-up for about $300, an oil change for $99 (10 gallons for most engines), a screwdriver, Vienna sausage, pork and beans, alarm clocks, shirts, caps, blankets, cassette tapes, radios, radar detectors, boots, video games, television, a chaplain and the same simple, unimaginative, generally tasteless, colorless highway food served up and down every interstate in America—burgers, fries, steaks, chops, fried chicken, all-you-can-eat buffets, pie and that great get-together symbol of the road, coffee.

Because more telephone calls are made from truck stops than any place except airports and military installations, at most big truck stops a telephone is located at every restaurant booth.

One of the largest centers, the Amoco All-American Auto/Truck Plaza at Exit 17W off Interstate 81 near Carlisle, Pa., takes up 37 acres, enough room to park almost 500 trucks. It pumps between 1.5 million and 2 million gallons of diesel fuel a month (the industry buys 36 billion gallons a year) and offers a complete repair and service center.

Other truck stops may offer a pawn shop, post office, chiropractor, barber shop, hot tub, chapel, branch bank, laundromat, shoeshine stand, parking lot wake-up service, live entertainment, golf cart shuttle from rig to restaurant, stocked fishing pond, movies, swimming pools, and legitimate massage. President Bush ate at a truck stop in Illinois during his 1988 campaign (and left a $50 tip).

Drivers walk stiffly into truck stops, rubbing their burning eyes and stretching, looking for anyone to talk to. Usually it's the waitresses, many of whom have completed truck-stop seminars on how to best serve their customers. They offer a happy face and coffee for starters, then listen to the drivers' troubles or laugh at their bad, off-color jokes heard a thousand times over:

Waitress: "Wanna screwdriver?"

Truck Driver: "Might as well. My truck won't start."

"Mostly," said a cashier here, "they are just hard-working, everyday people. They want to talk about three things–their trucks, their women and the weather, and their women are mostly in their imagination."

A popular bumper sticker on sale near the cashier's counter reads: THE MORE I LEARN ABOUT WOMEN, THE MORE I LOVE MY TRUCK.

LOUISVILLE, 4:52 P.M.–We are still on I-65 North in Kentucky, but it could be I-95 or I-81 and it could be Ohio or Michigan or North Carolina. After a while, each hill begins to look like the last one as the miles click by–329, 330, 331–and the passing towns are just dots on the map. Steve has driven through this city scores of times, several times on the first Saturday in May while the Kentucky Derby was being run at Churchill Downs, just off Interstate 264. It's as close as he has ever come to seeing a Derby. And he has driven through Indianapolis while the Indy 500 was being run and he never saw that, either. He often looks out over the steering wheel hour after lonely hour and thinks about doing those things someday. He plans trips he will never take, imagines conversations he will never hold, writes letters he will never put on paper.

Sometimes he thinks himself into depression, wondering why he hasn't done more with his life, reliving relationships gone bad, aching to be more a part of something, to know more of the country he passes through, envying the settled people he sees along the routes. "You have too much time to think out here," he says. "Before you know it, mole hills become mountains."

I-65 NEAR SEYMOUR, IND., 5:32 P.M.–Our headlights come on and soon we will be unable to look into the front seat of passing cars. Oh, yeah, it's standard entertainment for truckers, all of whom have at least one steamy erotic first-person story to tell. In fact, it is pretty much the same story: A woman pulls alongside with her skirt up and no pants on and it goes on from there. But on this trip we have seen nothing more exciting than a man in a business suit holding a cup of yogurt between his legs while he talked on his car phone.

PETRO TRUCK STOP, LOWELL, IND., 9:07 P.M.–His maximum driving hours almost used up, Steve pulls in for the night and parks in the gravel-and-mud lot about 200 yards from the restaurant with more than 50 other rigs, whose motors are idling and choking the air with heavy diesel fumes. It is standard procedure for drivers to leave motors running and their 20 to 30 multicolored marker lights on while they are parked, whether it is for five minutes or five hours. It's another practice about to change.

Truckers let engines run to keep their cabs warm or cool and because engines are hard to start in cold weather. But some companies are beginning to challenge that. With so many commercial trucks on the road, the fuel cost for allowing all of them to idle eight hours is almost $87 million and a waste of about 76 million gallons of fuel, not to mention the damage to the environment.

Schneider National Inc., a freight carrier out of Green Bay, Wis., is among the growing number of companies offering its drivers fuel-saving incentives. With monthly performance bonuses of up to $1,000 possible, few of the engines in Schneider's pumpkin-colored tractors are allowed to idle along the highways, and most of them cruise at a fuel-saving 55 m.p.h. J. B. Hunt, an Arkansas-based firm with better than 5,000 trucks on the road, now insists that its engines be cut off if the stop is for more than a few minutes, except when the temperature is 22 degrees or below. All of Hunt's long-distance tractors are governed for a top speed of 55 m.p.h.

At 9:12 Steve steps down from his Peterbilt with the engine idling and marker lights flashing. "The real reason a lot of them do it is because it looks good and sounds good," Steve said, looking back admiringly at his big red machine.

Steve has chicken-fried steak for dinner, french fries (his second plate of the day), salad and tea. After a telephone call home to his wife, he returns and crawls like a mole into the sleeper in back of his cab, pulls the curtain to and lets the vibration of the engine rock him to sleep. Not one prostitute knocks on his door.

Steve's sleeper is a miniature motel room. The bed, 3 feet off the floor, is 3 feet wide and 6 feet, 8 inches long. Before each trip Steve covers the firm mattress with fresh sheets and blankets brought from home and hangs a daily uniform change in closets at either end of the bed. The walls and ceiling are upholstered warmly, and there are overhead shelves on three sides. A control panel next to Steve's pillow regulates heat, air, stereo, a reading light and two overhead lights. He can stand on his bed and not touch the ceiling. It doesn't have a bath, but sleepers with showers, microwave ovens and refrigerators are now available.

MIDNIGHT: The number of trucks in the lot has grown beyond 100 now, and the diesel fumes sting one's eyes. The drivers don't notice. Most of them are asleep. A few sit alone in the darkness of their cabs and listen to the radio or watch little black-and-white TVs. A sign in the window of one truck reads: "I'm so horny I get excited at the crack of dawn."

Steve is up at 4 A.M. He walks to the truck stop across the parking lot with a fresh change of clothes, pays $5 for a private shower, sips two cups of coffee and is on his way at 5:10. His Snickers-and-Coke brunch will come later.

CHICAGO, MONDAY, 6:31 A.M.–Daylight breaks as we go rumbling through Chicago just ahead of work traffic. Every other vehicle seems to be a tractor-trailer, as if an army of them had camped just outside of town and converged on the city all at once. And perhaps that's so.

At 7:15 we roll onto the Mundelein terminal lot, drop the load, trailer and all, and call Chattanooga for instructions. Go to Milwaukee, 90 miles up I-94, we are told, and pick up a load of magazines at Moebius Printing and deliver them to Whittle Communications, publisher of *Esquire,* in Knoxville, Tenn.

MILWAUKEE, MONDAY, 9:17 A.M.–Two other Averitt trailers with the same orders are waiting to be loaded, and two Schneider drivers pull up while we are there. They sit around a stark waiting room and exchange horror stories–getting trapped in underpasses, getting lost, nodding off at the wheel. Nobody really listens, but they wait eagerly for their chance to tell a bigger lie than the one just told.

The Schneider drivers are in their late 40s or early 50s and, between them, have been driving less than two years. They pay about $3,000 to be trained by Schneider and get some of that investment back if they stay with the company more than a year. Their starting pay is 19 cents a mile, which is at the low end of the industry. Schneider will train you well into your 50s if you are in good health.

Steve makes 29 cents a mile for cross-country trips and 27 cents for shuttle trips. That translates into almost $35,000 a year or, with his 12-hour days, about $11 an hour. That is about as good as it gets for nonunion drivers. Union drivers make 39 to 40 cents a mile, but only about half of all general freight companies are union, including the four largest–United Parcel, Consolidated, Yellow and Roadway. UPS, which truckers have nicknamed "Buster Brown," pays by the hour, not by the mile, and pays top drivers more than $17 an hour.

Because J. B. Hunt is aggressive and has been involved in some small company buyouts and because it uses many beginner drivers, it is perhaps the most maligned company along the road. Handwritten signs in many truck-stop restrooms above the toilet-tissue dispenser read: APPLICATION FORMS FOR J. B. HUNT.

12:05 P.M.–We lose three hours in Milwaukee waiting to be loaded with 44,900 *Special Report* magazines. We turn south on I-94 and find a 76 Truck Stop that's so popular it charges $5 to park after the first four hours. Steve has breakfast, at last. Fried chicken. Truck drivers have three things in common, Steve says. They are overweight because of poor nutrition and lack of exercise, they have hemorrhoids or will have, and they suffer from broken marriages. Steve has gained about 20 pounds since he returned to driving, and he's in his third marriage. He didn't mention hemorrhoids and I didn't ask.

NEAR GARY, IND. 3:15 P.M.–The CB radio, usually a running septic tank of trash talk, has been strangely quiet this trip, Steve observes. Channel 19 is the truckers' channel, and it is useful mostly for traffic information, locating state patrol cars and conducting inconsequential conversations. Female drivers rarely use it, for fear of abuse, and few drivers need it for police locations any more because their speeds largely are under computer control. But a cop isn't on the interstate more than a few seconds before he makes the CB newsline: "Hey, we've got a bear in a plain black wrapper at the 120 get-off. Watch yer foot, boys, 'cause he's got his ears on and he's handing out fast-driving awards."

A local cop is a "local yokel," a county cop a "county mounty." A state police officer is "a full-grown bear." The loop around Atlanta is "Suicide Circle." Birmingham is "Smoke City." Nashville is "Guitar." New Jersey is "The Dirty Side," and Channel 19 is "Sesame Street."

LOWELL, IND., 5:30 P.M.—We stop and eat a meal we don't remember.

SOMEWHERE IN INDIANA, 8 P.M.—The road has become a black liquid. It weaves and pulses and breathes. We stop for coffee somewhere I don't remember.

SEYMOUR, IND., 10:30 P.M.—We stop for the night, Steve in his sleeper, me in a motel. But I cannot sleep. I close my eyes only to see the highway crawl like an endless flat concrete snake. Traffic is rushing at me with a murderous intensity. I see figures moving with no faces. The roadside is a blur. My back is aching.

The phone is ringing—my wakeup call.

TUESDAY, 6:16 A.M.—Steve begins another relentless, all-day drive, through Kentucky Bluegrass Country, past creosoted tobacco barns and white fences and horse farms—Louisville, Lexington, Frankfort, Corbin—carried along in the wave of endless traffic, rolling at an unbroken, hypnotic speed with an engine that has hardly been turned off for three days. Our conversation has been reduced to monosyllables.

KNOXVILLE, 1:17 P.M.—We drop the magazines and pick up a load of paper bound for a check-printing company in Norcross, Ga., by way of Chattanooga. It's a capacity load that puts us narrowly under the 40-ton limit. We stop at a truck stop for lunch, and talk to a shoeshine-stand operator who says she makes $200 some days.

CHATTANOOGA, TUESDAY, 6:07 P.M.—After 1,371 miles in six states, averaging about 56 miles an hour and 5.4 gallons per mile, we are home, Steve in his cushioned air-ride floating seat, me on that stump. We have no greater knowledge of the country we passed through, because we had no contact with it. We were never approached by an eager beaver, nor any other kind, never came in contact with a good buddy and never saw a drug deal or a pep pill. I never saw anything interesting in the front seats of passing automobiles, either. And I doubt that many ever do. It is mostly a dream, a trucker's fantasy, a hope that keeps an underpaid, overworked industry going that extra mile. If not this car, then the next.

In the four days we were gone, Steve smoked six packs of Salems, chewed a half-pack of Rolaids, took 10 aspirin, drank six Cokes and 20 cups of coffee, ate three plates of french fries, two cheeseburgers, a hamburger, a salad, fried chicken, chicken-fried steak, a plate of eggs, biscuits, gravy and grits and three Snickers. He slept 12 hours.

This is the way it gets done, the way 2.5 billion tons of freight is moved each year, twice as much as the railroad moves. Truckers will drive almost 300 billion miles this year, the equivalent of about 600,000 round trips to the moon.

And so that you may someday come to accept truckers, maybe even respect them, they are developing a better attitude and better skills and using better and safer equipment (their highway safety record has been twice as good as ours all along).

The Last American Cowboy isn't dead. He's just very, very tired.

Pull the Trigger

You want to understand Tom Junod? Then start with this: Junod loves to get inside, way inside, the minds of others. Oh sure, he writes in the third person, but that's a scam. The voice you hear belongs to his subject–whether that's John Travolta or Grant Hill or Lamar Alexander or John Wayne Bobbitt. "I hear harrowing stories and tell them as though they were my own. False confessions, disguised autobiography, ventriloquism–that's what I try to write, even when I'm writing about murderers," Junod says.

You want to know how to do this? "Sometimes I strangle the life out of my subjects, but sometimes–maybe on the fourth draft–subjects speak through me, and the tension between the opposites of storytelling–between structure and improvisation, between my subject and me–winds up giving the story its energy, inevitability, form, and grace."

Okay, so it's mystical. "You have to let go of the story you want to get the story you need–even if it tramples the sensitivities of your reader, your subject, yourself," Junod says. And it's risky. "The risks I took in writing 'Pull the Trigger'–well, there were a zillion–starting with the subject's father not wanting me to write it and he was one scary dude. And finding Tony Mobley–a guy willing to tell you he had a fine time blowing somebody's brains out–wasn't easy." But because "Pull the Trigger" was part of a triptych of stories about the consequences of America's love affair with handguns, Junod didn't have to provide background and could keep us listening to Tony, his amazing speech rhythms and outrageous mind games.

Junod attended Catholic schools on Long Island, then the state university system of New York, graduating as an English major magna cum laude *in 1980. "Faulkner started me on all this. I'm a style freak and I've never gotten his endless sentences out of my system," he says. Instead of going to grad school and becoming a scholar, he took a job selling handbags. Now he's writer-at-large for* GQ *and winner–two years running–of the National Magazine Award.*

You want to win prizes? "Learn to perform on the page," he advises. "And don't craft your stories for a market or a magazine or an editor. Dare, risk, fail, create yourself, be yourself. Oh, yeah–and keep a journal."

–CM

He shouldn't laugh, but that first time with the gun–it was *funny*, you know? That big old German bitch, that *frau*–she thought he had come to her nursery to buy a bush! He had sauntered down the hill, with the .357 in his waistband, under his jacket, and when she asked him who he was, what

---

he was there for, well, he doesn't know where these things come from, but there it was, in his head, in an instant, the *perfect* lie. He, Tony Mobley, was . . . Joe College. He was a college boy, yes, everything an 18-year-old *should* be, a college boy with a bright future, and he had just moved into his own apartment, and he needed some plants and bushes for atmosphere. Would she mind helping him? Oh, she would be delighted! She *liked* him, this woman, and he sort of liked her, too, the poor thing–she ran around the nursery, picking up bushes, putting them down, sweating, grunting, getting dirty . . . all for *him*, for Tony . . . until, of course, she wheeled the merchandise to the cash register and said, That will be $274, and he said, No, ma'am, that will be an armed robbery. Did she like him *now*, with a gun pointed at her? Did she like him *now*, as he circled the register, *styling*, the .357 at his side, dangling loose from his hand, Joe College replaced, slain, obliterated, by some lizard-eyed Joe Cool? Well, no, of course not, but she liked him when he left, that's for sure, because he let her live.

You want to understand Tony Mobley? You want to find out why he let all of them live, all his victims . . . all but one, a young man named John Collins? You want to be privy to Tony's secrets? You want to know him, master him, divine from the dreadful arc of his life the reason one man might use a handgun to destroy another? Then start with this: Tony loves to laugh. He is, in fact, helpless before the force of his laughter. He will laugh at funerals. He will laugh at court proceedings. He will laugh when he is talking about armed robbery, and he has been known to laugh when talking about murder. If something's funny, why shouldn't he laugh? Because the world doesn't want him to? Because the world deems his laughter *inappropriate*? Well, he has his answer tattooed on his shoulder. Three letters: "FTW." *You* figure it out.

See, if Tony had a choice, if he could live his dreams, he would be a comedian. Comedians are, in his opinion, the supreme artists. You don't want to laugh? Comedians *make* you laugh. They walk into crowded rooms, hostile rooms, and just . . . control them. Can you imagine how that must feel? Well, yes, come to think of it, Tony can, because that's what he does in his line of work: He works the room. Comedians have balls, man, and so do armed robbers. In fact, that's why Tony *loves* armed robbery and makes it his calling: because all you need to do it is a gun and a pair of balls. Hell, if your balls are big enough, you don't even need a gun; you just wiggle your finger under your jacket and say, Stick 'em up, motherfuckers! Gas stations, sandwich shops, Chinese restaurants, dry cleaners, pizzerias–they're all the same; everyone goes for the bluff, everyone folds. You walk into a place with the threat of heat, and nobody's going to ask questions; nobody, in fact, is going to say a word: The joint buzzes in silent harmony, in unspoken appreciation of your fucking *authority*. In an armed robbery, it's Tony's script and Tony's show; Tony gets all the lines; Tony's on the stage, Tony's in the audience, Tony's serving drinks, and Tony holds up the sign that tells the crowd when to laugh . . . and if, when it's all over, that fine little bitch who forked over the cash stands up and applauds, well, baby, you and Tony need to talk, you're his kind of girl.

He was born on Friday the thirteenth. Does that explain Tony Mobley, give him an excuse for who he is? Can he be a victim now, please, like the Menendez brothers? Tony was born premature and stayed in the hospital a month after his birth. He was anemic, sickly. He cried a lot. He was not what people call a "good baby." C'mon, folks—you want *reasons,* Tony's handing them out. Oh, he's not stupid; he's got a *mind* on him, that's what everyone says; he knows that people who come upon the wreck of his life will not be able to resist blaming his parents, his childhood or some slavering deviant who hid in Tony's closet and nudged him along the path of perversity. Well, get this: His father's worth millions. His father is Stephen Mobley, owner of a chain of sneaker stores called the Sport Shoe. You want balls? Stephen Mobley has balls. He was a door-to-door salesman who sold his house and put the stake into the first Sport Shoe and built his business from *nothing.* Deprivation? Want? Hey, they may explain your typical murderer, your average, everyday ghetto shooter, but they sure as hell don't explain *Tony Mobley.* Nothing does. Sure, his father's hard and his mother's harder; sure, they divorced when Tony was at a delicate age; sure, he resents the hell out of his older sister. But please, Dr. Freud, you have to believe him: There is nothing any of them did —father, mother, sister, grandpa, grandma, maiden aunt—to deserve *him.* He didn't get beat, he didn't get fucked; no, beating and fucking, they were what *he* did, and that's how it has always been.

Always. Tony has always been a slave to what the shrinks call his "impulses." If Tony was old enough to do it, he did it. As an infant, he cried; as a child, he lied and stole; as a boy, he got into fights, wrecked property, terrorized teachers; as a man, well . . . you name it. His parents didn't know what to do with him; their only sin was thinking they *could* do something with him, that their money could buy a solution, that the next expert, the next special school, might have the means to turn a crooked stick straight and true. They didn't realize they were doomed, doomed from the start, doomed by everything Tony was, his being. This school, that school; this shrink, that shrink: How could they possibly help him? How could anyone know what Tony needed, what he wanted? He didn't know himself. All he knew was this: Whatever he wanted, he wanted it *now.* Did he want to fuck men? Yeah, now. Did he want to fuck women? Yeah, now. Hey, Tony, you want to get high? You want to get drunk? Yeah, sure, sounds good, whatever: *now!* You know what Tony drinks? Jagermeister and Stoli. You know why? Because he doesn't want to waste time. Because he doesn't want to be one of those guys who buys a six-pack and then waits around to see *what happens.* He drinks to get fucking *drunk,* and he's always there when the fun starts.

He was 18 when the fun *really* started, when the shrinks at the last "therapeutic center" told his father that he was too old for them to keep, that they didn't know what to do with him, that they had no particular recommendations, save the old standby of hapless authority: disengagement. The boy needs to go out on his own, they told the old man; maybe one day, when he's about 40, he'll be able to curb his antisocial impulses and come around. The old man got Tony a job and an apartment, then wished him luck . . . and for a while, yes, indeed, Tony was lucky: He didn't get caught. He did his first job with the .357 . . . the *frau,* remember? . . . then his second. . . . Oh, you don't really want to hear about those years, do you, every robbery, every burglary, every kited check, every stolen car, every filched credit card, every parole violation, every job lost because the boss found his hand in the kitty? Let's just say Tony was a *bad* boy. Let's just say he robbed a gas station in Alabama, locked the attendant in the bathroom with a padlock, and for all he knows that motherfucker's still sitting there. Let's just say "this school, that school" turned into "this jail, that jail." Let's just say he didn't merely *burn* bridges to his family, he blew them up.

He found a new family, though, sort of. He met a man named Wayne, and Wayne became his patron. He moved in with Wayne's family and became a big brother to Wayne's teenage son. He went skating with the family, and there he was, smack in the middle of all this domestic bliss, with his freaking skates on, when the cops popped him for stealing a Camaro. *Bad* scene: Wayne's wife is crying, Wayne's kids are crying, everyone's crying–but they went to his trial and visited him in jail, and when he got out he moved back into their house. Aw, they loved him, and he loved them, as best he could. He used to take the boy out to Six Flags and blow hundreds of dollars, every penny he had, on rides and games and junk food; they'd ride home with a pickup truck full of stuffed animals, laughing, but then one day the kid saw some of Tony's cocaine, they argued, and Tony wound up sticking the .357 into his own mouth, to advance his position. You want to fight, son? Let's see how far you're willing to go. . . . Oh, you're *crying*? You're begging Tony to stop? *Please?* Okay, he'll stop, he won't blow his brains out, but he wins, you lose. Tony took the gun out of his mouth, and–it's true, it really happens–the gun just "went off." Fu-*uck:* hole in the wall, right over the water bed, guess Tony's got to be going, sorry for interrupting dinner, folks. He packed his bags, and when he hit the highway, he waved the .357 at a motorcyclist, drove him off the road and laughed all the way to his father's lake house.

He went to jail again–parole violation–and wound up, in 1990, at a halfway house in Macon, Georgia, for convicts with no family ties, no place to go. He was 24 years old. He got a job waiting tables at a classy restaurant, hired by a 300-pound homosexual who dug the danger, the delinquency, the desperation, everything Tony had to offer. And then: success. Can you believe it? He was good at something. He was a good waiter. Customers liked him; hell, they *asked* for him, Tony Mobley, by name, that charming boy with the beautiful smile. Beautiful: That's what the people in Macon called him, that beautiful, beautiful boy who made them laugh, who made them happy. . . . He fucked an honest-to-goodness beauty queen in Macon, did you know that? The bitch was slumming, but what the hell, she might as well slum with him, and he made the most of the opportunity, he made her scream. He still had most of his hair in Macon. He was still hard as a rock in Macon. . . . Shit, he used to go down to the queer bars on Broadway, take off his shirt, and it was amazing, fifty faggots asking him what he was drinking. They used to love his tattoos, the bulldog with the spiked collar on one arm, the boxing gloves on the other–you know, slap these fags around a little bit, they love you forever. . . .

Forever: Did Tony think that's how long it would last, his charmed life in Macon, those eight or nine months of party heaven, the absolute pinnacle of his cursed existence? No, shit, no–how could the party go on forever when Tony couldn't find anyone to keep up with him, to want what he wanted, to share the escalation of appetite? He was Tony Mobley, remember? He liked working; he *loved* robbing. He liked men; he *loved* boys, pretty young boys, the prettier the better. His enthusiasms were not like other people's enthusiasms; his impulses were not like other people's impulses. When they called to him, they demanded answers, and they demanded them right away–now, Tony, *now!* So on that night in February 1991–that *fateful* fucking night, the night he found the new gun and lost everything else–well, he was just answering his soul's insistent call . . . answering as he always had, answering the only way he knew how, with the word that usually wound up making his soul so happy and everyone else so sad: yes.

He wanted to get drunk, is all–that's how it started. He wanted to get drunk, and he ran into someone who wanted to get drunk, too–an old buddy from the halfway house named Gene. They drove to the grocery store with Gene's friend Daryl in Daryl's old Honda–Daryl driving, Gene in the passenger seat, Tony in the back. They hit a pothole, or something. Glove compartment popped open, and there it was, a statement in stainless steel, a study in concision, the Walther PPK .380, James Bond's gun. Gene took the gun out of the glove compartment. "Now this," he said, "is a *gun.*" He showed it to Tony. Daryl got nervous, told them to put it back. They went to the grocery store, and then to Tony's apartment. The cast of characters: Tony, Daryl, Gene, Gene's girlfriend, her baby and a 15-year-old boy, Todd. Oh, Todd was pretty, all right, the son of one of Tony's coworkers, a kid in whom Tony had taken an interest. Brotherly, nothing physical. They would go to the mall together. They would hang out at the arcade. They would watch TV. Hell, the kid was practically *living* at Tony's apartment. . . . *Drunk?* No, they didn't get drunk that night. They got fucking *stunned.* Black Russians, Killer B's, the freaking *baby* drinking liqueur in its milk, Tony playing his stereo as loud as it would go, the neighbors complaining, Tony telling them to shut the fuck up, banging the walls with his baseball bat . . . until everyone started getting sick, party's over, Todd and Tony, alone at last.

He beat the boy up. Why? Tony doesn't know why. Because he was there? Because he was too pretty, because he wasn't pretty enough, because he wouldn't stay, because he wouldn't leave–who knows why, Tony just did it, they got into a fight, and Tony broke a window with Todd's head. He threw the kid on the floor and stood over him, fists like stones–man, he wanted to fuck him *up*, he wanted to hurt him, give that boy something to remember him by, but he glanced in the corner of the room, and there it was, Todd's little backpack, full of schoolbooks, and Tony thought: I can't do this. He's just a kid, he hasn't even *shaved.* He called an old boyfriend, a pretty little pizza delivery boy who not so long before had broken his heart, and said, Take me to Atlanta.

Where else could he go? He had *tried* to stay away from Atlanta, he really had, because he knew that the city would be his ruin, that once he surrendered to it he would light a fire that would leave everything he knew in ashes. Now, though –big surprise, story of his life–it was *Macon* that lay in flames behind him, and he had nowhere else to go but up the interstate, to his grand finale. But first . . . well, if he was going to brave Atlanta, he needed something, he knew where it was, he didn't want to just *leave* it there–the gun. Four in the morning, he told the pizza boy to stop by Gene's place, he had forgotten something, and the pizza boy turned into the driveway, headlights shining into forever. The window of

Daryl's Honda—it just *gave in,* you know? Once, Tony had tried to punch out the window of a Monte Carlo, and he almost broke his fucking fist, but this—it just *succumbed,* and the .380 was his, and he was on his way to the big city, thinking *let's get it on, motherfuckers.*

The first thing he did, after settling back in at Wayne's house: bake a pie for his grandmother. The second thing: go looking for a place to rob. He was an outlaw now, full-time, and night or day, it didn't matter, that's what he'd do, "go to work," wearing his robbing clothes—black jeans, black shirt, red-and-blue jacket, a pair of black gloves, and the .380 snug in a cheap waistband holster. On your knees, please, head down, and don't *fucking* look at me—yeah, Tony had the rap *down,* and after one stickup this pretty little gal told the cops that Tony was a fine-looking man, that if he hadn't stuck a gun in her face she might have asked him for a date. Christ, even the authorities called him "the Happy Bandit"; he wasn't one of those vicious motherfuckers who went into places *blasting.* . . .

So why in the world did he do what he did? Tony Mobley killed a man! Ten days after he left Macon, he walked into a Domino's Pizza and, just past midnight, took the life of an innocent, John Collins—just *took* it, as though snatching it for himself. . . . Did Tony do it to get back at his mother? Well, he committed his murder on her birthday, just a few hours after delivering her one of his homemade pies. . . . Did Tony do it to get back at his father? Well, Tony drove all the way to Hall County, Georgia, where the Old Man happened to be living, to commit the crime. . . . Did Tony somehow know to *hate* John Collins, because he represented something Tony was not, or did he pull the trigger just to get it over with, to say the hell with it, to destroy everything he had ever been or would ever be, to kill his mother, his father, his sister, himself, Wayne, the pretty little pizza boy, John Collins, everybody, all in one shot, one instantaneous amalgamation of force and fire? On February 17, 1991, did someone have to die, just to leave a hole where Tony Mobley's life used to be?

No. You want to know what happened? Tony liked going bowling with Wayne's family, and he needed money to buy a bowling ball. On February 16, he brought the pie to his mother, and then drove, in Wayne's car, to Hall County, to find a place to rob. Why Domino's? Because it was open. Because it was an easy mark, sitting there in the middle of desolation row, one car in the parking lot, closing time, a last lonely light in the darkness. Tony parked in a lot on top of a hill, walked to the Domino's through a stand of trash trees and opened the side door: *Hel-*lo! Just what he wanted: all alone, an overweight guy in his red-and-blue Domino's uniform, all sweat and fear. ID on the nametag: "JOHN COLLINS"—college boy, same age as Tony, as a matter of fact, working his way through school, just a semester to go. . . . Well, Joe College, meet Joe Cool, he's got a gun, this is an armed robbery, now empty the fucking register. One hundred dollars? That's *it?* Are you sure that's it? Are you *positive?* Well, open up the office in back, John Collins, and let's hope you're right.

He wasn't right. In the office, in the back, on a desk, there was more money, a good deal more money, and Tony—well, Tony started *fucking* with John Collins, you know, messing with his head, just to do it, and John Collins snuck a glance at Tony Mobley, a look that said "Is this a robbery or a singing telegram?" And then:

DON'T LOOK AT ME, MOTHERFUCKER! And then: FACE THE FUCKING WALL! and then . . . No, no, Tony didn't want to *kill* him; he just wanted to put a good *scare* into him, but then the store suddenly filled with a cloud of light, and the light was so damned bright, Tony didn't know what to make of it. . . . What the fuck was *this?* Was it another pizza man, returning from his last delivery? Was it a cop? Was it a UFO? Was it fucking Elvis? The clock in Tony's head was ticking, *boom, boom, boom;* from two paces, he pointed the .380 at the juncture of John Collins's head and neck, averted his eyes from his target, and then, well, the buzzer sounded, and the game was over. You know, a long time ago, when Tony was around 15, he took his father's car for a spin, a restored beauty that Tony was forbidden to touch. He drove around for a while, and then, out of curiosity, decided to visit a house in his neighborhood that was the rumored domicile of Devil worshipers. He made it halfway up the driveway; then he ran out of gas and, knowing he was screwed, said "Fucking shit" and smashed the windshield with his fist. You want to know what it's like to pull the trigger and kill a man? Well, there you go: "Fucking shit," and a missile detonates the back of a human being's head; "Fucking shit," and you've put your stain on the fabric of eternity; "Fucking shit," and a man named John Collins is rendered a memory—no longer a son, no longer a brother, no longer a friend but, rather, an absence as insistent as a sinkhole; "Fucking shit," and you have become the enemy of every *living* thing, because you, Tony Mobley, are a murderer.

He ran. He ran, illuminated by the headlights that shone from the delivery-man's car, and he disappeared into the trees, into the darkness. In the belly of the beast: That's where he was now, sweating, stinking, smelling himself. He started the car and tried to drive slow. Who was going to pop him? Clint Eastwood? Starsky and Hutch, in that piece-of-shit Ford? But no. . . . See, after any crime, you have to cross the bridge; it doesn't have to be a *real* bridge—it could be a stop sign, a red light, an intersection, the entrance ramp to the highway. You *know* when you've crossed it, though, because until you do, you're sure you're going to get caught, and *after* you do, there's the rush you were looking for, the rush of wind, of freedom, of untouchability . . . the rush of *getting away with it.* Yeah, that was Tony that night, after he crossed *his* bridge, after he got on the highway—he had gotten away with it, he was Jonah spit from the mouth of the whale, and so, what the hell, he turned on the radio, hit the cruise control, stretched his legs, dug his hands in the garbage bag full of loot and began tossing Domino's receipts out the window. Oh, it was a scene, man, you had to be there: Tony's dumping receipts as fast as he can find them, but the money starts coming out of the bag, and there are dollar bills everywhere, caught in the wind, swirling around, turning the interior of the car into a ticker-tape parade.

The next morning, Tony grabbed a newspaper and read the little headline, something like "MAN ROBBED, KILLED AT DOMINO'S PIZZA." At first he thought, You mean, after I robbed him, somebody went in there and killed him? Guy had a bad *night.* He was just kidding himself, though, and when he closed the paper, he said, Tony, you fucked up this time. But you know what? He didn't *like* killing. He didn't sit around thinking about it; he's not Jeffrey Fucking Dahmer, there are no suspicious roasts in Tony Mobley's refrigerator. See, he prefers comedy to tragedy, and murder—it's tragedy, all the way; you murder someone, there are no laughs, no rounds of applause, no expressions of gratitude or relief; no, there's just this clanging *boom,* and then a silence that rings forever. The eternal crime: That's what murder is, and to make sure he didn't do it again, to reclaim his status as the Happy Bandit, Tony took the clip out of the Walther whenever he went robbing. He would park his car, scope the joint, and then *click!* he'd press the little button on the side of the gun, and *whish!* the clip would slide out onto the seat. He loved the little sound the clip made, because it meant that the gun was defanged, he couldn't kill again, that on *this* job it was just Tony Mobley, his brains and his balls.

He got caught, finally, about a month after he'd killed John Collins. A woman took down the license number of the car Tony was driving, Wayne's Buick; the cops tailed him, Tony crunched the gas, did a one-eighty, tossed the Walther out the window, and the chase began, his claim to fame, 45 minutes at 120 miles per hour, his foot to the floor, no pause, no letup, no surrender, just speed, pure speed, through the eye of the needle. Balls? Oh, man—Tony's balls were as big as balloons that night, as big as boulders. . . . He was in the *zone,* and the world, for the first and only time in his life, opened miraculously before him every time he needed safe passage. Roadblocks? You want to know how he got past the roadblocks? Listen: He's racing down the turn lane of Buford Highway, he's pumping that Buick fast as it can go, and, down the hill, he sees a cop car blocking his way, straddling the lane—so you know what Tony does? He turns his *lights off,* and then, when the cop's about a hundred yards away, he turns them back on. . . . You want to see a motherfucker get out of the *way?* This cop's *tires* are smoking, and then—*aah:* Everything's quiet, Tony's all alone, he's untouchable, he stops to *get gas.* Dig this: In the parking lot of the gas station, there's a cop sitting outside his car, a shotgun across his knees, but he's waiting for some car to come *speeding* in, he's expecting some desperate fucking character—and Tony, he's just *cool,* he drives up to the pump real slow and says, Good evening, officer. . . . He has to pay before he pumps, though, and so he walks into the gas station, tosses some fifties on the counter—he's been robbing, remember?—and when the attendant asks him if he wants change, Tony says, No, just a pack of Kools. Then he fills the tank and says, Have a good night, officer, and gets back on the road, *screeeeekkk!*

Oh, man, they threw everything at him that night, helicopters, cops from three freaking counties, but he might have made it, he might have outrun them all, if his tire hadn't blown. Now his ride is over; the helicopters are throbbing overhead, the bullhorns are blaring, a firing squad of rifles is going *click click click click click* behind him; he gets out of the car, but he doesn't turn around to face the heat; no, he figures that if the cops are going to shoot him, he's going to make them shoot him in the back, and so he keeps facing front, and what he sees is this: the interstate, absolutely empty, stretching north before him, an infinity of blacktop, a void so quiet he can hear it say *Aah.* He turns around, slowly; he sees cops, cars, blue lights, sharpshooters, rifles, pistols, you name it, but there, behind the law, he sees something else, something he has created: the world's biggest traffic jam, a line of cars backed up to fucking Pensacola, a captive audience just waiting for Tony Mobley to get on with the show.

Tony Mobley confessed to the murder of John Collins on March 13, 1991.
Tony Mobley was sentenced to death for his crime on February 20, 1994.
His sentence is being appealed.

Cal Fussman

Eleanor Ferguson
Is Very Good with Words

When Cal Fussman says he's working on a "story," he means it. "Most of my writing is in short story form," he says. Countering the tradition of news-at-the-top journalism, he entices readers to enter, then doesn't let them out. Finding his own style–it's not for everyone–took time. Some stories backfired, yielding bewildered editors and kill fees. But as he learned from a fortune cookie, "If your life is free of failure, you're not taking enough risks."

What's so special about the story form? News dies but a story lives on. "Years from now, someone can pick up this story, laugh some, and still have to read to the last word," he says. Fussman searches for the tension that could drive a work of fiction: someone vs. something. "If I can't find that friction," he says, "I'll do anything to squirm out of the assignment." With Mrs. Ferguson he used himself–touchy 36-year-old–and the game to make her background and reactions interesting. Along the way he tucked in a history of Long Island and a book review. No wonder it won a prize–from the American Association of Sunday and Feature Editors.

The story structure, he emphasizes, requires skilled editors who understand fictional forms and can locate narrative glitches, not just lop paragraphs. "I have to write for editors I trust, who want me to swim in deep water and will defend me like a Doberman," he says. When New York's Newsday *closed down, Fussman took the buyout option along with 250 other reporters and editors. Now he freelances, writing for* GQ, Life, *and ESPN's new magazine* Total Sports.

Fussman graduated in journalism from the University of Missouri (1978) and wishes he had spent more time in class and less at the campus paper. But he's been learning ever since–whether teaching 8th grade, odd-jobbing on three continents, running a marathon, sparring with a welterweight champion, retaking chemistry, or starting the accordion.

There's no time, though, for lowbrow literature. "Reading is a sacred part of the day," he says, "because what you read can change your life." It changed his. After reading Jorge Amado, book after book, he just had to go to Brazil. There he met his wife, and now he speaks Brazilian-Portuguese to his son. So savor great storytellers, he advises, like Guy de Maupassant and O. Henry and William Saroyan, and try John Sayles's The Anarchists' Convention. *And remember, God is in the details.*

–CM

Oh, no, she doesn't. She's not going to fool me. Look at her—sitting in front of the board, wrapped in that blue sweater against the autumn chill like the sweetest of old ladies. As if this is supposed to be a nice, friendly game of Scrabble. As if I—a 36-year-old writer at the zenith of his intellectual powers—will take it easy on her because she's a 91-year-old great-great-grandmother who can't hear very well and shuffles around in fuzzy Santa Claus slippers. So sorry, Mrs. Ferguson. I'm gonna mop the floor with you.

I've done my homework. I'm not going to be suckered in. I know that Eleanor Ferguson is no ordinary old lady. This is a woman who's just authored a book—a book called *My Long Island* that describes in elegant detail life from the turn of the century to World War II, life at a time when the Expressway was scrubland. I've read it through and through, know all about her: How as a farm girl she'd gobbled up the complete works of Robert Louis Stevenson, O. Henry and William Shakespeare; how her father, Hal B. Fullerton, a publicist for the Long Island Rail Road, was a lover of wild tales and the words that glued listeners to them. Yes, and I have spies who tell me that Mrs. Ferguson's been lying in the weeds for me, boning up on crossword puzzles and unscrambling words in that game called JUMBLE as she awaited my visit to the hospice in Vermont where she now lives. But it's more than her facility with the language that I fear. It's the endurance in her genes, the toughness in her bones. One of her daughters runs marathons. Another started competing in triathlons at the age of 61. And let's not forget her great-grandfather, the one who became infuriated when a newspaperman printed something he didn't like, the one who stalked off to punch the scribe out—at the age of 95.

So sorry, Mrs. Ferguson, but no prisoners will be taken. "It's a lovely afternoon for a game of Scrabble, isn't it?" I say in my most syrupy voice.

Her left eyebrow arches. "You're not the type of young man who invents words, are you?" she says. "Well, I warn you, I've got a copy of the Official Scrabble Dictionary right over there. And you'll notice it's rather well-used."

I feel myself biting my lower lip, can hear the song echoing in my head. All the way up the interstates from Long Island, I'd listened to a Billy Joel cassette, to the song that made me want to talk with Eleanor Ferguson in the first place, the one that starts:

> I've seen those big machines
> come rolling through the quiet pines
> Blue suits and bankers with their Volvos
> and their valentines
> Give us this day our daily discount outlet merchandise
> Raise up a multiplex and we will make a sacrifice.
> Now we're gonna get the big business
> Now we're gonna get the real thing
> Everybody's all excited about it
> Who remembers how it all began—out here in No Man's Land?

Mrs. Ferguson remembers. Yes, she could tell me exactly how Long Island was and how it turned into what it is. She's probably seen more change in her life than 99 percent of the people who've walked this planet. Born into a home of kerosene lamps, she gave birth to a son whose job was to inspect nuclear weapons loaded into planes that flew off the coast of Maine on constant alert during the Cold War. She had seen her father devote his life to luring people out to the blessed island with experimental farms that grew Halbert Honey watermelons, Black Red Ball beets, White Icicle Radishes, Howling Mob Sweet Corn and 996 other varieties of fruits and vegetables. She had even seen the Smith Haven Mall. Fourteen years ago, she left Long Island for Vermont to be close to her older daughter–to go back to nature. Yes, surely she could explain.

But now there is a Scrabble board between us. Hell with the interview, heck with the story. No way can I let a 91-year-old beat me. What was it that Lao Tzu said? That the art of warfare is based on deception? Well, then, divert her, outfox her, confuse her–then finish her off.

She motions to the pouch containing the tiny wood squares of letters. "Whoever draws the letter worth the most points goes first," she says. "First word gets double points."

I draw an M–three points. She pulls out an E–worth one.

"I'm more than willing to let you go first," I say, "but if you insist . . ." I use the starting advantage to total 12 points from the measly word GEM, then quickly scribble down the score before she has a chance to reconsider.

She looks over her letters. "You know, Mrs. Ferguson," I interrupt, "I was very impressed by that photo of you at four years old with the giant cabbage. I don't know anything about growing cabbages, but I've never seen anything at all like that in a supermarket. How did they make 'em grow that big back then?"

"Dynamite."

"Dynamite?"

"The explosions that cleared the stumps from the land," she says. "That's one of the reasons. The nitrogen got into the virgin soil and the vegetables really shot up."

She sets down the word PEAR for six points. YES! Keep her off balance, keep her talking.

"Clearing stumps for farmland?" I inquire. "About the only reason they clear land now is to develop malls."

"Malls!" Her face contorts as if she's bitten into a rotten peach. "We didn't *buy* things for Christmas. We made presents with what we had. And back then they were truly appreciated."

That's it, don't stop now.

"My great-grandson went out and got an electric eggbeater. Can you tell me what's so arduous about beating an egg?"

Rile her up!

"Back then work wasn't such a bad word. In the morning you started to work and you worked until you went to bed at night. I don't know what kind of parents the teenagers these days are going to be."

I lay down the word ZERO. "Let's see, Z is 10 points . . . E is 1 . . . R is 1 . . . O is 1 . . . double word score. That puts me ahead–61-44."

She studies her tiles.

"You know, Mrs. Ferguson," I say, "I wonder who'd have it tougher: You living nowadays on my Long Island. Or me living on your Long Island at the turn of the century?"

She looks up.

"Do you think you could ride on summer mornings bumper to bumper on the Long Island Expressway?" I ask. "Windows up to keep out the exhaust fumes and horns. Radiators boiling over."

"There are some things that might have made you uncomfortable had you lived in the early part of the century," she says. "For instance, there were no fire departments. Usually in the spring, sparks shot off the railroad tracks and caught fire. Sometimes the fires were small and you could stamp them out with your feet. But other times they'd jump firebreaks and roads and burn for acres and acres. One day a fire might be five miles to the east and the next it'd be in your own backyard."

She puts down two tiles. XI.

"Hold on here! XI! What kind of word is that?" I start to reach for the Official Scrabble dictionary.

"It's a Greek letter."

"Oh, yes, yes, of course," I say, trying to appear as if I'd never reached for that reference book at all. Look at that—she's wedged in that X worth 8 points so it sits next to an I in two directions.

Eighteen points from two letters!

We're tied. I stare down at my tiles. I'll show her—I'll come up with my own Greek letter. Let's see, there's Alpha, Beta, Gamma—damn, that's all I can recall. Why did I have to get so drunk at all those fraternity parties in college? All I can do is to turn READ into BREAD by adding the B.

She's playing like a farmer, getting the most out of her tools and territory. Listen to her voice—strong and confident. Look at how relaxed she is. The folks who come to this hospice are supposed to die within six months. And that's what doctors figured would happen when she arrived with that bad heart. But that was 2 years ago. The source of her strength is plain to see. She stays alive simply by appreciating the flowers around her, just as she'd done for the first eight years of her life in Huntington with the pond and the whale-bone seat in the backyard, and then at the experimental farm with the delicious cantaloupes that her father started in Medford, and then at the apple and peach orchard in Middle Island where she and her husband passed on the values of nature to their three children.

The book she wrote is not for a display window in a mall bookstore. It's not for money. She put pen to paper for the same reason she tended the flower beds. It was her daughter, Anne, who condensed and revised 22 times and spent thousands of dollars to get *My Long Island* published. No, it's not going to be on any best-seller list, maybe only a few copies will be sold through direct mail and at the Historical Society in Riverhead. But still, it's nice to come across passages like this:

When I hark back, it is sounds—sounds and smells—that shaped the world. Each sound had a chance to stand out, to make itself heard then. Now we live in such a maze of noise that you can't distinguish one sound from another and all the little ones are lost.

Let me shut that all out and think back to what I could hear on a summer day in Huntington in 1908. A lawnmower–hand-powered. A clinking, whirring sound accompanied by the smell of new-mown grass.

A horse-drawn wagon in the street. That nice clip-clop that the cupped hoof makes on a dirt road. Sometimes it was the water cart that came through sprinkling down the dust, and then you had that unique smell of wet dust. Or it was the ice wagon that stopped out front. There was the clink as the tongs grabbed hold of a cake of ice, steps on the brick walk, and you knew the ice was sliding into the cool maw of the icebox. . . .

Yes, the sense of peace radiating from her on the other side of this Scrabble board comes from that Long Island. I wonder if it's a peace that anybody growing up on Long Island now can have. I would love to have that serenity some day. But not now. I'm 26 points behind and looking at six vowels worth a point apiece. Hell with it. Time for something drastic. "Joey Buttafuoco and Amy Fisher. That's one thing you didn't have to deal with back in your Long Island."

"Who are they?"

"You've never heard of Joey Buttafuoco?"

"No."

"Allow me to explain . . ." Joyfully, I start spewing every sordid detail, but she cuts me off.

"Oh, we had our ten-day wonders."

"This is no ten-day wonder," I say. "We're talking daily headlines, television movies, radio talk shows. You can't get away from it and there's no end in sight."

She shakes her head. "Life's too short to pay attention to that sort of thing," she says. "Even if you're ninety-one years old."

She puts down the word QUEER in the corner over a box for double word score: 28 points.

"Of course," she says, "some skill is involved in Scrabble. But sometimes the winner is the one who gets the better letters."

DON'T PATRONIZE ME, Mrs. Ferguson, I want to scream. But I stare down at my letters in gloomy silence.

"I can remember when we first got the radio," she says. "We set the earphones in a crystal bowl to amplify the sounds and try to get stations as far off as Pittsburgh. What would you do now without your television and radios? Without a weatherman to tell you a blizzard was coming? What would you do if the electricity went off in your house and the snow piled up so high you couldn't get out? That's what happened to us once. For ten days. But we got by because we were self-sufficient. I'd been canning all summer. We had a cellar full of food. There was coal for the furnace and kerosene for the lamps. Do you know what? We had a wonderful time. My husband got out his mandolin. We played board games. If the electricity goes out and the computers go down now the whole world stops because nobody can do things without them anymore."

The pieces are running out. The board is clogged like eastbound traffic on the LIE at 5:30 in the afternoon. She's ahead by 24. It's hopeless. She's going to win.

"How did it happen to Long Island?" I ask. Games aren't important, Mrs. Ferguson. I've got an interview to do. "How did your Long Island turn into my Long Island so quickly?"

"I don't quite know," she says. "You probably could use Levittown as an example. We saw it coming up. We knew the boys coming back from the war needed the homes. But it was such a small part of Long Island. Next thing you know a lot of Long Island looked the same way. And people like you don't even know how to grow a head of cabbage."

She sighs. "If my father saw Long Island now he'd probably throw up his hands in despair. You don't realize how things are changing until they've already changed. Look at this." She points to a development coming up across the field outside her window. "That all used to be cow pasture."

Somehow I was not humiliated when she put down her last word and took my pieces. "I guess that is what I get for hanging around malls," I say. I look down at the board, up at her and smile. "Rematch next fall?"

"Sure."

"I hope to be better then," I say, vowing to start a garden next spring.

David Cohen

Diary of a Commuter

"I'm a safety net for the writer, a bridge to the reader," David Cohen says of his job as copy editor for The Boston Globe Magazine. *Deleting deadly clichés and omitting unnecessary words, he toils at the task of Sisyphus. So his own writing happens occasionally. His genre is the essay, a fluid form that carries an attitude–let's think about this. Cohen has thought about what it means to run over toads when mowing the lawn, whether he could have saved that man who jumped into the Mystic River, how to deal with stepping on his son's prized violin.*

For five years he thought about commuting and commuters. Engaging with those faces in the metro broke the rule of the rails, but some travelers talked and some gave performances. He and his editor struggled to select, to find the unifying thread. "You can't edit yourself," he says. One rule he applied ruthlessly: no embellishment or recreation after the fact. That meant leaving many crazy characters on the platform. But Cohen can document every word in his journal, tie every incident to his notes. He can also attest to the riskiness of blowing his own cover. "Hey, I'm a spy. I write things down," he revealed to his fellow riders.

A lifelong wordsmith, Cohen thinks working with writers and editors means diplomacy. Some of his protocols sound simple: activate the passives, split the compounds, kill the "which" clauses, read George Orwell. Some don't. "The easy way out is often the wrong way," he says. Cohen survives on a high print diet, reading magazines, political journals, novels, and short stories. Some stories he reads and rereads–Norman Maclean's A River Runs Through It *and* Young Men and Fire *and especially Hemingway's "Big Two Hearted River." Cohen can't get enough of that profound use of detail–like Nick's onion sandwich. Now that's writing: the shock of recognition as we see the ordinary in a whole new way.*

His one elective as a business major at the University of New Hampshire (1966) changed his life–101 Newswriting and Reporting, taught by Donald M. Murray. "He taught me a craft, and I've been in newsrooms ever since," Cohen says. Murray also helped Cohen write a cover letter for his résumé and suggested five words, "I know how to work." Another short sentence Murray and Cohen live by comes from Horace: Nulla dies sine linea.

–CM

The duke's nostrils flared and then whitened." I read this line in a novel that my seatmate was reading on a commuter train. She had boarded in Beverly and was so thoroughly absorbed in the book that she did not notice

David Cohen, Diary of a Commuter, *The Boston Globe Magazine,* September 4, 1994.
Reprinted courtesy of *The Boston Globe.*

my absorption in her. Though our shoulders and knees touched, we were never-theless strangers. I did not know or care why the duke's nostrils flared, but sitting beside the trim woman on the train, our bodies touching, our nearly identical black briefcases side by side on the floor, I tried to make my own nostrils flare. They would not.

Commuting to my job in Boston gives me a daily opportunity to be entertained by city life. Walking the streets, passing strangers by the hundreds, I revel in the variety of the people and their activity. But mostly, I savor the anonymity. At home, walking to the village store for a carton of milk, I might exchange a greet-ing or share a conversation with nearly every person I meet. On Boston's Con-gress Street, at Downtown Crossing, on the Red Line, at South Station, on a commuter train, I am an invisible man. The urban mask is a kind of luxury. In my North Shore neighborhood you cannot watch others without being watched in return. In the city you can stop, you can stare, you can listen. You can even take notes.

Like many who have spent their lives working on newspapers, I can read upside down. After boarding a subway in Dorchester during the evening rush, I spied a woman who was making an entry in what looked like a diary. I decided to read it. Inching closer, so that my head was directly over the seated woman's, I looked down. What I saw was the fastest handwriting I have ever witnessed and the tiniest letters I have ever seen. The characters that spilled from her speeding pen were so small that they lacked definition. Reading it was like trying to interpret a page full of ciphers. Making no sense of the writing, I concentrated on the writing instrument, an extraordinarily fat, yellow pen, the kind with a half-dozen buttons on top, for alternating the color of the ink. In the woman's small hand, the pen seemed as big as a banana.

Jostled by passengers on all sides, hanging over the woman in an almost predatory way, I tried to take it all in: the huge, yellow pen; the flying, indeci-pherable letters; the fact that she was *printing*, one tiny letter at a time, shooting them onto the page as if from a machine gun. She wrote in the yellow mode. The entry above was in another color, blue, I think, and the one before that, on the left-hand page, red. I saw green, too, and maybe orange. The lines of type were so close together that I could interpret no words, only bands of color. She seemed to be painting the page with her pen, spitting out the letters in an almost linear mechanical pointillism. I was mesmerized.

So was the man, wearing a Bruins jersey, squeezed in beside her. As he, too, watched the color pour from her pen, he shook his head from side to side. He looked up, and our eyes locked in one of those shared but wordless moments when you know that a stranger is thinking the same thing, or something approx-imating it, about an event that is unfolding. In our case the reaction was *wonder*. He looked away, the moment ended, and I heard myself say, almost to the air: "That is the tiniest handwriting I have ever seen."

The diarist looked up. She was in her 20s, a tidy young woman with a friendly, open face. She either didn't suspect or didn't care that I was trying to read her secrets. "I've been watching you write," I confessed. "I couldn't help myself. I've never seen anyone write that fast or that small. Is that a journal or diary?"

As the train made its stops and passengers got on and off, she told me her story. She had been keeping the diary since 1980, when she was in the sixth grade. "I use different inks, so I can delineate the days." *Delineate the days,* I thought. What a perfect way to describe what she was doing.

"I'm impressed by your printing," I said. Thus bidden, she held up the diary so I could see the words clearly. Now that I was exposed, I made no effort to read them. "What do you write?" I asked.

"Just the facts," she said.

"Really?" I said. "Just facts? No thoughts or feelings, no opinions or observations?"

"Just the facts," she repeated. "It's interesting to look back and see what I was doing three or four years ago."

At that point the train reached my stop, I bid the woman a hurried goodbye, and I exited the car. I'll never forget our brief exchange, and I'll never know if it warranted a letter-packed line in her diary.

My own irregular journal, hardly a diary, is a commuter's record of some urban moments. It goes back a dozen years, but the jottings are so haphazard that they would fail to show what I was doing even three or four days ago. The entries are made on scraps of paper, book jackets, magazine covers. Unlike the subway diarists' unembellished time line, my notes contain ambiguities and mysteries to delight the urban tourist.

Several weeks ago, on Congress Street, I saw what looked like smoke or steam pouring from a depression. I approached the spot, expecting to find a manhole, and found an actual hole, about 10 inches in diameter, that seemed to lead into nothingness. The urban infrastructure itself, crumbling before my very eyes! I looked around for someone with whom to share this moment, but despite the throngs of people heading for work, I was alone.

On subsequent mornings I inspected this hole, the steam rising like vapors from a fetid swamp, my imagination playing with the idea of scaly creatures lurking beneath the streets of the financial district. Then, finally, I spied my opposite number, a man walking through town with a toolbox instead of a briefcase but grasping a similar magnum mug of coffee. He was half a block from the hole when he saw the steam, veered instantly toward the spot, and, as I had days earlier, stopped to peer inside. I let him stand there for a few seconds, then joined him. He looked at me, then at the hole, then back at me, and then we silently looked at the hole together, smiling and shaking our heads in shared community as the steam from what could only be an unholy Otherworld wafted around us. Before he could say it, I did: "You know, at night, that's the hole the giant lizards use to enter the city." We roared as one, saluted each other with our mugs, and parted.

Comparing them unfavorably to New York's other denizens, E. B. White once disparaged commuters as the "queerest bird of all," providing the city its "tidal restlessness" but little else. While praising both natives and newcomers, White dismissed commuters as flecks in the stream who discover "nothing much about the city except the time of arrival and departure of trains and buses, and the path to a quick lunch."

Because most commuters have their work cut out, these words sting. Commuters may not be of the city, but many want to at least share in it. When my own commute becomes trancelike, and it does, I have but to recall White's words to break the spell. "The Long Island Rail Road alone carried forty million commuters last year," he wrote in the summer of 1948, "but many of them were the same fellow retracing his steps." As a commuter who refuses to wear the mantle of that meek fellow, I seek different paths.

On the eve of the last gubernatorial election, I came face to face with William Weld, the man who is now governor of Massachusetts. He was standing outside North Station, trying to get the attention of those like myself hurrying to catch trains. Most people rushed past, but a few accepted Weld's handshake or at least nodded at his greeting and appeal for votes. I could have stepped around him but, in an instant, decided I would shake the candidate's hand.

I had only just made up my mind whether to vote for him or his opponent, John Silber, and as Weld's hand gripped mine, I leaned in and, straight-faced, told him of my decision. Without releasing my hand, he regarded me soberly, smiled, and said . . . well, it doesn't matter what he said. What mattered was the extra second or two of contact in the crowd, the stop-time handshake, the tiny snatch of urban buzz I enjoy carrying home with me on the train.

A few hours after my encounter with Weld, members of my family viewed a television news segment about 11th-hour campaigning. As my family watched, there was John Silber, the college president, gesturing to a crowd; and in the next scene, there was Bill Weld, the former U.S. attorney, shaking hands with . . . *Dad.* Not only shaking hands, but talking, and, as seen by the videocam lens, appearing to talk intimately. The segment was repeated in a later broadcast, and I had to endure exaggerated ribbing at work the following day. For once, my urban mask had been stripped away.

Usually, the mask stays in place, providing the protection that has let me witness urban dramas with concern but immunity: a woman in labor, a blind man's tumble, a car crash, an arrest on the subway. More often, the mask provides the anonymity for brief exchanges that I might otherwise have avoided.

There was the disheveled man who approached me one hot morning on the Red Line platform at South Station. He could have been a street person or simply overdressed for the weather–he wore an overcoat–but he had his sights on me when he was 100 feet away, and he began talking to me when he was still 50 feet away. He ignored the other people on the crowded platform, who had to clear a path for him, and headed right for me. I could have moved away, I suppose, but because of the mask, I held my ground.

"Last night's [unintelligible]," he said. "I thought [unintelligible] having a baby [unintelligible]." With his face only inches from mine, he gave me a loopy grin and just stood there, perspiring.

"Oh," I exclaimed, dumbstruck but with perfect understanding. "*Quantum Leap.* I saw that. Last night. He had a *baby.*"

"I didn't like that at all," he said. "Sometimes the show [unintelligible.] But last night [unintelligible]."

"You know," I said, before the man suddenly turned and walked back the way he had come, "I didn't like that episode, either."

It's not all comedy and bizarre coincidence. My routes to and from work take me past at least a dozen beggars a day, and my journal reflects unease and ambivalence with these encounters.

At least once a week, I give beggars all my change. I am a repeat customer: The beggars I shun I tend to always shun; those I help I will help again and again. I favor passive types, but not so passive that they're sitting on the sidewalk. The man or woman who blocks my path usually gets nothing, but I will go out of my way to give a coin to, say, the man near the Haymarket subway station holding pictures of his children. "God bless you," he always says.

I am partial to middle-aged men claiming to be jobless breadwinners or victims of Agent Orange, and I am a sucker for elderly women with luggage and wild hair. I am turned off by people who panhandle with their children, and I won't give a dime to anyone panhandling with a dog. I am generous to old men who stand quietly with their hands out but steely to young, able-bodied types, the demonstrably drunk, and anyone with a shrill voice, especially when that voice is coupled with an annoying or confusing plea: Though sympathetic to her plight, whenever I heard the woman in the wheelchair at North Station screech the words, "Donate to bone cancer," I quickened my pace.

Depending on my mood, my response to panhandling is judgmental, emotional, gullible, disbelieving, moralistic, you name it. For some reason it matters what destitute strangers do with the money I give them, or at least what I think they do with it. I don't keep track of my handouts, but they can't exceed $50 in a year. What does *that* buy? So I feel guilty when I give and guilty when I don't give. I want them all to go away (homeless, go home?), but until they do, I can't look away.

A gangly and unkempt panhandler reached out to me rather aggressively last month near City Hall Plaza, thrusting his paper cup in my path and making wordless eye contact. I hesitated, felt in my pocket, found some coins, and dropped them, about 75 cents' worth, into the cup. "Good luck to you," I said, and continued on my way. I had walked about three paces when he screamed, "Why did you say 'Good luck'? What was *that* about? Why 'Good luck'?" He stood in the middle of the sidewalk, staggering menacingly while people streamed around him. The guy had dropped his cup of coins and was gesturing at me angrily. Down and out on the streets of Boston, possibly drunk, perhaps mad, and yet he was attempting to read between the lines of an innocuous remark.

The streets can indeed be mean. My journal records three times in the past year when a mob of pedestrians surrounded and pummeled the cars of impatient drivers. After one such melee, the car, which had grazed a pedestrian, was minus a taillight, and my briefcase was minus a handle, the only time I ever raised the satchel in anger. I have stood at the curb while a well-dressed man, nearly knocked down in a crosswalk, blocked the path of the errant car, pounded on the hood with his fists, and shouted obscenities, nearly reducing the driver to tears. I also have seen a man, angry that a woman would not yield for pedestrians on Causeway Street, smash the driver's-side window and threaten to drag the motorist from her car.

While I have yet to discern a pattern to the hostility that permeates the roadways of this city, on some days it is almost palpable. If there is ever a postmortem for the unwalkable, undrivable city, the chronicler will have to decide, once and for all, whether it was lawless pedestrians who made drivers homicidal or murderous drivers who made pedestrians maniacal.

Until a series of events dissuaded me, I was occasionally autobound myself. One of the events was a minor accident that sent me to Boston City Hospital in an ambulance. Wearing a neck brace, I lay on a gurney waiting to see a doctor. An emergency-room official with a clipboard checked on me from time to time, but no doctor came. After an hour or so, obviously much less in need of attention than the people around me—some had been punched, stabbed or worse—I got up and went home.

Another contributing event involved a taxi that I was following on the Southeast Expressway. The driver, cleaning out the cab as he inched along, was lobbing things out the window in a steady stream. It started with paper but soon escalated to food and cans and finally a footlong flashlight that the driver discarded a piece at a time: first the cap and lens (hook shot into the adjacent lane, *ka-bing*), then the bulb and its reflective dish (slam-dunk to the pavement, *ka-chunk*), then the flashlight casing (bullet pass to the car ahead, *ka-donk),* and finally the batteries, lofting through the air like depth charges (backhand flip to my windshield, *ka-pow*).

Whatever else it is, and it is darned scary, driving in and out of Boston is a form of isolation, demanding a defensive, even evasive, posture: The *last* thing the carbound commuter wants is contact with another driver. This is anathema to the curious, note-taking pedestrian. For him, contact is commuting's biggest reward.

The blocks between the North End and Dewey Square are a stage for the entire panoply of human experience. From the moment I exit a commuter train at North Station and begin my anonymous walk to South Station, where I board a Red Line car for Dorchester, I can witness pathos, violence, heartbreak—or imagine it unfolding. Even on those days when I make the trek in a somnambulist trance, like a TV viewer numb to the flickerings on the screen, I know I am being touched and made different, however slightly, by the experience.

A pedestrian stopped me near Post Office Square late one afternoon and asked how to get to a particular address. I told him I didn't know. He said, "Well, what street is this?" Though I had been using the same cross street for months, I couldn't identify it. This made me very sad. I had walked through the area time and again, at one point cataloging the number and kind of wardrobe elements that litter the gutter, and yet for all my attention to one kind of reality I had become blind to another. I could document that wrecked umbrellas, solitary gloves, and the odd shoe were the most conspicuous detritus between here and Government Center, but I couldn't name the street I was on.

The next morning, walking through Boston, I thought about the previous day's encounter. Retracing my steps, and mindful of E. B. White, I headed for the unidentified street and, once there, made a note (just the facts) for my journal: "Where, exactly, am I?"

Only in the city do I confront metaphysics before my second cup of coffee.

Melinda Ruley

Downeast: On Blackwater

Writers for alternative papers have a different take on risk. They brainstorm about how to be weird. When reporters at Durham's Independent Weekly *were unhappy with both candidates for governor of North Carolina, Melinda Ruley invented a better one, a female dream candidate. Readers thought she was real though, and even started sending checks.*

"On Blackwater" is all fact and the first of a three-part series about the crab industry "Downeast." It explores issues of race and gender, foreign and domestic workers, pollution and the environment. To get the story, Ruley got time away from her paper, a grant from the North Carolina Arts Commission, and moved to the shore. For two months she arrived at the crab house at 4 A.M. Eventually she accomplished what the owner had told her was impossible in this "closed society" –her subjects started to talk. For Ruley the risk was always about portraying these extraordinary women fairly and honestly, without condescension. The women knew the risk too. "They were very savvy and kept me straight," she says. So she made her presence–and the potential for distortion–part of the story and succeeded in conveying their power, wisdom, and dignity.

An English major, Ruley graduated from the University of North Carolina in 1983, then went on for an M.A., writing a thesis on Truman Capote. She thinks the novel is far from dead and reads a lot of them, from Jane Austen and Henry James and "a ton of the classics" to Cormac McCarthy, Grace Paley, Stanley Elkin, John Updike, and especially Don DeLillo–"the Charles Dickens of our time." Next she got hooked on freelancing. First were restaurant reviews, then book reviews, profiles, and features, until her stories were appearing in all kinds of places–from Out *and* Creative Loafing, *to* USA Today *and* The Washington Post. *She won a Livingston Award for Young Journalists in 1995. On the staff of the* Independent *since 1989, she's on leave now for a baby named Henry, but she'll be back, maybe as a columnist, maybe to write a book about the courts. She's always looking for the perfect trial–as well as the perfect candidate.*

Ruley advises writers to read voraciously, to write about everything, and above all, to take courage. "Don't be humble," she says. "Start with an attitude. Be aggressive. There's plenty of time to get meek and scared."

–CM

DURHAM, N.C.–Toward the end of our interview, Ruthellen stopped in midsentence and glared at me. She'd been talking about a difficult time in her life, a time of back-breaking work and hard decisions and uncer-

Melinda Ruley, Downeast: On Blackwater, *Independent* (Durham, NC) *Weekly,* June 29, 1994. Reprinted courtesy of the author.

tainty. I sat on the sofa and waited it out. She leaned forward, tapped a finger on my knee—hard—and said, "Don't write us as foolish womens when we tell you so much."

Ruthellen is onto the problem.

Last April I began work on a project on the lives of crab pickers in a small town in eastern North Carolina. The pickers were black, mostly poor, mostly uneducated. Few had traveled beyond the swampy coastal counties they were born in or held jobs outside the crab houses that line the creeks and rivers of those counties. Though many of the women knew my grandmother, who lived in their town and delivered some of their children, I was a stranger—white, curious, standing at the screen door with a Steno pad.

Most times, the screen door swung open and I was invited to sit at the kitchen table—or go fishing, or visit a relative in the hospital. As the weeks passed, family albums were opened, letters read, grandchildren introduced. I was asked to supper, invited to church and welcomed to sit at the picking tables at the crab house. Steno pads filled up and the tape recorder ran, recording hours' worth of stories about a group of women and a way of life that is ending.

Reading through the notebooks and listening to the tapes, I consider Ruthellen's warning and think how easy it is to exploit memories refracted by years and circumstance. Reporters fortunate enough to hold the material of people's lives in hand rarely see the quicksand spread around them, how easy it is to turn people into objects of our wisdom and our pity, and thus coerce them into caricatures.

When this happens, the last laugh is on the reporter who, eagerly describing what she hears and sees, overlooks the silences, the veiled comments and countercodes—the *woman,* in other words, who's talking so funny. Downeast, every remark, every anecdote, no matter how personal or intimate, is filtered through the politics of the small-town South. These crab pickers are not just a working-class subculture, they are elderly black women living in small towns and hinterlands claimed by tide and wind, a piece of the South in which Jim Crow prospers, in spirit if not law. The reporter who fancies herself a confidante to her sources, the beneficiary of unqualified truths, is kidding herself. When the project is over, you will leave and they will stay and nobody forgets it.

And yet the truth is told, a truth of hard work and poverty pieced together from the stories and the faces and the hands, deciphered from the shifting complexities of affection and exploitation. Only occasionally is there a frank appraisal—plumb on the mark and no apologies. "What you going to do if they don't treat you fair?" said Velma Murray, a crab picker for 52 years. "They got you between a tree and a stump."

The truth is also surprising. These woman are not without power and accomplishments, though it is not power and accomplishment as the world generally reckons them and has little to do with "empowerment," the buzzword of the '90s. Despite working a job that is tedious and smelly, that offers low wages and no benefits and currently is threatened by the influx of Mexican immigrants, the women I met were proud of their work.

"First-things-first is just different for some people," Ruthellen said, standing beside a clothesline festooned with wisteria. "I see womens on 'Oprah' talking about how they president of their companies and they ain't happy. Got a swimming pool and children in the college and they so unhappy they got to go on a TV talk show. I worked a honest living at the crab house and it was bad bad bad sometimes. Work was nasty, smelled bad. But they was always food for my babies and a little something for them to get started on when they got big. Do you see me on a TV talk show? I ain't ashamed: You can write that down: Ruthellen ain't ashamed.

Twenty miles north of Durham, the Tar River flows knee-high and warm as bath water. Teen-age girls stand on the banks with bamboo poles and cast into the current; elbows cocked, hipbones aslant, they issue idle threats to the tea-colored water. "Mista Fish I ain't here to feed you dinner, come on now." It is hot and when a truck rumbles over the bridge above, headed for a nearby tobacco field, the girls hush and wait for the breeze before recommencing. "*Mista* Fish *what* did I tell you?"

Born in the clay flats of Person County, the Tar River winds southeast through the piedmont and coastal plain, clearing by a good 15 miles the Triangle's metropolitan centers, its asphalt apron of Jiffy Lubes and octiplex cinemas. Instead, the river flows through tobacco fields and sidles up to towns like Pilot, Heartsease and Stanhope, places you can get to from Raleigh in a matter of hours and step out of your car onto ground that *smells* different. (Downeast is for a fact different, and here's how: In Raleigh, you get in your car and drive to the bank; if someone gets in your way you change lanes. The bank is the target. In Heartsease, you get in your car and drive up behind a piece of heavy equipment sidewinding down a two-way road. In Heartsease, you wait for the all-clear signal before you pass; while you wait you watch a hawk hang in the sky and remember a name you thought you had forgotten. The trip is the target. That's Zen. It's also downeast.)

In little Washington, just east of the Beaufort County line, the Tar River passes under a bridge, spreads out, slows down and becomes the Pamlico River. The river flows 33 miles before emptying into the Pamlico Sound, which in turn fans out to meet the Outer Banks and, beyond, the open Atlantic.

Near the mouth of the Sound, the Pungo River angles down out of the pocosins of Hyde County and joins the Pamlico. The rivers are fed by salt tides and blackwater creeks that snake through inland swamps and savannas. Though threatened by corporate farms and river-bottom mining, that estuarine combination of salt and freshwater continues to nurture a good deal of what we call seafood, including the Atlantic blue crab which, for much of this century, has been fished, cooked, picked and packed along the Pamlico and Pungo rivers.

THE "OUTLAW" PICKER

At 73, Mable Everette has seen a good deal of the century, much of it from her vantage point at the picking table. Mable met me in the middle of a rain storm at her house in Belhaven, a town of 2,300 on Pantego Creek. Because the banks of

Pantego Creek, an offshoot of the Pungo River, rise only four feet above sea level, rain is an uneasy blessing. Years ago, when my grandmother lived in Belhaven, we held our breath during hurricanes that would drown the chickens and carry porch furniture out to the Sound.

This, however, was a routine crisis, a steady spring rain that filled ditches, swamped front yards and floated small toys. A gray cat sat beneath the fig tree, looking damp and cross, but the rain was of little consequence to Mable, who sees most events, meteorological or otherwise, as blessings by virtue of the fact that she is alive to witness them. Like a lot of women I talked to, crab pickers in their seventies and eighties, Mable spoke as if she lived beneath a reprieve that might be lifted at any moment. Lord spare her, she would buy food tomorrow, clean the house Wednesday, see her grandson off to his prom Friday night.

Mable Everette is a kind of self-proclaimed icon of Belhaven's crab pickers and an "outlaw" picker. "That means fast," she says, "*fast* fast." Mable lives in a pink house with sky-blue walls and a glamour photograph of herself as a young woman, hair arranged in a glossy hive. "Hair and beauty is my *second* love," she says. "Crabs is No. 1 with me, and that's the way it is. I am the only one so far that has picked 101 pounds of crab meat in one day," she says. "I came out and took the record for that."

For most of her life, Mable has picked crabs for the George Baker family of Belhaven. In the '30s, she picked for "George Baker One," rumored to be the first person in Belhaven to pick a crab. She saw her current employer, George "Georgie" Baker III, through diapers while she worked for his daddy, "Big George Two." When Big George Two died, Mable was a flower girl at his funeral, a tribute to her friendship with him and her loyalty to the family, a loyalty that has survived nearly seven decades.

I started picking when I was 7 years of age. My sister and I lived with my old aunty Sally, and she was rearing us by herself and we did what we could to help. I would wake up at 2 and go in and work to the crab house until it got light. Then they would walk us up to some of the people's house to wash up and get us some breakfast and walk on up to school. It took some willpower to stay awake in school, but we did it.

I was always good at it, always fast with my hands—picking cotton, picking up potatoes. I'm just fast. I learned first to crack claws, that's easier and that's what they teach you when you're little. Then I learned to pick. They put what I earned on my aunt's time card.

I finished school and got married but that didn't stop me. It was instilled in me to go to the crab house. I went to the Madame K. Mitchell Beauty school in Portsmouth. My sister and I always had a lot of thick hair, and we had the lamps and the straightening combs and we would press our own hair. I have taught beauty culture and I love missionary work, but I have never stopped picking crabs. Every chance I got, I was down to the crab house.

People say to me, "Mable, why do you work so hard? Why do you keep so much food in your kitchen?" It's a part of me because I remember the summers when we'd come home from the crab factory, and we would be in the field chopping corn and cotton, and I was so hungry I didn't know what on earth to do. And I just looked right up, and I said, "Lord, if I ever live to see to get going on my own I'm gonna eat anything in the world that I want." And I do.

I'll be 74 in October, if God's willing. I have positive thinking. People say, "Don't go to the crab house, that's some nasty work." That crab house has caused many people to pay off their mortgages, it has sent children to school. It's been the only thing around here for women to do, and it's an honest living.

THE HOUSE OF CRAB

Baker's crab house sits in the northwest corner of town, where Battalina Creek cuts in from the Pungo. The building spans a stretch of dirt and creek bank at the edge of residential Belhaven. At 4:30 A.M., when the pickers begin to arrive, silvery eyes watch their headlights from the creek bank, and shapes pare away from the black background: deer, fox, raccoon.

The crab house itself hums with the machinery of its innards: steamers and cooling units, industrial-sized fans and power generators. The company truck sits in the gravel parking lot under a street light. There is an airbrushed seascape mural on the side of the truck: A tiny trawler cutting the water above an Atlantic blue crab and a colossal mermaid. The mermaid, an aquatic Farrah Fawcett-Majors, is the focus; she looks as if she could knock the vessel off the horizon with a flip of her hair.

By 5 o'clock on opening day, metal hoppers filled with steamed crabs are rolled into the picking room and work begins. (Crab picking is seasonal work, given a calendar by sun, rain and tide. The pickers usually work from April to December, and from 5 A.M. until 2 P.M. No one is sure why they start so early, though there is speculation that it is a holdover from pre-air-conditioned days.) There are only a handful of men in the crab house, and they surge to and fro in a small gang, tending to fuse boxes and conveyor belts, hoses and scales. The crab house is largely what Mable calls "a female place." Approximately 30 women, most of them following in the footsteps of their mothers or grandmothers, sit and stand at stainless steel tables that run the length of the room.

CAREFUL WITH THE LUMP

My mama used to pick crabs, says Lena Smith. I remember her coming home from the crab house and fixing supper. Just a routine thing, a job. My aunt picked crabs, my sister picked crabs. Just about all of my family have picked crabs. There's nothing here but crabs, shrimp and crabs and working in the fields. That's about the only thing there is.

I tried picking crabs when I was 16, but it didn't work. Some way or another I could never get the hang of it at that time. So I did house work and field work. I cleaned a little house for Georgie's mama. I worked in corn, cabbages, things like that. As I got older I started to gain in bills. I had a baby, and that was a big bill. I knew I had to get a job.

At first, I was a claw cracker but it came to a point that it started to work on my nerves. Cracking claws made me real nervous on the inside, that constant hammer motion. That's when I started learning to pick. I caught onto that. The main thing was keeping the bones out of the meat. I always have had to work on my bones; 'cause if the meat is bony the boss gets a lot of bad reports.

So I learned how, and I been going on about my business ever since. I do all right. I have made up to $60 a day. Every now and then I'll have a touch of arthritis, or my fingers may be stiff, but you go to work and forget all about it. Speed is where you make your money. I slow down with the lump because the prettier you can get that lump out the more money Georgie can get for it. He wants you to take your time on that lump 'cause that's where he gets his money.

PICKING SEASON BEGINS

There is a row of small windows and a wet concrete floor and a conveyor belt that carries crab carcasses to a dump truck outside. Each woman holds a single small knife and sits before a pile of crabs, scarlet red from the pressure cooker. The women wear plastic aprons over knit slacks or house dresses. They are expected to wear hair nets and leave fashion accessories at home, but there are always a few conspiracies. Women tuck their curlers into flowery shower caps or lacy hair nets. A few wear lipstick and earrings. The building smells like high school biology class the day the cat bags are opened.

Because it is opening day the women are minding the crabs, hunting a rhythm that will carry them through the next eight hours, the next eight months. To make minimum wage, each picker must pick three pounds an hour. Beyond that, they earn $1.50 a pound. Although a fast picker can make $300 a week, or $10,000 a year, many can pick only enough to make minimum wage. There are no health insurance benefits, no paid sick leave or pension benefits.

During much of the off-season, and in the spring when there are not enough crabs for a full week's work, pickers pick up extra work cleaning houses or receive unemployment checks. Occasionally, if the season starts late or the crabs are scarce, crab house owners will falsify work schedule records in order to qualify their pickers for unemployment benefits. It is a charitable gesture with a hidden agenda: "Bossmen don't want you finding no other work," says one picker. "They're afraid you won't come back to the crab house."

Early in the season, the crabs make minimum wage a challenge even for the fastest pickers. They are "mud crabs," small and hard, trawled at the mouth of the Pamlico River, or off the cold floor of the Sound. Later in the summer, local crabbers will supply more of the catch, and the crabs, the pickers say, will be "prettier"–bigger, softer.

For now, though, the crabs are hard and "bony," and, to make matters worse, most are "sooks," or female crabs–and most have eggs. "Sooks is the hardest to pick," says Mable, who nevertheless flies through the crabs, "backing," or pulling off the back fin and legs, plucking out the "jumbo lump"–the most expensive meat–then scrapping out the gills and eggs and picking the fine meat of the "ends" and "shoulders." "Sooks is built to protect the eggs. They're the most flavorful crabs but they're hard on your poor hands."

CRAB HOUSE TALK

Two hours pass and the sky comes through the windows, pink over the Creek. The weighers begin to process the plastic containers the women have filled. Maggie and Joyce sit at the "boning table," picking bits of shell and egg out of meat. The women begin to talk and laugh, catching up on news. Some nurse wads of tobacco or snack on crackers tucked into the tops of their aprons. When they spot Jody, a young man who walks around gathering tubs of claws, a discussion ensues on the consequences of his marital problems.

"I remember what he looked like when he first came here."

"He used to be beautiful. Used to could smell him come in the room."

"Had biceps all over him, looked like he just come out of college."

"That's what problems at home will do to you, is make you dwindle away."

"Got to have things right at home; I tell him there is more than one fish in the pond."

"Mm-mm-mm."

Although most of them live within walking distance of each other, opening day at the crab house is a kind of reunion, an opportunity for the exchange of information and gossip: Velma Murray's mother has not spoken from her hospital bed; Hilda Warren's daughter found a night-shift job in Washington; Maggie Moore was so excited about opening day she could not sleep all night.

There are updates on grandchildren, their appetites and illnesses, milestones and setbacks. Mable talks about her boyfriend, "Pink," who has checked into the hospital "probably for all his life." Velma sits on top of a stack of plastic chairs and trades insults with a picker across a mound of crabs.

"Velma, you are *in* my face."

"Hush up and act right. Can't you see I'm trying to get you straight?"

"I don't want to hurt you, Velma, Lord knows I don't."

"Ain't you a mess? You a bad girl."

"Go on, now, with your chubby self."

The other picker is Weasel, a distant cousin of Velma's, who claims kin, by blood or marriage, to most of the women she works with. "That's the way it runs," she says. "Crabs is a family tradition."

"We been knowing each other all our lives," says Mable, who cuts her eyes at Weasel whenever there are threats of bodily harm and advises me to ignore the battles, which usually end with giggles and kisses. "We are very close and special to each other," she says. "It is a togetherness place."

Everyone is excited. Georgie Baker walks around the picking room, teasing and laughing, taking an informal inventory of his workers: Who can he count on to work a full season? Who will quit before Labor Day? "Don't throw my claws out!" he hollers amiably. Mary Frances pops Maggie on the bottom with a wet towel and somebody makes a funny comment about the cluster of men working on the plumbing. Everyone is laughing. It is therefore surprising when one of the pickers looks up from her work at the boning table and says, quietly, "You put down in that notebook we are the lowest paid women in the world."

BELHAVEN USED TO BOOM

Business is poor in Belhaven. Tobacco does not grow in the humus, and textile mills have not made it east of little Washington. If you are lucky you work for the seed supply company or across the river at Texasgulf. Borden has left; Norfolk & Southern has left. Shops stand empty and waitresses, high school girls with limp perms and tangerine perfume, do their homework in the backs of restaurants. On the outskirts of town, men spend their days leaning over engines; children read below grade level and get hookworm; dogs live in a dirt circle beneath a mulberry tree.

In town, between Business 264 and Pantego Creek, the ruins of the old Cooperage Mill sprawl across acres of marshy bank, all of it For Sale. Cooperage was big business 60 years ago. When the timber boom supported lumberyards and mills, loggers cut old-growth cypress and the railroad brought workers in from the county. Well-to-do lumbermen and farmers moved to town and built houses with wraparound porches and gingerbread eaves. Edna Ferber was said to have visited, as were Orville and Wilbur Wright. Main Street prospered, and crab houses lined the creek banks and paid workers to do piece work: cut fish, shuck oysters, head shrimp and pick crabs. Each crab house had a distinct whistle to call employees to work.

Today bees live in the Cooperage Mill smokestack, and the crumbled bricks look snaky.

Belhaven used to be a fine place, a success. There was work for the menfolks back then, and it was a grand town. Crabs was plentiful and big, and there were lots of crab houses. It was a proud place to be living and raising a family. When Cooperage closed down it was a loss for the men that worked there.

MATTIE REMEMBERS

Mattie Ebron lives in a mill house purchased by her husband, John Booker T. Ebron, after Cooperage Mill closed down. The house is fastened to a wheat field on the northern edge of town, and standing in Mattie's front yard, your back to the town, there's nothing but lonely space, the flat earth and bands of shimmery color: emerald wheat, a smudge of scrub pines, then the sky, itself another sub-stratum, heavy and fragrant. It is not the bowl sky of the Midwest; downeast the sky descends, in a kind of perfumed siege. Mountain people are uneasy in Beaufort County, where even the creeks are vast and unwrinkled.

Mattie farmed with my great grandparents and kept house for my grandmother when she moved to town; the link between us affords certain privileges: For instance, every day I visit Mattie she asks me to feel the bones in her body knotted and pushed out of joint by arthritis and "general elderliness." She also snaps at me when I ask stupid questions.

Where else you think we womens worked except the crab house? They ain't nothing else. I worked in the field with a grub hoe, I cooked for the Navy shipyard and hung 'bacca in Rocky Mount. But my family was here, and I always came back here to the crab house. It was my life. Me and my sister Georgia both. Georgia was a outlaw picker. Lord, that woman could pick some crabs! I was fast but I wasn't like her. Womens worked so hard back then. To the crab house all day then come home and your feet all swolled up from standing. Got to jump on the yardwork and tend the garden and get the children fed. We was hard-workin', Lord knows we was.

Mattie is so small and frail her stockings sag around her ankles, and the bones of her skull show. Her dress is held together by safety pins. She refuses to be photographed, claiming she's gotten too "poorly." In fact, she is beautiful, but she discards the compliment like a bit of trash left on the kitchen table—the same quick brush of her hand—and, changing the subject, chastises me for driving around town by myself. Mattie is suspicious and fretful and keeps a two-by-four nailed to her front door. "Ain't you scared?" she says. "I see on the TV how they choke womens and leave 'em on the road. I don't go out by myself."

When Mattie's face is held to the light it's possible to imagine her years earlier, fearless and strong, working the crab house in the morning, spending her afternoons raising a white family, one eye on the ironing, another on the stove, listening for distress signals from children playing beneath the crepe myrtle trees. It's also possible to understand how Mattie and other black women, watching jobs disappear and their community run to seed, felt the only thing of strength and certainty was, as Mattie puts it, "courage and nerve power of womenfolks."

Men most generally don't help womens. The crab house was all womens. We ran the place and without us the place was nothing. The bossmen knew it. They would come along every day and tell us how good they liked us. They know a man won't do a job like that. A man'll get to thinking about the smell or he'll say I'm too good for this. A man'll walk off a job like that. Womens have more strength than men. Men don't want to do nothing but sit around or walk the road.

Chapter

Telling Stories
That Persuade

Keith B. Richburg

Continental Divide

Writers like Keith Richburg are changing our understanding of journalism, teaching by way of their self-reflection the shortcomings of the "just-the-facts" school. The facts, inevitably, are gathered from a point of view, a worldview. As Richburg explains: "I am a black man born in America, and everything I am today–culture, attitudes, sensitivities, loves, and desires–derives from that one simple and irrefutable truth." Such an admission in a newsroom is risky. But Richburg goes further and admits the unthinkable for a descendant of slaves, "I thank God my ancestor made that voyage."

In writing "Continental Divide," he says, "I knew I would incur the wrath of many who would accuse me of being a 'sellout,' a 'self-hating black man,' and more. But I wanted to write a piece that honestly reflected my feelings, without pulling any punches to satisfy popular sentiment or deflect criticism." That meant reporting from a personal perspective. "It was," he says, "a major departure from the style of my normal foreign dispatches." And a major success. The article drew such wide acclaim that he was asked to turn it into a book. So he wrote Out of America: A Black Man Confronts Africa.

Richburg was born and raised in Detroit, majored in political science at the University of Michigan, worked on The Michigan Daily, *was named Harry S Truman Scholar in 1978, graduated in 1980. Then he followed his urge to travel, to study–a graduate degree from the London School of Economics and a year at the East-West Center in Honolulu–and to write.*

With the world as his beat–currently he is The Washington Post *Hong Kong bureau chief–his reading is global too. He reads articles about places he doesn't cover, academic books about places he does, history and journalism and fiction, Graham Greene classics, and Paul Theroux's latest. "Read, read, and read some more," he advises. But wait to write. "By the time I turn on the computer, I have a clear idea from beginning to end. Colleagues ask how I write so fast. The writing is the easy part–deciding what to say takes time."*

Yes, it takes time, especially for a writer who asks hard questions–"Are you black first or a journalist first?"–and who knows that "the most important journey I took was the one inside my own mind and soul."

–CM

Keith B. Richburg, Continental Divide, *Washington Post Magazine*, March 26, 1995.
Reprinted with permission of *The Washington Post.* © 1995.

I watched the dead float down a river in Tanzania.

Of all the gut-wrenching emotions I wrestled with during three years of covering famine, war and misery around Africa, no feeling so gripped me as the one I felt that scorching hot day last April, standing on the Rusumo Falls bridge, in a remote corner of Tanzania, watching dozens of discolored, bloated bodies floating downstream, floating from the insanity that was Rwanda. .

The image of those bodies in the river lingered in my mind long after that, recurring during interminable nights in desolate hotel rooms without running water, or while I walked through the teeming refugee camps of eastern Zaire. And the same feeling kept coming back too, as much as I tried to force it from my mind. How can I describe it? Revulsion? Yes, but that doesn't begin to touch on what I really felt. Sorrow, or pity, at the monumental waste of human life? Yes, that's closer. But the feeling nagging at me was–is–something more, something far deeper. It's a sentiment that, when uttered aloud, might come across as callous, self-obsessed, maybe even racist.

But I've felt it before, that same nagging, terrible sensation. I felt it in Somalia, walking among the living dead of Baidoa and Baardheere–towns in the middle of a devastating famine. And I felt it again in those refugee camps in Zaire, as I watched bulldozers scoop up black corpses, and trucks dump them into open pits.

I know exactly the feeling that haunts me, but I've just been too embarrassed to say it. So let me drop the charade and put it as simply as I can: *There but for the grace of God go I.*

Somewhere, sometime, maybe 400 years ago, an ancestor of mine whose name I'll never know was shackled in leg irons, kept in a dark pit, possibly at Goree Island off the coast of Senegal, and then put with thousands of other Africans into the crowded, filthy cargo hold of a ship for the long and treacherous journey across the Atlantic. Many of them died along the way, of disease, of hunger. But my ancestor survived, maybe because he was strong, maybe stubborn enough to want to live, or maybe just lucky. He was ripped away from his country and his family, forced into slavery somewhere in the Caribbean. Then one of his descendants somehow made it up to South Carolina, and one of those descendants, my father, made it to Detroit during the Second World War, and there I was born, 36 years ago. And if that original ancestor hadn't been forced to make that horrific voyage, I would not have been standing there that day on the Rusumo Falls bridge, a journalist–a mere spectator–watching the bodies glide past me like river logs. No, I might have instead been one of them–or have met some similarly anonymous fate in any one of the countless ongoing civil wars or tribal clashes on this brutal continent. And so I thank God my ancestor made that voyage.

Does that sound shocking? Does it sound almost like a justification for the terrible crime of slavery? Does it sound like this black man has forgotten his African roots? Of course it does, all that and more. And that is precisely why I have tried to keep the emotion buried so deep for so long. But as I sit before the computer screen, trying to sum up my time in Africa, I have decided I cannot lie to you, the reader. After three years traveling around this continent as a reporter for *The*

Washington Post, I've become cynical, jaded. I have covered the famine and civil war in Somalia; I've seen a cholera epidemic in Zaire (hence the trucks dumping bodies into pits); I've interviewed evil "warlords," I've encountered machete-wielding Hutu mass murderers; I've talked to a guy in a wig and a shower cap, smoking a joint and holding an AK-47, on a bridge just outside Monrovia. I've seen some cities in rubble because they had been bombed, and some cities in rubble because corrupt leaders had let them rot and decay. I've seen monumental greed and corruption, brutality, tyranny and evil.

I've also seen heroism, honor and dignity in Africa, particularly in the stories of small people, anonymous people—Africans battling insurmountable odds to publish an independent newspaper, to organize a political party, usually just to survive. I interviewed an opposition leader in the back seat of a car driving around the darkened streets of Blantyre, in Malawi, because it was then too dangerous for us even to park, lest we be spotted by the ubiquitous security forces. In Zaire, I talked to an opposition leader whose son had just been doused with gasoline and burned to death, a message from dictator Mobutu Sese Seko's henchmen. And in the Rift Valley of central Kenya, I met the Rev. Festus Okonyene, an elderly African priest with the Dutch Reformed Church who endured terrible racism under the Afrikaner settlers there, and who taught me something about the meaning of tolerance, forgiveness, dignity and restraint.

But even with all the good I've found here, my perceptions have been hopelessly skewed by the bad. My tour in Africa coincided with two of the world's worst tragedies, Somalia and Rwanda. I've had friends and colleagues killed, beaten to death by mobs, shot and left to bleed to death on a Mogadishu street.

Now, after three years, I'm beaten down and tired. And I'm no longer even going to pretend to block that feeling from my mind. I empathize with Africa's pain. I recoil in horror at the mindless waste of human life, and human potential. I salute the gallantry and dignity and sheer perseverance of the Africans. But most of all, I feel secretly glad that my ancestor made it out—because, now, I am not one of them.

First, a little personal background that may be relevant to the story at hand.

I grew up as a black kid in 1960s white America, not really poor, but not particularly rich either. Like most blacks who settled in Detroit, my father had come up from the South because of the opportunities offered in the automobile plants, which in the 1940s were gearing up to meet the demands of America's World War II military machine. He joined the United Auto Workers, and stayed involved in union politics for more than 40 years.

There were actually two black Detroits while I was growing up, the east side and the west. The dividing line was Woodward Avenue, our own version of Beirut's infamous Green Line. But the division was more psychological than geographic, centered mainly on black attitudes, the strange caste system in black America at the time, and where you could place your roots in the South. Roughly put, the split was between South Carolina blacks on the west side and Alabama blacks on the east. These were, in a way, our "tribes."

It sounds strange even to me as I look back on it. But those divisions were very real to the black people living in Detroit when I was young, at a time when the city was transforming itself from predominantly white to predominantly black. It was drummed into me that South Carolina blacks, like my family, owned their homes and rarely rented. They had small patches of yard in the front and kept their fences mended. They came from Charleston, Anderson, Greenville, sometimes Columbia. They saved their money, went to church on Sunday, bought their kids new clothes at Easter and for the start of the school year. They kept their hair cut close, to avoid the nappy look. They ate turkey and ham and grits and sweet potato pie. They were well-brought-up, and they expected their children to be the same.

Don't cross Woodward Avenue, we were told, because those blacks over there came up from Alabama. They talked loudly, they drank heavily, and they cursed in public. They had darker skin and nappier hair. They didn't own homes, they rented, and they let the grass in the front run down to dirt, and their fences were all falling part. They ate pigs' feet, and often had more than a dozen relatives, all from Alabama, stacked up in a few small rooms. They were, as my father would have called them back then, "niggers"–South Carolina blacks being good colored people. The greatest insult was "He ain't nothin'–he just came up here from Alabama!"

Detroit can get oppressively hot in the summers, and those little houses that black families owned then didn't have anything like air conditioning. So to stay cool, my brother and I would walk (you could walk in those days) down Grand River Avenue to the Globe Theater, where for less than a buck you could sit all day, watching the same movie over and over in air-conditioned splendor until it was time for dinner. I especially remember when the movie *Zulu* was playing, and we watched Michael Caine lead a group of British solders against attacking Zulu tribesmen in what is now South Africa. We took turns cheering for the British side and the Zulus. But neither of us really wanted to cheer for the losers. Whoever was rooting for the Africans would usually sit sullenly, knowing what fate held in store. Then came the credits and the heady knowledge that when the movie played again, after a cartoon break, you would be able to cheer for the British once more.

Beyond what I learned from *Zulu*, I can't say I had much knowledge of Africa as a kid. I probably couldn't have named a single African country until high school. The word "black" came into vogue in the 1960s, thanks to, among others, James Brown. In 1967, Detroiters burned a large part of the city to the ground, and then all the white people I knew in my neighborhood starting moving out to suburbs that seemed really far away. A lot of people my father called "black radicals" took to wearing African-style dashikis and stocking caps in red, black and green, the colors of African liberation. But, when you were a kid from a quiet, South Carolina family growing up on the west side, these seemed like frightening symbols of militancy, defiance, even violence. Any connection to a strange and unknown continent seemed tenuous.

Why am I telling you all this? What does Detroit more than a quarter-century ago have to do with contemporary Africa? Maybe I'm hoping that bit of personal history will help explain the attitude of many black Americans to the concept of their own blackness, their African-ness.

You see? I just wrote "black Americans." I couldn't even bring myself to write "African Americans." It's a phrase that, for me, still doesn't roll easily off the tongue, or look natural on the screen of the computer terminal. Going from "colored" to "black" took some time to get used to. But now "African American"? Is that what we really are? Is there anything African left in the descendants of those original slaves who made that long journey over? Are white Americans whose ancestors came here as long ago as the slaves did "English Americans" or "Dutch Americans"? Haven't the centuries erased all those connections, so that we are all now simply "Americans"?

But I am digressing. Let's continue with the story at hand.

Somewhere along the line, I decided to become a journalist. It was during my undergraduate years at the University of Michigan, while working on the school newspaper, the *Michigan Daily*. My father would have preferred that I study law, then go into politics. Blacks in the 1970s were just coming into their own in politics, taking over city halls across the country and winning congressional seats in newly defined black districts. And that's what articulate, well-educated black kids did: They became lawyers and politicians.

But I wanted to write, and to travel. The travel urge, I think—a longing to cross an ocean—is shared by a lot of midwesterners. I became a reporter for *The Post*, and would take trips overseas whenever I could save up the money and vacation time. Paris. Morocco. Brazil. London for a year of graduate school. Train journeys across Europe. Trips to Hong Kong, Taiwan, later Japan and China.

But never sub-Saharan Africa (defined as "black Africa"). Whenever friends asked me why, in all my travels, I had avoided the continent of my ancestry, I would usually reply that it was so big, so diverse, that it would take many weeks if not months. I had studied African politics in school, even written a graduate school thesis on the problem of single-party states in Africa. I considered myself a wide-eyed realist, not given to any romantic notions about the place.

The real reason I avoided Africa had more to do with my personal reaction—or, more accurately, my fear of how I would react. I knew that Africa was a continent with much poverty and despair. But what would it be like, really like, to see it as a black person, knowing my ancestors came from there? What if I found myself frightened or, worse, disgusted or repulsed?

And what would it be like, for once in my life, not to stand out in a crowd? To be just one of a vast number of anonymous faces? For better or for worse, a black man in America, or a black man in Asia, stands out.

A friend of mine in Hawaii, a fourth-generation Japanese American, told me once of her fear of traveling to Japan. "I don't know what it would be like to be just another face in the crowd," she said rather innocently. It was a sentiment I immediately shared. When, in early 1991, my editors at *The Post* asked me if I wanted to cover Africa, that same feeling welled up inside me. I was in Asia on vacation when I got the assignment, and I sought out a Reuter reporter named Kevin Cooney, who was based in Bangkok but had spent several months working in Nairobi. He put it to me bluntly. "In Africa," he said, after we both had a few too many beers, "you'll be just another nigger."

It was a well-intentioned warning, I would find myself recalling often over three sometimes-tumultuous years.

"Where are you from?" the Zairian immigration officer asked suspiciously in French, fingering through the pages of my passport.

I found the question a bit nonsensical, since he was holding proof of my nationality in his hand. I replied in French, "United States."

"I think you are a Zairian," he said, moving his eyes from the passport photo to me to the photo again. "You look like a Zairian."

"I'm not a Zairian," I said again. I was tired, it was late, I had just spent the day in the Rwandan border town of Cyangugu, just across from Bukavu in Zaire. And all I wanted to do was get back to my room at the Hotel Residence, where, at least if the water was running, a shower awaited. "Look," I said, trying to control my temper, "that's an American passport. I'm an American."

"What about your father—was he Zairian?" The immigration man was not convinced.

"My parents, my grandparents, everybody was American," I said, trying not to shout. "Maybe, 400 years ago, there was a Zairian somewhere, but I can assure you, I'm American."

"You have the face of a Zairian," he said, calling over his colleague so they could try to assess which tribe, which region of Zaire, I might spring from.

Finally, I thought of one thing to convince him. "Okay," I said, pushing my French to its limit. "Suppose I was a Zairian. And suppose I did manage to get myself a fake American passport." I could see his eyes light up at the thought. "So, I'm a Zairian with a fake American passport. Tell me, why on earth would I be trying to sneak back into Zaire?"

The immigration officer pondered this for a moment, churning over in his mind the dizzying array of possibilities a fake U.S. passport might offer; surely, using it to come into Zaire was not among the likely options. "You are right," he concluded, as he picked up his rubber stamp and pounded in my entry. "You are American—black American."

And so it went around Africa. I was constantly met with raised eyebrows and suspicions upon explaining that I really was, really am, an American. "I know you're a Kenyan," said one woman in a bar—a hooker, I think, in retrospect. "You're just trying to pretend you don't speak Swahili."

"Okay," I told her, "you found me out. I'm really a Kenyan."

"Aha!" she said. "I knew it!"

Being able to pass for an African had some advantages. In Somalia, for example, when anti-Americanism was flaring as U.S. Cobra helicopters were bombing militia strongholds of Gen. Mohamed Farah Aideed, I was able to venture into some of the most dangerous neighborhoods without attracting undue attention. I would simply don a pair of sunglasses and ride in the back seat of my beat-up white Toyota, with my Somali driver and AK-47-toting bodyguard up front. My biggest worry was getting caught in the cross hairs of some U.S. Army marksman or helicopter gunner who would only see what, I suppose, we were: three African-looking men riding around Mogadishu's mean streets in a car with an automatic weapon sticking out one of the windows.

But mostly, I concluded, being black in Somalia was a disadvantage. This came home to me late in 1993. I was one of the reporters at the first public rally Aideed had held since coming out of four months of hiding. The arrest order on him had been lifted, and the Clinton administration had called off the humiliating and futile manhunt that had earlier left 18 U.S. soldiers dead in a single encounter. The mood at the rally was, predictably, euphoric. I was among a group of reporters standing on the stage awaiting Aideed's arrival.

Suddenly, one of the Somali gunmen guarding the stage raced up to me and shoved me hard in the chest, forcing me down onto my back. I looked up, stunned, into his wild eyes, and he seemed to be pulling his AK-47 off his shoulder to take aim at me. He was shouting in Somali, and I couldn't understand him. A crowd gathered, and there was more shouting back and forth. Finally, one of Aideed's aides, whom I recognized, helped me to my feet. "I apologize," the aide said, as others hustled my attacker away. "You look like a Somali. He thought you were someone else."

Being black in Africa: I had to fight myself to keep my composure, to keep from bursting into tears.

Many months later, I found out it wasn't only black Americans who felt the way I did. That was when I ran across Sam Msibi, a black South African cameraman for Britain-based Worldwide Television News. I was stuck in Gikongoro, in southwestern Rwanda, and I needed a ride back to Bukavu in Zaire. Msibi was driving that way and gave me a lift.

Msibi had started out in the early 1980s at the South African Broadcasting Corp., then joined a German station, and had worked for a while as a cameraman for the TV station in the "independent" homeland of Bophuthatswana. Since joining WTN, he had covered the worst of South Africa's township wars, back when the African National Congress and the Zulu-based Inkatha Freedom Party were still battling for political dominance.

Msibi knew better than I what it was like to be a black journalist amid Africa's violence; he had been shot five times, in Tokoza township, and managed to live to tell the tale. "It's a problem in Africa," he said, as he navigated the winding mountain road. "When you're black, you have to worry about black-on-black violence."

"Sometimes I want to stop to take pictures," he said, surveying the scene of refugees on the move toward the border, often with their herds of cattle and goats in front, always with small children trailing behind. "But I don't know how these people will react." I explained to him, naively, that I had just traveled the same road a week or so earlier with a Belgian TV crew that had no problem filming along the highway. "Yeah, but they're white," Msibi said. "These people might think I'm a Hutu or something."

I grew quite fond of Msibi during that nearly four-hour drive; I found that he, a black South African, and I, a black American, were thinking many of the same thoughts, venturing together into the heart of an African tragedy that was about as different from downtown Johannesburg as it was from Detroit or Washington, D.C.

"Africa is the worst place—Somalia, Zaire," Msibi said, more to himself than to me. "When you see something like this, you pray your own country will never go this way. Who wants to see his children walking like that?

"I feel I'm related to these people. I feel they're my own people. I pity them—and not just here. In Kenya, Zambia, in Angola. I always feel pain in my heart to see this."

"In South Africa," he said, "you hear on the radio that a million people got killed somewhere in Africa, and there you are brushing your teeth, and it doesn't mean anything to you." Then he added, "It's like in America."

Are you black first, or a journalist first?

The question succinctly sums up the dilemma facing almost every black journalist working for the "mainstream" (read: white) press. Are you supposed to report and write accurately, and critically, about what you see and hear? Or are you supposed to be pushing some kind of black agenda, protecting black American leaders from tough scrutiny, treating black people and black issues in a different way?

Many of those questions were at the heart of the debate stirred up a decade ago by my *Post* colleague, Milton Coleman, when he reported remarks of Jesse Jackson referring to Jews as "Hymie." Coleman was accused of using material that was off the record; more troubling, he was accused of betraying his race. For being a hard-nosed journalist, he suffered the wrath of much of the black community, and even had to endure veiled threats from Louis Farrakhan's henchmen.

I have had to deal with many of the same questions over the years, including those asked by family members during Thanksgiving or Christmas gatherings in Detroit. "Let me ask you something," my favorite cousin, Loretta, began once. "Why does the media have to tear down our black leaders?" She was referring to Marion Barry and his cocaine arrest, and to Coleman Young, the longtime Detroit mayor who was always under a cloud for something or other. I tried to explain that journalists only do their job and should expose wrongdoing no matter if the wrongdoer is black or white. My cousin wasn't convinced. "But they are the only role models we have," she said.

It was an argument that couldn't be won. And it was an argument that trailed after me as a black reporter covering black Africa. Was I supposed to travel around looking for the "good news" stories out of the continent, or was I supposed to find the kind of compelling, hard-hitting stories that I would look for any other place in the world? Was I not to call a dictator a dictator, just because he happened to be black? Was I supposed to be an apologist for corrupt, ruthless, undemocratic, illegitimate black regimes?

Apparently so, if you subscribe to the kind of Pan Africanism that permeates much of black American thinking. Pan Africanism, as I see it, prescribes a kind of code of political correctness in dealing with Africa, an attitude that says black

America should bury its head in the sand to all that is wrong in Africa, and play up the worn-out demons of colonialism, slavery and Western exploitation of minerals. Anyone who does, or writes, otherwise is said to be playing into the old "white conspiracy." That attitude was confirmed to me in Gabon, in May 1993, when I first met C. Payne Lucas of Africare, a Washington-based development and relief organization. "You mean you're a *black* man writing all of that stuff about Africa?" he said.

Lucas was in Gabon for the second African-American Summit, a meeting bringing black American civil rights activists and business leaders together with African government officials and others. It was an odd affair, this "summit," for at a time of profound change across Africa—more and more African countries struggling to shed long-entrenched dictatorships—not one of the American civil rights luminaries ever talked about "democracy" or "good governance" or "political pluralism" in my hearing. These same American leaders who were so quick off the mark to condemn injustice in South Africa, when the repression was white-on-black, suddenly lost their voices when the dictatorships were black.

Instead, what came out was a nauseating outpouring of praise from black Americans for a coterie of some of Africa's most ruthless strongmen and dictators. There were such famous champions of civil rights as Jesse Jackson heaping accolades on the likes of Nigeria's number one military thug at the time, Gen. Ibrahim Babangida, who had just shut down a critical newspaper and was about to renege on his pledge to transfer his country to democratic rule. There was speaker after speaker on the American side complimenting the host, Omar Bongo, a corrupt little dictator in platform shoes who at that very moment was busy shutting down his country's only private (read: opposition) radio station.

But the most sickening spectacle of all came when the baby dictator of Sierra Leone entered the conference hall. Capt. Valentine Strasser, a young tough in Ray-Ban sunglasses, walked in to swoons and cheers from the assembled American dignitaries, who were obviously more impressed by the macho military figure he cut than by the knowledge that back home Strasser was summarily executing former government officials and opponents of his new military regime.

I had seen that kind of display before around Africa: black Americans coming to the land of their ancestors with a kind of touchy-feely sentimentality straight out of *Roots*. The problem is, it flies smack into the face of a cold reality.

Last March in the Sudanese capital of Khartoum, I ran into a large group of black Americans who were also staying at the Khartoum Hilton. They were there on some kind of a fact-finding trip, and being given VIP treatment by the Sudanese regimen. Some of the men went all-out and dressed the part, donning long white Sudanese robes and turbans. Several of the women in the group covered themselves in Muslim wrap.

The U.S. ambassador in Khartoum had the group over to his house, and the next day, the government-controlled newspaper ran a front-page story on how the group berated the ambassador over U.S. policy toward Sudan. Apparently, some members of the group told the ambassador that it was unfair to label the Khartoum regime as a sponsor of terrorists and one of the world's most violent, repressive governments. After all, they said, they themselves had been granted nothing but courtesy, and they had found the dusty streets of the capital safer than most crime-ridden American cities.

I was nearly shaking with rage. Couldn't they see they were being used, manipulated by one of the world's most oppressive regimes? Human Rights Watch/Africa—hardly a water carrier for U.S. policy—had recently labeled Khartoum's human rights record as "abysmal," and reported that "all forms of political opposition remain banned both legally and through systematic terror." And here were these black Americans, these willing tools, heaping praise on an unsavory clique of ruling thugs. I wanted to confront them, but instead I deliberately avoided them, crossing to the other side of the lobby when I had to, just to avoid the temptation of shouting some sense into them.

I went back to my room at the Hilton, turned on CNN—and learned that my Italian journalist friend, Ilaria Alpi, and her cameraman had been slain in a shootout in Mogadishu, left to bleed to death in their bullet-riddled car. I couldn't go get a drink—alcohol is forbidden in Sudan. I didn't want to go pace the bleak lobby and encounter those instant Sudan experts with their romanticized notions. So I stayed there in my room, alone, and cried for Ilaria.

Do I sound cynical? Maybe I am. Maybe that's because, unlike some of the African American tourists who have come out here on a two-week visit to the land of their roots, I've *lived* here.

Do you think I'm alone in my view? Then meet Linda Thomas-Greenfield, and hear her story.

Thomas-Greenfield is a black American diplomat at the U.S. Embassy in Nairobi, her third African posting; she spent 3 years in Gambia and 2½ in Nigeria. After completing her studies at the University of Wisconsin, she had spent time in Liberia, and she remembers how elated she felt then making her first voyage to her ancestral homeland. "I remember the plane coming down," she said. "I couldn't wait to touch down."

But when I talked to Thomas-Greenfield last summer, she had just finished nine months in Kenya. And she was burned out, fed up and ready to go home.

Her house in Nairobi had been burglarized five times. She had had an electric fence installed. "When they put up the electric fence, I told them to put in enough volts to barbecue anybody who came over." When she continued to complain that even the fence didn't stop the intruders, the local Kenyan police station posted two officers on her grounds. But then the police began extorting payment for their services. "I've gotten to the point where I'm more afraid not to give them money," she said. "They're sitting outside with automatic weapons."

Now she was having a higher, 10-foot-tall fence built around her grounds. And she had become so exasperated, she told me, that "I'm ready to sit outside myself with an AK-47."

In April, Thomas-Greenfield traveled to Rwanda for an embassy assignment. She had been in the country only a day when the presidential plane was shot down and an orgy of tribal bloodletting began. Most of the victims were Tutsi, and Thomas-Greenfield, a towering 6-foot-plus black woman, was immediately mistaken for a Tutsi. She recalls cowering in fear with machine guns pointed in her face, pleading repeatedly: "I don't have anything to do with this. I'm not a Rwandan. I'm an American."

In the end, it was not just the crime and her close call in Rwanda but the attitude of the Africans that wore down even this one-time Africa-lover. Thomas-Greenfield had never been invited into a Kenyan home. And doing the daily chores of life, she had been met constantly with the Kenyans' own perverse form of racism, under which whites are granted preferential treatment over blacks.

"There's nothing that annoys me more than sitting in a restaurant and seeing two white people getting waited on, and I can't get any service," she said. Once, at a beach hotel on the Kenyan coast, she complained to the manager about the abysmal service from the waiters and staff. The manager explained to her, apologetically, "It's because they think you're a Kenyan."

"I think it's an absolute disadvantage" being black in Africa, said Thomas-Greenfield, who, at the time we talked, said she was considering cutting short her assignment. "Here, as anywhere else in Africa, the cleavages are not racial, they are ethnic. People think they can tell what ethnic group you are by looking at you. And if there's any conflict going on between the ethnic groups, you need to let them know you're an American."

She added, "I'd rather be black in South Africa under apartheid than to go through what I'm going through here in Kenya."

This is not the story I sat down to write. Originally, I had wanted to expound on Africa's politics, the prospects of freedom and development, the hopes for the future. My tour in Africa, after all, came during what was supposed to be the continent's "decade of democracy"—after the fall of one-party communist states of Eastern Europe, the argument went, and the consolidation of democracy in Latin America, could Africa's one-party dictatorships and military regimes be far behind? At least this was the view of many Africa analysts, and of hopeful African democrats themselves, when I began the assignment.

But three years of following African elections, in countries as diverse as Nigeria, Cameroon, Kenya, Ethiopia, Malawi and Mozambique, has left me—and many of those early, hopeful African democrats—far less than optimistic. I've seen elections hijacked or stolen outright, elections canceled, elections bought and elections that have proved to be essentially meaningless. How can you talk about elections in countries where whole chunks of territory are under the sway of armed guerrillas? Where whole villages get burned down because of competing political loyalties? And where traditional belief runs so deep that a politician can be charged in public with casting magic spells over poor villagers to force them to vote for him?

African autocrats are proving far more entrenched, far more brutal and far more adept at the manipulation of state machinery than their Eastern European communist counterparts. Africa's militaries—as compared with those in, say, South America—are proving less willing to return to the barracks and bow to the popular will. In country after country, even oppositionists demonstrate themselves to be grasping, quarrelsome and in most cases incapable of running things if they ever do manage to make it to power. Politics in Africa is about lucrative spoils and fresh opportunities for corruption, and much of opposition politics across the continent consists of an out group wanting its turn at the feeding trough.

It's become a cliche to call tribalism the affliction of modern Africa, but, unfortunately, my years of covering African politics has convinced me that it is true. Tribalism is a corrosive influence impeding democratic change and development. In Kenya, where the opposition had perhaps the best chance of any in Africa to wrest power from a strongman (Daniel arap Moi), it splintered along ethnic lines in the December 1992 elections. One well-educated Kikuyu woman, a secretary working for a foreign news agency, told me she would never vote for the man then considered the lead opposition candidate, Jaramogi Oginga Odinga, for the simple reason that Odinga was a Luo, and Luos, you see, traditionally do not circumcise. "I will never live under a Luo president," she told me, explaining the importance of this operation to "manhood." For want of a circumcision, an election was lost. Moi was reelected with barely a third of the vote, in a split field that saw two Kikuyus dividing the Kikuyu vote and Odinga winning Luoland.

Even in places where opposition parties have managed to overcome the odds and win power in democratic elections, the results so far have been mixed. In Zambia's case, the 1991 election of Frederick Chiluba was supposed to herald a beginning of a new democratic era. But what I found there last year was a country reeling from corruption and incompetence. Government officials have been implicated in drug dealing, others have resigned in disgust claiming the old democratic movement has lost its direction. In a depressing sign of the times, the autocratic former leader, defeated president Kenneth Kaunda, took the opportunity of my visit to announce to me his intentions to launch a comeback bid.

And finally, finding hope becomes even more difficult when you look at the basket cases—places like Zaire, which is in perpetual meltdown; Liberia, still carved up between competing armies; Sudan, ground down by seemingly endless civil war; Rwanda, which was convulsed by one of the worst episodes of tribal genocide in modern times; and Somalia, poor Somalia, which has virtually ceased to exist as a nation-state.

My final journey in Africa was to Somalia—fittingly, I thought, because it was the place I spent most of my time over the past three years. I found it fascinating to cover a country in which all forms of government had collapsed, and to watch as the most ambitious post–Cold War experiment in aggressive peacekeeping tried to patch it together. I was one of those on the early bandwagon for intervention; all Somalia needed was a few Marines and some international aid, I thought, and the gunmen and militias would fade into the background. Somalia got the Marines, 12,000 of them, plus about 15,000 other U.S. troops, and upwards of $4 billion in international aid. But the place today is as violent and chaotic as when the troops first landed more than two years ago. And now the world has withdrawn, closed the door and turned out the lights, leaving what essentially is a blank spot on the northeastern tip of the continent, a violent no-man's land, a burial ground for one of the most costly and ultimately futile interventions in the history of "peacekeeping."

My final journey was to Somalia. But I found that in my time on the continent, the most important journey I took was the one inside my own mind and soul.

In trying to explain Africa to you, I needed first to try to explain it to myself. I want to love the place, love the people. I can tell you I see hope amid the chaos, and I do, in places like Malawi, even Mozambique. But the Rwandas and Somalias and Liberias and Zaires keep intruding into my mind. Three years–three long years–have left me cold and heartless. Africa is a killing field of good intentions, as Somalia alone is enough to prove.

And where does that leave the black man who has come "home" to Africa? I write this surrounded by my own high fence, protected by two large dogs, a paid security guard, a silent alarm system and a large metal door that I bolt shut at night to keep "Africa" from coming across the yard and bashing in my brains with a panga knife for the $200 in my desk drawer. I am tired and, like Linda Thomas-Greenfield, ready to go.

Another black American, writer Eddy L. Harris, the author of *Native Stranger,* ventured into the dark continent, to discover that the place where he felt most at home was South Africa, that most modern, most Western of African countries. So I'll end this journey there too, recalling my last trip to Cape Town, Africa's southern tip. I traveled the wine route, and sat and drank what I'd purchased while the sun set over the beautiful sand beaches. Cape Town is one of the world's most beautiful cities, and one can feel perfectly at peace on the veranda of the Bay Hotel. But all I remember thinking was: Imagine all the horror that lies between here and Cairo, in that vast stretch of earth we call black Africa.

So, do you think I'm a cynic? An Africa-basher? A racist even, or at least a self-hating black man who has forgotten his African roots? Maybe I am all that and more. But by an accident of birth, I am a black man born in America, and everything I am today–culture, attitudes, sensitivities, loves and desires–derives from that one simple and irrefutable truth.

Dave Barry

The Name Game

Editors' note: *As risk takers, we decided to let humor columnist Dave Barry profile himself. But we will add this: A deliberate writer, he often works through 20 drafts. "I want to have control over every word," he says. "But because humor is spontaneous, I have to rely on my first instinct that this is funny."*

Barry regularly takes risks with tone and content. In "The Name Game," he wanted to shock with language, calling a CEO dirty names, commenting on sexual behavior. In "Dude," he pricked the industry as a media insider. Self-critical, he wondered–too insider? Citing "overwhelmingly positive" reader response, Barry remains confident. "I don't worry about offending readers without a sense of humor."

–AK

Dave Barry was born in Armonk, New York, in 1947 and has been steadily growing older ever since without actually reaching maturity. He attended public schools, where he distinguished himself by not getting in nearly as much trouble as he would have if authorities had been aware of everything. He is proud to have been elected Class Clown by the Pleasantville High School class of 1965.

Barry went to Haverford College, where he was an English major and wrote lengthy scholarly papers filled with sentences that even he did not understand. He graduated in 1969 and eventually got a job with a newspaper named–this is a real name–the Daily Local News, *in West Chester, Pennsylvania, where he covered a series of incredibly dull meetings, some of which are still going on.*

In 1975, Barry joined Burger Associates, a consulting firm that teaches effective writing to businesspersons. He spent nearly eight years trying to get various businesspersons to for God's sake stop writing things like "Enclosed please find the enclosed enclosure," but he eventually realized that it was hopeless. So, in 1983, he took a job at The Miami Herald, *and he has been there ever since. In 1988, he won the Pulitzer Prize for commentary, pending a recount. His column appears in several hundred newspapers, yet another indication of the worsening drug crisis.*

Barry has written a number of short but harmful books, hailed by critics as "containing a tremendous amount of white space." The CBS television series, "Dave's World," is based on two. Also, he owns a guitar that was once played by Bruce Springsteen.

–DB

Dave Barry, The Name Game, *The Miami Herald*, July 28, 1996. Reprinted courtesy of the author.

I want to stress that I'm not bitter about what the Philip Morris Corp. is trying to do with the name "Dave."

In case you didn't know, Philip Morris is test-marketing a new brand of cigarettes called "Dave's." Over the last year I've seen big billboard advertisements for "Dave's" cigarettes in Seattle and Denver. These are folksy ads; one of them features a tractor. The message is that "Dave's" is a folksy brand of cigarette, produced by a down-to-earth, tractor-driving guy named "Dave" for ordinary people who work hard and make an honest living, at least until they start coughing up big folksy chunks of trachea.

Of course, there is no actual "Dave." The people at Philip Morris are just calling the new brand "Dave's" because they think the name "Dave" sounds trustworthy and non-corporate. This is pretty funny when you consider that Philip Morris is the world's largest tobacco company and has enough marketing experts and advertising consultants and lawyers and lobbyists to sink an aircraft carrier, not that I'm suggesting anything.

According to an article in *Advertising Age,* Philip Morris made up a whole story—described by a Philip Morris spokesperson as "a tale of fictional imagery"—about how the "Dave's" brand of cigarettes got started. Here's the story, as quoted by *Advertising Age* from Philip Morris promotional materials:

"Down in Concord, N.C., there's a guy named Dave. He lives in the heart of tobacco farmland. Dave enjoys acres of land, plenty of freedom and his yellow '57 pickup truck. Dave was fed up with cheap, fast-burning smokes. Instead of just getting mad, he did something about it . . . Dave's tobacco company was born."

Is that a heartwarming and inspirational tale of fictional imagery, or what? A guy—a regular guy; a guy exactly like you, except that he doesn't exist—gets FED UP with the "status quo." So instead of just sitting around and complaining, he gets up off his imaginary butt and—in the great "can-do" tradition of Americans such as John Wayne, who courageously pretended to be many brave heroes before he died with just the one remaining lung—"Dave" decides to *make his own brand of cigarettes.*

Philip Morris does not provide details regarding how, exactly, "Dave" raised the money to build his cigarette factory. Maybe "Dave" robbed a nursing home; maybe "Dave" borrowed the money from other members of his neo-Nazi group; maybe "Dave" sold his huge collection of child pornography. You could make up any story you wanted about what "Dave" did, because "Dave" is not real! That's the kind of fun you and Philip Morris can have with tales of fictional imagery.

On the other hand, you must be very, very careful when you talk about real people. An example of a real person would be Geoffrey C. Bible, who is the chief executive officer of Philip Morris.

Because Geoffrey C. Bible is real, you should not use the name "Geoffrey C. Bible" in a derogatory way. You should not, for example, say, "Darn it! The dog made Geoffrey C. Bible on the carpet again!" Nor should you permit your youngsters to use expressions such as "Tommy stuck his finger way up into his nose and pulled out a big old Geoffrey C. Bible!" Nor should you say that a person caught engaging in an unnatural act of romance with a sheep was "doing the Geoffrey C. Bible." That would be wrong.

It would also be wrong to make up a tale of fictional imagery about Geoffrey C. Bible, such as:

"Down in the heart of Philip Morris corporate headquarters there's a guy named Geoffrey C. Bible. Geoffrey C. Bible enjoys plenty of employees and a corporate jet. Geoffrey C. Bible was fed up with so-called 'scientists' saying that cigarettes kill more people every year than alcohol, cocaine, crack, heroin, homicide, suicide and O. J. Simpson. Instead of just getting mad, Geoffrey C. Bible did something about it. He deposited his enormous paycheck."

So does everybody understand the ethical point here? You must NOT take liberties with the name "Geoffrey C. Bible." You may, however, take the name "Dave" and do pretty much whatever you want to it. As I say, I'm not at all bitter that Philip Morris has decided to appropriate my name, and my father's name, and the name that a lot of regular guys who really exist have used over the years. A name that has apparently earned some measure of trust, which is why Philip Morris wants to attach its new cigarette brand to this name, the way a leech attaches itself to your leg. Who knows? If this strategy works out, maybe it'll inspire a whole bunch of new cigarette brands with trustworthy names. I bet that even as you read this, some marketing people, somewhere, are batting around the concept of "Jesus" cigarettes.

They need to keep coming up with ideas. They're in a tough business: The people who use their products—and I am NOT implying that there's a connection—keep dying of lung cancer. It's an unfortunate situation, and I for one am getting fed up. But instead of getting mad, I'm going to do something about it.

I'm going to start calling lung cancer "Geoffrey's disease."

Read All About It, Dude

Here in the newspaper industry we are seriously worried. Newspaper readership is declining like crazy. In fact, there's a good chance that nobody is reading this column. I could write a pornographic sex scene here and nobody would notice.

"Oh, Dirk," moaned Camille as she writhed nakedly on the bed. "Yes yes yes YES YES YES YES YESSSSSSS!"

"Wait up," shouted Dirk, "I'm still in the bathroom!"

It was not always this way. There was a time when everybody read newspapers, whereas today, most people do not. What caused this big change?

Dave Barry, Read All About It, Dude, *The Miami Herald*, November 13, 1994. Reprinted courtesy of the author.

One big factor, of course, is that people are a lot stupider than they used to be, although we here in the newspaper industry would never say so in print.

Certainly another factor is that many people now get their news from television. This is unfortunate. TV news can only present the "bare bones" of a story; it takes a newspaper to render the story truly boring.

But if we want to identify the "root cause" of the decline in newspaper readership, I believe we have to point the finger of blame at the foolish decline by many newspapers to stop running the comic strip "Henry." Remember Henry? The bald boy who looks like Dwight Eisenhower?

I believe that readers like the "Henry" strip because, in times of change and uncertainty, it always had the same plot:

PANEL ONE: Henry is walking along the street.

PANEL TWO: Suddenly, Henry spies an object. You can tell he's spying it because a dotted line is going from his eyeball to the object. Often the object is a pie cooling on a windowsill.

PANEL THREE: Things get really wacky as Henry eats the pie.

PANEL FOUR: The woman who baked the pie comes to the window and discovers that the pie is gone. The woman is surprised. You can tell this because exclamation points are shooting out of her head.

This timeless humor has been delighting readers for thousands of years, but for some reason most newspapers stopped running the strip and readership has been in the toilet ever since. I don't think it's a coincidence.

Whatever the cause, the readership decline is producing major underarm dampness here in the newspaper industry. We're especially concerned about the fact that we're losing young readers—the so-called Generation X.

Go to any newspaper today and you'll see herds of editors trying to think up ways to make newspapers more relevant to today's youth culture. This is pretty funny if you know anything about newspaper editors, the vast majority of whom are middle-aged Dockers-wearing white guys who cannot recognize any song recorded after "Yellow Submarine."

But they're trying. If you read your newspaper carefully, you'll notice that you're seeing fewer stories with uninviting, incomprehensible, newspaperese headlines such as PANEL NIXES TRADE PACT and more punchy, with-it headlines designed to appeal to today's young people such as PANEL NIXES TRADE PACT, DUDE.

As a middle-aged Dockers-wearing white guy, I want to do my part by making my column more hep and appealing to young people. So I'm going to conclude by presenting the views of some students of Daniel Kennedy's English class at Clearfield, Pennsylvania, High School. I recently wrote a column in which I said that some young people today have unattractive haircuts and don't know who Davy Crockett was. Mr. Kennedy's class read this column and wrote me letters in response; here are some unretouched excerpts, which I am not making up:

"Maybe one of these days you should look in the mirror, Dave. Dave, you need a new hairstyle, man! You have a puff-cut, Dave."

"You say that I don't no anything Davy Crockett. Well I know that he fought at the Alamo. He also played in several movies."

Let me just say that we in the newspaper industry totally agree with you young people on these points you wish to make, and if you will please start reading the newspaper, we'll be best friends, okay? Young people? Hello?

You're not even reading this, you little twerps.

"Oh, Dirk," moaned Camille, "I am overcome by desire at the sight of your, your, what do you call those?"

"Dockers," said Dirk.

Innocence Lost

"Taking risks? They come with my territory," says Eugene Izzi. "I only write nonfiction concerning what interests or angers me, so it's always written from the same mind-set–rage. No one has ever accused me of being objective."

A Chicago writer with 16 novels in print and 5 more under contract, Izzi is known for his moral intensity. His subjects: gang leaders, drug dealers, convicts, and hustlers. He writes about those on the edge, and he thinks he has some answers–about what creates criminals, for example. "You don't get a violent criminal without first having an abused kid," he says. He also thinks writing can change things. Sometimes his has. An article about an ex-husband in prison for stalking his wife started such a media blitz that the authorities had to parole the man out of state. That probably saved the woman's life.

At 38, Izzi wrote "Innocence Lost" for the Chicago Tribune Magazine *because of his intense hatred for the sort of "humans" who betray the trust–and innocence –of a child. "They usually get away with it, but this time the bastard didn't," he says. Izzi's presence changed the story's outcome. "The prosecutor used me as bait to trap the judge into a conviction."*

Izzi finds writing nonfiction demanding. It imposes too many constraints. "In fiction, I can interview people, as I always do–cops, crooks, phone sex operators, prisoners, whatever–then do whatever I want with what I've learned. In nonfiction, I have to be far more careful." So he takes journalism very seriously. "Most people read novels for entertainment but newspapers or magazines for enlightenment," he says. Once he lived on the street for six weeks to tell the story of homelessness from the inside.

His best advice to writers is Winston Churchill's remark, "Never, ever quit." Izzi's first published novel was the seventh one he had written. A high school dropout– "Frankly, school bored me to death"–and an Army veteran at 19, he worked full-time jobs, writing before and after work. Today, between writing novels, he reads Andrew Vachss, John MacDonald, Elmore Leonard, and the best, Mark Twain. That leaves neither time nor inclination for social life–"Nothing there for me to learn"–and besides, it's a privilege, not a birthright, to be a writer. "I want readers to feel my fury, make it their own."

–CM

Editors' note: *Four months after being interviewed for this profile, Eugene Izzi was found dead, hanging from his 14th story office window in downtown*

Eugene Izzi, Innocence Lost, *Chicago Tribune Magazine*, April 29, 1991. Reprinted courtesy of the author.

Chicago. He was wearing a bulletproof vest and his pockets contained cash, brass knuckles, and three computer disks with the draft of a novel–the story of a Chicago mystery writer, nearly murdered when thrown out of his office window with a rope around his neck. Izzi's death was ruled a suicide.

The little girl is wearing a white dress with patent-leather shoes. Her black hair is in pigtails, anchored with pink bows. She is sitting before a conference table, in a chair that is too large for her, a doll engulfed by brown wood, shyly looking up at all of the adults in the room, her large brown eyes flitting from person to person, filled with something far less than joy; maybe fear. She will not make eye contact with me, as I am not of her clan and she's learned the hard way what strangers can do, even those she'd been told she could trust. It took some time after her violation before she could trust even her father again.

She was sexually abused a year ago, when she was 3, and now she is being prepared to possibly take the witness stand and testify against the human who assaulted her. A once normal and carefree child, she is now painfully timid. She has recurrent nightmares, and most nights she wets the bed. Her mother sits next to her, one hand always on the little girl's back, as if terrified that if she doesn't maintain physical contact her little girl will disappear. From time to time her father stops pacing and leans down and kisses her, his smile nothing but teeth showing through a rigid mask.

Her soul has been stolen, her life altered irretrievably. She has been invaded by an adult whom she was told she could trust, and now she trusts no one.

The accused is 60 years old, with white hair and a lined, pockmarked face. He's been down this road before, though he has never been convicted. He has often glanced back at me from his position at the defense table in the courtroom, never holding my eyes when ours meet, like the child won't, but for different reasons. He can afford to hire high-priced legal talent, and the lawyer brings a couple of assistants with him every day, all of them ordering the client around, telling him at recesses how to act, how to look, not to smile. They caution him with sidewise glances my way; although the defense attorney has been known to court publicity, he doesn't yet know which side of the ring I'm working. At least he can look me in the eye.

We live in a city where anyone with any knowledge of the legal system is aware that some judges have been bought, where, for years before Greylord, justice had been done in the hallways rather than the courtroom–an envelope changed hands and you didn't even have to wait for your case to be called–then we throw up our hands in dismay, shocked when the details of this system hit the front pages of our newspapers. What surprise is there in that? I always thought I knew the score, but I was never aware of how few rights certain victims have in a courtroom, especially if that victim is a child.

In the previous days the defense team has been bickering with the assistant state's attorney, arguing before a jury is picked about whether the prosecutor will be able to use the term "victim," because it can plant in the jurors' minds the idea that a crime has been committed. Another point of contention has been whether the child's disclosure to emergency-room doctors, and later with counselors, can be considered "hearsay." The judge has called several recesses so he can study precedents in other cases before making his ruling. The defense is buying all the time it can get–they are well aware that kids give in under pressure.

The divorced mother had looked upon him as a kindly neighbor, a godsend who'd sit with the child at no charge while she ran errands. Now she sees him as being sent from hell. She is visibly bowed from the guilt, while the accused appears guiltless. She allowed her child to be alone with the accused. The father is slightly built, several years his ex-wife's junior.

His feelings are mixed. He feels resentment against the ex-wife for leaving the child with the molester; anger and hatred against that human for hurting his child and altering all of their lives. The accused, it seems, is the only one involved–including myself–who hasn't lost innocence, maybe because he had none to be stolen from him. The father hates this man, can't understand how anyone could ever do that to a child, or why the police questioned *him* about the molestation first. He resents the police for that, sees it as a waste of their time. Most of all, though, the father just wants revenge.

"I wish I could have got to him before the cops did," he says, nervously pacing, calming down as he kisses his child's head. Strange things are happening in his eyes, conflicting emotions dominating him. He wants to know what the holdup is, why the jury hasn't been called. The prosecutor can't tell him her suspicions just yet. He walks away from the child, expressing his pain in a soft whisper, out of the little girl's range of hearing.

"He deserves to die," the father hisses.

The prosecutor smokes cigarettes in the tiny office she shares with two others, away from the family, talking softly, worry lines on her brow.

"It's gonna get blown out of the water," she predicts. Two floors below us, the judge has recessed for lunch. The defense attorney has given a powerful opening statement, discussing this "new frontier" of law, and urging strong cautions about the credibility of small children. He left the courtroom smiling.

The prosecutor isn't smiling. Nor is the arresting officer. After the arrest, he had to take a couple of days off to get his mind right.

"It was a good bust," the cop says. "The evidence is indisputable, the doctor's report and the fact that he was the only male ever left alone with the kid. You've got a kid in *therapy* here, and she isn't even old enough to know what the word means." He lifts an anatomically correct doll off the prosecutor's desk and flips it into my lap.

"You should have seen what she showed me using this doll.

"There was no other man in her life, except her father, and we questioned him first, because in a case like this the father's usually the perpetrator. We ruled him out.

"No one else could have done it. We played it straight, by the book. I tried for hours, on several different occasions before the arrest, to get him to open up to me, to confess. He'd never open his mouth. We got the reports together and pinched him, but it looks like it won't be good enough."

But they're going to give it their best shot.

A child-abuse expert on the North Side tells me that this is not at all uncommon. Most child-abuse cases never even get to court, the parents unwilling to subject their child to the trauma of reliving the ordeal.

"Pedophiles are criminals of opportunity," she tells me. "They pick their victims carefully."

She also tells me that one child in 10 is sexually abused before they grow out of adolescence, while other experts aren't as conservative, putting the figure at one in four. The guilt and emotional suffering the children feel, even for the fortunate few who receive adequate therapy, can haunt them throughout their entire lives. No one has told them the one simple truth: that child abuse is never the child's fault.

I am allowed to witness "therapy" sessions with several of the invaders, squirming as I listen to a grossly obese, greasy, unemployed truck driver explain how his 12-year-old daughter seduced him; to a skinny Southerner who tells how he was just teaching his pre-teenaged daughter how to conduct herself when the time comes for her to go out on dates; to another who disdains such sophistry and who flatly argues that his children are *his* property, and why would he let anyone else have a shot at them?

They are all there due to court order, predatory pedophiles feeling remorse only when they are caught. There is no confirmed "cure" for their depravity. Theirs is not a consensual act of sexuality; it is a crime of terrible betrayal and brutal manipulation, the demonic preying on the innocent. Some child-abuse experts see it as a volitional choice the pedophile makes; others see it as an emotional disorder, a sickness.

One internationally recognized expert I spoke to put it in terms I understood best. "To think about sex with children is sick; to act upon those thoughts is evil." But evil isn't a word that is yet in the psychiatric manuals, so the search is still on for a "cure," and some of the pedophiles are allowed to talk their way through therapy, see the error of their ways and be reunited with the families that they have destroyed.

I also learn that adult males who have sex with female children are truly and only pedophiles; it is not an act of heterosexuality, any more than an adult male who preys on young boys is gay. It is a tag they use often, though, milking the gay community's well-known liberal attitude for all they can get, hitching their wagon to the gay caravan and hoping respectability will rub off upon them.

The child who has had her innocence stolen now sits on top of the table, having crawled there from her chair. The mood in the room is lighter, the prosecutor having just broken the news that the child will not be testifying after all. They will be relying on their experts, the doctors and psychiatrists, the arresting officer, the counselors, all of them ready to testify to fact and evidence, adults who are used to lawyers badgering them, trying to confuse them.

The child does not know about vengeance, nor about courage. She has received quite an education, however, concerning personal safety.

There are nightmares that still haunt me, childhood traumas that will never be completely out of my mind. I am no stranger to the pain that adults can inflict upon helpless children. But I am an adult now, and relatively safe. I have gained strength—built walls and defenses against the monsters, hip to the evil ones who corrupt the guileless, are cunning enough to know they can get away with it and evil enough to make the child take the blame because in their little minds they just don't know any better.

Who will give this child strength, I wonder, where can she turn for justice? To courtrooms? I am no stranger to them either. Have been inside more of them than I care to remember. I've attended drug trials and murder trials, burglary and assault and attempted-murder trials, and not always as just a curious observer. But I've never seen anything like this, the posturing, the legal maneuvering. I figure this child deserves better.

God only knows what her nightmares are; God shudders at the thought of others who might look at her and believe that she has a normal childhood, compared to their own.

Back in the courtroom I sit behind the child's grandparents. The parents are not here, have taken the child home. It is late and there is a holiday coming up, and the judge is calling it a day.

The accused walks past me with a curious glance at my notebook, safe in the knowledge that kids can't vote, knowing that he's gotten away with it before and confident in the inevitable outcome.

If it's true that one child in four is sexually abused, this guy will never be out of work, although he ought to be. I can't help but wonder if we, as a society, have the power to put him, and all the others like him, out of work permanently.

The defense attorney wishes the prosecutor a happy holiday, and leaves the defense table, walking through the low swinging doors and approaching me, smiling. He extends his hand and introduces himself, and I rise from my seat, hold his eyes so he knows it's no mistake, and walk past him, out of the courtroom.

Laura Miller

Parkland's
Pink Pinafore Problem

Laura Miller has built a career on columns that irritate news makers and news managers alike. The Dallas journalist calls herself "overly intense, occasionally maniacal"–a reporter who tends to "jump into things on impulse and then, at the sight of the first obstacle, become downright obsessed."

Her frenzy emerged in the mid-'80s at The New York Daily News *and continued in Dallas at the now-defunct* Times Herald *and* D Magazine. *Since 1991, she's regularly delivered blastout columns, 2500 to 10,000 words each, for the* Dallas Observer, *an alternative weekly newspaper in one of the country's hottest media markets.*

This determination is nothing new. As student editor, she provoked a high school principal to kill a story on the faculty vs. prom band. A journalism and political science major, she covered her campus at the University of Wisconsin for Time *magazine before graduating in 1980. She then headed to* The Miami Herald *and* The Dallas Morning News, *with freelance stints abroad, covering royal funerals and the Falklands war.*

Now, at 35, she pours out investigations stuffed with facts about those known and those about-to-be. In "Parkland's Pink Pinafore Problem," Miller delivered what she calls "lots of attitude, lots of in-your-face precision" about odd hospital policies. When a doctor's wife screamed just inches from her face, Miller admitted: "It was passionate." After all, she concedes, "telling it exactly like it is without slapping on any varnish" can be risky.

Fearful of wrong conclusions, Miller overreports, then ruthlessly self-edits while sipping a margarita at her favorite cheddar-fries hangout. Her concentration is formidable. "I push the envelope on deadline for every single story I write," she once explained. "I must be sure I'm right." Her columns draw raves, including the 1995 H. L. Mencken writing award for "Pinafore" and two others.

The chase thrills Miller. "I get real jazzed," she told a reporter at a competing paper. "I love the prying, the talking, the cajoling. I can work a phone for eight hours straight and not move from that desk." Then, she added: "If something is going on in this city that stinks, I'll try to find out about it. And I'm pretty damn good at finding out things I set my mind to. Pretty damn good."

–AK

Laura Miller, Parkland's Pink Pinafore Problem, *Dallas Observer*, May 12–18, 1994.
Reprinted courtesy of *Dallas Observer*.

Miss Honey Grove, Texas, is sitting in a plastic booth at McDonald's wishing she had something to sip, but the lines at the front counter are too long to wait in.

This whole place is a bit long in the tooth actually–grimy, smelly, and cheerless. But then, this is no ordinary McDonald's–there's no kiddie playground out back, no busy drive-through, no sunny picture windows facing the mall-filled prairie.

This is the McDonald's in Parkland Memorial Hospital–the tax-supported county hospital, the biggest baby producer under one roof in America, and the hands-down best place in the city to come after a head-on collision. Plenty of good medicine is done here.

But it's pretty much of a sludge pit.

As Miss Honey Grove–Janet Lawhon by name–sits in a uniquely clean booth in deep conversation with two other people, a tall, reed-thin man approaches her table. He is shaking violently–head bobbing erratically, hands and arms atremble. His clothes are a mess; his eyes protrude. He's in bad shape. He's also in need of money, he says.

Across the hall in the ladies' room, a young woman is trying unsuccessfully to bum a tampon off patrons. She has just washed her arms and hands–in a curiously protracted way for a non-hospital employee–but there is no paper towel to dry them off, and the two hand blowers on the wall are broken. For that matter, most of the soap dispensers are broken or torn off the wall, too, and the stalls reek of old urine and are covered with graffiti.

After five minutes in this bathroom, in this fast-food restaurant, in this hospital, I have an overwhelming urge to get the hell out of here. Forever.

Not Miss Honey Grove. She tells me quite earnestly that she wants to *stick around here* on a regular basis. She wants to minister to the poor and the sick as a volunteer–cuddle sick babies, make people smile, even commune on a regular basis with the beggar man and the tampon lady.

There's only one problem, she tells me. She's not wearing that pink pinafore.

Being a volunteer anywhere–a battered women's shelter, a soup kitchen, a nursing home–is one of the nicest things a person can do. Being a volunteer at Parkland is downright angelic–or insane, depending on how you look at it.

Janet Lawhon and Steve Whitehead even look like angels. Both are clean-cut, articulate, blond, thirtysomething pre-med students who are seeking meaningful hospital experience before applying to medical schools in the fall.

Whitehead, 41, was born in Indiana. For the past 15 years, he worked at Texas Instruments, helping build high-powered missiles. Three years ago, he began thinking more about saving lives than snuffing them out, so he began taking pre-med courses at Brookhaven Community College. That's where he met Lawhon.

Lawhon, 34, was born in a town that could have been in *The Last Picture Show*. Her grandfather and dad were pharmacists; her two brothers and a sister are pharmacists; her mom runs the downtown family pharmacy. In case you don't know where Honey Grove is, it's between Pecan Gap and Bug Tussle. (That's about 85 miles northeast of Dallas.)

At an early age, Lawhon got a strong dose of what being blonde and beautiful means in the South.

"If you were from a small town in Texas and a woman and you looked good, you were supposed to take advantage of it," Lawhon says. "So I was in the pageant. And guess what? I realized it wasn't that great."

It wasn't just that the town fathers wouldn't allow the previous 1973 winner to crown her—she was, God forbid, with child in 1976, the year Lawhon was crowned. (Miss Honey Grove 1923 was summoned out of retirement to do the honors.) And it wasn't just the constant appearances at the garden and bridge clubs. "I didn't like being a beauty queen type," she says. "Because later in life when you want to be taken seriously, it's an uphill battle. No matter what you accomplish, somebody's always there telling you you got where you are because you're a pretty blonde."

Enter Parkland Hospital. Eighteen years later.

Lawhon, an award-winning TV medical reporter in Knoxville and New Orleans, had gotten tired of watching other people save lives. Determined to go to medical school, she was looking for experience and had heard about an infant screening program at Parkland. In the program, at-risk newborns were checked for hearing problems by hooking the babies up to electronic monitors that checked brain activity. Audiologists did the analysis, but volunteers obtained the data from the babies.

Whitehead was interested, too. He had been a Parkland volunteer three years earlier when he was first thinking about switching professions. It had been an exhilarating, albeit hellish, experience. "I volunteered for the midnight to 4 A.M. shift in surgery ER—the bowels of it all," Whitehead says, referring to the emergency room. "There was always blood spurting all over the place. I wheeled dead bodies to the morgue. I was never there when there wasn't a shooting or stabbing or cardiac arrest coming in the door. I saw male rapes. Female rapes. Lots of car accidents with children. You see it all—it's the real world."

Unfortunately, it's not the real world in Parkland's volunteer department.

Enter another southern belle. "Dad was in real estate," Lisa Little, a 1968 graduate of Highland Park High School told me brightly last week.

Little, 43, was herself a real estate agent and a lowly Parkland volunteer 15 years ago when hospital management, taken with her supreme dedication to the job, offered her a full-time position, now paying $48,000 a year, heading up the volunteer program. She has been like a kid in a candy store ever since, she says, except that she doesn't wear a candy-stripe outfit.

No, she makes other people do that. And I do mean *makes*.

Specifically, female volunteers must wear a Parkland-issued pink jumper—similar, I imagine, to the ones high school candy-stripers wore back when Donna Reed was a big hit on TV. Volunteers have to buy the pinafore from Parkland for $19.05.

Upon hearing this, of course, Lawhon had flashes of the Honey Grove beauty pageant ceremony, complete with floor-length gown and rhinestone tiara. She quickly asked Little if it would be all right to wear what the men were told to wear—a red vest and navy-blue scrub pants.

Absolutely not, Little told her in a lengthy interview for the post in late February. "She said that other *progressive* women had objected to the policy before, but she had told them that if they didn't like it, they could volunteer elsewhere—and so could I," Lawhon recalled.

Not only would Lawhon have to wear the pinafore, she wouldn't be allowed onto the hospital grounds unless she was in it. If, say, she was coming from somewhere in the real world, where pinafores no longer exist, she would have to change clothes in her *car* before stepping onto the hospital campus, Little told her.

Lawhon—and Whitehead, who was in the meeting with her—did not take this well, in part because their interview had been, well, Germanic, from the get-go. For the opportunity of volunteering to check little person's ears, Little had demanded to know Lawhon's and Whitehead's GPAs at the *community college;* she had warned them that if they didn't follow the hospital's volunteer policy she would see to it that they "never got into any medical school anywhere"; and she had pooh-poohed Lawhon's current volunteer work at Texas Scottish Rite Hospital for Children, saying it wasn't good enough to be used as a reference.

Lawhon and Whitehead were, to put it mildly, stunned—all they wanted, they kept thinking to themselves, was the opportunity *to work for no money.*

"I know that wearing a baby-doll outfit for a 15-year-old doesn't bother some other women, but I've been out in the real world, and I do know what it's like to be treated like a little girl when I have the ability and the talent to compete with men," Lawhon says. "And to think you have to *buy* the silly pinafore—it's like, 'you'll take your medicine *and* you'll like it.'"

No one's saying that Little isn't nice—she's *terribly* nice, in the way that only well-bred Texas women can be nice. Right before they slit your throat.

"Oh, you're just *so* nice to think of us—thank you, thank you." Ms. Little was gushing into the telephone as I entered the volunteer office last Friday unannounced. "Well, that would be *divine.* Thank you, honey—*wonderful.*"

As Little spoke and smiled, spoke and smiled, I pulled out my reporter's notebook. Her smile fell to the floor—I could almost hear the crash—and Little stopped abruptly in mid-compliment, cutting off her listener to ask me who in the heck I was and what in the world I wanted.

Soon we were sitting comfortably across from each other in chairs. I was here, I told Little, because of the pinafore problem.

The clouds descended; the lightning was not far behind. "Oh, I can't *believe* this person is doing this," Little glowered. "I mean, somebody who goes to such *lengths*. . . . She was such a nice girl, a smart girl, a *beautiful* girl. And I thought I was such a good judge of character," Little added wistfully.

And what lengths was she speaking of—punctured tires, late-night phone threats, voodoo dolls?

"For someone to write the chairman of the board, the president and CEO, and the hospital attorney—I don't understand this," Little ruminated. "It's been such a headache. It just seems like there's a bigger, better picture in the world. Or should be."

Lawhon did, in fact, write letters—a pretty common thing to do, actually, for a person with a complaint. She got one response, from hospital president Dr. Ron Anderson, a bona fide hero for doing what he does for a living, but a bit too well-coached by the hospital lawyer on this one. "The pink pinafore policy does not violate federal or state laws," he wrote Lawhon.

Well, *that's* a relief.

Little's not laughing. She does not dispute the conversation she had with Lawhon and Whitehead, as relayed by me in some detail. She was simply doing what she's been doing for the past 15 years. "I'm not a good person," she told me at one point, in her best poor-little-ol'-me voice. "I know I'm not a good person, but I try to be."

Little shut down our conversation pretty quickly—right after I pointed out that a 76-year-old Oak Cliff grandmother, who had been volunteering in the newborn nursery for three years and had loved it, had been suddenly ordered to wear the dreaded, stupid pinafore. The grandmother had refused, pointing out that she'd been allowed to wear her street clothes and a volunteer jacket—or sterile scrubs when needed—without causing any problems. Today, because of the pinafore problem, Parkland no longer has her loving arms around those babies.

Asked about the grandmother, Little pinched up as though she were sucking on lemons. "You're getting a little deep into this," she told me. "I just don't care. I'm sorry."

So was I—talking to her was much more entertaining than talking to hospital spokeswoman Sue Mundell. Mundell explained that after the much-publicized kidnapping of a Parkland newborn last year, Little had gotten nervous about her volunteers.

"Lisa thought, 'Oh my God, what if it had been one of the volunteers?'" Mundell told me. "So she felt it was important for *everyone* to have a uniform that was easily identifiable and also a little harder to get on than a jacket."

So Little asked hospital administrators to tighten up the pinafore policy—previously, pinafores had been recommended, but, as the grandmother (who, Mundell told me disapprovingly, had worn stiletto heels and tight pants) knew, a long pink jacket over street clothes was okay, too.

No more.

But since the complete stranger who snatched the baby was dressed like a doctor or a nurse—in blue scrub top, dark pants, surgical mask, cap and paper shoe covers—how would it improve security to dress volunteers like kewpie dolls? Why not go back to the old policy? How about a simple ID picture badge?

Mundell shrugged. She was not in disagreement. "We may come to that," she said. "I think maybe we didn't anticipate any real criticism of this. We could well consider that—but, again, that's Lisa's decision, and I think her position is that she's been doing her job for 15 years, and she doesn't want anybody else telling her how to do it."

Walking around the dingy, dirty hospital last Friday, I bumped into nary a volunteer over a three-hour period. It made me wonder just how many people Parkland had scared off—after all, over at Scottish Rite, where I'd been earlier that day, you practically trip over volunteers, who literally swarm the building like cheerful neighbors, helping patients to their rooms, manning the popcorn machine, greeting people at the front door.

All in street clothes with simple jackets over them–that they don't have to buy.

"These people don't have any other incentive to be here except the pleasure they bring to the children and the belief that they're doing rewarding work–and that the hospital appreciates it," says Scottish Rite spokeswoman Peggy Black. "We try to make it as easy as possible for them to be here."

And people like Lawhon, a faithful Scottish Rite volunteer, are very happy there–in their *pink* jacket.

"My question to Parkland is, 'Do they have so many volunteers that they can afford to treat each one like a prison inmate?'" Lawhon sighs.

Apparently so. "The thing is, quite frankly," Sue Mundell told me, "we don't have a shortage of volunteers. We have enough that we have people who will wear a loin cloth, if we asked them to. . . . This woman might be great. Someone in a pinafore might be also."

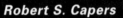
Robert S. Capers

You Can't Look It Up: An Outdated, White World at Milner

As The Hartford Courant *began downsizing, Bob Capers began another career. After 20 successful years as a journalist, he carefully packed away a favorite quote tacked near his desk. Even now, as a graduate student in botany, he eagerly paraphrases writing coach Donald M. Murray: "All good writing is risky." Capers provides the followup: "Without taking risks, there is no growth. And without growth, at least for me, there is no life."*

That philosophy propelled Capers when the Colby College graduate–an English major who never took a journalism course–became a Courant *editor in 1978. He urged reporters to be analytical and interpretive, insisting that's their responsibility. Then, when he traded editor eyeshade for reporter notebook 10 years later, Capers followed his own advice.*

At 45, covering education, Capers took a shelf-by-shelf look at the library in an inner city school. In "You Can't Look It Up: An Outdated, White World at Milner," he tried to be "fair and effective, but highly selective." Capers wrote the first chunk over three days, fueled by outrage. "I've written stories with attitude before," he says, "but this has more attitude." His effort involved "writing and rewriting, listening to the sound of the words as they assembled themselves–listening as a reader would, asking subliminally, 'How do I feel?'" It also involved negotiations with editors: writing a more traditional mainbar to preserve this sidebar.

Though reserved and soft-spoken, Capers will flail his arms, even if only metaphorically. "As a journalist, did I go too far in saying not just that this is what it is, but that this is wrong? I don't think so. As a news writer, I don't write editorials, and this isn't a column, but my position on the matter is no less clear. And taking a stand like that is scary."

With a colleague, Capers netted a Pulitzer Prize in 1992 for a series about the flawed Hubble space telescope. Though judges rewarded the probe of America's space program, the reporter saw the personal tragedy of the man who polished the satellite's mirror. How did Capers learn to care, to make readers care? On the job. "It's not easy to go out there and open yourself day after day to the emotional load the world serves up," he says. "But such is the job of a journalist. Be brave."

–AK

I n the world of the Milner School library, it's the 1950s and '60s. America is rich and powerful, people are all happy, and youths will grow up to have good jobs and nice families.

It's a wonderful world, a quaint world, here in the library. It's also a racist world. Here in the Milner library, people are white.

Outside the walls of this world, in the classrooms of Milner School, there are about 700 children, more than 99 percent of whom are black or Hispanic.

These are the pupils who come to this library to read about the world and to do their academic research.

The world they find in the books here in the library isn't like the world they know. The people they find here don't look like the people they know.

Here in the Milner library, books tell about jobs children might like to have when they grow up.

They could grow up to be firefighters. There's a 1962 book that tells about it. All the firefighters are white.

In fact, all the people at the farm that burns are white, too. And all the people who live in the city where there's a fire–they're all white too.

So are school children. You can tell from the picture that shows a firefighter speaking about fire safety to a classroom full of children.

Careers With a Television Station tells about many jobs people can get–as engineers, performers, artists, sales people–if they are white. In the world of the Milner library, there are no black or brown people at TV stations.

The world of Milner library tells about other opportunities, too. One book is called *I Want To Be a Homemaker.* There are two copies of that one.

There's also information here about what the world offers in the way of free-time activities.

People can go to the symphony, for instance. Not if they're black, though. You can tell from the pictures that no one at a classical music concert is black. No brown people either.

No one who plays an instrument in the orchestra is black or brown either. Not even yellow. You can tell that from looking at *Music Makers,* a book published in 1957, which has pictures of 60 people who play in the orchestra. They're all white.

There are other library books–newer library books–that pupils can take out. A couple hundred of them are piled up on a cart where they've been for weeks–maybe months–after being returned.

Nancy Gary, who was the librarian until being reassigned recently to Simpson-Waverly School, didn't have time to put them back on the shelves. She was at Milner only 2½ days a week, and no one else worked in the library.

Gary didn't have time to keep the card catalog up to date, either. It appears the library has no books on Magic Johnson, Jose Canseco, Rod Carew, Rickey Henderson, Ken Griffey Jr., Carl Lewis, Arthur Ashe or Muhammad Ali.

She said the library *does* have a book on Michael Jordan, even though he's not listed in the card catalog.

She said she threw away the really old books when she started working in the library in 1987.

"That's why the shelves are so empty," she said.

The more than 2,000 books that Gary kept include *On The Mound*, which is about three professional baseball pitchers: Bob Feller, Carl Hubbell and Howard Ehmke. All are white. Ehmke retired in 1930.

In the world of the Milner library, students learn that some telephones now have push buttons and that the United States has just picked its first seven astronauts.

"One of them will be the first American astronaut to travel in outer space," the book says. "The Soviet Union is also training men who may someday be astronauts."

Being an American Can Be Fun tells about the United States and about the wonderful opportunities people all have and how youths can all grow up and get jobs and do meaningful work and be happy. It says everyone is descended from people "who came from some other country to live here and become Americans."

There are some books here about those other countries.

In the world of the Milner library, Jomo Kenyatta is president of Kenya, which is described as "a once troubled spot." The library books say a still-troubled place in Africa is called The Congo. It's north of Rhodesia.

A book called *The Ibo of Biafra* says some of these people have learned English but still use "colorful expressions" from their nature language.

The woman who wrote that book also did one called *The Pygmies*. She thinks these people "seem rather handsome and appealing." She says, "They are totally unselfconscious in their brief bark breechclothes and belts."

There are a few books about Latin America, too. In the world of Milner library, the president of Nicaragua is Anastasio Somoza. Guerrillas had been causing problems there, but Somoza's troops wiped them out in only one month of fighting in 1967.

Children Around the World has information and pictures about 22 countries and the people who live in them.

This world does not include China. Nor does it include any nations in South America. Africa does not exist in this world.

Cuba exists, but all the people there are white. You can tell from the picture.

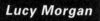
Lucy Morgan

Death Came Too Slowly,
Agonizingly

"I got my first reporting job in 1965 because the city librarian told a newspaper editor that I read more books than anyone in town and might be able to write," Lucy Morgan says. *The librarian was right. After three years at the* Ocala Star-Banner *in Florida, Morgan moved to the* St. Petersburg Times. *Here she found her life's work, covering—actually uncovering—the endless processes of crime and government and their all too frequent symbiosis.*

Morgan likes to take apart the obvious, to write the stories no one else is writing. She thrives on risk. Once she was sentenced to eight months in jail for refusing to name a source. Her case went all the way to the Florida Supreme Court, the sentence was overturned, and reporters gained some rights to protect their sources. Next came an assignment to special projects—public corruption, drug smuggling, and organized crime—and a lot of participants discovered that having her on their case was not only news but bad news. A finalist for a Pulitzer in 1982, she won the prize in 1985 for her investigative series about a county sheriff who was soon out of work.

When Morgan's mother got old and sick and entered a nursing home, a whole new world of public corruption revealed itself, medical overtreatment of the elderly. Thousands of dollars spent on useless therapies made Morgan mad, and when she gets mad, she writes. "Putting it down on paper seemed to help," she says, "just as it has helped to write about other personal events, even the death of my 18-year-old son." The response from readers who were also mad was so phenomenal—and the bills for her mother's treatment so excessive—that she went after the medical records. That fight took a year and a court order, but Morgan won, wrote more detailed stories, and got more responses—hundreds. It's not over yet. Getting readers all the information they need is never over.

Too busy asking the right questions to finish college, Morgan might complete a degree when she retires. Meanwhile, she's writing stories and serving as associate editor and chief of the Times *Capital Bureau in Tallahassee, as well as board member of the* Times *Publishing Company.*

But she's still reading books—two at a time—history, mysteries, nonfiction, bestsellers. After all, that full library card paid off.

—CM

Lucy Morgan, Death Came Too Slowly, Agonizingly, *St. Petersburg Times,* September 7, 1994. Reprinted courtesy of *St. Petersburg Times.*

The look was angry. The tear that gathered in the corner of one eye would easily define the phrase "bitter tears."

Mother was curled into a fetal position. Blisters turning to sores were popping up all over her 91-year-old body. She had lost 12 pounds in a week and was refusing to eat. Fluid filled her lungs.

She was dying, if only everyone would let her go.

Mother had been unable to speak a word any of us could understand for two years. She didn't know her children and grandchildren and was way beyond answering yes or no to even the simplest question.

She died one crumb at a time. Death began with a stroke in 1979 and continued to creep up on her each day. I thought the end was near last month as I watched that single tear roll down her face, but ample doses of antibiotics prolonged her days once again.

There was little left of the mother we knew. She was like a vegetable that had to be watered, kept alive by modern medicine that cost a fortune.

Mother couldn't tell me what she thought about it all, but I know.

I know the woman who scrimped and saved to amass more than $30,000 for her "final illness" would have been appalled to see how quickly the money disappeared and how many state and federal tax dollars were spent to keep her alive long past the day she would have wanted to be breathing.

She would have wanted all that money to be used in some other way: to educate a grandchild, provide medical care for the younger generation or even to finance a trip to Europe. She did not want to live past that day when she could read and write and talk and enjoy good music.

If makes me cry to think of all the things she did without to save her money: the trips not taken, the clothes she made instead of buying. She might as well have thrown the money off a cliff.

She had a living will, plus two daughters and a sister who all were dedicated to blocking any act that would unnaturally prolong life. She gave us a power of attorney to handle her affairs and make whatever decisions needed to be made about her health care. She had told us over and over that she did not want to linger on this earth once she was unable to enjoy life.

Despite all that, we failed. Nothing we were able to do helped her leave this earth in a timely fashion. There were days we longed for Dr. Jack Kevorkian to make a house call.

Time and time again, she approached the brink of death only to be brought back by powerful antibiotics or other medical miracles. Finally, as she stopped eating and the nursing home started talking about feeding tubes and other measures, we hired a lawyer and got help writing a letter invoking laws that are designed to let people die with dignity.

Even then we had to find two doctors willing to declare her terminally ill and remain on guard against all the measures that doctors and health care institutions wanted to take to keep her alive.

She took matters into her own hands last weekend. She quit eating or drinking anything. On Monday, she quit breathing and was gone. On Tuesday, a funeral home took her frail body back to Hattiesburg, Miss.

Lucile Sanders Keen will be buried in the town where she was born. In life, she ran a family drugstore, was assistant dean of women at the University of Southern Mississippi and national director of sales training for two cosmetics companies.

She and others like her are money machines, living, breathing corpses that if kept alive, feed the medical kitty that runs nursing homes, hospitals and doctors' offices.

Even as doctors were declaring her terminally ill, the nursing home was billing Medicare more than $9,000 for speech therapy and occupational therapy. The sad thing is that Medicare paid them $7,641.60 for the service, which was performed on a 91-year-old woman who tried to quit eating.

They were trying to help her swallow better, a speech pathologist told me. It obviously had not occurred to them that she might have enough will left inside her frail body to quit eating.

"Well, she does seem to spit it back up at us a lot," the pathologist responded when I suggested that her refusal to swallow food might be deliberate.

I consistently refused to take her out of the nursing home, haul her across town and have an annual mammogram performed despite letters from the nursing home that reminded me of my duty to do it. That's one indignity I could spare her and the state's taxpayers.

Mother never knew it would be so hard to die, or so costly.

We don't even know how much money has been spent. Her money was gone in a couple of years, paid out in monthly installments to a nursing home, pharmacy and doctors. Medicare and Medicaid paid thousands of dollars in the five years that elapsed after she ran out of her own money and agreed to contribute her monthly Social Security and retirement checks.

We caught only glimpses of how much money was involved because Medicaid doesn't want to tell patients or their families how much money they are spending. I complained once, when her supplemental insurer was billed for a "broken femur" in a year when she broke nothing. It took a dozen or more phone calls, a letter and a copy of our power of attorney for me to see one measly piece of paper, which inadequately described the service performed for the $5,000 charge shared by Medicare, Medicaid and insurance.

In the end, nobody did anything but continue paying the bills.

Why does our health care system continue providing so much medical care to people who are so clearly dying? No amount of money could bring Mother and many of her fellow nursing home patients back to any sort of life they would want to live.

It's our tax money at work. Nobody seems to care how much money is spent to keep people breathing. It makes me wish that at the end, Mother could still talk. She'd have given them a piece of her mind.

Hank Stuever

Oklahoma Story

Hank Stuever works sentence by sentence, an admission that amuses even him because his "lifestyle reporting" projects often explode to 3000 words. Yet he insists "every sentence is no less important than the first."

Stuever is as passionate about media mania: He hates it. "I avoid the story everyone else is doing and do the one I can." In Oklahoma City, for example, he avoided the civic center, coroner's office, and funerals that chronicled the Murrah Building bombing in 1995. Instead, he roamed as an observer, a narrator, trusting his mind, telling a very personal tale, and all the while fretting: "Could this be a big pile of nothing? Am I blowing this?"

He persisted, gathering notes on laptop and steno pads, with green pages numbered front and back. He left the site only after spending crucial time in the library, a habit from days at Loyola University in New Orleans, where he majored in journalism and learned how to research "for a professor brave enough to give me a D." Why track all those facts? "Context is everything."

At The Albuquerque Tribune, *Stuever attacked his notes with a yellow Highlighter and tapped out more than 100 inches of "Oklahoma Story" in one sitting. Fueled only by Diet Pepsi, he finished the first draft in 13 hours. Over the next half day, he edited: scrolling, scrolling, scrolling on the computer, with periodic printouts to tame his urge to see type.*

In 1990, after internships at The Washington Post *and* Los Angeles Times, *Stuever arrived at* The Tribune, *a feisty afternoon paper in a rare two-newspaper town. He trained on the metro desk, with the "sofa beat" of arroyo drownings, drive-by shootings, gangland slayings, even a manhunt for a serial murderer. Of those days, Stuever says, "You always end up sitting on the couch when you talk with a victim's family."*

By 26, when he headed to Oklahoma City, he'd begun writing and editing features as part of a team. A finalist for the Pulitzer Prize in 1993 and (for this story) in 1996, Stuever welcomes praise. And job offers. He now reports for the Austin American-Statesman. *He even welcomes criticism. "Readers may hate what I write," Stuever says, "but they read it all the way through."*

–AK

Hank Stuever, Oklahoma Story, *The Albuquerque Tribune,* May 6, 1995. Reprinted courtesy of *The Albuquerque Tribune.*

My great-grandfather, John Jacob Schneider, is fixing windmill blades on the family's western Oklahoma wheat farm on a November day in 1922 when, somehow, he loses his grip, falls, breaks his neck and dies.

This is a long way and many years from the Alfred P. Murrah Federal Building and what happened there at 9:02 A.M. on April 19, but it is an Oklahoma story all the same.

Without the windmill accident, my grandfather, Joseph Leo Schneider, does not quit junior college in Kansas and return home to Oklahoma to help his mother run the farm and raise the babies. Without the farm, he never buys his first J. I. Case Co. tractor, and therefore never becomes the traveling Case salesman he was for 40 years, never landing himself and his family in a three-bedroom brick house on Northwest 37th Street. Without the windmill, he never marries Gladys Irene New in 1931 and they never stay through the Dust Bowl, the Depression and the war years. Four children and nine grandchildren and 10 great-grandchildren are not born.

So it happens that my grandfather, J. L. Schneider, now 91, returns home from daily Mass and is carrying his laundry from his bedroom to the washing machine when he hears the explosion 32 blocks away.

As the world descends into sounds of sirens and helicopters, Grandpa knows something is going wrong downtown.

As an Oklahoman, I associate the place with luck and sorrow and a steady acceptance that life is as random as wind.

Five days after the blast, I get to Oklahoma City, walk up Blue Hill and hear a gospel choir singing. They are 27 strong tonight from the Christian Life Missionary Baptist Church and brought here by Jesus, their pastor says. They are standing across Northwest Seventh Street by the perimeter fence. A green military truck full of National Guardsmen rolls by. All eyes are fixed on what remains of the Murrah Building two blocks over, shining horribly under floodlights like a gaping cadaver. The body count on the news says 79, so far.

"*There, too, my heart / Singing glory to His name. . . .*"

When their song is over, the pastor, Jayel Jacobs, gathers his flock to pray: "Lord, help the right to come out of this!"

Yes, the faithful shout. "Lord, remember those who are not with us–*Yes!*– Remember those still wanting–*Yes!*–Those still hurting, Lord!–*Yes!*–Jesus! Jesus! Jesus!

"Jesus got it goin' on in this situation!"

The small things are overwhelmed by the big thing. The appropriateness of normal life is now in question, where "OK" had been a lifestyle: OK to dine out? OK to go see a movie? OK to continue with the 28th annual Festival of the Arts downtown? (Answered: Yes to dinner, but no raucous laughter. Yes to a movie, if it's a comedy. No to the popular arts festival, because they're still bringing bodies out just two blocks from the exhibition tents.)

My friend Mary Heffron Ramsey is afraid to go to Penn Square Mall to buy skin moisturizer because, she says, she doesn't feel like being in a large building with a lot of people around. "It sounds vain," she says, apologetically, "but I'm just really on edge. I don't want to go anywhere." She is sitting at her desk at work. This is how it happened, she thinks to herself: A boring hump day in front of a computer, pushing paper, talking on the phone, unwinding a paper clip.

Another close friend, because of her job, has 20, possibly 30 funerals to attend in the coming days and weeks. That is the number of all funerals she had ever attended in her life, times seven. She doesn't own that many things black or navy to wear to all these funerals, and why would anybody? "And yet," she says, "you could go some places in this town and if you didn't know it had happened, you wouldn't know *anything* had happened." Her job, in public relations, is to keep the hordes of media away from the grieving families and funeral homes. She must keep her distance from me as well.

Another friend, Ceci Chapman, worries she didn't pray enough on the Tuesday before it happened. She worries about the spiritual undertow of it: "I tried to watch 'Crossfire' last night and they were so heady . . . debating what happened. What happened here is passion, a passionate thing. It's just impossible to have that kind of head logic. There's a place for that, but that place can't be here right now."

My grandfather keeps a small, stained spiral notebook next to my grandmother's bed at St. Ann's nursing home in the northwest part of town. He was told to write down each day what my grandmother manages to eat from the spoon he holds for her, while she peers at him from the fog of pain where she now lives, defeated by strokes and collapsed bones, weighing less than 100 pounds. Grandpa's methodical scrawl fills the pages, the handwriting I know from birthday cards and exacting repair logs he keeps in the glove compartment. Page after page, it's "20 percent meat loaf, 75 percent mashed potatoes, very upset today. . . ." Page after page, with little else remarked on: "Christmas Day" or "Gladys disturbed and in much pain." On April 19, Grandpa wrote: "FEDERAL BLDG. EXPLODES . . . 20 percent lasagna, 50 percent pudding. . . ."

The small things are in fact the big thing.

We stood on stage at Bishop McGuinness, the Catholic high school, a thousand years ago, dressed as hayseeds with our faces rouged-up pink, singing Rodgers and Hammerstein's "Oklahoma!" while our parents clapped wildly from the audience. We held hands and prayed in circles, asking God for better SAT scores and football trounces and, for others we barely knew, miraculous deliveries from car wreck comas and pancreatic cancer.

We guzzled furtive beers by Lake Hefner, cheap beer, suburban brats singing songs by Prince, the Cars and AC/DC, standing on a picnic table near Stars and Stripes Park. We were restless to the teen-age core, keeping an eye out for the cop who would inevitably come down this dirt road to chase us away.

There were dreams about getting out of here. You could see the water tower blinking through the trees. You could feel the wind on your face. A weathered bust of Dwight D. Eisenhower stared out over choppy Lake Hefner, the city's fonder tribute to God, family and country.

What you need to know about the urban heartland is how it can weigh upon you. What you need to know about the Bible Belt is how tightly it can cinch. What you need to know about a comfortable place is how discomforting predictability can be.

Some of us did move away. Others stayed in Oklahoma, opting for a literal and emotional "OK," something unchanging and reliable, something bland and boxed-up and there.

You either heard the blast or you didn't.

You were here for it or you weren't.

People do their best to describe it to the more than 400 reporters and photographers from all over the world who didn't hear it: Not thunder. Not a jet. Not a crash. Not a boom, but a *bam*. To the bone. Framed pictures lifting up and slamming back against the wall. A noise "up there." They all thought it was on their own roof, or on the floor above, or just next door, when it was blocks or miles away. No one explains it exactly, no matter how many times you ask.

Before Murrah. After Murrah.

The small things are completely different now.

" . . . MANY PEOPLE LINK important themes in their lives to a global sense of being Oklahoman, even to the extent of making Oklahomaness the object of their "primary role identification" (Roher and Edmonson, 1964), and when taken to the extreme, this identity becomes a narrow, overly invested, constricted one that feels like a highly defended fortress."

*HOWARD F. STEIN AND ROBERT F. HILL, anthropologists,
from an introduction to* The Culture of Oklahoma, *1988*

Oklahoma City sits on 623 square miles, a space larger than Chicago and New York combined. The population is 444,719, but that is misleading: About 1 million live in a tri-county area around and including the city, 74 percent of them White, 17 percent African-American, 3 percent American Indian and 6 percent everyone else. In its worst hour of pain, my sprawling hometown was descended upon by the world's prying yet sympathetic cameras and labeled, at last, "the Heartland."

Which it never was to me.

"Heart" implies a pumping, constant vitality, something Oklahoma City has not. Since farming and agriculture account for only 2 percent of the jobs, "heart" is perhaps a better analogy to the region's legendary gushers, the oil fields that brought prosperity and, ultimately, financial despair. The pride that swelled up *After Murrah* is rooted in the everyday humility *Before Murrah.*

Oklahoma City is worn down by the oil bust of 12 years ago and ignored by the rest of the world for decades, on the map as neither "South" nor "Midwest" nor "West." It has a negative self-image contrary to a dozen city government attempts (including a current $28 million downtown revitalization plan) to restore enthusiasm and bring attention to the place.

Here is a city that, for a time, consumed more fast-food per capita than anywhere else. Here is a world with 11 Wal-Marts, 43 McDonald's restaurants, 33 Taco Bells, 4 shopping malls and, by one count, 522 Baptist churches. Here is a metropolis that in its wildest dreams aspired to be more like Dallas.

It is a vast, quietly urban, politically and culturally conservative place. Its bustle is crisscrossed by fleeting moments of bucolic, weedy perfection on two-lane roads, punctuated by the kitsch of indecisive midcentury architecture—a bank that looks like a golden honeycomb dome; a 20-foot-tall Townley's milk bottle towering above a street corner; rounded space-age skyscrapers that reach for a future that wasn't.

Some people say: "You don't talk like you're from Oklahoma." I have always supposed they meant it as a compliment, but the ever-present, ferrous red dirt of Oklahoma's ground never fully bleaches out of white socks.

I go home one or two times a year now, returning to ride in my grandfather's airplane, a 1966 single-engine Cessna he still flies; returning to watch "Days of Our Lives" with my grandmother before the strokes took her cruelly away without taking her fully; returning for the weddings of high school friends, assuring myself that nothing ever happens in Oklahoma City.

No more. Driving on the familiar roads of town, I am swept into a mournful flurry of headlights in daytime. This is everyone's way of keeping vigil. Headlights on Classen Boulevard, on Northwest Expressway, on Western, on Route 66. Headlights shimmering in the midday sun. Headlights flickering like votive candles against the asphalt, so you can't forget, even when you try.

Six days after the blast, the TV news totals 91 bodies recovered with perhaps 100 still missing, with footage of rescue Labrador retrievers stressed out and howling.

I come back to the perimeter line at Seventh Street and Harvey Avenue on Blue Hill, to again press my face to the fence and stare over the network TV vans at the Alfred P. Murrah Federal Building with the increasing, and quietly reverent, crowds. Funeral wreaths are being propped up on street corners. Blue and purple ribbons adorn every fence and telephone pole. Innocuous words wear new meanings: *credit union, day care, HUD, Ryder, bureaucrat* and especially *Oklahoma.*

The building was another faceless slab of glass and concrete, a specialty here, a monument to red tape named after a deceased judge. Now everyone knows its twisted innards and floor plans intimately, from newspaper and magazine maps. You hear parts of conversations in restaurants, lively discussions about how Housing and Urban Development was on sections of the fifth, sixth, seventh and eighth floors; the Secret Service was on the ninth floor and the snack bar was on the fourth and the General Accounting Office was on the third.

Everyone in a grocery store line is acquainted with the difference between "the Pancake," where Floors 4 through 9 collapsed on top of one another, and "the Pit," where the bowels of the Murrah Building collected underground, and "the Cave," where the third floor collapsed against the second, behind the America's Kids day-care center, forming a dark tunnel along the building's south end.

Everyone seems to know (or knows the nurse who knows) the doctor who amputated the trapped woman's leg in front of God and The Associated Press, a bone surgeon who heretofore was known best for his efforts to convert the city's athletic youth from football to soccer, in order to reduce sports injuries. You hear that he had to finish the job with his pocketknife. You hear that he had to borrow another doctor's shoes on the way to Murrah.

By the end of Day 6, I count at least four deaths or injuries that are somehow connected to my world. A woman who once helped my mother sew church banners at St. Charles Borromeo, dead. A woman who graduated from Bishop McGuinness High School four years behind me, dead. A man who was in church youth group a few years ahead of me, alive, who was heard to have said, after he rode his desk through the air from the seventh floor to the fourth: "Sorry to drop in on you like this." His father, meanwhile, is missing, presumed dead.

A man named Steven Garrett holds his daughter Ashlyn, 4, on his shoulders for a better look at the Murrah Building. The wind blows hard through the downtown streets, and Garrett tells me he had to come down and see it for himself.

"Because I know it will never be the same, living here. I've lived here all my life and I know how we tend to move on. You can feel people trying to be normal and it just doesn't fit to be normal anymore," he says.

I tell him I grew up here, too.

"So you know, right? he says. "It's like you're proud of this place, but something's never going to be right again? That's not a lack of hope or anything. We'll live. But different, you know?"

The house on 37th Street seems at first indifferent to the mournful mood outside. My great-great-grandfather still stares with translucent eyes from his portrait above the fireplace. The clock still chimes every 15 minutes. My mother and my aunts are still young brides in black-and-white studio shots; I am forever 17 and shaking the archbishop of Oklahoma City's hand at graduation.

While Grandpa sits in his chair and looks at more Murrah aftermath on the "Today" show (he limits himself to some news in the morning, maybe some at lunch and the entire newscast at 10), I take in the wallpaper and the smells of furniture polish and coffee, and reassure myself of the availability of Hershey Kisses on the kitchen buffet, my Grandma's touch. What she clipped out of newspapers—a Presidents Day salute, a recipe, a mention of my cousin the lawyer—has yellowed on the refrigerator, in futile wait for her return from St. Ann's.

Grandpa says the windows barely shook.

The house, he says, is sturdy.

"I was already feeling depressed," he tells me. "There are a lot people in this town hurting right now, but you know, I have been feeling kind of down." A 91-year-old man keeps his own authority on grief. He returned from ushering Sunday Mass with a free pamphlet on "The Grieving Process" and put it on the kitchen table.

Ella Hite comes on Tuesday mornings to clean my grandparents' house. She sweeps, dusts, vacuums, runs the washer and dryer, and even irons my grandfather's shirts against his polite protest, and now, she says, "I go around and catch myself staring off into space, thinking about all that has happened. I'm still saying, 'Why?'"

Ella lost at least two friends from her church, Mount Carmel Baptist. More than that, her daughter had worked in the Murrah Building up until the Friday before the explosion. Ella herself worked a janitorial shift at Murrah, back in the 1970s. Her connections to it seem unending.

The pastor at Mount Carmel had said the Lord promised these cruel and terrible things would happen. Ella listened and it sunk in like this: "The Lord's on his way," she says. "We got to love, hope and *look up.*"

Grandpa is now at the kitchen table, listening in. Murrah is where he took his Social Security paperwork. When he managed a low-income apartment house for my uncle, he was often in and out of HUD.

"You start to think," he says, looking at a picture of one of the alleged conspirators, Timothy James McVeigh, on the cover of the *Daily Oklahoman,* "whether or not God has something to do with this guy being pulled over by that officer in Perry. That there's some kind of miracle in that happening so quick."

While Ella vacuums and Grandpa mows the back yard, I walk three blocks to the First Christian Church on Northwest 36th and Walker Avenue, another curious piece of imposing Oklahoma architecture, commonly called the Egg Church because it looks like a giant white egg with a steeple on top.

The Red Cross, with 622 volunteers today, has set up a "family center" in the Egg for relatives of those killed in the blast. The media convene in the church hall adjacent to the Egg, waiting for new shreds of grief to be empathized with and broadcast around the world. Satellite trucks idle in the parking lot. Newspaper reporters cram into a small performance theater to plug in their laptops.

But the buzz among reporters hanging out at First Christian is that there are no stories left here, no tears easily quoted from behind closed doors.

A pool of three reporters—one from the local AP bureau, one from the *Tulsa World* and one from the local ABC affiliate—is escorted into the family center by an Army major and a Red Cross official.

A press conference is later called so the pool reporters can tell the rest of us, about 20 reporters and photographers, what they saw.

They describe the "total human care" within, the trays of free food from local restaurants, the heaps of donated toys for bereaved children to play with. They explain what they saw in the "notification center," the makeshift medical examiner office where a fax machine delivers body IDs from downtown to an employee who, we are told, "breaks down in most instances." A sound bite from him, too: "I have to pause and gather myself and I think (the families) are appreciative of that."

We are told of the little Capuchin monkey who has been brought in to "soothe" grieving families and children. We are told of one woman in particular, who, once informed of her husband's death, began to cry. The monkey, we are told, touched her tears, tasted them and gave her a hug.

"Can you describe the notification office in more detail?" a reporter asks.

"Is there just one fax machine?" asks another.

"Are the conditions of the bodies discussed with the family then, or does that happen at the funeral home?"

"What do the families talk about to each other? Do they talk to each other? Do they leave once the body they're waiting for is ID'd? Do they drive themselves home or does the Red Cross take them home?"

Later, outside the Egg Church, a woman from a West Coast TV station smokes a cigarette. Her station, she says, is pulling out of the "Terror in the Heartland" story as soon as half the bodies are found and they get shots from a few funerals —one day longer, at most. The meat of the matter, she says, has moved to Michigan militia groups and Kansas motels. She asks me:

"Did you actually believe the monkey story?"

Walking home, I am passed by two funeral processions on 36th Street, heading opposite ways.

Connie Chung, the CBS co-anchor, has become a sort of anti-media rallying point in a tired, weeping city that's almost quoted out. After the famous newswoman apparently insulted Oklahomans by asking in the first news conference if the city would be able to "handle such a disaster," Chung rumors began to fly: Connie Chung was handcuffed for crossing the perimeter line. Connie Chung sneaked into a funeral dressed as a nun. Connie Chung is going to do the newscast from the remains of the day-care center.

On Day 7, there is even an anti-Chung T-shirt: "Connie, Go Home."

"That's the kind of weird thing—all this attention coming down on Oklahoma City," says my friend Mary Heffron Ramsey, a little miffed. "Then they'll all go home after a while. When did reporters ever come to Oklahoma City? Even you— you'll be gone in a few days, too, and the rest of us will still be here dealing with it."

Home is Jesus, *Jesus got it goin' on in this situation,* Jesus on bumper stickers, Jesus in the expansive megachurches along suburban interstate exits. Oklahoma City's believers are, in descending order, Baptist, Southern Baptist, Methodist and then all other Protestant religions combined, followed by a 5 percent minority of Roman Catholics.

"I used to be right up there complaining about the Bible Belt-this, the Bible Belt-that," says a friend, raised Catholic and Catholic-schooled like me. "Now faith and church seem like the thing that's holding Oklahoma City together. I look at it completely different now."

Catholics camped on Blue Hill the first night of the Great Land Run, the opening of Unassigned Lands of Indian Territory on April 22, 1889, the mad dash of high hopes and patriotic lawlessness that created this place.

A priest, according to church historians, likened the grassy hill, which was adorned with spring's bluest wildflowers, to the Blessed Virgin's mantle. They held Mass in a tent on Blue Hill 13 days after the Land Run. The site seemed proper for a cathedral, which was completed in 1903 and dedicated to St. Joseph.

Much of Blue Hill was church-owned. Two decades ago, the Archdiocese of Oklahoma City sold the land next door to St. Joe's at Northwest Fifth Street and Harvey Avenue, land that held a grade school and a convent, to the federal government so that a new office building could be built. That was Murrah.

Every stained glass window in old St. Joe's was blown out and smashed by the explosion. The parish priest, the Rev. Louis Lamb, was around the corner at the bank when Murrah exploded, holding a deposit receipt that reportedly reads 9:02 A.M.; the parish secretary, not so luckily, was injured in the blast wave. The structural fate of the cathedral itself is now in question, another sorrow on a heap of sorrows, something that will have to be dealt with later.

Churches are united here now in ways unfamiliar to me. For once in Oklahoma City, it doesn't matter if you're Baptist or Buddhist. On the other side of

Murrah from old St. Joe's, the First United Methodist Church also lost its ancient stained glass. Seven blocks from the blast, the just renovated First Baptist Church lost its stained glass, too, like a row of shiny bullets pushed over. Churches have become the primary focus of "the healing process," jetting in "grief issues" experts and holding nightly, tearful huddles.

Children at my parochial grade school, St. Charles Borromeo, are coloring pictures to explain how they feel: "Confused" says one, in simple purple, blue and yellow letters. Another is a Magic Marker sketch of McVeigh, an arrow drawn to his face and captioned, "We care about everything–but he dosen't (sic)" and "Bomb, we don't like you."

I feel St. Charles–the asphalt playground, the girls in plaid jumpers, the boys in blue slacks, the crucifixes on the walls–within the most innocent part of myself. The kids will be fine, says the school principal, Joe Sine, if a little distressed. Bureau of Alcohol, Tobacco and Firearms officers took time out from the rescue effort to visit the cafeteria during lunch and got the hero treatment. The school held a fire drill and a tornado drill, if only to suggest that disorder and chaos have a proper response in Oklahoma. The student council sells soda pop on the school steps to raise money for disaster relief and a Murrah memorial.

"But what we need now is closure," Sine says. "To get the bodies out, to talk about it, to move on."

At Bishop McGuinness High School, in Room 8, a freshman English class is getting ready to take a test on *A Raisin in the Sun.*

The students set down their pencils at 9:02 and stand to pray; it's been one week since Murrah, since the school building shook, and the kids, who were passing between second- and third-period classes, stopped and looked at one another. The day was panicky as the children of lawyers and judges and business types tried in vain at the cafeteria pay phones to reach their downtown parents.

A week later, the governor, Frank Keating, whose son, Chip, happens to be in Room 8 taking the English test, has ordered the city be entirely stopped, traffic and everything, for one minute. All we hear are church bells.

I sit on the principal's couch. The same couch, shiny and black and deep. The same principal, Steve Parsons, reminds me what McGuinness is and how it is not all that affected:

"It gets back to that whole sense of people having free will," Parsons says. "We still teach respect, treating others with respect. It's a moral world. Lord's sake, you must have heard that enough when you were around here. That's what sees us through."

I f anything, I was a strange and bored child of God in my own Unassigned Lands. I jumped off the roof wearing a Hefty bag for a parachute. I buried myself in comic books. I imagined living on other planets, in other places, with other families.

The raw newness of this April in Oklahoma–the luminescent green and burgeoning cumulonimbus clouds–reminds me that we are in storm season. Frightening weather is a point of pride here in Tornado Alley. My mother used to love to drive out west of town to watch for funnels and lightning; invariably our station wagon would be pelted by hail while the muddy red creeks swelled and the air turned a shade of violet. That was about the only escape Oklahoma ever provided.

Tonight, the end of Day 7, is hampered by the wind. Murrah is increasingly unsafe for rescue workers, and at least 60 bodies are still missing.

Day 8 now, and Grandpa looks over at me from the top of his *Daily Oklahoman* while I eat Cheerios. "One hundred and three," he says.

Businesses downtown, outside the Murrah perimeter, are slowly repairing. All the windows in the Kaiser's Ice Cream Shop and Soda Fountain building, a landmark since 1910 at Northwest 10th and Walker, are being replaced.

Kaiser's is a kind of example of the urban rebirth city leaders are hoping for, having been closed down for a time until 1993, when a cooperative of homeless people opened it as a gourmet coffee shop called the Grateful Bean.

Peter Schaffer, a lawyer who helps run the Grateful Bean, says some windows blew inward, while others blew outward, no rhyme or reason to it. No one was hurt. The sheet music stand on the cafe's piano blew clean off.

Being in Kaiser's reminds me of bored summer vacation days, when my mother, driven to placate me, would tell me to get dressed up for a trip downtown. We'd walk the streets and ride elevators and eat lunch in a restaurant. I felt utterly cosmopolitan.

Beneath Oklahoma City, for reasons no one seems able to pinpoint, city leaders of the late 1960s constructed an underground series of tunnels called the Metro Concourse. Despite its preponderance of outdated orange walls and creepy twists and turns, most downtown workers still use the Concourse for a quick lunch and short route between skyscrapers.

I follow the Concourse from the Liberty Tower and north several blocks, past subterranean luncheonettes and hair salons and cash machines. The hallway leading to the courthouse and the Alfred P. Murrah Federal Building grows desolate, dark, ending at glass doors where you can see nothing but endless, evil blackness.

"Don't go in there," barks an unseen intercom voice when I merely touch the door.

The public library downtown is also closed off, missing many windows, and so I head to Oklahoma City University, a private Methodist college on Northwest 23rd Street, to sort through the state lore I left behind in Mrs. Laverne Crumley's ninth-grade Oklahoma history class.

All ninth-graders take Oklahoma history, by law. In it, you learn of the Indian relocation of the 19th century, *Tsa La Gi*, the Trail of Tears. You learn of the "Five Civilized Tribes" (Choctaw, Cherokee, Chickasaw, Creek, Seminole) and Sequoyah's syllabary alphabet. You take a test to name all 77 counties. (Pushmataha, Pottawatomie. . . .) You simulate the Land Run, dressed as pioneers, staking your claim on the school football field; half the class, according to tradition, must jump the gun and be "Sooners," winning the better land. You read Steinbeck's *The Grapes of Wrath* and watch old newsreels of Will Rogers twirling a lariat.

The narratives do not come together until much later, in adulthood, if at all; usually it's the cynics who manage to form Oklahoma history into larger themes of building up and tearing down, of lawlessness in the face of government, of isolation and hard luck, of dreams deferred.

While trying to come by a simple explanation of why the dirt here is so very red (it's rich in iron, for starters), I happened on a picture of Oklahoma City's Main Street snapped 53 years ago by the Farm Security Administration:

"All the buildings in the photograph have since been demolished. . . ." Included in the photo is the 17-story Biltmore Hotel, which triggers a memory of my father, of sitting on his shoulders in 1977, part of the large crowd that turned out to watch the blowing-up of the Biltmore in a cloud of reddish orange dust.

Making my way through the crowds on Day 9, 112 bodies recovered they say, to once more press my face to the perimeter fence and fathom Murrah.

A wind knocks off my baseball cap, and it sails several feet before knocking into a woman's shoulder. She jumps in fear, and says, "You liked to scare me to death! I'm still so jumpy." It turns out she heard the blast in her office four blocks away. It turns out she lost two friends and knows of another six dead people.

All is still jumpy. Grandpa doesn't want to see the Murrah. Neither does my friend Ceci. She'd rather pray in her apartment, "I don't feel like I belong there," she says, with plain sorrow.

Others go to the perimeter fence twice and three times a day. This is, after all, a town with not much to do but cry. Someone is having his first cigarette in 10 years. Others cope in obscure ways, cleaning out their garages, polishing their tools, repapering the kitchen shelves, taking the kids to play on the rocket slide at Stars and Stripes.

Funeral processions hold up traffic.

Headlights in daytime.

Mary goes to the mall for her skin cream after all.

And I have not been the reporter I wanted to be here. I have avoided the funerals. I didn't dicker for a badge to get closer to the mammoth, ruinous thing.

When it comes down to it, I didn't hear the boom. For that, I am hardly Oklahoman anymore, not part of this citywide group hug. The place is farther from me now, After Murrah, an innocence lost.

I am in my grandfather's backyard, perplexed. The apple tree is dying. We lost the big tree out front, and the bigger one out back near the garage, the one with the swing. Now the apple tree, which gave us decades of sour green apples, has parasitic borers. Grandma would work those apples all summer into pies and applesauce. I worked those apples with my mother as recently as two summers back.

A man came out and looked at the tree and recommended it come down. "No, save my tree," Grandpa told him. "Don't cut down my tree."

So the man pruned the tree back to severe nubs. He dug a ditch around it and sprinkled an anti-bacterial crystal into the ground. Maybe the roots will suck that up and the tree will make it through.

"Time will tell, Hank," is all Grandpa says. "God doesn't give you more than you can handle. We all have a cross to bear."

An insignificant apple tree is 32 blocks from the Murrah Building, but it is an Oklahoma story all the same.

Chapter

Telling
Our Stories

Jim Fussell

Living with Tourette

Jim Fussell approaches work at The Kansas City Star *ferociously: report, report, report, trim 90 percent; write, write, write, trim 90 percent. "That perfectionism drives me crazy," he says, "but I hate putting something on the page that is substandard."*

The reporter's own story, "Living with Tourette," began at 33 with self-examination–what he calls a "painful, surprising, cathartic" process. But he plunged on, determined to communicate. "I had to start digging." After all, he explains, "I can't write unless I understand fully."

He asked the same tough questions of himself as he regularly asks of others. "I now know how it feels to have every inch of life culled over," he says. "It's difficult exposing myself to readers. It's difficult to be that honest." Yet he took the risk. "If you're not taking chances, challenging yourself, pushing the reader, doing something different," he says, "then you're not really alive."

In pursuit of himself, Fussell took notes on computer and on yellow legal pads, a holdover from one year in law school. He also called on training. A few years after graduating from the University of Nebraska in 1980, he returned to pursue a journalism degree. When Fussell wandered into the student newsroom, he promptly decided: "I'm home." Then, in 1985, he turned an internship into a job at The Miami Herald. *A year later, he began reporting for* The Star, *roaming from bureaus to metro desk to features, where, he insists, "I'm home again."*

Fussell thrives on the offbeat, describing himself as "a weird guy doing some weird stories." Indeed, he counts on Tourette as "rather off-putting." Skillfully, relentlessly, Fussell turns his uncontrollable neurological disorder–wiggling tongue, bobbing head, twisting neck–into controlled interviewing. "It never fails to relax them," he says of those he profiles. "The person who is being entrusted with their story is a person who has vulnerabilities."

"Tourette" ran before The Star *began officially discouraging first-person stories. (Editors there promptly reneged, allowing Fussell to describe his do-it-yourself home delivery of a baby daughter.) But the reporter himself hates those "I" stories that fail, "thunking harder than third-person duds." He also hates broad policy. "It's important to open up and be human," he says. "Too often, readers don't know the folks who are bringing them their news. These pieces connect."*

–AK

Jim Fussell, Living with Tourette, *Star Magazine, The Kansas City Star,* May 13, 1990.
Reprinted for informational purposes only with permission of *The Kansas City Star.*

The petite brunette unbuttoned my shirt to my navel, and placed her hand on my chest.

"I'm Jennifer," she said, kissing me softly on my cheek. "And I have to do this."

I smiled nervously.

"This is embarrassing," she said, yanking my shirttails out of my trousers. "But you've got to understand. It's just what I do. I can't help it."

This was turning into quite a day. I thought I'd seen it all after I'd met a woman who munched on my shoulder, a man who threw punches at my head and a woman who yelled "I'm a virgin!" at passing strangers.

But this?

"I can't help it," she repeated as her finger traced a line down the right side of my face and went straight for my beltbuckle. "I just can't help it."

I knew that. None of the people I met that day could help it. But they all shared something that I was in Washington D.C. to learn more about.

It's called Tourette Syndrome, a neurological disorder that causes people to exhibit strange tics and/or bizarre behaviors they cannot control.

It was the second day of the three-day national conference of the Tourette Syndrome Association, and so far I had met a score of people with varying types and severities of the disorder.

My favorite had been Bob. Every few seconds Bob would fling his arm out as if shooting an imaginary basketball.

"I just found out yesterday I've got Tourette," he told me at the hotel. "I drove 10 hours to get here before the conference ended."

Bob and I talked until 2 A.M. in the hotel bar. When I had to leave, he looked at me as if I had just saved his life.

"God bless you," he said. "You don't know how it felt to feel so weird, so strange and so alone for all these years–like I was the only person in the world that did these strange things.

"Then again," he said. "I guess you do."

As if on cue, I shook my head wildly left and right and slammed it backward.

Yes, I knew. I've lived with Tourette Syndrome for 31 years.

If you have never heard of Tourette Syndrome, you are not alone. Many doctors who have misdiagnosed me as "anxious" can attest to that.

Tourette Syndrome is thought to be caused by a chemical imbalance in the brain. Estimates of how many suffer from the syndrome vary wildly. Some experts claim about 100,000 people in this country have it. Others say there could be 2 million. But the numbers are nowhere near as dramatic as the variety of physical and vocal tics, odd behaviors, thoughts and compulsions the disorder spawns. It may cause you to blink your eyes, blurt out swear words, howl like a banshee, hop like a bunny rabbit, have racing thoughts, unbutton people's shirts, or repeat the last word of a sentence endlessly–endlessly, endlessly, endlessly.

Or it may cause you to shake your head as I do.

There is no cure for Tourette Syndrome, but some drugs can lessen the severity of its symptoms. Researchers believe Tourette is genetic, and there is evidence it runs in families, although not in mine.

In the Middle Ages, such tics were seen as a sign of demonic possession. When exorcisms failed to drive the spirits from the body, people were burned as witches.

Today, people just make fun of you.

"Hey, you," a scruffy Olathe high school student yelled at me once. "Are you a spaz-meister or what?"

"No," I said, "I'm a reporter for *The Kansas City Star.*"

He flipped me the middle finger, jerked his head backward and wiggled his body in mock contortions.

"I have Tourette Syndrome," I said. "It's a medical condition."

He ran off, getting high fives from his buddies.

I got into my car and considered running him over.

I hate people sometimes.

And I hate having Tourette Syndrome.

For me, the syndrome is like having a 200-pound man sit on my shoulders all day. A sadistic 200-pound man.

The man grabs my head and jerks it back about once very five seconds. Then he twists it left and right. He does this about 10,000 times a day. I am sore all the time. My only respite is when I sleep or make love.

Still, I am able to function. I've been married for 10 years, have a job, a house, a cocker spaniel, a sense of humor, a nasty golf slice, a stock plan and a 1-year-old son named Patrick.

I wear no cast, no brace, and I don't sit in a wheelchair. On some days there appears to be nothing wrong with me at all. As a result, most people know almost nothing about the real me.

A friend asked me once about a bizarre Tourette-related condition I don't have called coprolalia. I told him the story of a man who, because of his Tourette, couldn't inhibit swear words and racial epithets from coming out of his mouth.

"Now you see," he said. "Aren't you glad you only shake your head and you don't do that?"

"No," I said. "What he does is no worse than what I do. It's just different."

"You can't be serious," he said. "You just move your head a little. It's no big thing."

"It is to me," I said.

And I will never forget what he said next—"Stop whining. You could have something that was really hard to live with. Hey, you're lucky."

"Oh, yeah, I'm the lucky one," I said. "I just shake my head a little. Well, what if you shook your head like this every moment of your life?" I yelled. "Go ahead, try it for a day. Try it for an hour. Or for a lousy 10 minutes!" And I was really screaming now.

"Do it in front of your parents, and in front of your son with the big wondering eyes. Do it in front of the woman you love or eating or reading or drinking in a bar or on a bus or in a movie or when you're trying to sleep."

"I'm sorry," he said. "I didn't know."

"Nobody knows," I said.

As I write this, I am in the newsroom of *The Star*. My shoulders are tight as a rusty door hinge. My head shakes so hard I can hear the "THUD" my brain makes when it smashes into my skull. My neck twists so hard I can feel the vertebrae cracking.

It is 8 P.M. Done for the day, I walk quickly out of the building.

"Night, Jim," a co-worker calls.

I ignore her.

In my car, I think about my head motions and my lower lip quivers. I shake, and a tear rolls down my face.

I start the engine then lay on the horn for five seconds.

I roll over into the passenger seat and cover my eyes with my left arm.

"Are you OK?" a man says, tapping at the window.

"Just go away," I tell him.

Twenty minutes later, I am fine. I drive home.

I kiss my wife and tell her a joke. I play with Patrick and we laugh and tumble, and for a moment, I *do* feel lucky.

A journalism classmate of mine once described me as a "walking contradiction in terms: happy and in agony at the same time."

I am the first one to admit that living with Tourette often can be as funny as it is agonizing.

When I was first hired by a newspaper in Florida, my new editor took me to a crowded seafood restaurant. After waiting 25 minutes he called out to a waitress, who held up her index finger and scurried past our table. Ten minutes later she came back.

"Ready to order?" she asked, striding breathless to our table.

Before we could speak, my head shook violently from side to side. The waitress we had waited a half hour for turned and scuttled away.

"WAIT!" we yelled, lunging from the table.

Too late.

My head motions also recently attracted the attention of the U.S. Secret Service during a presidential visit to Kansas City.

"Stop right there," said the man with the dark suit. "What do you think you're doing?"

"I'm a reporter," I said, fumbling with my press pass. "See?"

"I mean what are you doing with your head like that?" he said.

"I have Tourette Syndrome," I said. "It's a medical condition."

Finally, he let me go, and I may be paranoid, but I swear he watched me the rest of the day.

Then there was the devil woman of Lenexa.

The woman flagged me down in a parking lot one day and told me she could stop my head shaking.

"Oh, joy," I thought. "What is it this time. Vitamins? Chiropractic? Biofeedback?"

"I watch Pat Robertson," she said. "Of the 700 Club. I'm going to pray for you and maybe the devil will come right out of you."

I left before she tied me to a stake.

I don't remember the first time I shook my head, but the consensus of my family was that it was sometime around age 7. I was living in Swarthmore then, a quiet suburb of Philadelphia, Pa.

Swarthmore was a beautiful community with an excellent school system, but all I remember about it was the time I was run out of second grade for disturbing my classmates. It was the shrieking.

I wanted to stop. I put my hand over my mouth to muffle the sounds. I held my breath until I was dizzy. Nothing worked. Finally, frustrated school officials asked my parents to keep me at home for a while.

I stayed home for two months, and shrieked a little less, I think. I had mixed emotions about being home. I was a good student and I liked school, but it was embarrassing to be around other kids. So home I stayed: lonely and comfortable; happy, but sad.

Eventually the shrieking stopped. It was replaced by eye blinking and sniffling.

My father tried to help me by getting me to talk about my troubles.

"What's bothering you, Jim?" he would plead night after night, eyes scouring my face for a telling expression.

And I would cry. Every night I would look into his eyes and see the way he was hurting. I just wanted to stop so that he could stop.

Shortly after we moved to Lincoln, Neb., in 1968, I began to shake my head. In seventh grade I shook my head near a boy, and he spit on me.

"You're a chicken head," he said. "A damn chicken head. Shake for us, chicken head. Show us how weird you are."

And even though I tried not to, I always would.

One night, when I was in high school, my father got more frustrated than I have ever seen him.

"Don't tell me there's nothing wrong, Anita," he yelled at my mother. "Look at him, he's shaking like a chicken with its head cut off! What is he doing that for?"

I stomped around the room. I was angry, frustrated, confused.

"I don't know what you want me to say!" I said. "Maybe I'm just crazy like they all say."

My father stood up, realizing things had gotten out of control.

"You're not crazy, Jim," he said, putting his arm around me. "You're my son, and I'm proud of you. And I promise you with everything in my heart, we'll lick this someday."

Someday came on a crisp fall day in 1984.

Four years after I married my wife and a semester before I finished a journalism degree at Nebraska, I picked up a *Time* magazine and stared at a full page advertisement bearing a large picture of William Shatner–Captain Kirk in the television show *Star Trek*.

The headline above his head read: "Does Your Child Have Tourette Syndrome? Do You Even Know What It Is?"

"No, Captain," I said.

I read the ad and shuddered.

I read it again. And again. I tore it out.

"This is me," I said out loud.

A week later, I sat in a neurologist's office and listened as he changed my life.

"It's nothing much to worry about," he said, his voice trailing off. "You have a disorder called Tourette Syndrome."

"What?" I said. "What was the name?"

"Oh, the name's not important," he said. "It's a tic disorder. You've got tics."

"Dammit," I said, jumping from my seat and staring at him. "Don't tell me the name's not important. TELL ME THE NAME!"

"Tourette Syndrome," he said.

"Really?" I said. "You mean it's in the medical books? I haven't made it up? I'm not crazy?"

"You have tics," he said again.

"Stop saying that," I said. "I have a name for it now. I have something to tell people. I can have a telethon for God's sake! I have Tourette Syndrome!"

I ran to my car and shut the door.

"Dad," I thought as I turned the key. "It wasn't our fault. We didn't cause this."

I soon thought a lot of impossible things could come true.

I held my breath as my neurologist gave me a prescription for a drug called Haldol that he said could lessen the effects of my head shaking, or maybe, he said, stop it altogether.

It was almost too much to conceive. A new lease on life? No more shakes? To be normal?

I drove home to my Lincoln apartment, dreaming about a life without head shaking.

At home I hugged Susan when I showed her the pills.

I knew she would love me whether they worked or not, but when I saw her face and the look in her eyes, I wanted them to work right then.

I walked into the bathroom and took a pill.

Three weeks passed with little or no reaction. The doctor increased my dosage.

Soon after taking the increased dosage, I didn't want to shake my head.

I wanted to die.

The pills made me horribly restless.

"You know the swirling energy that's usually in my head?" I asked Susan.

"Yes," she said.

"Well, now it's in my chest and my stomach," I said, pacing. "I can't relax. I've got to move. I want to jump out of my skin."

Into the kitchen, onto the sofa, through the hallway, into the bathroom, out of the bathroom. I looked out the window, rolled on the floor, did jumping jacks and cooked two breakfasts that I didn't want.

Susan tried to hold me, but I couldn't stay in her arms. I wanted to move, I wanted to scream, I wanted to run.

That's it, I wanted to run.

I went outside in my socks. Twelve degrees and snowing.

I ran in large circles in snow up to my calves. The cold and the exercise felt good. I ran for 20 minutes until I had cleared a smooth, circular path in the apartment parking lot.

I came inside, exhausted.

I don't remember how I got to sleep that night. But in the morning, I threw the Haldol away.

Since that experience I have tried other drugs, including a drug that was supposed to block the side effects I experienced on Haldol, but didn't.

Currently I am not taking any drugs. But another new drug recently has been approved by the Food and Drug Administration. It's called Anafranil.

"Cross your fingers," I told my wife recently. "I'm going to try it."

That night I dreamed about taking the new drug. In my dream it was a magic potion, an elixir that bubbled and foamed and smoked above a golden chalice.

I drank, and my head motions disappeared.

All around me I saw a calm new world. My neck was free. My head was free. People congratulated me as I strode with a rock-still head wherever I wanted to go. It was incredible, it was wonderful.

It was a dream.

Even though I was diagnosed six years ago, it was only after my wife and I attended the national conference of the Tourette Syndrome Association that I saw proof that there were others like me—normal people whose bodies did things beyond their control.

We went to the conference as representatives of the Kansas City chapter of the Tourette Syndrome Association.

It's hard to imagine having to travel thousands of miles to a place you've never been before to truly feel at home for the first time in your life, but that's what happened to me.

And to Jennifer. And to Bob.

Roaming the large lobby of our hotel, we got to know each other by the crazy things we did.

Jennifer was the the toucher. I was the shaker. Steve was the puncher.

I met Steve at the conference's keynote address by a Virginia congressman.

"I have a gun," Steve announced, taking his hand out of his pocket and thrusting his fist within inches of my head. "I have a knife."

"Hi, Steve," I said.

"I didn't mean that, you know," he told me.

"I know," I said.

Steve has the type of Tourette's that causes him to blurt out inappropriate things. He often punches the air with his right arm and says "I'm going to knock you out."

He never does.

My first introduction to Steve was at the general membership meeting when a Virginia congressman was waxing pretentious about how he had learned his love of social issues at the side of President John F. Kennedy. Steve, doing his best Lloyd Bentsen, yelled out "You ain't no Jack Kennedy," to the delight of the audience.

Later in the speech, the congressman said, "I know that a lot of you probably think politicians are crooks . . ."

To which Steve said "Gimme my wallet!"

I liked Steve.

But I was late for my meeting. As I turned to leave, I saw a slender young woman in an ankle-length print dress shake her head almost to the floor.

"I . . . I . . . I'm a virgin, I really am," she declared to no one in particular. Then she hit a high note and held it for at least 10 seconds.

As she did that, a man in a crowd to my right yelled HELLLPP! at the top of his lungs. Another mooed like a cow. Yet another barked like a dog.

As I turned my head toward the sounds, I bumped into a round-faced woman who placed her mouth on my shoulder. And began to chew.

I flinched.

"Oh, don't worry," she said. "I don't bite. I just like to graze a little."

"You just like to–graze?" I said, making sure I had heard her right.

"Yes, I'm sorry," she said.

I looked to my right and a woman nodded as if to say, "It's all right, go ahead."

"OK," I said. "Graze away."

The grazer smiled at me.

"You have a nice shoulder," she said.

"Thank you," I said as she gummed my sweater.

After she finished, I saw the brunette who had earlier unbuttoned my shirt. This time, she put her hand on my stomach and rubbed softly.

"I'm sorry," she said, with eyes drooping like a beagle.

"No reason to be," I said, shaking my head in a painful circle. "You don't have to explain to me."

She laughed, and kissed me softly on the side of the cheek. Then she grabbed at the top of my sweater as if trying to unbutton it.

The sweater was a crew neck.

"Weird, huh?" she said as she pretended to scold her bad hand. "I can't stop it."

"That's all right," I said, steadying my head with my hands. "Neither can I."

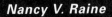

Nancy V. Raine

Returns of the Day

Over Nancy Raine's desk is a line from her favorite writer, Virginia Woolf: "One doesn't want to be things. One wants merely to be allowed to see them." But throughout her career in the arts she has hardly been an onlooker. Always involved, she has made documentary films and directed radio networks, worked as consultant, administrator, and fund-raiser for dozens of arts organizations and several universities. And always writing, she has produced in genre after genre— proposals, reports, and speeches for others, essays, articles, and poems of her own.

Before she wrote "Returns of the Day," she was halfway through a comic novel when, she recalls, "Suddenly I felt resistance." So she put the novel aside and started doing daily writing exercises—the kind that composition and creative writing teachers assign. What emerged was a meditation on having been raped. "One day I sat down and wrote the entire first draft," she says. "So this story took me seven years and two days to write. I had a great deal pushing to get out, as Faulkner once said."

Raine writes with a deep respect for the reader, believing Thoreau's remark that truth requires two people: one to speak and one to listen. "I felt I was asking a great deal from my reader because of the subject—something rarely talked about in personal terms. The response to the published piece was profoundly moving because I realized I had spoken for others," she says. Now she is working on a memoir, a book-length reflection on living with rape. And it all began with an exercise. "That was itself a valuable lesson about the creative process."

In the late '60s, Raine majored in philosophy at the University of Iowa because she thought she should study something that didn't come easily. So she learned ancient Greek, read the pre-Socratics, and worked her way through Western philosophy, including the philosophy of science. "I found balance by writing poetry every day and reading science fiction," she says. "The intellectual rigor of my studies provided tools that I have drawn on ever since." Of course, Iowa is known for writing. "I met many writers, took writing courses, and learned early on that writing requires self-discipline, practice, and patience—you have to love it for itself."

–CM

On an autumn afternoon in Boston seven years ago, when the cherry tree in my garden was the color of orange marmalade and the sky was a flawless blue, a man slipped through the back door of my ground-floor apartment while I was taking out the trash.

I don't know how long he skulked in my home, or in what shadows. Long enough for me to lock the back door, turn my back, walk over to the sink and begin to wash the pan I'd cooked oatmeal in that morning. I was scrubbing it when he grabbed me from behind. "I'm going to kill you," he said. He dragged me into my bedroom and, using duct tape, blindfolded and bound me. He then beat me and raped me. I never saw him. Only his enormous feet.

The anniversary of my rape is the brooding axis of my year, more significant than my birthday. After all, I don't remember my own birth struggle. But I remember every second of those three hours. Like the majority of rapists, he was never caught, tried or imprisoned. Like all survivors, I am growing accustomed to living with an anniversary that can be marked only by silence, a silence that tastes a lot like shame.

Every year I feel the anniversary coming even before my conscious mind recognizes it. When the air crisps and the leaves begin to turn, I get this thing about taking out the trash. About oatmeal. The eyes in the back of my head, the ones that are never shut, begin to burn like the autumn colors, filling me with emotions I still can't encompass.

I know how to mark my birthday, my wedding anniversary, even the anniversary of my brother's death. But the day I was raped? How should I observe the passing of another year? After all, I did take the trash out yesterday, and just this morning–*the* morning–I ate oatmeal standing at my kitchen window while contemplating the wild plum trees in my California garden that were turning the color of . . . orange marmalade.

Of course, anniversaries are celebrations. Celebrate is what I do on my birthday, with friends and family who make a fuss that I outwardly protest and secretly relish. Celebrate is what I do on my wedding anniversary, when my husband and I slip out of the humdrum and go off and do something silly that makes us appreciate our routine again. And on the anniversary of my kid brother's death, I call my mother and we retell the story of how he carried his pet alligator to the zoo when it outgrew the bathtub–in a paper bag on a Washington bus. I am never alone when I celebrate these anniversaries, because someone else remembers them, too.

Is it possible to celebrate this anniversary alone, as alone as I was that afternoon? Celebrate in silence my slow coming to terms with the fact that I can never again be that woman who locked her door and felt safe? My husband, my mother, my friends still suffer their own brand of helplessness when they try to imagine the content of my memory. My father, who spent his life in law enforcement, leaves the room if the subject of rape in general, or my rape in particular, creeps into the conversation. Why remind them? And dare they remind me, when they secretly hope I might be "over it" at last?

Silently every year on this date I remember with particular lucidity what it was like to be only mindless instinct, a collection of synapses and fibers, muscle and bone, organized around a single desire: to live another second. This reduction to such bare necessities of body was an alchemy that spun not gold but something dark and polar, a terrible knowledge that to this day sits in the center of my heart like glacial ice. Why remind people who love me it is still there?

On this anniversary, more or less safe in the cradle of the day's routine, I began to think back. To the first anniversary, when I realized that I had to stop talking about what happened to me because the people who loved me could not bear to hear it. The second, when I pretended to myself I was "over it." The third, when I realized I wasn't. The fourth, when I was in treatment for post-traumatic stress syndrome. The fifth, when I was convinced my treatment wasn't helping and secretly wondered if I had the guts to kill myself. The sixth, during a lunch date, when I told a woman I barely knew that our meeting was occurring on the anniversary of my rape. I spoke matter-of-factly, afraid she might gather up her black briefcase and suddenly remember a dentist's appointment. "My 10th was in June," she replied.

As the seventh anniversary hour, 3:30 P.M., approached, I made a cup of tea. I remembered a story I'd heard 25 years earlier from my friend George. In those days, work crews marked construction sites by putting out smudge pots with open flames. George's 4-year-old daughter got too close to one and her pants caught fire like the Straw Man's stuffing. The scars running the length and breadth of Sarah's legs looked like pieces of a jigsaw puzzle. In the third grade she was asked, "If you could have one wish, what would it be?" Sarah wrote: "I want everyone to have legs like mine."

Yes, I thought.

When George first told this story I knew it contained a profound truth, but not what that truth was, nor that I would need it someday. Today, I understand that the self consumes misfortune like a sacred potion until the glass is empty. And this bitter elixir changes who we are. Sarah could not imagine herself without her scars. But she *could* imagine those scars not setting her apart. She could imagine not being alone. She was not wishing her misfortune on others, but wishing they could share it with her.

I finished my tea and realized I was too anxious to take my daily walk. The odds of being raped don't go down because you've been raped once. A little past 3:30, the doorbell rang. I crept to the peep hole and looked out. It was only the local florist, a woman. The bouquet she presented was huge—yellow roses, pale orange lilies and blue irises. It was from my goddaughter, a university student, who was viciously attacked and sexually molested two years ago by a pack of American college boys in a bar in Mexico. The note read: "You are not alone. Love K."

No. I am not alone. There are millions of us celebrating our silent anniversaries, I thought.

Someday we will all march to the Capitol carrying flowers, and we will leave them on the steps. We will celebrate our anniversaries. We will give our names. The month, the day, the year, the hour. We will stop being silent. We will stop being alone. It doesn't have to be in autumn. I'm not picky.

Andrew Lam

Growing Up Vietnamese
in America

Andrew Lam's professional schizophrenia was born in Asia and bred in America. He began "Growing Up Vietnamese in America" at 11, a refugee from wartorn Saigon. Early on, he shattered both cultural and family expectations, trading science for art. Now a journalist dedicated to facts, he delights in fiction that, for him, "moves beyond the issues to some kind of rattling of the soul." And though he interprets the Asian-American experience, he aims for universality.

The contradictions started in 1986, when Lam graduated from the University of California at Berkeley as a biochemistry major. A restless researcher of cancer, he headed to night school for diversion. When his first efforts at autobiography made classmates cry, he was hooked. He eventually earned a 1991 Master's in creative writing from San Francisco State University. Meanwhile, in 1989, a classmate introduced him to the Pacific News Service, and Lam became "an accidental journalist."

On the job, Lam uses the structures of fiction to enhance straight reporting. "One can be literary in journalism," he insists. "It's art; the purpose is revelation." But in "Growing," he blurs techniques of fact and fiction. And that can be risky. Though he hoped to make sense of a senseless shoot-out, Lam, the 30-year-old American reporter, failed. At a crucial knock, Lam, the Asian, hesitated. "I still chastise myself," he says now. Yet he pursued the story in the only way he knew how: "to move inside." As he explains: "Their history became my history." One version netted him a first place in a 1995 competition sponsored by the Asian American Journalists Association.

Now an associate editor, Lam travels widely from a base in San Francisco. His stories travel even further, to stateside papers and magazines and abroad to El Hispano, Tokyo Weekly, The International Herald Tribune. Lam frequently revisits Vietnam, in person and in words. He inevitably wears the face of Viet Kieu, Vietnamese nationals living abroad. "If I am to them Santa Claus or Odysseus, I feel to myself helpless, overwhelmed by mass misery and self-pity," he wrote once upon return. The pity has since vanished. "There's only so much I can do. I'm following my spirit path to be a writer."

–AK

Andrew Lam, Growing Up Vietnamese in America, *The Sacramento Bee*, March 27, 1994. Reprinted courtesy of the author.

On the afternoon of April 4, 1991, 15 years, 11 months and 27 days after the end of the Vietnam War, four Vietnamese youths armed with semiautomatic pistols stormed into a Good Guys electronic store on Stockton Boulevard in Sacramento and held 41 people hostage. Speaking heavily accented and broken English, they issued what *The Bee* described as "a series of bizarre demands." They wanted a helicopter to fly to Thailand so they could fight the Viet Cong, $4 million, four bulletproof vests and 40 pieces of 1,000-year-old ginseng roots.

While a crowd, some enthusiasts equipped with their own camcorders, gathered across the street, TV reporters informed viewers that three of the gunmen were brothers–Loi Khac Nguyen, 21; Pham Khac Nguyen, 19; and Long Khac Nguyen, 17–and that the last, Cuong Tran, 16, was Long Nguyen's best friend. The Nguyen brothers had come from a poor Vietnamese Catholic family headed by an ex-sergeant of the South Vietnamese army. All four were altar boys. Three of the youths had dropped out of school or had been expelled. None had been able to find a steady job.

The gunmen could be seen on live television behind the store's glass doors, strolling back and forth with their firearms, bound hostages at their feet. Sacramento County Sheriff Glen Craig, who had implanted listening devices in the store, reported that the gunmen were jubilant at seeing themselves and hearing their names on TV–"Oh, ah, we're going to be movie stars!"

As the siege wore on, negotiations reached a stalemate. The gunmen had grown increasingly edgy and refused to negotiate after authorities met only part of one demand–providing them with a single bulletproof jacket. Sheriff Craig, on the other hand, told reporters that the four would not "focus on any single demand. They were attempting to gain notoriety, attention and, perhaps, some transportation out of the country."

Eight-and-a-half hours later, after the gunmen wounded two of the hostages, a SWAT team raided the store on live television. Three of the young men were killed immediately, but not before one of them sprayed the hostages with bullets, killing two employees–John Lee Fritz and Kris Sohne–and a customer–Fernando Gutierrez–and wounding eight more. Loi Nguyen, the oldest, and the one who wore the bulletproof jacket, was seriously wounded. His trial on 49 felony counts and three counts of murder is set for July 11. He is pleading not guilty.

As I watched this tragedy unfold on my TV set that night, I remember being overwhelmed by an irrational fear. It was the fear that the Vietnam War had somehow been renewed by those gunmen and by those helicopters hovering over the store. And though I was on the safe side of the TV screen now and judging their barbaric acts, I was not without this singular sense of foreboding: Six years ago I could have been one of them.

If the story of the Good Guys ended in carnage on the linoleum floor of an electronics store, it began an ocean and an epic journey away, nourished by numerous subterranean streams. It is those streams I am foundering in. I am at once too close and too far from their story. Though an American journalist now, I came to this country as a Vietnamese refugee, the son of a South Vietnamese army officer. The young men and I, through our fathers, are veterans of a civil war we never actually fought. In their demands, I hear the thematic echo of vengeance, which forms and shapes all Vietnamese youths who grow up in America.

Visiting that same Good Guys store today, the first thing you notice is yourself. Walk through the glass door and a dozen camcorders give back your reflections on the various TV sets. For as little as $549, you could be (oh, ah) your own movie star.

I saw but tried not to look at my own faces on these TV screens. I do not believe in instant fame, had always thought Andy Warhol's prediction an odd American curse. But teenagers are daily worshipers in this secular temple of high-tech consumerism, their eyes mesmerized by the *son et lumière*.

At the Nintendo counter, five Asian teens vied to compete for world championship of Street Fighter II. At the cellular phone display, two Latino girls pretended to gossip, using those palm-sized communicators. And at the store's far end, a hundred or so TV sets formed a kind of electronic wall that talked and sang and showed the shopper the panorama of America—talk shows, soap operas, commercials.

It is here, in this American postmodern public square, that the ethnic private meets the mainstream public. At dinnertime on the night of the Good Guys siege, Papa and Mama Nguyen suddenly saw their three eldest boys holding American hostages at the neighborhood electronics store. One can assume that their sons were simultaneously watching their own drama on dozens of TV sets. It is a kind of instantaneous real-life opera made popular by television these days, the blood opera with all nuances flattened so that viewers get only a reporter's sound bites and vivid endings. Narrative is shaved to the bone, history and background ignored.

That sort of ignorance is peculiarly American, or so it seems to many of the 12,000 Vietnamese in the Sacramento area. A few who watched the siege recall a dangerous combination of arrogance and confusion among the TV reporters and especially the authorities. "They ran around like chickens without heads," said one Vietnamese man who volunteered to help the police but was turned away. "The boys were Vietnamese Catholics and the sheriff initially had a Laotian monk at the scene," he said.

Yet clues that would have helped the sheriffs and the journalists unlock the gunmen's psyches were just minutes from the Good Guys, in Little Saigon. In a mini-mall a mile or so away, a videostore called Ngoc Thao (Precious Herb) catered to a Vietnamese clientele. Colorful posters of gangsters and cops holding Uzis and of ancient swordsmen in silk brocades flying above temple rooftops covered the walls and glass windows.

Here, as in many other video stores frequented by local Vietnamese in Sacramento, one can find 1,000-year-old ginseng roots—the precious cure-all usually discovered by the lucky hero in kung fu epics—or other magical panaceas and cursed swords. They're in hundreds of Hong Kong videos, dubbed in Vietnamese, that line the shelves.

The cashier, a heavily made-up woman, was having a busy day. Like a high priestess with holy water, she dispensed pieces of Asia's fabled past to hordes of homesick Vietnamese.

"Sister, when is the Royal Tramp video coming out? I've been waiting for months."

"Sister, we want *Dragon Palms* and *The Revenge of Black Orchid.* I hear the woman in *Orchid* is the best fighter and, like a man, kills everyone who assassinated her parents."

"Aunty, how much does a karaoke machine cost? Everybody in my family is dying to be a rock 'n' roll star."

At the entrance, an 8-year-old holding a plastic bag filled with kung fu video was his old man's pride and joy. Papa urged youngest son to say something to a friend, an army buddy wearing a fatigue jacket. Youngest son shrugged, then, without enthusiasm, recited a quote from a movie:

"Honorable father, I must leave you now and find a mentor to learn the martial art way. I will avenge our family honor after I have mastered the Iron Palms of Death."

The two men laughed and applauded the mythological voice of China, a voice that provides a kind of parochial snare in the Americanization process. Thanks to CNN, satellite dishes, cable TVs, VCRs, jumbo jets, camcorders and fax machines, integration turns retro-future-active. Technology renews old myths, shrinks oceans, packages memories, melts borders, rejuvenates old passions, redefines the assimilation process.

For Asian children immigrating to America today, their parents' homelands are no longer as far away as they were for children in earlier times. The American-born Vietnamese boy who mouths ancient wisdoms may not know their meaning, may never, for that matter, master the Iron Palms of Death, but somehow Asia has already exuded mysticism into his soul. Indeed, the alluring incense, the singsong languages, the communal and familial Confucian values of loyalty and obligation, the old-world gestures of self-sacrifice and revenge—all that earlier generations of American-born Asians tried so hard to exorcise—is now in style, evidenced in the Little Saigons and Little Seouls that dot so many California urban landscapes.

Two days after the Good Guys siege, a *Bee* photo that ran the length of the page showed the Nguyen brothers' parents standing in their living room as if facing a firing squad. Though stricken with grief, Bim Khac and Sao Thi Nguyen admitted journalists into their tiny two-bedroom unit in the Laura Dawn Manor Apartments, a two-story structure rented out mostly to Southeast Asian families.

The photo shows a sagging sofa, a VCR and, of course, a large TV set. On top of the TV stands a South Vietnamese flag—three red horizonal stripes against a gold background—representing a country that no longer exists. On the opposite wall, a three-tier shrine displays crucifixes, statues of Mary, Joseph and Jesus and various martyred saints, all with mournful faces.

The Nguyens and their six children spent four months in a refugee camp in Indonesia before coming to the United Sates in the early 1980s. In Sacramento, they were receiving Aid to Families with Dependent Children. The ex-sergeant from the South Vietnamese army, who is active in church, said through an interpreter that he was no help to his children when it came to explaining American things such as homework or news on TV. Still, wasn't what he wanted for his children the same as what any Vietnamese parent wants—that they do well in school but keep "Vietnamese traditions"?

"Please tell the people of Sacramento I am very sorry for what my sons have done," the patriarch offered. Asked how his quiet, obedient boys wound up becoming hostage-takers, Nguyen and his wife provided only a miserable silence.

This is the silence of an older generation of Vietnamese refugees who no longer feel anchored anywhere but in their impoverished homes. The exterior landscape belongs to America, strange and nonsensical, not their true home. Inside, many Vietnamese refugees tend to raise their children with stern rules—the way they themselves were raised back home. Vietnamese is spoken, with familiar personal pronouns—youngest son, older sister, aunt, father, great uncle and so on—lacing every sentence to remind the speakers and the listeners of their status in the Confucian hierarchical scheme of things. These parents are unprepared for children who lead dual lives, who may in fact commit rash and incomprehensibly violent acts—not at all the docile and obedient Vietnamese children they had hoped to raise.

"They are no longer really Vietnamese, nor are they really Americans," said a former teacher, who recently came from Vietnam and now lives on welfare in Sacramento, of his own children. He called their tangled assimilation "crippled Americanization."

For Loi, Pham and Long Nguyen and Cuong Tran, who failed school and grew up between the Good Guys electronics store and the Ngoc Thao, there existed two separate notions—notoriety and revenge, revenge being the stronger impulse. One encourages public displays that may lead mainstream America to acknowledge that they exist. The other fulfills the old man's extraterritorial passion—"helicopters to Thailand to kill Viet Cong"—and rejects America as the wasteland.

To grow up Vietnamese in America, after all, is to grow up with the legacy of belonging to the loser's side and to endure all that entails. To grow up in America is to desire individual fame and glory, a larger sense of the self.

After Good Guys, the media offered a variety of explanations. One had to do with the chronology of waves, as in waves of Vietnamese immigrants. The first wave of refugees who came to America in 1975, my wave, comprised intellectuals, educators, army officers, skilled civil servants, professionals—Vietnam's best and brightest—those who had not experienced Vietnam under Communist rule. This wave adjusted readily to American life, to an America of the 1970s that was economically stable and motivated, in part by guilt, to be generous to the newly arrived: There were English as a Second Language teachers, low-interest loans, job-training programs.

The later wave, the boat people who came in the '80s, were a different group–people who had been traumatized by re-education camps, cannibalism, rape, robbery, drowning at the hands of sea pirates, people who had suffered a chaotic and broken society back home under Communist hands. These less-skilled, less-educated refugees were ill equipped to adjust to a less generous America.

But there were deeper currents that fed this second-wave refugee family that the media failed to detect. According to one Vietnamese who has been a social worker and knows the family well, the Nguyen parents had been burned not once but twice by communism. They fled to the South in 1954 when Catholics were persecuted by Ho Chi Minh and his army, and they fled Saigon as boat people a few years after the Communists ransacked the South in 1975. Communist crimes, Viet Cong crimes, human-rights abuses by the Hanoi regime–all are meticulously documented by Vietnamese Catholic newspapers and magazines in the United States. The Viet Cong, whom the eldest Nguyen boy barely remembered, nevertheless figured as the prime villains in the household cosmology–the chief cause of their family's suffering in America, the robbers of their father's dignity, the blasphemers of the crucifix in their church, called the Vietnamese Catholic Martyrs.

The Nguyen brothers and Cuong Pham (whose more-affluent Chinese Vietnamese parents, unlike the Nguyens, refused to open their doors to journalists) were reportedly Hong Kong movie fanatics. All four youths watched the highly stylized films whose sword-crossing heroes and gun-toting detectives and gangsters duked it out amid Hong Kong high-rises, filling their waking dreams with homilies to honor, fraternal loyalty, betrayal and, of course, revenge.

To many Vietnamese living in Sacramento, these Hong Kong videos are the real culprit in the Good Guys shootout. Gangster films like John Woo's *A Better Tomorrow* and *Bullet in the Head* were the rage among Vietnamese youth in the late 1980s. It was in re-enacting these gang-shooting scenes, some speculate, that the gunmen coolly flipped coins to decide which of the hostages would take the first bullet.

In *Bullet in the Head*, three best friends–blood brothers from Hong Kong looking to make a name for themselves (they have been losers up to this point)–travel to Vietnam during the war to smuggle illegal ampicillin. With the help of an assassin, they end up fighting everyone, including the Viet Cong. Though profit was their original quest, they are searching for their lost souls–they cannot decide whether they are good guys or bad guys. Along the way, the brothers are captured by the Viet Cong and tortured. They escape when Army of Republic of Vietnam helicopters arrive and attack the Viet Cong stronghold.

What moves the plot along, and prompts young Vietnamese viewers to whooping-oohing cheers, is the escalating interplay of terror and death from one scene to the next, culminating in a betrayal of camaraderie and leading to vengeance. A few weeks after Good Guys, Sacramento police received a mysterious letter signed by the Brothers of the Dragon.

"On 4-4-91 you have killed our brothers in Sacramento for no reason," it announced. "For this reason there must be revenge. The Brothers of the Dragon have decided in a meeting a lesson will be made." On the margins of the letter were the Vietnamese words that embody the Hong Kong video gangster mythos, words that many Vietnamese gang members have tattooed on their own skin: *Tinh, Tien, Tu, Toi, Thu—Love, Money, Prison, Sin, Revenge.*

I try but cannot reach Loi Nguyen. His defense lawyer, Linda M. Parisi, refuses to answer my letters and phone calls. Then I go to interview his parents, both under psychiatric care. Although I imagine myself to be an American journalist, the closer I come to their home, the more I realize this has been a false assumption. Sitting in my car outside the Laura Dawn Manor, I am overwhelmed by fear and guilt. Once the door opens and the old couple welcomes me in, in my mother's language, I know I will lose all perspective. An American journalist would ask the old couple, "How do you feel?" but I can't. Among Vietnamese, a collective understanding assumes that we have all suffered an epic loss, so it is pointless to ask. Once inside, I might as well put away the note pad and declare my loyalty to the old couple, whatever their shortcomings.

I am also aware that I will somehow benefit from their tragedy. If the youths were inarticulate and failed to become stars, I, the one who has a public voice, am about to gain a measure of notoriety as the teller of their sensational tale. Irrational as it may be, I feel like a cannibal. And this, perhaps more than any other reason, is why I can't bring myself to knock on their door.

Defeated, I return to San Francisco, where I live. It is, I realize, a different narrative that I am after now, one that moves from the incidental toward the historical. I go to Tu Lan, a Vietnamese coffee shop in the Tenderloin area where Vietnamese men wearing unkempt army jackets argue about Vietnamese politics in low voices on a weekday afternoon. Cigarette smoke hangs in the air like a white mosquito net. A song entitled "Mother Vietnam: We Are Still Here" echoes from the stereo.

Thuan, a 22-year-old who came to the United States five years ago, stares at my laptop with large, sad eyes as I jot down some notes. Of course he has heard about the Good Guys siege, which has become a legend among his friends.

"What those guys tried to do is to make America notice us. To me they're martyrs. Brother, America doesn't care if we live or die. At night, I see Vietnamese kids wandering the streets like ghosts. Some run away from home, some have no home to go to. Some travel from one city to the next looking for something, not knowing what. Maybe if I had come early and become articulate and educated like you, it would be different. But it's too late. Now I'm just a nobody. No education. I'm just stupid like a pig."

Thuan, whose father died in a Communist re-education camp, has an easy explanation for the hostage-takers' demands. "The ginseng roots are to increase your internal strength tenfold. Everybody knows that. Some say you can see in the dark if you drink enough tea made from it. The older the roots are, the more potent and powerful. The helicopters are for revenge. If I were the sheriff, brother, I'd have given them the helicopter and ammunition and sent them to Vietnam to kill all the Viet Cong in the world."

I understand my brother in the coffee shop. But while he speaks of vengeance, I have learned a different lesson, the American lesson: the knack of re-inventing oneself. To survive in the New World, we must, likewise, challenge the old world's blood-for-blood ethos and search for a new story line.

I have changed. I have, like many I know, driven down that hyphen that stretches like a freeway from the mythological kingdom with its 1,000-year-old ginseng roots toward the cosmopolitan city, the wind in my hair and Springsteen on the radio. English is a bendable language now, English my own song.

Perhaps only a loser knows real freedom. Forced outside of history, away from home and hearth, he can choose to remake himself. One night America seeps in, and out goes the Vietnamese soul of sorrow. For the Vietnamese refugee family, the past is an enigma best left (at least temporarily) alone.

As I think about those young men and what they did, I realize that I, in Vietnamese eyes, haven't been a very good son. I had denounced my father's passion for his homeland as parochialism, had learned to listen to his war stories as tales of nostalgia, had, in fact, taken the private angst of his generation and disseminated it in public light—an unfilial act.

I imagine the Nguyen brothers adoring their father, the ex-sergeant of the South Vietnamese army. They must have loved and trusted his war stories. According to *The Bee*, the Nguyen brothers had folded their arms, the Vietnamese filial pious gesture, and asked their parents for permission to leave the house that fateful day. This image haunts me. They tried to bring dignity to their father by fighting his war. They coveted being good Vietnamese sons: To assuage the old man's grief, the young man must defeat his old man's enemy.

A mile or so from the Good Guys store at the newest plot in St. Mary's Cemetery, flanked by a large statue of St. Pius and an American flag, Long and Pham Nguyen are buried side by side. It takes a while to find their tombstones behind the pink mausoleum. It is late afternoon, and a few birds chirp as the sprinklers spray mist that forms rainbows. The only other visitors at St. Mary's are a Vietnamese family busy burning incense sticks. The smoke, blown by a warm breeze, wavers alluringly.

Searching for the Nguyen brothers' tombstones, I find names that leave a kind of phosphorescence on my mind—names like Le, Tran, Vuong, Nguyen—Vietnamese last names that once belonged to emperors of millennia passed, etched on new tombstones on plots where the grass has not yet fully grown.

Between the two brothers' tombstones I place ginseng roots, $10.99 a box in a Vietnamese grocery store. The box has a plastic cover with the American Stars and Stripes painted on it. And printed in the lower righthand corner is the word *USA*.

Anonymous

In Search of a Perfect Valentine

Anonymous will remain so.

The first valentine he ever sent her was the best, they both agreed. It was no store-bought greeting but a carefully composed poem that caught the fervor of his longing, her dark beauty and entrancing traits, the intensity and laughter of their times together. It was all in slightly sophomoric rhythms, to be sure. But unwittingly he had found the secret of the perfect valentine. Intensely personal, relentlessly complimentary and speckled with allusions only he and she could understand.

Better still, its timing had been perfect. He had mailed it from New York, where he lived and worked, to her home in Washington, D.C. It arrived the very day his chief rival was taking the lady out to dinner, and it blew the rival's evening into irrelevance. Without that first powerful valentine, the New Yorker often thought, they might not be married today.

The next year, he blundered catastrophically, forgetting the essence of a valentine. As they edged toward marriage, he had begun to dither, and his ambivalence crept into the poem. Her eager eyes froze as she repeated one offending verse over and over in disbelief. It was a lesson he never forgot. Valentines are not what is, but what ought to be.

In succeeding years, he found the Muse harder and harder to summon. Now he was writing against the mythic lyricism of his first perfect poem, which she lovingly tended in her scrapbook, along with its successors. He dared not repeat words or images, lest he seem unimaginative or the lady appear unchanging. And he dared not lose that fervor, lest her scrapbook chart some imagined decline in this devotion.

Each February, he would be paralyzed by anxiety until, at the last moment, he would frantically scribble verses and read them aloud over dinner, with heartfelt pledges to deliver a perfected version for the scrapbook. He seldom did.

Last week his lady, as fresh, beautiful and mischievous as the day he met her, reported that a women's magazine had dissected men from various professions. Journalists, the magazine alleged, were notorious for insisting that the only authentic dining experience was in cheap ethnic restaurants. But journalists did have one virtue: they wrote superb poems to their ladies.

The pressure was becoming intolerable. Now he would be writing against an even more impossible standard—the poetic heroics of his entire profession. Clearly, it was time to give up the struggle and look for a new art form. Possibly a billboard above Times Square, proclaiming his love for all to see. Or a classified ad in the personals columns. Or, maybe, an editorial.

Anonymous, In Search of a Perfect Valentine, *The New York Times,* February 14, 1991. Reprinted with permission of *The New York Times.*

Christopher Scanlan

Daddy's Rage

"Can I get the interview I need? Can I write the story? Did I get it right?" In 22 years of reporting, Chip Scanlan recalls very few days when he wasn't bedeviled by such doubts. To survive, he relied on a tip gleaned in 1974 while earning a Master's in journalism from Columbia University. "Be counter-phobic," a taskmaster there suggested. Do what you fear.

Scanlan follows this advice in "Daddy's Rage," freelanced to Sunday magazines and later published on the Web (www.reporter.org/poynter/home/index.htm). Indeed, he took the challenge that he tosses out as director of writing programs at The Poynter Institute for Media Studies. Since 1994, he's asked seminar participants there to write and coach such personal essays.

Before joining Poynter, Scanlan reported for two small Northeast dailies and The Providence *(RI)* Journal-Bulletin, *wrote features for the* St. Petersburg Times, *and reported nationally for Knight-Ridder Newspapers. Editor of* How I Wrote the Story, *he now produces Poynter's annual series of* Best Newspaper Writing.

Despite that record, Scanlan can cite only a handful of his personal vignettes: a year in the Peace Corps, a volunteer stint at a mental hospital. "But in all of these, I stayed back, my presence little more than a personal pronoun . . . ," he acknowledges. "Like most journalists, I feared the word 'I'." After all, he says, such writing means overcoming fear, focusing on self rather than source.

To tackle a tough subject, Scanlan first filled pages with disjointed thoughts, scribbling at night, in bed. The next day, sitting beside students tapping at Poynter computers, he attacked the screen with a plaintive opener: "I do not want to write this." Yet he persisted, writing nonstop without thinking, discovering what he wanted to say. The process grew familiar. "I choked back my usual disgust at my first draft," he explains. "I rewrote."

At 44, Scanlan retraced decades, peeling away feelings about his father and their relationship. "You don't have a personal essay unless you have a religious experience," warned the editor of Northeast, The Hartford Courant's *Sunday magazine, where this story appeared. "Then it's the task of the writer to recreate the moment."*

Scanlan did. Backed by friends and family, he then took his biggest risk: going public.

—AK

Christopher Scanlan, Daddy's Rage, *Northeast, The Hartford Courant Sunday Magazine,* September 17, 1995. Reprinted courtesy of the author.

It's late at night, and I'm screaming at my kids again. Yelling at the top of my lungs at three little girls lying still and terrified in their beds. Like a referee in a lopsided boxing match, my wife is trying to pull me away, but I am in the grip of a fury I am unwilling to relinquish. "And if you don't get to sleep right now," I shout, "there are going to be consequences you're not going to like."

With that vague but ominous threat, I slam the door so hard that I hear plaster falling behind the walls and throw myself on my own bed, out of breath, pulse jackhammering in my temples, throat bruised and burning, a growing tide of remorse and revulsion rising within. From the children's room, howls descend into sobs and then sniffling whimpers as my wife murmurs a lullaby of explanations. "Daddy loves you very much," I hear Kathy tell them, a bedtime story in which I appear as a monster whose true, kinder side is obscured by fatigue and worry. "He's just tired, and he wants you to go to sleep. No, you're right, he shouldn't lose his temper, but sometimes parents get upset, and they do things they shouldn't."

All my life, I have struggled with anger and its manifestations in fits of temper.

In college, I once punched a kitchen cabinet in anger, and while I no longer recall what I was so frustrated about, I have never forgotten how, for months afterward, I couldn't shake hands without wincing. But it was only after I became a parent—we have a 7-year-old and two 5-year-old fraternal twins—that my rages grew worse and more frequent.

I have never hit my wife, but I have punched walls during arguments with her.

I love my kids, but I have left my handprint, a faint blush, on the backs of their thighs when I've spanked them. I have seen them recoil from me in terror.

At the office, I'm friendly, easygoing, generally considered a nice guy. It's only at home that I display this vein-popping, larynx-scraping rage. It's not just that I never show this secret, ugly side of my personality to others; I don't even seem to feel it in any other spheres of my life. Why must loved ones bear the brunt of anger?

It's 6:15 A.M. Two of the kids are slurping their way, with a solemn determination, through their Ripple Crisps and Cheerios. The laggard remains in bed, curled under her comforter, thumb planted firmly in her mouth.

"I'm counting to three," I call up from the landing. Silence.

"One."

The whiny protest is muffled, by the blanket and the finger. "Don't count!"

"You're going to miss the bus. You can't be late. Two."

Nothing.

"If I get to three, no 'Scooby Doo' tonight." Denying them this inane cartoon, their latest favorite, has proved to be a potent threat, and from the howl it sparks, I know I have hit a nerve. She doesn't move. Inside my head, some unseen force is unleashed, and my anger spews forth, like a race car's fiery exhaust. "That's it," I roar, my anger all out of proportion to the offense. "THREEEEEEE."

With that, the recalcitrant child is howling, and her twin joins in, while the eldest begins berating me. The peaceful breakfast is now a war zone.

I didn't want to believe anything was wrong. I shrugged off my wife's complaints that I had become the out-of-control parent her father had been. "I don't want my kids to have a father they're afraid of," she said after one of my outbursts.

"Wait a minute," I countered. "The kids know I love them." Didn't I always apologize after my anger had spent itself? Wasn't I unstinting with hugs and kisses?

"Maybe you should talk to somebody about it," she said, but I rebuffed that gentle hint. Everybody loses his temper sometimes. People get angry. Kids can drive you crazy. It's not as if I beat my wife or kids.

Kathy began clipping the occasional newspaper article about anger and pinning it to the refrigerator door. Eventually, she told me flat-out that she wouldn't tolerate any more verbal abuse. Her ultimatum, along with a particularly awful late-night screaming assault on the kids that left me ashamed, and, most of all, afraid, finally broke through the wall of denial. I did what I always do when I'm trying to get hold of something elusive: I wrote about it. Two years ago, I sat down in front of my computer and began what became a series of meditations. I called it my Temper Log.

I didn't write in it every day or every week, not even every month. But a pattern emerged from the sporadic entries. I was then working as a newspaper reporter in Washington, D.C. I constantly felt under the gun of deadlines at work, worries about supporting a family of five on a single paycheck and the incessant demands of the children. I seemed to lose it most often early in the morning, in the rush to get sleepy children to school, or at the end of a long day and a deadening ride home on the Metro. I was usually tired, hungry, overwhelmed by the frustrations that studded my workday, beset by the responsibilities of a family. Half of me wanted to be Super Dad; the other half wanted to be left alone. And for the first time, I had someone I could yell at without immediate consequences—someone who wouldn't fire me, or hang up and give the story I was after to a competitor, someone who loved me so much that they took this crap that they shouldn't have to take.

FROM THE TEMPER LOG

"Tuesday night, shortly before midnight.

"The last two days, I have lost my temper with the children as I got ready for work and tried to get them up. Today I got so furious with Michaela when she wouldn't put on her OshKosh jumper, I picked her up and dropped her on the bed against the bunched-up comforter. This is how 'normal' people wind up on the child-abuse hot line, accused of mistreating their children. I am sick at heart for acting this way. I love my children so much, and I don't want them to remember bad things about me, the way I remember Daddy breaking the rosary that night in the kitchen."

I am no more than 9, and I am standing just outside our family kitchen. My father has come home drunk again. He is in his mid-40s, (about the age I am today). By now, he has had three strokes, land mines in his brain that he seems to shrug off, like his hangovers, but which in a year will kill him. He has lost his job selling paper products, which he detested, and has had no luck finding another. He and my mother begin arguing in the kitchen. Somehow he has gotten hold of her rosary beads. I hear his anger, her protests, and then, suddenly, they are struggling over the black necklace. (Has he found her at the kitchen table, praying for him? I can imagine his rage. "If your God is so good, why are the sheriffs coming to the door about the bills I can't pay? Why am I broke? Why can't I find a job? Why am I so sick? Why, dammit? Why?") Out of control now, he tears the rosary apart. I can still hear the beads dancing like marbles on the linoleum.

I don't want to make this another one of those "It's all my parents' fault" stories, the convenient apologia of the Adult Child of an Alcoholic. Like me, my father was the product–and the victim–of his own upbringing: the only child born to a mother who had numerous miscarriages before him and a second-generation Irish-American father who squandered several fortunes and ended up alone with his memories in a furnished room at the YMCA.

While my own memories of my father are fragmentary, my mother's stories describe a vibrant, winning man, rich with an aura of promise that became deadened by alcohol and the burden of supporting a large family on a salesman's uncertain salary. No wonder he was angry.

Whatever psychic wounds my father's death caused when I was 10 seem to have frozen over my recollection of him. I have few conscious memories; those I have are starkly-etched scenes of drunkenness, grief and rage that left me with a reservoir of unresolved anger. This limitless supply feeds the frustrations of my own life, as do my templates of parental behavior that I, the loyal son, can reen-act with my own children. For many years, I thought that I hated the dimly-remembered stranger who was my father. I believed that I hated him for dying before I could learn who he was, for scaring me when he was drunk, but now I realize I hate him only because he left me before I could say "I love you."

FROM THE TEMPER LOG

"I told Caitlin that I am trying to control my temper because I don't want to frighten her and Lianna and Michaela. Last night, she angered me because she didn't want to go to bed, but I tried to put myself in her shoes and realized she was worried because Mommy wasn't home yet. So I lay down with her until she fell asleep.

"It's a balancing act, I see now, between my needs and theirs. Sometimes mine will have to take precedence. And sometimes, like last night when Caitlin just wasn't ready to sleep because she was afraid, I have to let the anger go and focus on what they need."

They read like confessions, these recitations of my outbursts, and the act of setting them down, however painful, has helped me. I've also gotten better, with my wife's help, at recognizing the flash points; like an early warning system, she can detect the first signs of a blow-up—the edge in my voice, my impatience with the bedtime-delaying antics of the children—and steer me clear.

I've finally begun to take her advice to just walk away, shut the door, go for a walk, without feeling guilty. Unlike, or perhaps because of, my father, I rarely drink. I talk about my temper with the kids. They know Daddy has a problem and he's working on it. I'd like to be able to say that I never lose my temper anymore, but I can't. Kids are constantly testing you, and often, I know now, they can inspire deserved anger.

The night my father broke my mother's rosary, my younger brother and I lay crying in our beds. The door opened, and light spilled in. In the placid cruelty of what passes for reason in a drunk's mind, he told us, "Don't worry, boys, your mother and I are getting a divorce," which, of course, sent our wails even higher. There have been moments when I have remembered that scene, and the memory has checked me from saying something equally terrible to my own children huddled in their beds.

Even then, I knew that he was terrified of something, and now I see that my worst anger seems to come when I am most deeply afraid—about work, about money, about whether I will amount to anything or if I will die as he did, bitter and unfulfilled. I don't want my children to remember me the way I remember my father, as this looming, frightened man.

"At every corner," the poet Robert Lowell wrote, "I meet my father, my age, still alive." The other morning, the barber who cuts my hair stood behind me with an oval mirror to show off his handiwork. I found myself looking at the same bald spot on the back of my head that I used to stare at from the back seat of our family Ford, when my father was at the wheel. There are mornings when I wake up afraid and wonder: How many mornings was he afraid? How many nights was he squeezed to the breaking point? I meet my father now in the dark of my children's bedroom, hearing in my shouts the echoes of his rage, the legacy of anger passed from father to son. As our children have grown from cribs to their own beds, I have begun to hear myself in their outbursts: temper tantrums from the oldest, impulsive slaps from the youngest. Rivers of rage run from one generation to another, and it may be impossible to staunch the flow. But I have to keep trying. One breakfast, one bedtime, one day at a time.

Jonathan Dahl

Missing in America

"Missing in America" ran in the coveted Middle Column on The Wall Street Journal's *front page, an unusual twist for reporter Jonathan Dahl, as well as for his missing brother, Jeff. Poverty, addiction, mental illness, homelessness—all became personal as Dahl searched four states for an elusive Jeff. Dahl's hunt began in 1989, when he sacrificed vacation time to follow tips. He later marshaled* Journal *prestige and resources. After all, he says, "you cannot just put an adult's picture on a milk carton."*

The reporting was a struggle, but the writing was not. Dahl relied on the classic Journal *format—open anecdotally, segue to the organizing nut graph, move chronologically, return to anecdote—to provide a familiar context for readers. Noting his "blend of very formalistic and very personal," he insists that journalists never lose objectivity, even in first-person pieces. As with other stories, he parceled his writing energy predictably: "80 percent on the lead and nut graph, 20 percent on everything else." He wrote for two weeks, paring years of material, making larger points, yet never straying far from Jeff.*

Publication sparked 500 letters. Then, as a special senior reporter at 30, Dahl discovered professional limits. "No one came forward with anything to help. Everyone came forward with their own experiences," he says. So the reporter envied doctors and lawyers who successfully solved problems. Naively, Dahl now concedes, he wanted journalism to solve his problem. "On a personal level," he says, "it didn't."

Dahl, of course, took all the right professional steps. After graduating from Columbia University in 1980, he added a Master's in journalism a year later. Then he headed to The Houston Chronicle *for a rookie reporter's traditional start: the cops beat. Bureau hopping—Dallas to Chicago to New York City—began when he joined* The Journal *in 1984 to cover transportation.*

Now an editor, Dahl warns, "Don't forget how powerful, both in positive and negative ways, words can be. Years later, people won't forget what you've written." He notes how his brother never forgave the reference in "Missing" to "ditties." But whatever the risks, whatever the consequences, Dahl-the-editor is adamant that reporters cannot be cowed. Of his own story, he reports: "It was not a happy ending." In October 1995, Jeff Dahl committed suicide.

—AK

One tense day in August 1982, my brother vanished.

Strung out on drugs, Jeff kicked in our parents' car door that afternoon –because they wouldn't give him $35. Years of drug treatment hadn't helped; he had smashed furniture, taken off with the family car and threatened to burn down the house. Afraid and frustrated, my father told his 27-year-old son never to come home.

Jeff took Dad at his word. From that day on, we didn't hear from my brother or know if he was dead or alive. My mother was haunted by police photos of a local bank robber resembling Jeff. I imagined my brother, three years my senior, holed up in a crack house. But no one suffered more than our father, who agonized over evicting his son. Shortly before he died in May 1988, Dad made one final wish: Find Jeff.

This is the story of how I tried to fulfill that wish. For more than a year, I traveled off and on through New York, Connecticut, Colorado and Florida in search of my missing brother. With a creased photo of a smiling Jeff in my wallet, I hit dozens of police stations, shelters and bars, picking up leads from oddball characters like "Skinhead Bob." All along, I put off the nagging question of what I would do if I found Jeff.

A COMMON JOURNEY

I wasn't alone in my ordeal. Nobody knows how many missing adults there are, but more than 40,000 people a year ask the government or the Salvation Army to help find loved ones. Some of the missing are refugees from adoptions, divorces or separations. Many are part of the nation's growing number of anonymous drifters and homeless. But while it's easy to get lost in America, finding missing adults is a journey through frustration and helplessness. These people's faces don't get put on milk cartons. No major support group exists. Most government agencies won't give out information because of privacy laws. So anxious families are left to search aimlessly on their own.

My search for Jeff–who once bloodied the noses of sixth-grade bullies for me –started in the fall of 1989. I began tracking down his high school friends, scattered in Washington, Texas and New York. I also randomly picked Jeff Dahls from phone directories around the country. One night I phoned a Jeff and Sandra Dahl in Bellingham, Wash., where one of Jeff's close friends had moved. Maybe he's married and settled down with a good job, I hoped. "It's not your Jeff," a woman said softly.

Eventually, one of Jeff's friends told me to try a public park in Westport, Conn., where Jeff was rumored to be playing guitar, his favorite hobby. Westport is only about 10 miles from where Jeff and I grew up in Darien, Conn.

So in November 1989, I drove from my home in New York to Westport, home to million-dollar colonials and Paul Newman. For no logical reason, I pulled into the first gas station and flashed Jeff's photo at an attendant. He suggested I speak to a local pastor, the Rev. Theodore Hoskins. A silver-haired man with a Lincolnesque beard, Mr. Hoskins once attracted national attention by letting vagrants live in the pine woods behind his church—a move that embarrassed the citizenry into building a homeless shelter.

For a moment, Mr. Hoskins studied Jeff's picture. "I hope you know," he said, trying to break the news gently, "that Jeff has been one of our street people."

Jeff, it turned out, had scavenged in those church woods and slept in a junked Pinto about the time I was living in a spacious high-rise overlooking Lake Michigan in Chicago. My parents had always assumed their son had run far away. But Mr. Hoskins said my brother, following the habits of many homeless people, stayed near his hometown for years, crashing on friends' couches and flopping in shelters. Drugs, mostly marijuana but also cocaine and heroin, still dominated his life. "Your brother," he said, "really wants to get better, but . . ."

Mr. Hoskins sent me to the Gillespie Center, a one-story brick shelter for the homeless furnished with three sagging couches, wobbly card tables and a large-screen television. The pastor thought Jeff might be staying there. And in the eerie half-light, any of the silhouettes on the cots could have been my brother. I quickly scanned the faces of three snoring men and of a grizzled old man who offered a cup filled with spit. Finally, I came upon a counselor who recognized Jeff's picture. He told me Jeff had left Westport just three weeks before.

My brother was on the run, skipping town owing a local drug dealer $4,000. The dealer, alternately described as a harmless "pothead" and a thug who collected bayonets and crossbows, had handed out crude "Wanted" posters offering a $200 reward for my brother. "Jeff could be anywhere," the counselor said, squeezing my shoulder as I tried to imagine how I would ever find my brother in a sea of three million homeless.

Jeff's life wasn't supposed to turn out this way. As children of an IBM executive, we took winter vacations in the Bahamas and spent summer weekends on the meticulously swept clay courts of the Tokeneke Club in Darien. Jeff was the middle and brightest of three children, the one who won the President's Cup at Tokeneke for best swimmer and had a 130-plus IQ. He was also the closest to me: He tied my shoes at the bus stop and made toys for me by hand. Once while we were climbing tress he rescued me from choking on a toy-gun strap that had caught on a branch—an incident that went down in family lore as the day Jeff saved his brother's life. Together, we drove our oldest brother so crazy he wrote a sixth-grade essay on our antics: "Those Two."

Jeff did well in school. His eighth-grade English teacher once called our mother to say his writing was good enough to publish. He had a steady girlfriend, Gigi, and he shared the same interest in film making our father did. After dinner, the two often spent hours studying film strips and slide shows that Dad produced for IBM conferences.

A TURNING POINT

But Jeff became unusually moody and depressed in high school; he stopped dating and lost interest in swimming. At 19, he took up marijuana, first as a diversion from a boring lifeguard job, later as an obsession. He hid his habit from us for two years as he progressed to harder drugs and then dropped out of the University of Delaware. Heartbroken, my parents spent much of the next six years checking Jeff in and out of the Silver Hill Foundation, a psychiatric center in New Canaan. He was diagnosed as an obsessive-compulsive neurotic, a disorder that in his case was marked by uncontrolled urges and sudden outbursts. It was never clear what the main cause of his problem was–drugs or mental illness. But psychiatrists said the family couldn't really help until Jeff got off drugs on his own.

After Jeff left, our family looked for him briefly but soon ran out of leads. Eventually, he became the family myth: the "artist living in Washington state" to anyone who asked. The President's Cup was packed off to Goodwill. But some years later, my father began to think Jeff's problems were mental and beyond his control. "If he had lost an arm, we wouldn't have thrown him out," he would say. When my search began, I wanted Jeff to know about Dad's remorse. In Westport, the Rev. Hoskins encouraged me to find him for another reason: Your brother needs you.

For the next seven months, I called shelters and police departments in random cities. I scoured New York subway stations, music stores and $1 movie theaters. Disheartened, I sometimes gave up for long periods. But I also often returned to the Gillespie Center, hoping some of Jeff's friends–street people and drifters with names like "Human Skull," "Boss" and "Whiplash Watson"–would stop by. They seldom did. But some of the drifters I did find mentioned that Jeff had talked about going to Florida. So last October, I headed south.

A FAMILIAR NAME

I picked Clearwater on the hunch that somehow Jeff had discovered my parents had moved there. My first stop was the Homeless Emergency Project, a bleak compound with a decrepit bus, a rotting gazebo and an overcrowded dormitory. "The name sounds real familiar," said Barbara Green, the administrator, as a squad car dropped off a vagrant shaking from hunger.

That vague comment alone was enough to fill me with frantic hope. I lingered at shelters for hours, fearing I might just miss him, and shoved my handwritten "Lost Brother" posters at startled Tony Roma waiters. I checked out every rumor, no matter how wild.

At the St. Vincent de Paul soup kitchen in downtown Clearwater, Sylvia, a one-armed woman in psychedelic bellbottoms, promised to deliver Jeff the next morning. "We're friends," she said with a toothless smile. She never showed up and I should have known better: She had been wrong about my brother's age by 15 years. Later, I drove 20 miles to the Silver Nugget bar near a seedy part of Tampa purely at the suggestion of a wino. Removing my tie, I awkwardly tried to blend in with the unshaven pool hustlers, hoping nobody would notice my penny-loafers.

"That's him," teased a baseball-capped barfly after glancing at my brother's picture. Laughing loudly, he pointed to a friend slumped on a bar stool.

HOME OF PRESIDENTS

Still hoping Jeff was in Clearwater, I promised myself that I would pore over every log book in every shelter, police station and drug center in the county;

never mind that some shelters don't require identification ("Ronald Reagan" signed in at one shelter four times). But there wasn't enough time to check all 27 homeless care facilities, much less search the records of the 18 police agencies.

Drug rehabs were even more impenetrable; they refused to release any information about patients because of confidentiality laws. At Operation PAR, a drug rehab with palm-shaded cabins, I waited two hours petulantly demanding to talk to "someone important." "Your brother could be here right now, and I couldn't tell you," a staffer said. After that, I just wanted to go home.

On a return trip to Florida, I discovered other people sharing my frustration. At the Abundant Life Church in a drug-ravaged neighborhood in Tampa, an elderly Esther Fonseca surveyed 10 homeless men stretched out on pews–their beds for the night. Her 59-year-old cousin, Milton Braga, whom she had raised, disappeared in 1986. She still keeps his clothes neatly folded at home and religiously tours local shelters. For her, a missing relative is almost worse than a dead one. "The misery never stops," she said.

A CALL HOME

The church manager himself, Ray Greene, was once among the missing. He drank himself into homelessness in 1988 and went into hiding for two years. His 10 adult children ran his photo in the *Tampa Tribune* with the heading: "We Love this Man." They also tried the Salvation Army's missing person bureau and the Social Security Administration. But both agencies are better equipped to find people who use Social Security numbers, which many homeless don't. So Mr. Greene's children never did find their father; he called them when he sobered up.

"It's amazing there's almost nothing to help these families," said the husky, sad-eyed Mr. Greene. The 60-year-old ultimately decided to stay at the church to work with the homeless; his own bed, now, is the altar's nylon carpet.

With no leads in Florida, I focused on Westport again. In November, I had a breakthrough. Joe Downer–a longtime friend of Jeff's–surfaced at the Gillespie Center. A veteran drifter with a walrus mustache and droopy jeans, Joe gave me a name in San Antonio and another in San Francisco. From these people, I got my first reassurance in a long time that Jeff was still alive–and almost within reach. "You just missed him," said Jack Klee in San Antonio. "He came in with a pillowcase of clothes and left when he started to wear out his welcome."

My brother had told Jack he was going to Denver, and I hoped that Joe might have a lead there. But before I could find him again, Joe came down with what he described as encephalitis, a brain disease that can damage memory. I panicked when I realized a crucial link in my search might be slipping away.

'A' IS FOR . . .

I raced out to Westport early on a Sunday morning. Inside the shelter, Joe was folding towels, his face chalky, his speech slurred. For three hours, we struggled to talk above a blaring TV set. But all Joe could remember was that one of Jeff's pals, Gary Watson, lived in a Colorado town near Denver beginning with "A." Was it Aurora? No. I left the shelter and dashed past the local Benetton and Chez Pierre restaurant, searching for a place that sold maps on Sundays. Joe studied one I found. "I'm sorry," he mumbled.

Seeing Joe so sick made me panic even more. Life is short for people on the streets, and Jeff had been there eight years. "Most of them don't last that long," said Paul Villella, a night supervisor at the Gillespie Center. One of Jeff's Westport friends had shot himself, another had died from a heroin overdose and a third had choked on his own vomit. I had learned Jeff was still using hard drugs and had been talking about suicide. "He's very lonely," said his friend Jack Klee.

The next day Joe remembered: "A" was for Arvada.

The only address I had in Arvada was for Gary Watson's mother. On Dec. 17, I drove from the Denver airport to her split-level home, where she ushered me into a living room of neatly appointed furniture. She said Jeff had been in Denver recently, had been over for dinner and had cleaned up, "to an extent of course." Then she nervously blurted out: "I don't know if I should be telling you this, but your brother was in the hospital." I asked if Jeff had been in an accident. Mrs. Watson held up her hands, palms out, and slowly pantomimed slashing a wrist. I felt nauseous.

Mrs. Watson tried to be comforting, but we were strangers. In her driveway, I sat in my rented car and took in the snowy panorama of Mount Evans. People in Colorado always say the mountains give them a feeling of well-being; that must not have been true for Jeff. I had just heard that my brother almost killed himself. But after all these years of being apart, Jeff seemed more a ghost than a brother.

JEFF'S NEW BROTHER

I set out to find Gary Watson, who, his mother had said with some embarrassment, worked at a porno shop. At Kitty's Pleasure Palace in Denver, her skinny and soft-spoken son was busy ringing up sales while two topless women with brassy hair and neon G-strings gyrated in glass booths. Gary shook my hand and smiled: "I've heard so much about you."

He had known Jeff more than 10 years and almost thought of himself as Jeff's little brother. He even kept a scrapbook of Jeff's scrawled cartoons and songs. While the skinflick *Night Dreams* played on a monitor overhead, Gary described a Jeff I wanted back: a friend who taught him about bass guitar and John Irving novels. In all their years together, Jeff was always too hurt to talk much about our family. "But he was always talking about how his little brother works for the *New York Times*," Gary said, referring to a childhood ambition of mine.

Just a few months before, though, Gary and Jeff had parted ways after a fight over a maintenance job they both wanted. Gary pointed to a bus stop where he'd last seen Jeff. "My feeling is he's out of the state," he said. It was the fourth time I had just missed Jeff.

Just like that, my search had run aground again. At the Comfort Inn, I made plans to head home. Christmas was a week away. But Gary called in the middle of the night with a new lead: "Skinhead Bob," a local punk-rock musician who knows Jeff, was insisting my brother was in Denver. But when I called Skinhead

Bob, he said he was leaving town in a few hours and didn't feel like talking on the phone. He gave me the choice of a 2 A.M. meeting at his place, or nothing at all.

SECOND THOUGHTS

The moment I started groping through the dark entrance to his apartment building, I wanted out. His boyish face and hair were mild-mannered enough, but Skinhead Bob immediately boasted about his days with a street gang called the Slap Shots. He proudly waved a wooden cane with the chiseled inscription on the handle: "Chief Psycho."

When I asked for Jeff's phone number, he changed the subject. I showed him my driver's license to reassure him I wasn't the drug dealer on Jeff's trail. He grinned. I told him about Jeff saving my life as a kid. More grins. When he started talking about a local girl giving birth to the anti-Christ, I decided he was too unstable to pressure. For half an hour, he rambled on about death and Richard Nixon. He casually mentioned that I was sitting on the same lumpy couch that Jeff sat on the day before.

Finally, Skinhead Bob cut off his monologue and without any explanation scribbled down a phone number. I never did get his real name.

I didn't call the number for six hours. In a sleepless mental haze, I drove all night through Denver's Capitol Hill section. Gary had warned that Dad's death "was going to hit Jeff real hard." But I was stalling for other reasons, too. In many ways, coming face-to-face with the missing is the hardest part of the search. Call it the Rip Van Winkle syndrome. After all those years apart, you don't know if finding the relative will be good or bad—for either of you. Sometimes it's almost a relief when the search hits a dead end. But it was too late to turn back. I went to a pay phone.

"Hello," a man said after four rings. It was my brother's voice, unchanged after all these years. I hung up immediately, paced for five minutes and dialed again.

"Hello, Jeff. This is Jonathan, your brother."

"Jonathan?" He paused as though he were about to cry. "Oh my God."

FAMILIAR FACE

Ten minutes later, I drove up to a two-story apartment house with windows covered with crumpled newspapers. A tall man in a T-shirt and black sneakers lumbered down the staircase to greet me. At 35, Jeff still wore his blond hair in the same Elvis Presley hairdo from high school; his eyes were the Windex-blue I remembered. But his face looked haggard and bloated, and his swimmer's build had become potbellied. The kid in my wallet photo had become a middle-aged man. We had missed a quarter of each other's lives. Hesitantly, I reached to hug him, but it was like embracing a statue. Even in the good times, we were never big huggers.

"You still have your hair," he said.

Upstairs, my brother gulped vodka from an old peanut-butter jar and collapsed onto a futon couch. His accommodations were even worse than I expected: He and another man shared a one-room apartment near downtown with peeling paint, a roach-infested stove and a Christmas tree decorated with condom wrappers. Too nervous to sit, I paced and peeked into a utility closet, tripping over a bare mattress on the floor. This was Jeff's bedroom. Jeff finally broke the silence. "So, how are Mom and Dad?"

My pause and opening few words–"I'm sorry"– were all Jeff needed to hear. "I suppose that's one reason I never called," he said, rubbing his teary eyes.

There would be many more painful moments. I would learn right off that Jeff had never tried to contact our family–not once. Although the family remembers Dad telling Jeff to leave until he got off drugs, Jeff insisted he was told to stay away for good. With an icy stare, he also pointed out that I too had once rejected him, refusing to let him stay at my college fraternity house before he left home. "I was an embarrassment," he said tersely. Then he softened. "I was waiting to call with good news. It just never happened."

Jeff, in fact, had never escaped from drugs or alcohol for more than a few months. Because they're cheaper, he was using marijuana and vodka now, but he said he had tried everything from Angel Dust to cough medicine to avoid "the horrible pain of being sober." Addiction is a word that doesn't really sink in until you see your brother constantly drawing on an asthma-spray inhaler because his lungs are so shot from pot smoking.

Because of his addiction, my brother had spent almost half his adult life at drug rehabs, drunk tanks and mental wards. After the final fight with my parents, Jeff checked himself into a state hospital, where he spent Christmas heavily sedated–and alone. He then tried a few rehab centers in New York; one made him scrub a rock with a toothbrush as punishment, he said, and another shaved his head.

After that, Jeff spent much of the next six years in Westport, then thumbed across the country and "got stuck" in Denver. He slept in Greyhound bathroom stalls until the police rousted him with nightclubs, and spent a few days in jail because he couldn't afford a $10 fine for hitchhiking. Occasionally, he scraped by on dishwashing jobs and lived in boarding houses. But that never lasted more than a few weeks. One of his "best times" was spent wearing a Friar Tuck robe and taking a vow of silence as a monk's helper at Denver's St. Andrews Church.

PLAYER IN THE PARK

As it turned out, my brother had never gone to Clearwater. He lingered in Westport not to be near Darien but because the town let him play guitar in the public park. The *Westport News* even ran a picture of him performing for spare change. And though he didn't like to talk about it, he had tried to kill himself, more than once. "I just didn't think anyone cared about me," he said.

I listened to Jeff talk about the past without knowing what to do about the future. By finding my brother, I had traded one painful mystery for another. Should he return with me to New York? Should I give him money? A dozen psychiatrists and counselors I talked to told me Jeff needed to get into a long-term drug center or mental hospital. My brother didn't think either would help. He couldn't be forced to go, the psychiatrists said, because he isn't clearly mentally incompetent.

The rest of my family had no answers. My mother and oldest brother supported my search, but they thought Jeff needed to reform on his own. None of us wanted to take him in for now because we didn't think we could handle or solve his problems. My mother also vividly remembered Jeff's violent threats. "I wish him well," she said. "But until he gets off the drugs, the son I knew and loved died at 19."

GETTING ACQUAINTED

I gave up looking for any quick answers and decided to make the best of my week in Denver with Jeff. We spent most of the time driving around aimlessly, making awkward small talk and eating at Taco Bell. The first day, I gave him $40, which he spent on food, pot and vodka. He occasionally hinted for more money and we argued when I refused. One day we took a road trip through the Rockies, but otherwise I limited our meetings to just a few hours at a time. While looking for my brother, I had dreamed of the days we would spend together. But now all I wanted to do was hide in my hotel and shut out the pain of his past.

On Christmas, Jeff gave me a handdrawn cartoon with the caption, "Man seeking lost brother finds Elvis." I gave him a guitar case and a harmonica. On my last night in Denver, he played guitar at a local bar, belting out "Put Me in the Rehab," "I Killed a Yuppie Today" and other ditties he had written. Afterward, he took me aside. "It's great to have my brother back," he said.

But are we really back? Since I left Denver, Jeff has called me only sporadically and I usually don't know how to reach him. He has moved seven times—flopping at Gary Watson's one day, at a ratty motel on Denver's west side the next. He recently called me at three in the morning, crying because he was stuck in a shelter where the homeless sleep in stalls divided by torn shower curtains. He told me he may never be able to get off the streets. When Jeff hung up, I worried that he might disappear again. Then what would I do?

Part of me wants to help him, but part of me realizes I can't be my brother's keeper. Until I figure out what to do, I think about Jeff all the time—how he struggles with his drug habit, how he weaves in and out of homelessness. For me, the tattered figures curled up on New York's sidewalks and the panhandlers rattling cups on 42nd Street all have the same face.

My brother's.

The Inside Story:
Writers on Reading

Why risk camaraderie when competition is so acceptable? Because, as the staff of the Rapid City Journal *discovered, writing collectively offers benefits for writers as well as readers. At the prodding of a visiting newsroom coach, the avid readers on staff turned into avid writers to produce a tabloid celebrating International Literacy Day. First, they received the vaguest instructions– "Move your readers. Make 'em laugh. Make 'em cry." Then, they procrastinated. But Diane Montz, editor of the special section, persisted: "Who better to ask about reading than those who write?"*

Over two weeks, staffers snatched minutes between breaking stories to challenge formula thinking, formula reporting, formula writing. No one escaped. The newsroom receptionist, who rereads her favorite book annually, proudly confessed that. Editor Joe Karius dodged, then delivered an emotionally tough ending. With prodding from the desk chief, anonymous copy editors reestablished credibility as writers. Indeed, Laura Tonkyn, staff writer and part-time copy editor, led off with a reassuring pledge on the Journal's *front page: "There is nothing I will not read."*

Curious or anxious, writers hacked into computer queues to spy on each other's words. Capitol bureau reporter Bob Mercer, known for writing politics in bulk, delivered two satisfying column-inches. Dick Rebbeck, a 20-year veteran, agonized from hotel to hotel while on the road, finally faxing perfected phrases from a drugstore on the prairie. "A tough assignment," he later groused. And, after graphic artist Marty Two Bulls found his writing voice, he documented the stories of others with his visual voice.

Reporters at this small daily displayed a typical range of ability (semi- to very organized), of attitude (skeptical to enthusiastic), of experience (1 month to 37 years). And with time, enough time, these writers enjoyed the rare opportunity to rewrite: polishing text, solving problems of style and structure. Working off deadline, without the pressure of production, the editors also enjoyed cooperation, not competition, to coach an entire newsroom.

And staffers discovered that they did not want to hide behind oh-so-anonymous photo credits or bylines. But, even after publication, they weren't ready to tell all. "Don't tell anyone how much fun this is!" they cautioned. So the visiting coach promised to keep quiet. (She lied.)

–AK

Staff, The Inside Story: Writers on Reading, *Rapid City Journal*, September 8, 1993.
Reprinted courtesy of *Rapid City Journal*.

SO MANY WORDS, SO LITTLE TIME
--Laura Tonkyn
Journal Staff Writer

There is nothing I will not read.

I read classified ads, real estate listings; the other day when breakfast loomed without anything else at hand, I even read the papers explaining my car insurance policy. I always read when I watch TV and generally when I take a bath. Of course, I read the back of cereal boxes.

I read in the car while on vacation, throwing my husband into despair. Apparently I should look at the scenery. My father used to say that, too. Speaking of vacations, I have the perfect one planned. Me, a beach, a chair with an umbrella and 20 or 30 books.

I read in the car while waiting for my son's school to get out. I read in the car while slopping 2-for-1 tacos down my shirt. If I can't find a paper to read at McDonald's, I waste 50 cents and buy one.

If I consider a book well-written, I will read it regardless of topic. But I read very fast and not always thoroughly, so it's an open question as to whether I am well-read.

I've loved to read since I was 4 years old. I imagine an old age filled with books and the time to read them. In the meantime, I read in snitches and snatches; the good, the bad and the boring; but never so boring, so confined, so small as a world without reading.

WRITTEN WORD PACKS A PUNCH
--Rick Snedeker
Journal Copy Editor

Ironically, the news came in a letter.

Because during the three years Eric and I shared a villa in Saudi Arabia, he never wrote one. He was a literate guy but leery of words he couldn't take back.

So, when he went back to England and I sailed for America in 1988, no word came from the kingdom by the sea for months.

But when Betty, his old girlfriend from the desert, died, he called long distance to talk. She was 43 and full of life before the breast cancer, and the three of us drank many a glass of foul, bootleg wine together.

We buried her on the phone. I never heard from Eric again.

But not long ago a letter came with Queen Elizabeth on the stamp. The sender was Eric's friend Paul, on whose boat we once glided across the English Channel on a brilliant summer day to a little pub on the Isle of Wight. Just for a pint of bitter.

Paul called it the hardest letter he ever wrote. An aneurysm formed on Eric's brain in the spring, and the doctors were buoyantly optimistic about surgery. But they were mistaken. With his family waiting in the recovery room, Eric died.

Eric would have wanted me to know, Paul said. Who would have guessed?

I just stared at the word on the page. Died. When it's real and close, there's no more powerful word in English. It empties your soul.

That afternoon, I wrote to Eric's teen-age daughter, whom he saw infrequently but doted on. I told her she was the one pure joy of his life. I wrote the words down so she could read them any time.

So they could never be taken back.

MEET MY FRIENDS

--BOB MERCER

JOURNAL CAPITAL BUREAU

I have this friend. Call him Jerry. One day his newspaper almost killed Jerry.

That's what happens when you read the sports section while cruising 65 mph down Interstate 90.

I have these other friends. Call them Mona and Buzz. He ranches in Stanley County. Mona is his wife. One day Mona decided to buy a book for a girlfriend. "What for?" Buzz asked. "She's already got a book." He probably was kidding.

UNKNOWN GIRLS OF SUMMER INSPIRED LIFELONG ADDICTION

--DICK REBBECK

JOURNAL STAFF WRITER

Oh, that first book, and the second, and the third that I scanned so easily in those long-ago summer days of adolescence.

Too young to get a regular job, I idled away the hours at the swimming pool and peered from behind a book at the trim, tanned high school girls, remote as movie queens on the far side of our age gap. Soon enough, I also decided I was too young—or too skinny, or too shy or something—to get such a girl.

What I did get, though, was addicted to reading—a lifelong addiction, for the journey out of puberty goes on and on.

So now, many years later, I sit in the sun, yet another adventure book on my lap, and think of the women who were the girls I never knew.

DICTIONARY CONFIRMS A SLIP OF THE TONGUE

--TED BROCKISH

JOURNAL EDITORIAL PAGE EDITOR

I don't recall why I was so enraged with my older brother. But I distinctly remember bursting into the kitchen. As soon as the words flew off my tongue, I knew I had made a mistake.

"You know what that $%*&?! did?" I bellowed, not really to anyone in particular.

My mother reacted as if the words were meant for her ears. Obviously, the money she and my father were spending on their eighth-grade son's parochial school education wasn't getting the job done completely.

"What did you say?" she demanded. Before I could answer, she had another question. "Do you know what that means?"

"Er . . . it has something to do with . . . er . . . the needles on a cactus . . . I think," I stammered. Actually I had a vague idea . . . well, actually not so vague . . . but if she didn't know, well, I wasn't about to tell her.

Following a stern lecture about engaging the muscle between my ears before the muscle between my cheeks starts wagging, I decided I needed to know for sure what that word means.

So I consulted the *Webster's Dictionary* perpetually stationed among the *Book of Knowledge* encyclopedias on the family room bookshelf.

Hmmmm. There it was. ". . . a mark or shallow hole made by a pointed instrument . . . penis–usually considered vulgar . . . a disagreeable or contemptible person."

Yeah, that was it. That's what I meant. "Disagreeable" and "contemptible" certainly fit my brother.

But I decided it best not to further enlighten my mother.

BREAKING NEWS HIT HOME HARD
--Joe Karius
Journal Editor

Every once in a while, usually while driving at night, I'll hear that rapid clacking sound from the old black Associated Press teletype machine.

I'll see the words forming into a sentence on the cheap white paper.

It was 1965, 28 years ago. But I remember in vivid detail the scene that night. Back from covering a common council meeting in the small central Wisconsin city, I was headed to the second floor newsroom.

But the typewriter-like sound of that AP machine in the downstairs radio station offices stopped me. I decided to see if there was some late-breaking story. In only my second year of reporting, I loved the excitement of reading news before almost anyone else.

Of the thousands of stories I've read off those old teletypes and, later, the computer systems that followed, I remember that one most of all.

"MILWAUKEE (ap) A 21-year-old West Allis woman drowned Tuesday in a boating accident on Lake Michigan, just north of Sheboygan . . ."

Her name was Virginia.

Four years earlier, I had taken her to the prom at St. Mary's Academy. Later that summer she gave me her class ring–we talked about getting married.

Eventually, we broke up. I don't remember exactly why.

But I'll never forget reading that story. Each time my mind replays that scene, I can't help wondering what I wondered that night. Would she still be alive if we each hadn't gone our own way?

CONFESSIONS OF A WIRE CRUISER
--Bill Harlan
Journal Staff Writer

Hi. My name is Bill. I'm a wire cruiser.

"Cruising the wires" is the newsroom equivalent of "channel surfing"—a nasty, shameful habit.

Just as cable-television channel surfers ride their remote controls from *Revenge of the Teen-age Space Vixens* to the Northeastern Box LaCrosse championships, wire-cruising reporters navigate their computer terminals deep into the bowels of the *Journal*'s newswire files.

The *Journal* receives hundreds of stories each week that never make the paper because, frankly, who cares about gangland crime in Moscow or the oyster-fishing problems in Virginia?

A reading junky cares. ("It's a jungle out there," Vyacheslav Yegorov said.)

A news-a-holic cares. (It's not just oysters. Shad and sturgeon are in trouble, too!)

I knew I was "cruising" for trouble when I started looking forward to the *Washington Post*'s weekly summaries of magazine stories.

You say reading articles about articles is sick?

Hey, I don't subscribe to *Cigar Afficianado*, so how else would I discover that the value of Cuban Davidoffs is skyrocketing?

If I hadn't read the story about *Beer: The Magazine*, I never would have learned that ". . . beer is a gift given in return for the curse of self-awareness, the knowledge of our doom—we're gonna die someday."

Which is sort of how I feel about reading news stories.

That's why I cruise.

And I can quit any time. Honest.

SHE READ THEM ALL

--TIM REILLY ·
JOURNAL STAFF WRITER

I never read much when I was growing up. But my freshman year in high school, while I looked for classes to slide through, I stumbled into a reading class taught by Mrs. Olsen.

This looked like just the ticket for someone who didn't want to work. To get an A, I simply had to read a million and a half words, or about 10 paperbacks. There was a catch. I would have to give Mrs. Olsen oral reports.

Mrs. Olsen could have been a nun. She was old. She wore black cat-eyed glasses and had bad teeth, which to me meant bad breath. But, I figured I could just skim the books, lie my way through the reports and skate out of the class with my A.

I was wrong.

I first reported on "Jory," a rather risque western. When I said the title, I half expected her to smack my hand with her ruler and tell me I shouldn't waste my time on such trash.

Instead, she asked me a pointed question about the sex in the book and how it made me feel. I was stunned. This old woman had not only read "Jory," but she spoke to me in an adult manner and wanted to know which was more important to a young man—sex or freedom? This was more than I could take.

The race was on. I searched for books that I was sure she hadn't read. Tom Wolfe's *Electric Kool-Aid Acid Test*–read it. Carlos Castenada's *A Separate Reality* –done that. Jack Kerouac's *On the Road*–been there.

I couldn't win. She had read everything and she knew what to ask. I couldn't lie. I had to read the books. I hated it. I got a B.

Looking back, I realize she opened a door for me, and I am grateful. If by chance, I write a book, I'll dedicate it to her: "Mrs. Olsen, I know you haven't read this one."

MEMORIES TO SAVOR MADE OF WRITTEN WORDS
--Heidi Bell
Journal Staff Writer

You can't file phone calls in a shoebox. That's why I love letters.

People are busy, and it's easier to pick up the phone than to write a note. I know–sometimes I resort to phone calls, too. But I'm a saver. I keep ticket stubs and valentines, pressed flowers and school pictures . . . and letters.

I like them written in real handwriting. I love it when the writer's ideas are smeared with peanut butter from breakfast or splashed with coffee.

Maybe letters meant the most when I was away at college, as a link to home that I could hold. My mom sent notes in familiar, flowing handwriting, with drawings of her, the dogs and the cat in the margins. My sisters sent news and encouragement. My niece drew pictures and explained them to her mom, who wrote her exact words underneath. On paper I saw a baby grow into an amazing 3-year-old who could draw things like "a slender stick in the wild."

I've had a few long-distance romances, maybe because I loved getting the letters. I'd savor the possibilities, sometimes carrying a letter in my pocket all day until I could read it undisturbed. Anticipation was usually (but not always) better than reality. I'd read and re-read them, lingering over the best parts, sleeping with them under my pillow.

I've probably had great phone calls, but no way can I remember any details. Letters are different. They're a diary. They remind me of forgotten things–some that still bring pain, others that make me laugh. I file them all away in cardboard, these pieces of my life. Someday I might need them.

AN ARTIST READS
--Marty Two Bulls
Journal Artist

Not long ago, I was browsing through a small county library in eastern South Dakota. In its large section devoted to pulp paperbacks, the smell of decaying paper and cedar bookshelves was surprisingly pleasant and reassuring.

The scent brought back my thoughts as a young boy fascinated with reading. Reading opened a wonderful world to me, a world I had no idea existed.

Through the words of Ray Bradbury, I flew a rocket ship to Mars. Robert E. Howard pounded and welded Conan's adventures to life, and I walked with JRR

Tolkien to Moria. What most fascinated me was realizing this material was created long before I was born.

Returning from the library, I studied my old drawings. I am an artist, the kind who paints and draws. As I grew up, I got singled out as a good artist. Someday, I hope to be a great artist.

In the beginning, my subjects were science fiction–the rocket ships and lasers blazing from my sketch books. These were a direct link to what I was reading.

The boyhood dreams of glory flowed from my optimistic pen. I dove head first into fantasy, but I found the waters shallow. I soon waded into books about history, radical theories and poetry.

My art work took a darker, more serious turn as I entered high school and the adult world. It wasn't until I met and fell in love with my wife, that my work lightened up. Now I see a brighter world through our three children. And I watch them work on their coloring books, just entering this world of enchantment. I smile and wonder if they will become artists, too.

I still remember the effect reading had on me. That same feeling drives me to create art that may inspire someone else, the same way books inspired me.

IMPACT LINGERS INTO THE NIGHT
--ROBIN MCMACKEN
JOURNAL FEATURES EDITOR

I mourned tiny Claudia's death.

For 400 years she lived in the same yellow silk dress, the same child's body, a dispirited soul with no family.

Louis, Madeleine and Claudia were the aristocrats of the id who I invited into my bedroom every night for three weeks.

I listened to their luridly erotic tales from New Orleans. The blood feasts. The nights at the opera. Now visiting time was over.

Sadly, I closed *Interview with the Vampire,* and set the alarm. Too tired to wash off my makeup, I burrowed deeply into my comforter.

I lay in bed for at least half an hour.

My midnight neuroses and Claudia's faint calling from the final pages of my book would never let me sleep.

I jumped out of bed, frantically scouring my jewelry box for a pair of crucifix earrings. I bought the tacky costume jewelry in Denver during the pre-"Sex," post-"Like a Virgin" Madonna era, crusty gold filigree crosses with giant faux rubies in the center. I never wore them. I found only one earring, and rubbed the dust off the smooth glass.

Carefully, I aligned the earring perpendicular to the edge of my nightstand. I crawled back into bed and closed my eyes.

That was my ritual for three nights, but I never forgot the image of a vampire swooping down on my neck.

How could I? In Anne Rice's books, crucifixes don't kill or even frighten vampires. That's just a rumor.

Cancer Becomes Me

When Marjorie Gross's piece, "Cancer Becomes Me," appeared in The New Yorker, *readers in the United States and Canada laughed–and gasped. Her quips in the face of the Big C revealed an amazing talent, an outrageous nerve. Letters poured in from patients and publishers. "How about three hundred grand? Write whatever you want," one best-seller monger offered. But Gross never performed for the money. In fact, she lived by three mottoes: Never be a hack. Never write for money. Always write from pain.*

Pain–that was part of her too brief life. A shy kid growing up in Toronto, she got used to teachers calling her an underachiever. She called them boring and retreated to the family basement to make comic videos. Skipping college, she headed for New York City to study acting. At 18 she was doing stand-up comedy at The Improv–not your ordinary teenager–and that was in 1974, when the few women comics on the scene joked about their hairdos. Fresh and funny and left of center, "Young Marge" could make them laugh without four letter words.

After missing out on Saturday Night Live–*a friend named Gilda Radner got the last spot–she broke into network TV as a writer for a hip teen show called* Square Pegs. *The show lasted two years–long enough for her to appear as a guest on Letterman. Then, committed to writing, she moved to Los Angeles, wrote for* Bob Newhart, *and* The Larry Sanders Show, *and discovered her talent for survival in "The Room." Here a dozen or so writers sit around a table in 10-hour stretches and tear up sitcom scripts, questioning situations, savaging lines, rewriting jokes, competing for funniness. Life in "The Room" is tough. Eventually she found a room she really liked, writing for* Seinfeld. *It was the best of times.*

Like many great clowns, she was a troubled loner, hard to love but harder not to. Self-educated, she read screenplays by the score and volumes of history. She loved Martin Amis, Truman Capote, John Updike, F. Scott Fitzgerald's Pat Hobby stories, and indulged herself in Beatlemania, paying ten grand for an authentic shirt at Sotheby's. Her brother Jonathan describes her gifts with an old saying, "Talent does whatever it wants, genius does only what it can." Her genius was comic. Her time was short. She died of her disease in June 1996, at 40. What a loss.

–CM

So I'm sitting in the doctor's office, he walks in, just tells me straight out, "I was right–it's ovarian cancer, so I win. Pay up." And I say, "Oh, no, you're not gonna hold me to that, are you?" And he says, "Hey, a bet's a bet." You

---

Marjorie Gross, Cancer Becomes Me, *The New Yorker*, April 15, 1996. Reprinted courtesy of the estate of Marjorie Gross from *The New Yorker*.

don't know what it's like to leave a doctor's office knowing you're lost a hundred dollars: suddenly everything's changed.

Well, O.K., I've exaggerated a little. What really happens is the doctor walks in and gives you the sympathetic head tilt that right away tells you, "Don't buy in bulk." The degree of tilt corresponds directly with the level of bad news. You know, a little tilt: "We've caught it in time"; sixty-degree angle: "Spread to the lymph nodes"; forty-five degree angle: "Spread to your clothes." In her book about cancer, Betty Rollin wrote, "First, you cry." However, she didn't mention what you do second, which is "Spend, spend, spend." You're sort of freed up, in a weird way. Suddenly, everything has a lifetime guarantee.

So I had a hysterectomy, and they found a tumor that they said was the size of an orange. (See, for women they use the citrus-fruit comparison; for men it's sporting goods: "Oh, it's the size of a softball," or, in England, a cricket ball.) I languished in the hospital for ten days, on a floor where everybody had cancer, so the sympathy playing field was level. You can't say, "Hey, can you keep it down? I just had my operation." You might get, "So what? I'm on my fifth." "Poor thing" doesn't really come into play much on this floor. My mother, who also had this disease (yeah, I inherited the cancer gene; my older brother got the blue eyes, but I'm not bitter)—anyway, my mother told me that for some women a hospital stay is a welcome relief. You know, to have someone bringing you food, asking how you are, catering to your every vital sign. See, she wound up in a room with five other women, and they would sit around talking on one bed, and the minute the doctor walked in they would jump into their own beds and re-create the "incoming wounded" scene from *M*A*S*H*, insuring that they would not be sent home early.

Which now leads us quixotically but inevitably to chemotherapy. What can I say about chemotherapy that hasn't already been said, in a million pop songs? I was prepared for the chemo side effects. I had my bald plans all in place. I decided to eschew wigs—all except the rainbow wig. Once in a while, I'd put that on when I didn't want to be stared at. Luckily, in my life style (Lesbeterian) you can be bald and still remain sexually attractive. In fact, the word "sexy" has been thrown my way more times this year than ever before. I've had dreams where my hair grows back and I'm profoundly disappointed. The bald thing works on other levels as well. The shortened shower time—in and out in three minutes easy. Shampoo-free travel. Plus, I get to annoy my father for the first time in twenty years. He hates to see me flaunting my baldness. I thought I'd lost the power to disgust him, but it was right there under my follicles all along.

The other side effect is that I've lost twenty pounds, which has sent my women friends into spasms of jealousy. I think I even heard "Lucky stiff." I said, "I think I'm closer to being a stiff than lucky!" But it fell on deaf ears. I suppose it's a testament to the over-all self-esteem of my fellow-women that, after hearing all about the operations, the chemo, and the nausea, the only thing that registers is "Wow, twenty pounds!" and "You look fabulous!" It's a really good weight-loss system for the terminally lazy. I mean, a StairMaster would have been preferable, but mine wound up as a pants tree.

Then, there are my other friends, who are bugging me to go alternative. So now I'm inundated with articles, books, and pamphlets on healers, nutritionists, and visualization (which I know doesn't work, because if it did, Uma Thurman would be running around my house naked asking me what I want for breakfast). I was also given a crystal by a friend who was going through a messy divorce. She was given the crystal by a guy who died of AIDS. As far as I was concerned, this crystal had a terrible résumé. As far as the healing power of crystals goes, let me just say that I grew up eating dinner under a crystal chandelier every night, and look what came of *that*: two cancers, a busted marriage, and an autistic little brother. There, the healing power of crystals. Enjoy.

This is not to say I'm completely devoid of spirituality. I mean, when you're faced with the dark spectre of death you formulate an afterlife theory in a hurry. I decided to go with reincarnation, mixed with some sort of Heaven-like holding area. Then, of course, we could also just turn to dust and that's it. I come from a family of dust believers. They believe in dust and money: the tangibles. The thing about death that bugs me the most is that I don't want to get there before all my friends. I don't even like to be the first one at the restaurant.

The hardest part of this whole thing is that it has completely ruined my loner life style. I've never felt the need to have anyone around constantly. I mean, I never wear anything that zips up in the back, and I hate cowboy boots. And now I get ten times as many phone calls–people wanting to come over and see me. When I'm well, I can go months without seeing someone. Why the rush to see me nauseated? I especially don't believe in the hospital visit. People come in, you're lying there, you can't do anything, and they start talking about their plans for the night.

I hope with all this negative talk I haven't painted too bleak a picture and therefore discouraged you from getting cancer. I mean, there are some really good things about it. Like:

(1) You automatically get called courageous. The rest of you people have to save somebody from drowning. We just have to wake up.

(2) You are never called rude again. You can cancel appointments left and right, leave boring dinners after ten minutes, and still not become a social pariah.

(3) Everyone returns your calls immediately–having cancer is like being Mike Ovitz. And you're definitely not put on hold for long.

(4) People don't ask you to help them move.

(5) If you're really shameless, you never have to wait in line for anything again. Take off the hat and get whisked to the front.

So it hasn't been all bad. I've done things I never would have done before. I even got to go to Europe with a creamy-white pop star. I used to use the word "someday," but now I figure someday is for people with better gene pools.

True West

Richard Rodriguez's favorite trope is paradox. "No belief is more cherished by Americans," he writes, "than the belief that one can choose to be free of American culture." Knowing such freedom is illusory, Rodriguez works at the task of understanding.

His parents came from Mexico and raised their family in Sacramento, where Rodriguez learned English from Irish nuns, quickly becoming a star student. In his first book, Hunger of Memory, *he offers a visceral account of what losing the intimacy of a private language and gaining the citizenship of a public one feels like. "The loss implies the gain," he concludes, arguing against bilingual education for Mexican children.*

After years of study—too many he now thinks—at Stanford, Columbia, Berkeley, and a Fulbright in London, Rodriguez planned to become an academic, but that club seemed small and lonely. Then, too, the bitter irony of being labeled a minority after endless toil to enter the majority struck him as intolerable. Instead, he became a public writer, an essayist and culture critic, intent on making his journalism meet the requirements of literature. His model for this marriage is George Orwell.

But the voice is his alone. Rodriguez writes in a style as effortless and natural as a simple sentence; yet his clear clauses resonate with allusions, dazzle with metaphor and metonymy, elevate details into aphorisms, concentrate perceptions into new truths. Then they compose themselves into exquisitely polished paragraphs, strung like beads on an invisible string he lets his reader create.

Rodriguez lives in San Francisco, works as an editor for Pacific News Service. When he writes for newspaper and television audiences, he tries for what he calls "transparent prose." But, he says, "some of my writing lately has turned almost baroque in structure." In his latest book, Days of Obligation, *he casts a cold eye on the contrasts that make up his complex themes: Mexico and America, Catholic and Protestant, private and public, class and race, communal and individual. Though his sense of irony and his perception of paradox make him the least sentimental of writers, nothing runs deeper than his abiding commitment to citizenship.*

Here is a true American. In "True West," published in Harper's Magazine, *Rodriguez at 50 offers an exploratory—perhaps unfinished—meditation on what that means. It is a fitting piece to end—or begin—this collection, pointing the way to the journalism of the future, as it argues for a new definition of community.*

—CM

Relocating the horizon of the American frontier

Growing up in Sacramento, any imagination I had of the West (a landscape suggested by studio backlots in Burbank, which was south) lay east of the Sierras. The Sierras appeared on the eastern horizon, sheer and dreadful portals from which the Donner party would never descend. In summer, the mountains were obscured by Zeusy yellow clouds; sometimes storms of lightning–Olympian ruminations never communicated to the valley floor.

Except in the writings of John Muir. In 1869, Muir spent a summer in the Sierras. He had arrived at California by ship to grasp the implications of the coastline. America, he saw, comes to an end here.

In the 1950s, California was filled with westering Americans who were confident they had arrived. My parents were from Mexico. My father described California, always, as "*el norte*." My father's description had latitude, allowing for more America. To have grown up with a father who spoke of California as the North, a Chicago-accented neighbor who spoke of California as the West, to have grown up thinking of the West as lying east of here, is already to have noticed that "West" is imaginary.

American myth has traditionally been written east to west, describing an elect people's manifest destiny accruing from Constitution Hall to St. Jo' to the Brown Palace to the Golden Gate. A classics professor in Oregon rebuts my assertion that California is not the West. His family moved from Queens to Anaheim in the Fifties. They moved WEST. Simple. The way the East Coast has always imagined its point of view settled the nation.

In Warner Brothers' cartoons, the sun went down with a ker-plop and a hiss into an ocean that had to be the Pacific. Because I assumed I knew where the day ended, the more interesting question was "Where does the West begin?" I grew up with my back to the sea. From high school I had been mindful of Fenimore Cooper's description of a lighted window on the frontier. Nowhere else in American literature does a candle burn so brightly. That small calix of flame was a beacon of the East–all the fame of it. Where the light from that candle was extinguished by darkness, there the West began.

A couple of years ago, at a restaurant in the old train station in Pittsburgh (as coal cars rumbled past our table), my host divulged an unexpected meridian: "Pittsburgh is the gateway to the West." The same in St. Louis, the same in Kansas City. In Texas: Dallas is where the East begins; Fort Worth is where the West begins.

I was trained East. Louis L'Amour and Zane Grey wrote "westerns." Westerns sold for twenty five cents to old men with wires running from their ears down to the batteries in their shirt pockets; men who would otherwise spend their evenings staring at the linoleum.

Josiah Royce, Nick Carraway, Damon Runyon–for those of us who had grown up in the West, New York was finishing school. Eating clubs at Princeton, authority, memory–all the un-American themes.

I remember thinking nothing could be more glamorous than to be the *New Yorker* correspondent who would hold any hinterland–be it Paris, Rome, or Sacramento–up to the amused monocle of Eustace Tilley. The entire literature of the West was made up of such correspondents: Harte, Muir, Twain. Coldest winter I ever spent was one summer in Saaaan Francisco HAW HAW HAW.

I was trained East, an inveterate reader of "easterns"–Wharton, James, Kazin, Baldwin, Mailer. I noticed that the highest easterns–Wharton, James–were written as though they were westerns (westerns traditionally began with an innocent arriving from the East). Isabel Archer of Albany, New York, journeys to Europe, where she achieves inexperience amidst the etiolated foliage, the thicker light, the charged conversations.

Go east, young woman! I think we are just now beginning to discern the anti-narrative–an American detective story told from west to east, against manifest destiny, against the Protestant point of view, against New York, old ivy, the Civil War, the assurances of New England divines.

A florid, balding gymnopaede bellows to me from an adjacent StairMaster in San Francisco that is abandoning California. "Too–" he raises fur-epauleted shoulders to portray constriction. He is moving out West–that is the expression he uses–to a house thirty minutes from downtown Boise where there are still trees and sky.

The Boston Brahmin who sought an aperture as her life constricted to ice cubes and cable television didn't consider California when she thought of retiring in the West. Of her last trip to California she remembers only despair within a gold-veined mirror. She settled on Santa Fe, with its ancient, reassuring patina, recently applied with little sponges. She wears blue jeans, nods to "Howdy"; she goes to the opera, sometimes to Mass.

The apparent flattery the East Coast pays California is that the future begins here. Hula hoops, Proposition 13, college sit-ins, LSD, Malibu Buddhism, skateboards, beach boys, silicon chips. California, the laboratory. New York, the patent office. The price Californians pay for such flattery is that we agree to be seen as people lacking in experience, judgment, and temper. It seems not to have occurred to the East that because the West has had the knowledge of the coastline, the westerner is the elder, the less innocent party in the conversation. It is no coincidence that the most elegant literature cloudless Los Angeles has produced in this century is celebrated worldwide as *noir.*

Californians have been trying to tell eastern America that the country is, after all, finite. Only within the last few years–a full century after the closing of the frontier–have we gotten a bite on the cliché: *Tonight Peter Jennings asks, Is the Golden State tarnished?*

A few years ago, after an earthquake in Los Angeles, a television producer from the Canadian Broadcasting Corporation asked me for an interview on the future of California. The Canadian producer decided we would have our televised conversation at Venice Beach, the place tourists come on Sundays to experience comic extremity by the sea. I would sit in an Adirondacks chair, the blue Pacific over my shoulder. And, by and by, there I was on Venice Beach, wired for sound and my hair blowing east. I had become a correspondent. But this was Tuesday, a gray afternoon, the fog pouring in on a gale. Black teenagers wearing Raiders jackets stomped over cables that were lying about, kids so accustomed to TV crews they didn't pause to gander. An old guy wanted five bucks to stay out of the shot. A trio of German tourists, two men and a woman, and they all looked like Beethoven, stopped at each of the hundred and one T-shirt and counterfeit stands that lined the beach. The tarot readers set up their card tables and sat with their backs to the gray ocean, limp-haired priestesses of that huge, turgid brain. Panning the scene for something golden, we did eventually find one happy face. At the concrete muscle-beach exhibition booth, we came upon a sunburned old salt with sagging breasts, eager to pose for the camera in his red nylon bikini, winking insanely with every revolution and flex.

II.

Several seasons ago Ralph Lauren produced fashion layouts of high-WASP nostalgia that were also confused parables of Original Sin. Bored, beautiful children pose upon the blue lawns of Long Island together with their scented, shriven parents. All are washed in the Blood of the Lamb. Their parents have rewon Eden for the sake of the children. The knowing children, however, have obviously found a disused apple under the hedge and have swallowed it.

Mr. Lauren's more recent work attempts a less complicated innocence; he has had himself photographed astride a horse. The *mise en scène* is the American West. According to *W* magazine, in real life (as we say, allowing for variance), whenever Mr. Lauren wants to escape the mythology business he repairs to his Double RL Ranch, a 14,000-acre spread outside Telluride, Colorado. On a meadow within that reserve, he has constructed a Plains Indian teepee inside which he has place genuine Navajo rugs and club chairs from London–"There's stuff inside there an Indian never dreamed of," as one tickled ranch hand remarked.

I do not intend to mock Mr. Lauren's Trianon *sauvage*. It may represent an authentic instinct for survival, like the family-built nuclear shelters of the 1950s. Leaving all that alone, I should confess I have not made my own peace with wilderness, never liking to be more than two miles from restaurants and theaters. From an air-conditioned car, I often regret suburban sprawl. Mine is an aesthetic regret. But as a westerner, I approve the human domination of Nature.

I have been to Telluride only once–for the film festival. But I have often enough visited chic little towns that nestle in the mountain states of the West. At a weekend wedding in Idaho most recently, the guests had flown in from Los Angeles and London. On the Saturday morning, nearly everyone rode into the foothills on horseback.

I trudged one mile, perhaps two, in the direction of loneliness. A noise stopped me. A crackle or something; a pine cone dropping; a blue jay. I discovered an anxiety the white pioneers could have known in these same woods a century ago. Whose woods these are? Injuns'? Well, I am an Indian, and my shoes were getting scuffed. Snow White and the Seven Militiamen? And then an idea, more unsettling: the forest was empty. I turned and quickly walked back to the lodge, where Ella Fitzgerald's voice flitted through speakers in the eaves of the lobby.

Mr. Lauren, quoted in *W*, speaks in oracular puffs from beneath designer blankets: "I'm just borrowing the land." (. . .) "You can never really own it." (. . .) "It's only yours for a short time." (. . .) The *W* article notes the Double RL Ranch is circumscribed by fifteen miles of white fence.

In nineteenth-century daguerreotypes of the American West, the land is the dropped rind from a transcendently fresh sky. Time is evident; centuries have bleached the landscape. There is no evidence of history except the presence of the camera. The camera is debris; the pristine image "taken" is contamination. The camera can look only backward. Our backward glance is pure and naively fond. To see the future we must look through Ray-Ban darkly.

The Puritan theology of America predisposed pioneers to receive the land as "virgin." The happy providence of God had provided them a new Eden. The gift must have inspired exhilaration as well as terror. Evidence of exhilaration remains. Settlers dammed the waters, leveled mountains, broke their backs to build our regret.

Some neighbor's house in Sacramento, a summer evening. I have come to collect for the newspaper. "Come on in, honey," the wife said through the screen door. "Hold a sec. I've got goop on my hands." I watched as she finished rubbing liniment into her husband's shoulder. She noticed my fascination (though she interpreted it incorrectly), said, "Labors of Hercules," which even as a child I could interpret as meaning she was comically rearming her husband for battle with Nature. Nature meant labor. All he'd been doing was working on the lawn.

An acquaintance in his eighties had pits of cancer dug out of the side of his nose. My friend lamented his disfiguring fate in the present—"I use sunscreen; never go out without a hat." The young doctor's prognosis harkened to a pristine West: "This damage was done a long time ago, when you were a little boy and stayed too long in the sun."

I believe those weathered westerners who tell me over the roar of their air conditioners that the wilderness is no friend. They seem to me to have at least as true a knowledge of the West as the Sierra Club church. A friend, an ex–New Yorker, now a Californian, tells me she was saved from a full-scale panic attack while driving at night through a remote stretch of New Mexico by the sudden appearance of writing in the sky: BEST WESTERN.

Something in the heart of the westerner must glory in the clamor of hammering, the squealing of saws, the rattle of marbles in aerosol cans. Something in the heart of the westerner must yearn for lost wilderness, once wilderness has been routed. That in us which is both most and least human—I mean the soul—cannot live at ease with oblivious nature, nor do we live easily with what we have made. We hate both the world without us and the world we create. So we mythologize. Ralph Lauren has built roads on his ranch, sunk ponds, cleared pastures. "My goal is to keep and preserve the West."

Ralph Lauren's teepee of "commercially farmed buffalo hides" was painted by "a local mountain man" with figures representing Mr. and Mrs. Lauren and their three children.

Such is the rate of change in the West, you end up sounding like some hoary ancient if you recollect the fragrance of almond orchards where the mystic computer chip clicks; if you remember cattle where almond trees now bloom. I meet such middle-aged ancients. The man in Albuquerque has seen his hometown completely changed in forty-two years, even the sky. "They" have altered everything. They, presumably, are his own parents.

Once the shopping center is up and the meadows are paved over and the fries are under the heat lamp, we park in a slot, take our bearings, and proceed to the Cineplex to watch Pocahontas's hair commune with the Great Conditioner. We feel ourselves very sympathetic with the Indian, a sympathy we extend only to the dead Indian. Necrophilia thrives throughout America, especially in the West, certainly as one approaches the Mexican border, or Borders Books. The *New York Times* best-seller list abounds with pale-face channelers of Cro-Magnon metaphysic–the medium in Sedona, Shirley MacLaine's agented alter ego in Beverly Hills, the *brujo* in the novel of Cormac McCarthy.

That part of me I will always name western first thrilled at the West in Vista-Vision at the Alhambra Theater in Sacramento, in those last years before the Alhambra was torn down for a Safeway. In the KOOL summer dark, I took the cowboy's side. The odds have shifted. All over the West today Indians have opened casinos where the white man might test the odds.

The dead Indian, Weeping Conscience, has become the patron saint of an environmental movement largely made up of the descendants of the pioneers. More curiously, the dead Indian has come to represent pristine Nature in an argument made by some environmentalists against "overpopulation" (the fact that so many live Indians in Latin America are having so many babies and are moving north).

Another summer day, late in the 1960s, I was driving a delivery truck to a construction site at the edge of suburban Sacramento. Making a sharp turn right, I saw a gray snake keeling upon the watery concrete. I make no apology for the snake. It is no literary device I conjure to make a theological point. It was really there in my path on that hot summer afternoon for the same reason that Wyoming sunsets resemble bad paintings.

I hadn't time enough to swerve or to stop. Bump. Bump. Front wheels; rear wheels. Looking into the rearview mirror, I saw the snake writhing, an intaglio of pain. I drove on.

Eventually I found the lot where I made my delivery. After a few minutes, I returned to my truck, retraced my way out of the maze. Only then did I remember the snake and look for it where I had slain it.

Several construction workers were standing alongside a sandwich truck, drinking sodas. One man, a dark Mexican, shirtless, had draped the snake I killed over his shoulders–an idea that had not yet occurred to Ralph Lauren, who at this time was just beginning to be preoccupied with WASP nostalgia.

III.

On the afternoon of my fiftieth birthday, I have come to Point Reyes, a promontory from which one can see for miles along the coast of California, north and south. The ocean, seen from this height, is tarpaulin.

Just below the lighthouse warning signs have been posted by the National Park Service. There are photos of nineteenth-century shipwrecks. Cautions to swimmers. Undertow. Sharks. Beware, beware . . .

I descend to the water. Appropriate for an aging man to turn up his collar, roll his cuffs, and play at the edge. The ocean, as it should be, is young–unraveling and then snatching back its grays and pinks, celadons, and the occasional bonny blue. The relentless flirtation of it loses charm. One begins to imagine pagodas and lanterns, gardens of spices that lie beyond.

Adam and Eve were driven by the Angel of the Fiery Sword to a land east of Eden, there to assume the burden of time, which is work and death. All photosynthetic beings on earth live in thrall to the movement of the sun, from east to west. Most babies are born in the early morning; most old people die at sunset, at least in novels of large theme. We know our chariot sun is only one of many such hissing baubles juggled about, according to immutable laws. So much for immutable laws.

So much for mutability, for that matter. I have just had my face peeled. I go to the gym daily. I run. I swallow fistfuls of vitamin pills. I resort to scruffing lotions and toners. Anywhere else in the world I could pass for what-would-you-say. In California I look fifty.

Besides. The older I become, the farther I feel myself from death. It is the young who are dying. I remain unreconciled to the logic of an alleged nature. I am unnatural. As a boy I read Richard Henry Dana's *Two Years Before the Mast.* What I remember was the furious storm as the ship tossed about the Horn, all Nature pitched against us. My Dana was not the Dana whom D. H. Lawrence mocked for returning to Boston, to Harvard, to a clerk's position, a clerk's hearth, a clerk's fizzing kettle. My Dana was a white-throated, red-lipped romantic who sailed away.

Around the rock where I am sitting now, seabirds gather to rotate their silly heads, zoom unblinking lenses toward my fists, patient for manna. It is the last day of July, the feast of St. Ignatius. The wind is picking up and the waves come pounding in from the gray towers of Asia.

Imagine how California must have appeared to the first Europeans–the Spaniards, the English, the Russians–who saw the writing of the continent in reverse, from the perspective of Asia, adjusting the view of California through a glass, silent and as predatory as these birds.

By the time he returned to the East Coast, Dana was about the same age I was when I moved to Los Angeles. I was determined to throw off all clerkishness. Twenty-five years ago in L.A., one could sense anxiety over some coming "change" of history. Rereading Dana, I am struck by the obvious. Dana saw California as an extension of Latin America. Santa Barbara, Monterey, San Francisco –these were Mexican ports of call. Dana would not be surprised, I think, to find Los Angeles today a Third World capital teeming with Aztecs and Mayans. He would not be surprised to see that California has become what it already was in the 1830s.

From its American occupation, Los Angeles took its reflection from the sea rather than the desert; imagined itself a Riviera. Knowledge of the desert would have been akin to a confession of Original Sin–land connection to Mexico was a connection to a culture of death. In the 1960s, overcrowded Los Angeles attempted to preserve its optimism as Orange County. Ten years later, Orange County was running out of Protestant lawns for sale. Only desert remained—Riverside and San Bernardino counties.

More than aridity, California fears fecundity. Perhaps as early as the 1950s film *Invasion of the Body Snatchers,* nightmare images of pregnant pods and displacing aliens converge. Fecundity is death. (To manufacture life is to proliferate death.) Who's going to pay for fecundity? The question reminds us of scarcity, for we live at the edge of the sea. What is scarce is water. Metaphors Californians now summon to describe their fear of the South are, appropriately, fluid. Waves of people. Tides of immigrants. Floods of illegals. Sand, the primordial image of barrenness, uncivilization, becomes an image of unchecked fertility.

William tells me—he's a movie guy—in a smoke-free, vegan cantina (high-ho, Silicon), that cowboy movies will shortly make a comeback—"big time." The busboy, an Indian, approaches our table balancing two possible futures: "Regular or decaf?"

In the 1970s, decorators in Beverly Hills urged their clients toward realism: an aesthetic cooperation with the desert. Floorboards can be bleached, windows uncovered. The difference of L.A. is winter light. No chintz, no wrought-iron chaise, no snuggery. Sand, creams, taupes, apricots. Californians welcomed cactus into their houses even as Mexicans were pushing their dusty heads under the cyclone fence. The desert decor became a way, I suppose, of transforming the troubling future into something Californians might be able to live with.

It occurs to me that the admission of Alaska and Hawaii into the union further undermined the myth of the West by destroying the symmetry of the map. What happens to the notion of sovereignty when you have states outside the border? Heretofore, the United States was a literal description.

Watch. In tonight's weather report, the United States of America is letter-box formatted to exclude Canada and Mexico. America is conceived by Americans longitudinally, excluding North and South. There is no weather in Guadalajara. There is no weather today in Montreal. Alaska is an isle of Lapanto hovering above the continent. Hawaii is a sidebar, somewhere to the left of the Arizona desert. Both states seem to be held in reserve—Alaska for the future, Hawaii for a blue Christmas.

One Sunday in December 1941, Hawaii became the point on the map most Americans would thereafter remember as our vulnerability to Asia. After the war, Hawaii became our boast: the Pacific is ours. But the reverse would also become true. We had waded out too far, we had been lured into complicated Asian waters.

We have always resisted the Asian prospect. Coolie labor built much of the American West in the nineteenth century. Nevertheless, the Asian was persecuted by California for coming at the continent from the fishy side. Celestials, we called them, had a devilish language of crossed sticks and broken banjo strings. The custody they exercised over their eyes implied they had discovered evil here but were keeping the knowledge to themselves. Inscrutable, we said at the time. Now we say Asians work inhumanly hard.

"Asians work too hard," says a friend of mine who has been towing a boat behind him for years. Asians are America's fastest-growing minority. Hispanics will soon be California's majority. Everyone knows Mexicans are fat mañanamen (even Karl Marx thought it better that the United States took California, because Americans would make more of it). But now it's Hawaiian-shirt time for American's Can-do-know-how-thumbs-up-Charlie-jig-jig of World War II fame. José Manuel Santo de Dios takes over the maintenance of the California landscape. When he's not washing dishes. Or flipping hotcakes. And Mae Wah Wong exemplifies work habits we used to approve as northern European. José What's-His-Name is up at dawn and drives a hundred miles to work. Mae's hundred and seven grandchildren have taken all the slots at Berkeley, the Athens of the West. Western canon go boom-boom.

Shots not heard in Hawaii. I think Karl Marx was not thinking of Keanu Reeves, but it was Marx, scribbling away through the winter of the British Museum, who believed the California Gold Rush was a more significant event than the discovery of the Americas by Columbus. After the Gold Rush, the Pacific would replace the Atlantic as the economic theater of the world. San Francisco is only now becoming the first mainland Honolulu, a breeding ground for Asian-Caucasian mixtures, with the additional complexity of Africa and Latin America. California's is one of the richest economies in the world. Marx would be interested.

The United States never had a true North until now. The American Civil War divided the nation; impressed upon the Union the distinctiveness of the regional South. But the North was never more than a political idea and a recipe for clam chowder. Economics prompted diplomats to sign the North American Free Trade Agreement. For the United States, NAFTA represents a revolutionary recalibration to north and south.

Mexico and Canada, so different from each other, are similarly north/south countries—neither has a myth of the West. In Canada, the North represents continuity, the unchanging character of the nation. Canadians, in autumn, still speak of the approaching North, relishing in that phrase the renewal of isolation. Whereas the Canadian South is little distinct from the United States. Mexico is the same in reverse: in Mexico, the great stone civilizations weighed upon the South. The North was a province of nomads and revolutionaries and, later, American confluence.

Coming upon the continent from the Atlantic, English Protestants imagined the land as prehistoric, themselves cast onto Eden. The Indian they named Savage rather than Innocent. The Atlantic myth of wilderness worked so powerfully on the first American imagination that future generations retained an assumption of innocence—a remarkably resilient psychic cherry. Every generation of Americans since has had to re-enact the loss of its innocence. Vietnam was the loss of our innocence. Gettysburg was the loss of our innocence. Oklahoma City was the loss of our innocence. Ingrid Bergman's out-of-wedlock baby. Watergate. World War II. Other countries take cynicism with mothers' milk. America has preferred the child's game of "discovering" evil—Europe's or Asia's or her own or grandfather's. (Every generation of Americans likes to imagine that the generation preceding lived in the 1950s and that its own decade, the 1960s, is postlapsarian.)

The east-west dialectic in American history was the story of man's license to dominate Nature. Railroad tracks binding the continent are vestigial stitches of the smoke-belching Judeo Christian engine, Primacy of Man. Having achieved the Pacific Coast, settlers could turn to regret the loss of Nature. (Though eastern America once named itself New Eden–New England, New York, New Canaan, New Bedford, new everything–in the California gazetteer there is nothing new.)

Twice a year, along the Pacific coast, people gather to watch the great migration of whales, north to south, south to north. The route of the whale has great allure for postmodern Californians because it is prehistoric, therefore antihistorical. The Pacific totem pole might be an emblem for a New Age, marking the primacy of Nature over man–a new animistic north-south dialectic that follows a biological, solstitial, rather than an historical imperative.

The old east-west dialectic moved between city and country, the settled and the unsettled. The plaid-suited city slicker disembarked at the western terminus of the nineteenth century to find himself an innocent amidst the etiolated foliage, the brighter light, the conversations in Spanish. Today's children of the suburbs hitch between tundra and desert, Idaho and Baja, cold and hot–versions of wilderness beyond which unpolluted Nature lies or oblivion or God.

The liturgy of the Mass still gathers a people "from age to age . . . so that from east to west a perfect offering may be made." But the future of Christianity attaches to a new, ecliptic north-south axis. Africa embraces the Catholicism disused by secular Europe; U.S. Protestantism has cajoled the penitential Latin American centuries to tambourines. Or consider America's cowboy religion: Mormons followed prophecy from east to west, away from persecution, into the desert. By 2012, the Mormon majority will be Spanish-speaking. Meanwhile, Native-American animism (Father Whale, Mother Panda) thrives among the great-grandchildren of American pioneers. The sole orthodoxy permitted in our public schools is the separation of paper from plastic.

In something like the way the East Coast invented the West, California today is inventing a rectified North. From the perspective of California, Oregon is a northern state and Seattle is a northern city. Vancouver becomes a part of the continuum without regard to international borders. Several states now seem to cluster under the white belly of Alaska: Washington, Idaho, northern sections of Utah and Colorado, Wyoming, Oregon, and Montana, famous for secessionists.

I believe the journey to Alaska is a death wish, insofar as it is a wish to escape civilization rather than extend it. In the late 1950s (at the same time that California became the most populous state), Alaska became the horizon–an albino hope, a gray-rolled cumulus, a glacial obsession–like Melville's great whale. Alaska absorbed all the nouns that lay bleaching along the Oregon Trail. Solitude. Vacancy. Wilderness. Alaska became the destination for the footloose and the loner and the seeker of silence. Americans decided Alaska would be governed as a pagan reserve–Nature sacrosanct.

Wisdom and a necessary humility inform the environmental movement, but there is an arrogant self-hatred too: the idea that we can create landscapes vacant of human will when, in fact, protection is human intrusion. The ultimate domestication of Nature is the modern ability to say of Nature: Rage on here, but not elsewhere.

Seattle rises as the capital of the new North, as Los Angeles is abandoned to the Third World. Seattle is proudest of its internationalism—Boeing, Microsoft. But for many Californians, Seattle offers a refuge from cosmopolitanism. Those who abandon L.A. for Seattle abandon civilization for civility, perhaps for one of those sanitary, bright book-cafés where fed-up white people can sit alone, savoring the black bitter draughts of the South: Mexico, Colombia, Sumatra.

From the perspective of Mexico City, Los Angeles is a pale, comic city. From the perspective of Seattle, paint-peeling Los Angeles is the tragic antipode of the coast. L.A. assumes most of California, large portions of Texas, Nevada, the bottom halves of Utah and Colorado, all of New Mexico, Arizona, and stray Dade County, Florida.

I live within the precinct of Los Angeles, I suppose. Although it's true I drink bottled water, I am connected to the South, to desert, to death. True as well that as a citizen of this coast, I feel my future more closely aligned to British Columbia than to Massachusetts. I have become accustomed to the odd orientation within a nexus that occurs at the end of any epic historical route or at the beginning. The most important highway in California is Interstate 5, the northern route, connecting desire and fear. The skinhead crosses into Oregon to get away from the Guatemalan who is heading for California. America begins overhead: that jet is coming in from Asia. America comes to an end here.

See how the metaphor of the West dissolves into foam at my feet.

(P)Review

At the Media's Edge

Telling Stories/Taking Risks, we hope you'll agree, is a book filled with edges. This anthology celebrates journalists who push hard—often to the edge—to amass facts, facts, more facts, hoping for some truth, who then push even harder as they begin to write. What they do is often dangerous to body and agonizing to soul. We offer their work as a guide, an introduction to journalists excited about journalism, looking, longing for stories that provoke, that surprise, and that are never, ever bland.

Many publications unfortunately play it safe, producing what New Journalist Tom Wolfe once called a "paralyzing snoremonger." And many journalists unfortunately rely on formula—a stuffed lead, an inverted pyramid of factoids, that far-too-simple exposition. Indeed, this may be rooted in classrooms, where too many composition teachers promote only the ornate and complex, where too many journalism educators favor the trite: Hype the lead. Hook with an anecdote. String those quotes. Crank it out. Even new media, hopeful of new talent, bring no relief as on-line producers face static *shovelware.*

If you're a newcomer, you might feel a bit uncertain about the rules, journalism's whowhatwhenwherewhy. Indeed, you might well ask, what *do* I need to master—or avoid? What *should* a profile include? How *do* I write an obit? Is "I" *ever* acceptable? With enough reading, with some practice, you'll learn the conventions. You may even grow comfortable. But too many rules, too much comfort, can squelch the joy and excitement, as well as the future, of journalism. Who *wants* to be comfortable? Certainly not the risk takers in this book. So once you refine the basics, you should—as these writers here have—pursue the adventurous.

Of course, as you try new reporting and writing tactics, you may fail. That's the one risk you'll *always* face. But stretching—taking chances, testing limits—makes growth possible. For journalists trapped in newsrooms filled with taboos, this is never easy. It's tough to fight personal laziness or myopic editors. But in the classroom, you're *supposed* to take risks. So go ahead, do it—with a coach's blessing. "If we want good writing," Donald M. Murray insists, "then we must support writers who have the courage and imagination to achieve large failures of vision, form, and language." But, too often, as Murray frets in "Pushing the Edge," we write "at the safe center of tradition," while "the best writing—by inexperienced and experienced writers—is written at the edge."

As Jonathan Alter, a senior editor at *Newsweek,* argues: "Good journalism has to have an edge." Can we find that edge? Can we provide context, with style? Can we entice readers to take time, to make time, by offering subjects that matter, with content that counts? After all, this *is* the Late Age of Print. Would-be readers browse a bit on-line, listen to radio *in transito,* channel surf in nanoseconds—but *read?* Our stories have to be good to compete and great to transfix.

Our stories, whether delivered in black-on-white or backlit blue, will be measured by our risks. "Aren't those who say *take a risk* really saying *be a writer?*" suggests Paula LaRocque, coach at *The Dallas Morning News.* Writing in *Quill,* she adds "Know things. Make connections. Write smooth, energetic sentences. Put aside forever the trite, the threadbare, the formulaic. Use your imagination. In short, be at least as smart and entertaining a storyteller in print as you are in person. That's what *writers* do."

This we can do, this we must do. Take your cues from these good writers, and from good teachers and editors everywhere. They know the risk it takes to be, to coach, more probing reporters and much better writers. Join them at the edge.

Alice M. Klement, journalist and newsroom coach